REENGINEERING MIS

Aligning Information Technology and Business Operations

Kevin G. Coleman
Jim Ettwein
Clelland Johnson
Dick Pigman
Deborah Pulak

IGP

IDEA GROUP PUBLISHING

Harrisburg, USA • London, UK

Senior Editor: Mehdi Khosrowpour
Managing Editor: Jan Travers
Copy Editor: Beth Green
Printed at: BookCrafters

Published in the United States of America by
Idea Group Publishing
Olde Liberty Square
4811 Jonestown Road, Suite 230
Harrisburg, PA 17109
Tel: 800/345-4332 or 717-541-9150
Fax: 717-541-9159
E-mail: 75364,3150@compuserve.com

and in the United Kingdom by
Idea Group Publishing
3 Henrietta Street
Covent Garden
London WC2E 8LU
Tel: 071-240 0856
Fax: 071-379 0609

Library of Congress Cataloging-in-Publication Data

Reengineering MIS: aligning information technology and business operations/Kevin G. Coleman...[et al.].
p. cm.
Includes index.
ISBN 1-878289-30-6
1. Management information systems. 2. Organizational change—Management.
I. Coleman, Kevin G., 1957-
HD 30.213.R439 1996
658.4'038—dc20 95-38963
CIP

British Cataloguing in Publication Data
A Cataloguing in Publication record for this book is available from the British Library

Reengineering MIS: Aligning IT and Business Operations

TABLE of CONTENTS

PREFACE

Reengineering Management Information systems

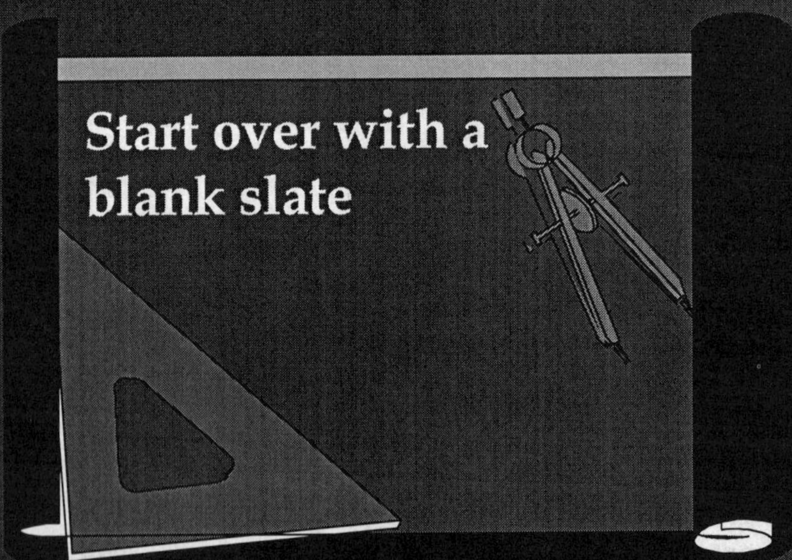

Preface

No one would dispute that we are experiencing a substantial amount of change in the business world. Only one thing remains constant; change. Change is inevitable. The challenge is to anticipate change, plan for it and use it to our advantage to expand our businesses. Management information systems (MIS), a critical part of the business organization, has fallen short in this area. Business can no longer afford the lavish expenditures perpetrated in the name of technology. The time has come for MIS to contribute to the bottom line of business.

Globalization is one of the most powerful factors driving the changes taking place in the business world today. We are competing in a world market in which technology has closed the gaps from one country to another. No longer do we operate in a vast world where distance is a factor when conducting business. For this reason, we must adapt and change our strategies and philosophies for conducting business competitively.

With the tremendous impact of the new requirements, businesses are forced to re-examine the way in which they operate. This is no more evident than with IBM. "The "King" has fallen," many brokers proclaimed. The significant drop in the price of IBM's stock sent shivers not only through the financial and investment community, but also through the business community. CIO's were quite concerned over their substantial dollar investment in IBM hardware, software and services and feared the impact from the dramatic changes IBM was going through could have on the MIS as an organization. When initially invested, these dollars were destined to support the business for decades. Changes necessary within IBM could require a new direction in terms of technological environment for corporate MIS. This is one example of how unforeseen external factors can impact not only MIS but also the core business processes that have become so heavily reliant on information systems. The events experienced by IBM should serve as fair warning to all organizations, not just MIS, that continuous change is necessary to sustain a position in the marketplace of tomorrow.

Global business and economic changes have educated and toughened the consumer and the business executive. We now are dealing with educated consumers and with keen, business savvy, international executives. No longer is mediocrity an acceptable level of service if businesses are to survive and prosper. Quality, customer service and added-value features represent the new criteria used when evaluating and selecting with whom we want to conduct business and initial cost has fallen to a secondary factor. Businesses will continue to adapt to the evolution of the global society. As we move toward the 21st century, the globalization of the marketplace is forcing companies to:

- Integrate customer service and product suppliers
- Shorten time to market for products and services
- Design and manufacture quality into products and services
- Focus our marketing efforts
- Manage for global competition
- Reduce costs
- Explore innovative techniques for gaining competitive advantage
- Aggressively apply information technology as an agent of change

We have just scratched the surface in discussing the influences behind change in business. These changes have indeed been brought about by many more factors. The economy, political environment, improvements in technology, shifts in values of the consumers and evolution influence the way in which we conduct business. As the business environment evolves, the organization, culture, values and beliefs of our businesses must be modified. To keep up with the evolutionary process of business and to meet the challenges of the 21st century, organizations began to apply an innovative management technique called reengineering. Reengineering techniques set bold goals and allow organizations to shed the burden of tradition. In an effort to rapidly bring about radical change in the business necessary to realign operations with the current and future markets, the majority of businesses have initiated reengineering projects.

Radical change is defined as a total departure from the management mentality that has been with us for several decades. In simpler terms it includes moving from task-based operations instituted in the industrial revolution to value-added activity or process-focused operations by focusing on processes and making them more efficient and productive as well as increasing customer service by changing business processes. Organizations are beginning to modernize. Updating their policies and procedures, restructuring and down sizing in an effort to bring them into alignment with the current business climate are all secondary to process redesign. Our research has shown that over 32 percent of reengineered processes deal directly with customers and 20 percent are related to customers but do not directly reach them. Businesses expect these changes to bring previously unheard of financial benefits to the organization. In some cases, benefits as great as ten times the improvement in critical measures of performance can be achieved. The radical change required causes organizations to change their internal philosophy, values, beliefs and organizational culture with regard to business. Early efforts ran into heavy resistance because of the lack of understanding and knowledge about changing the inherent culture of the organization in order to reinforce the underlying philosophy of the redesigns. Once this short coming was identified, many change management companies sprang up to assist organizations in perpetuating cultural change throughout the organization. Information technology is the tool business needs to change the processes for delivering new products and services. Yes, clearly it is an enabler to change within business. MIS, in the present state, is ill-equipped to meet the growing needs of business brought about by reengineering! The key to reengineering is proper application of information technologies. Information technology allows the redefinition of business processes, the breaking of old rules and the establishing of new ones. Information systems can serve to position our organizations to take full advantage of the global market. However, failure to align our technologies in support of globalization of our core business processes will surely serve to seal our fate and expedite our extinction. In many cases, early symptoms of not only misaligned MIS departments but totally misapplied technology has been witnessed and has been identified as the most significant stumbling block in the business organizations efforts to improve processes.

MIS must radically change. And the time to change is now. Since the advent of computers, information systems have moderately adapted to marketplace pressures and the economy. This adaptation has brought about the need to rethink our position within the organization. Patches and work-arounds have been the way of life for most MIS departments. This has taken place out of necessity, not choice. As a result of these steady modifications, processes and systems have evolved into inflexible fragile mosaics of code that in most cases fail to support the organization and become obstacles in the organization's efforts to conduct business. Just as business has needed to evolve, the MIS organization has needed to evolve, but has stagnated in every area except the use of the latest technology. Continuous infusion of new technologies into the business information systems has increased the complexity of work. The continuous expansion of technology generated islands of knowledge about specific areas of technology and made the MIS organization highly fragmented, inflexible and politically charged. Factor in the significant changes brought about by reengineering the business and suddenly you find out that your ability to compete in the vicious marketplace we are in today is significantly impaired by MIS's inability to rapidly change. MIS departments are trying to survive another day. Fighting fires is the normal mode of operation. There is no time to plan for the future. MIS spends over 50 percent of time and budget on maintenance. Little time is left for planning and positioning business processes and systems for what lies ahead.

The ability of organizations to compete will depend upon how well they prepare themselves for the future. For this reason, we have begun reengineering our organizations, processes, information systems and our culture and beliefs as they relate to business. To advance in tomorrow's market, business and technological strategies must be aligned and unified with the customers' expectations. In an effort to meet the challenges, organizations are redefining processes, roles and responsibilities and the way in which they measure their effectiveness. Organizational restructuring, technology planning, reskilling and integration of new technology will enable organizations to meet the challenges that lie ahead. Technological advances are providing us with the tools necessary to substantially improve our process efficiencies as well as with functions and features we dared only dream of less than a decade ago.

The changes that are taking place have far-reaching effects on MIS. As we change the way we conduct business, we must also reconstruct the MIS organization within our businesses. The ability to collect, process, analyze and efficiently disseminate meaningful information will enable organizations to become more competitive. To quote Sherlock Holmes: "To reason with inadequate information is dangerous", and I would like to extend this by adding: "To reason with inaccurate or out-dated information is suicidal." Clearly, the role of information technology in business has increased. MIS will be held accountable if we do not change the way we operate.

Highly successful organizations of the next century will be the ones that uncover the hidden powers that technology brings to business processes and operation. Information technology, for many, will be a competitive advantage. But just how do we achieve competitive advantage brought about through information technology is questionable. First, let's define what we are talking about by obtaining competitive advantage through information technology.

> *IT Competitive Advantage is:*
> *"The ability to provide customers, internal as well as external, the functions, features and capabilities they would want, if they only knew they could have them."*
> Kevin G. Coleman—CSC Leading Edge Forum

People cannot articulate the need or want for something if they cannot imagine it being possible. Our view of the way business can be conducted is constrained by what we believe to be possible. Once the users recognize that something is possible, they immediately change and cannot live without it. We must educate business leaders and become a catalyst for innovative application of information technology to all processes within our business. We must give the users the power they need to be successful. Through a partnership with the business process owners, not only will we both grow and learn, but we will also cement our place in the organization's future. To achieve this competitive advantage through information technology we must reengineer MIS.

The reengineering efforts to date have focused on the business side of the organization and the information systems that support the business processes but not on the MIS organization itself. This places MIS, as a contributor to the business, at a significant disadvantage. The '80s saw substantial investment in information technology. This investment, in many cases, was as much as 50 percent of capital budgets. The investment was made in the name of business improvement. However, many executives are struggling with how to define the gains anticipated for the infusion of information technology. Not only did business leaders not understand the implications of information technologies, but they also never achieved this goal. So, to the surprise of many, business leaders saw little change in MIS and clearly little or no added value. Many executives now view MIS as a runaway expense rather than an asset.

The reengineering of MIS will transform the current organization to an energized catalyst for change, fully integrated and engaged in business operations. Therefore, the new mission of MIS varies significantly from that of the existing organizations. There are four key areas that have been identified as being misaligned in MIS organizations. These are the areas within MIS requiring modification.

FROM	**TO**
• Trying to survive another day	• Looking ahead, planning and anticipating the organizations future needs
• Technology Focused	• Focusing on Process Transformation
• Transaction Based	• Process Enabling
• Justifying through Cost/Benefit Ratios	• Justification by Process Performance Improvement
• A Support Organization	• Integrated & Contributory Business Partner

The reengineering of MIS will serve to challenge traditional tools, techniques, organizational structure and measures currently associated with MIS. The changes suggested here will enable MIS to dramatically improve their processes and to facilitate the organization's gaining a competitive advantage through the use of technology.

Where to start and what will change are the two most frequently posed questions when teams embark on the journey of reengineering. The first activity to complete is establishing a bold new focus and goals for this undertaking.

FOCUS

- Contribution of MIS to business
- Cross functional value-added MIS processes
- Technological alignment with business. Does this meet our definition of Reengineering? You better believe it. The very essence of what MIS is within the organization is going to change, not to mention the way MIS is structured and delivers services.

GOALS

- Reduce systems development from years to months
- Integrate and align with business process groups
- Increase the capabilities of core business functions through technology

These are three quite simple goals. Simple but very difficult to reach given the current state, the goals are quite a distance off. Is this dramatically different from where we are today? Some people may say not really. But in reality we take entirely too long to develop systems and, in most cases, we act in our own selfish best interests when it comes to selecting technology. We are just big kids looking at bright, shiny new toys and saying I must have that as long as it fits nicely into the current skill set I have. Anything outside of the current skill set is seen as a threat, and reason upon reason is given why we must not venture into this foreign territory.

As stated earlier, reengineering is about processes. In order for the goals and objectives to be met, each of these processes will need to undergo change. What are the processes associated with MIS? It turns out there are only four. Few in number, but they are absolutely critical if we are to efficiently conduct business.

- System Development
- System Support
- MIS Operations & Delivery
- Business Process Transformation

Business Reengineering Impact on MIS

Changes brought about through business reengineering require substantial rethinking of MIS overall. Defining what changes that typically accompany business reengineering and how MIS needs to be positioned will expedite the reengineering of MIS. Chapter 1 of this book will look at what changes are needed because of business reengineering.

System Development

Changes to the methodology used for systems development will be needed to achieve our objectives of reduced development time. A lab approach to using accelerated, iterative development is defined in Chapter 3. In addition, the restructuring of MIS will provide a closer working relationship with the business process owner, thus increasing cross fertilization of the development team and bringing about an infusion of new ideas.

Now that we have changed the way we are conducting development projects, we need to change the way we manage these efforts. Traditionally, MIS projects have been late and over budget. Chapter 9 will cover an approach that is integrated with the accelerated lab approach.

System Support

Support of the business users will allow better alignment and increased levels of understanding and cooperation within the entire organization. Changes to the organizational infrastructure needed for increased support are defined in Chapter 2. The very structure and scope of the MIS organization will be transformed into a complex series of cooperative associations.

MIS Operation

The way that people act is governed by the way that they are gauged and rewarded. To transform the behaviors and facilitate transition from the traditional culture, new culture measures of performance and rewards are needed. These requirements are covered in Chapter 7. In addition, because of impact on technical infrastructure, reskilling of the staff is required. This is without question one of the two top challenges that we face. This topic is discussed in Chapter 8.

System Enhancement

The capabilities that need to be achieved for competitive advantage requires changes to the technical architecture, tools and techniques. Selection of an appropriate architecture and the tools and techniques required to support the new development and functionality are discussed in Chapters 4 and 6 respectively.

Now that we have defined our new environment and processes we need to integrate the suite of technological-based services and capabilities into a working business environment that is not static. This critical event will be discussed in Chapter 5.

Reengineering of MIS as part of the organization is critical to the success of businesses today. This book will provide the background and foundation necessary to bring about radical change within the MIS organization. Additionally, this book provides models that depict good and poor examples of structure, processes and measures as well as lessons learned from reengineering engagements.

The authors assembled here represent authorities in their specific areas. The data contained here is a composite of nearly a century of experience which includes over a dozen reengineering engagements. Their knowledge and capabilities have been leveraged by some of the world's most prestigious companies. The guidance provided throughout this book will enable organizations to realize the true potential and value of Management Information Systems.

INTRODUCTION

Reengineering Management Information Systems

Chapter 1

Introduction

History of Reengineering

The early 90's saw significant activity focused on making business operate more efficiently with better service for their customers. Organizations were challenged to completely rethink their operations. The question typically asked was: "How can we perform this work better, quicker and more economically?". Then they were also asking: "Why are we doing this at all?" The technique of choice was labeled Reengineering. Reengineering allows organizations to completely reinvent themselves as if they were starting over from scratch. The added question of: "Why are we doing this at all?" made business look at the essence of their existence. Recent studies have concluded that as many as 70 percent of America's largest businesses are currently involved in reengineering.

The case for action is clearly survival. New approaches and methods, which often are drastically different from legacy methods, are required to sustain the current position of organizations in the world market. Often times this dramatic change is met with great

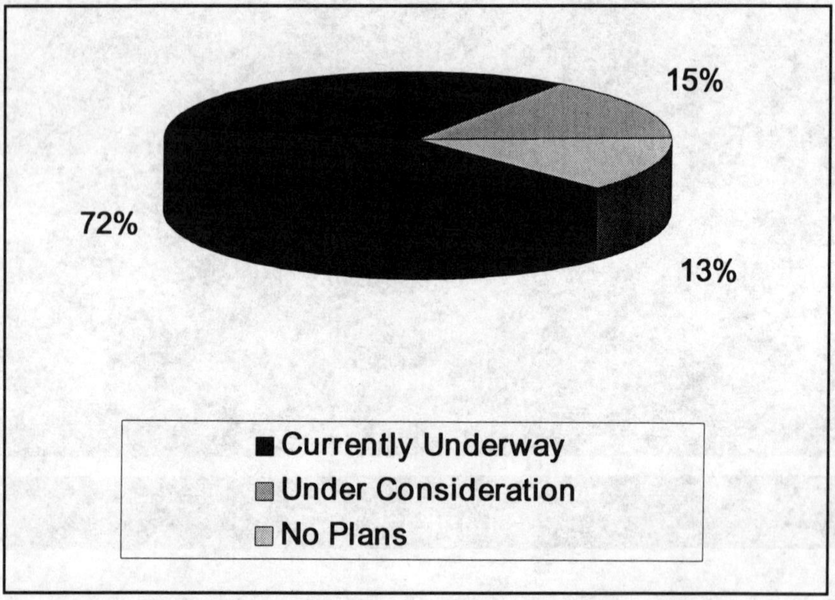

Figure 1-1 The greatest percentage of America's largest businesses have reengineering projects underway. In this study 72 percent of the respondents were currently involved in reengineering their organization.

resistance by not only the workers, but also the middle and upper management. The standard answer executive sponsors of these efforts gave when confronted with this issue was a resounding: "What choice do we have?". Change or become obsolete, even extinct is the order of the day. At this point we are merely talking about survival. We have not addressed the issue of providing competitive advantage to our organization.

Innovation provides competitive advantage in the new marketplace. Identification of technology and techniques that would be considered enablers would allow organizations to compete under advantageous conditions. For this reason, the view of MIS's importance to the organization has grown substantially during recent years. The view and influence of MIS has continuously changed as technology has matured and the true value that information systems provide when conducting business has been recognized.

Information is the key to successful business operations. One executive, when asked what advice he would give some struggling business, said: "Get more information about your business." Information about every aspect of business operation will help you run and control your operations. All too often we operate without critical facts that would have had an impact on our business decisions. The lack of information results in operational problems, lost opportunities and even business failures.

When information technology was first introduced, many organizations became quite excited and proclaimed all the problems of business would now be solved. At that time technology was permitted to drive the direction of business. Businesses modified themselves and adapted their processes to permit the use of early computer systems. However, this period was very short lived. As technology became significant to the operation of business, technical gurus were moved into upper-level business management positions. Though these individuals were technically competent, they lacked key business, vision and managerial skills needed to achieve long-lasting success. As economic times became rough, the strain placed on organizations increased and the abilities of the purely technical managers were highly suspect.

A shift was clearly necessary to reposition business properly. The flood of business school graduates with the all powerful MBA behind them took the helm from the technical managers of the previous period. Many technical managers and some senior level executives for that period claimed that the MBA stood for "More Bad Answers" because of the lack of understanding about technical aspects of not only the information systems, but also technical aspects of products and services. At this point we became business focused and MIS took on a new role. MIS was viewed, more or less, as a necessary evil. MIS was a means of collecting and distributing the reports and information necessary for management to operate and control our business. Key measures for monitoring the effectiveness of MIS during this period was the timely processing and distribution of reports.

The third distinctive period which MIS went through evolved around the emergence of the new information-processing technologies. Artificial Intelligence, Computer-Aided Software Engineering, and Object Oriented techniques were all proclaimed to be the salvation of information systems. Tremendous investments were made into incorporating new techniques into existing systems and even the custom development of new systems. This decision was made because of the great benefits said to accompany the installation and operation of these systems. At the same time, a corporate chief information officer (CIO) position evolved to manage this critical information resource of the corporation.

In addition, small empires were built within the MIS organization around individuals with a great understanding and knowledge about a specific technology that emerged and became part of the corporate suite of technology. Rapidly, it became evident that these technologies and techniques were of value but were not the end for all the problems facing business. The inability of technology to deliver the promised benefits saw increased turnover in the CIO role. As the stress was placed on business to become more responsive to customer demands and to become more efficient and cost-effective, the CIO turn-over rate soared as high as 30 percent according to studies conducted by industry experts. CIO, in many cases, changed its meaning from Chief Information Officer to "Career Is Over". Technical and business individuals shared this position, and the stress that went along with it. Striving to meet the challenges given them by the business, MIS executives struggled to keep their heads above water.

Current philosophies around information technology dictated that various techniques are required to enhance the ability of organizations to conduct business. Technology is an enabler, not a driver. Both business and technical expertise are required to achieve the organization's goals and objectives. Subsequently, properly applied technology can actually provide a competitive advantage. However, in many cases, the alignment of MIS with the vision of the organization was off. Also, MIS was not part of the inner circle, and as business direction and focus changed, the message of change often did not reach MIS.

As one might imagine, businesses are very dynamic. The dynamics force business to adapt and modify their operations over time. In fact, the process of doing business is evolutionary. Minor changes have been made on top of other changes on top of other modifications. What has resulted is bastardized processes that are

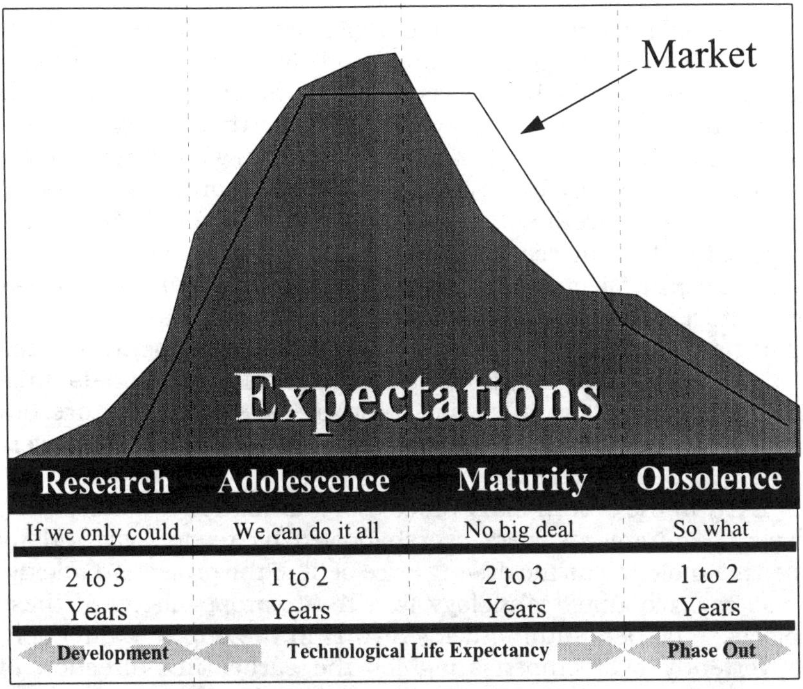

Figure 1-2 A timeline that represents the way in which MIS matured and the corresponding changes that have taken place.

difficult to manage, impossible to monitor and extremely inefficient. Many times efforts are made to develop new processes. However, these efforts are only moderately successful because of failure to include all touch points that affect or are affected by business and internal politics.

Touch points are areas that are affected by a change in operation. A change in one area may or may not affect others. Experience tells us that for the most part numerous areas will indeed be affected when core business processes, such as order management, are modified.

What makes reengineering different? The reengineering approach takes a global look at the organization and starts over with a clean slate. This allows processes and operational procedures to be designed with the goals and objectives of the organization in mind. Through the identification, use and monitoring of best practices, not only in the specific business or market area that you operate, but in other unrelated industries with the same type of functions, businesses are growing and learning from each other. Looking at the best in functional class provides not only a baseline for measurement but also an operational foundation upon which to build. "Good enough" is no longer the way we do business.

The understanding of the organizational goals and objectives are critical in any reengineering project. The vision of the future organization must be incorporated uniformly within the process and operational design stage of the project. This will provide a common thread throughout the business processes and information systems that support those processes regarding the way that the organization will conduct business and, more importantly, what business the organization is really in. This allows all parts of the business to become aligned around the strategic vision of the organization. Recognizing the far-reaching effects this has on organizations, reengineering project managers must include programs in soft areas like culture, values and beliefs as well as how we as part of the organization will be measured and rewarded for our performance.

To achieve this goal, information systems professionals must clearly understand not only what the business requirements are, but also why these are necessary. They must also understand the drivers behind the need to change.

Early in the evolutionary process of information systems, businesses' requirements were overshadowed by technology. Many times technology was the driving force behind the projects. Quickly, it was realized that technology was the improper focus of these projects. The pendulum quickly swung in the opposite direction, inadvertently overcompensating for the earlier mis-direction of projects. Business became the driving force behind the operation redesign projects. However, this ran into difficulty when technology was not properly applied or when emerging technologies were omitted because of lack of understanding or insight to the benefits of these technologies. As a result, the competition who used new technologies gained competitive advantage. Reengineering has realigned the pendulum. Centered, technology is an enabler for businesses to change and become more efficient and competitive. Unification of technology and business process requirements are critical to successful reengineering. Unification matches the appropriate technology so a business practice can benefit and ensures proper human resource management resulting in a business solution.

Σ Information technology + Business practices + Human resources = Business Solution

Too often we have attempted to use technological solutions as the mechanism for addressing issues surrounding the way in which we conduct business. Unfortunately, this is not a total solution. Technological solutions only address one of the three areas required for a complete and acceptable answer to the issues that we are facing in business. The additional areas that are included in a reengineering solution provides the supporting activities to assure an answer that will be accepted and functional.

The subtle differences are what make reengineering significantly more successful as an approach than other traditional methods. If the project managers start over from scratch with a global view, the design of the business and supporting systems is not influenced based on past practices. Reengineering enables us to rethink our approaches and promote innovative "out of box" thinking that will provide the organization a competitive edge.

Reengineering Project At A Glance

Projects related to reengineering vary greatly in breadth and depth. The structure and specific techniques employed are broad-based as well. The closest in terms of span are the results. Significant. A $4 billion firm received a $1 billion jump start in revenue over a three-year period. This is the type of quick-and hard-hitting return organizations are interested in because it contributes significantly to the bottom line. As a result, the incremental returns of cutting fat and reducing overhead have been consumed over the past decade.

The projects that increase sales and drastically improve margin

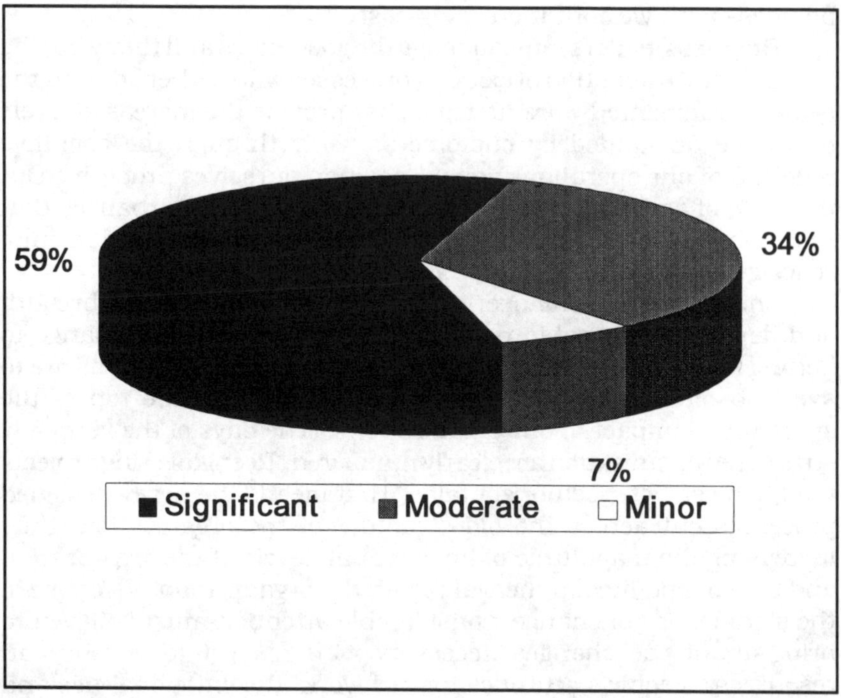

Figure 1-3 The goal of reengineering initiatives is to make major improvements. When poled, the response clearly shows only seven percent of the initiatives are for minor or incremental improvements.

seem to be the norm when we talk about reengineering. However, this type of improvement neither comes cheap nor without risk.

Being almost-as-good as our competitors will not be tolerated in today's business climate. If we are only as good as our competition, the marginal growth that swings back and forth between the major players is the only gain that can be achieved. Organizations must be best in their class in order to survive the turbulent times that we encounter periodically. The class in which we operate is comprised of businesses throughout the world. We are operating in a borderless marketplace where the entire world is competing for customers. For all too long businesses have run thinking customers would purchase from whoever had the cheapest price. That is no longer the case. The consumer has been educated in all markets and will look at the entire life cycle involving pre-sales activities through post-sales support. Quality, service and the ease with which a customer can do business with a vendor are considered prior to making the commitment to a vendor. Customers no longer make purchases, they make commitments to do business with an organization over the life of the product. The levels of service most businesses offer today must be increased in order to compete globally. But how do you increase customer service levels and make our organization easy to do business with without increasing cost?

Business leaders must manage the good times as if they were the lean times. Automation of existing processes will neither address the issue of fragmented work activities nor provide the increased levels of service demanded by customers. Only through the cognitive redesign of our operations can we position ourselves properly. But this type of activity is not for the weak of heart. Disturbances that rock the core of our business will be felt from this fundamental redesign of business operations.

The impact of reengineering projects vary greatly to the breadth and depth. Manageable risks ranging from significant change to betting the farm, so to speak, are unavoidable if organizations are to avert obsolescence. Clearly, we are operating at the top of the spectrum of impact to our organizations. The days of the vertically structured organization are clearly numbered. Reengineering projects tend to be structured horizontally. That means the newly designed processes cut across the old structure of the organization, thus increasing the magnitude of impact at all levels of the organization and causing political upheaval within the organization. Because of the significance of change, considerable attention must be given to bring about the changes necessary with respect to our human resources. People's attitudes toward work, the emotional ties and philosophical approach to conducting business must be changed to become aligned with the new organization.

For example, under traditional thinking, customer orders are

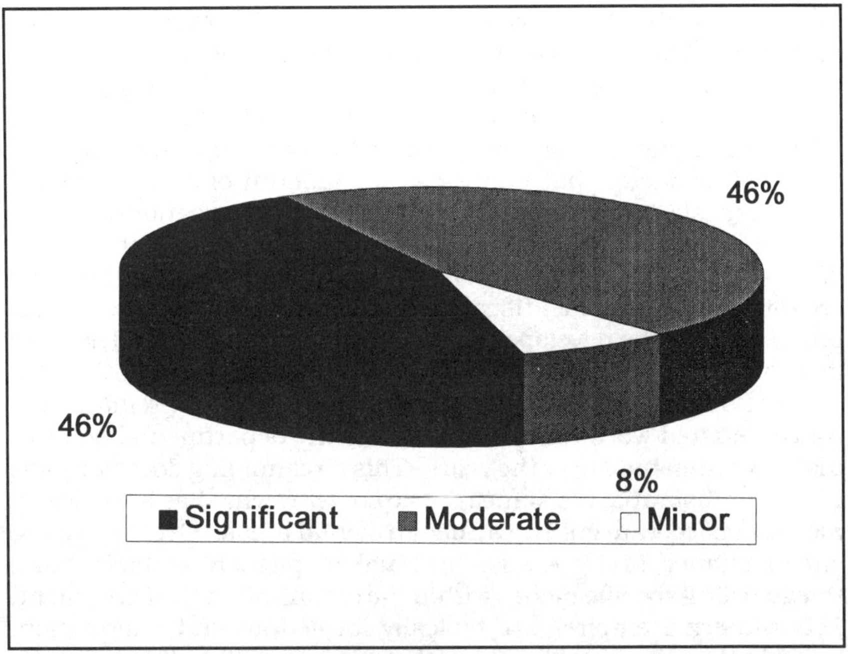

Figure 1-4 With the dramatic change in business processes, borders of authority need to be re-drawn. Only eight percent of those involved in reengineering initiatives saw only minor changes to the organizational structure after implementing the new processes.

placed with one department, materials are allocated by another department, products are packed and shipped by still another department and the products are priced and invoiced by still another department. This is even further complicated when the sales force is segmented by different products. Sales force segmentation occurs when purchasing a product and supplies forces the customer to talk to two different sales persons and the number of hand-offs and interaction with other departments would be multiplied by the number of products mixed on an order. Application of a reengineered technique to this scenario would result in a possible order-owner concept. Supported by information systems, the order-owner takes orders for all products and services, prices the order, allocates the inventory, specifies and cuts shipping papers and, finally, cuts the invoice. A complete sales cycle would be handled by one individual or department.

What we have done is redesigned the sales organization and merged it with distribution and shipping. The reduction in hand-offs and interaction decreases the likelihood of someone dropping the ball and allows the customers a single point of contact in reference to their order. In addition, orders tend to be processed much faster and with fewer errors. This example is one of high risk and high impact. The elevation of risk is due in part to the touch points the process has with the customer. Although high, the risk is manageable through the involvement of key accounts in the design of the order management process and review of the sales order process and other techniques that will be discussed later on in other chapters.

Another factor that influences the amount of risk associated with a redesign is the amount of change the organization will have to incur as a whole. Metrics must be available to estimate the impact of change to the various areas within business and supporting organizations. After identification and measurement of the change, programs must be developed that cultivate that change and nurture its acceptance.

The streamlining, such as that mentioned above, removes the concantenated work tasks and devolves the departmental empires that have been built over the years. This streamlining does not come without substantial resistance due to crossing what has been deeply rooted in corporate culture as departmental areas. Over the years, out of chance or by design, internal empires have been built, safeguarding specific niches within the organizational environment. These internal empires are typically formed around information. Individuals, in an effort to secure their position within the company, act not as part of a team, but with their own benefit in mind.

Departments also operate with their own best interest in mind, not the companies. Department "A" may be faced with a problem that falls under the domain of Department "B". Department "B", whose area catches the problem, does not need to address this problem in order to be successful as defined by their goals and the measures identified for the department. However, sales may be lost if the identified problem is not addressed. But the cost of fixing the problem has not been included in the budget of Department "B". Therefore, it would negatively impact the budget of the supporting department, decreasing their overall performance as currently measured. This is easily traced to the task orientation of our business brought about by the changes required at the onset of the industrial age.

One individual holds and limits access to information or the source of information and, therefore, has built an inherent reliance on that individual by others. This is even more true of the MIS organization as technology develops pockets of expertise. In many cases, knowledge about specific technologies did not exist within the organization, so outside expertise was brought in. This builds small empires. A prime example is evident in a multi-billion dollar international organization.

The MIS shop was highly fragmented around technologies. In order to do a complete system wide back-up, the PC Server Group, the Network Administrator, the Data Base Administrators (4 different DBMS), the Main Frame Group and Operations all would work on backing-up their domain. The result was a process that yielded individual back-ups that were not synchronized and took two days for the organization to recover from a system failure. Breaking down barriers and boundaries that no longer have a place in today's organization requires more attention than it is often given.

The culture that is highly embedded within the organization, the way we measure success, our values and the beliefs must be modified to obliterate the bureaucracies of the industrial age. Old style management has left scars on today's senior work force. If this is not bad enough, the middle segment of workers have been indoctrinated by senior personnel thus transferring the fears and rules of the corporate games.

In order to be successful at redesigning the corporation, the cultural aspects must be addressed. This area is neither easy to change nor does it receive the attention that it deserves. Over the past decade, many organizations have been spawned to assist corporations in successfully cultivating corporate change. The change of corporate culture also takes considerable time to plan and implement. Efforts to change the way people act and how they perceive the business must be planned and communicated in a manner that is easy for people at all levels to understand. Often overlooked is communicating what has precipitated the need to make these changes. Without this important factor, individuals often have difficulty in grasping and embracing the changes that all too often are accompanied by work force reduction.

A review of the reengineering initiatives that have been completed or are in the final stages show tremendous impact to the corporate culture. Corporate culture deals with what departments, managers and staff value and the way they act and treat others, including the customer. Alignment of the cultural aspects of the organization with the vision and measures set to monitor and control the business is critical. All too often the measures contradict the new culture defined for the organization. A term that has been thrown around for the last decade is the "right-side-up" company. An inverted pyramid is the symbol of the "right-side-up" company which places the workers on top with the customers and the management on the bottom.

A belief that also goes along with this corporate style is the belief in the employee. The employee is honest, hardworking and conscientious for the company. This culture, with stringent monitoring of employees and strict reporting controls, is quite contradictory and causes confusion and an opinion that management is all talk and just for show.

The way we expect the organization to act with regard to business, how we serve our clients, how the business focuses, and

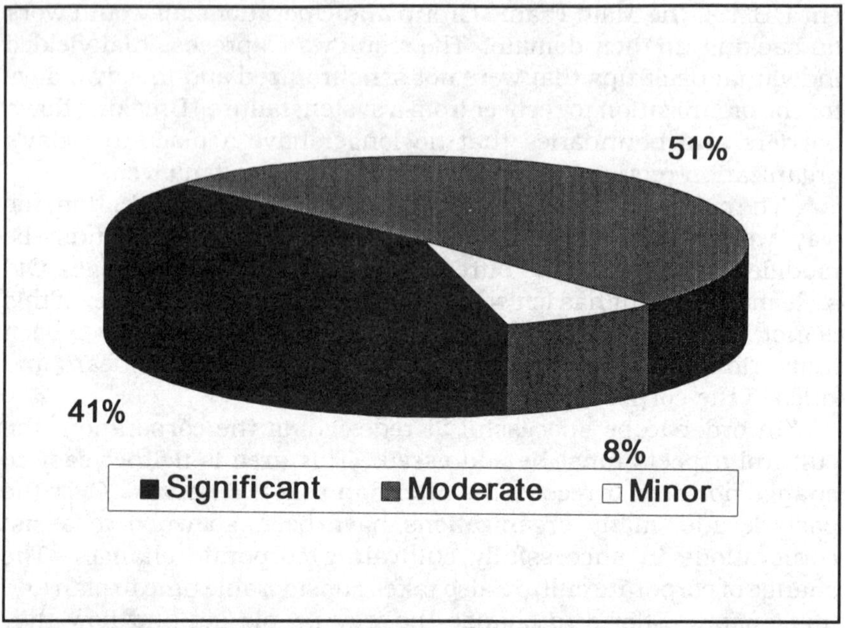

Figure 1-5 Reengineering projects often turn the world of the organization inside out. For this and other reasons, major modifications of corporate culture must take place.

how and what we value in terms of contributions of our staff need to change to align with the business environment today. Companies must remain flexible and responsive to the needs of the changing market. We must be able to do business as required by our customers. Transforming the organization into what is perceived as a company that is easy to do business with is a key to success that will secure the organization's place in the business community of the future, resulting in significant pressure for the organization to increase overall performance.

Corporate officers are fighting to secure a place in the marketplace for their organization. Increased demands from the stockholders coupled with a changing customer and the global economic situation have forced executives to take an active role in transforming the organization to become competitive in the new business environment. Organizations have become more profitable by looking for cost savings within the business. Efforts to increase productivity, trim fat and reduce waste have allowed organizations to remain solid. These efforts have all but exhausted that area of savings. Now businesses must look to other areas within to provide greater positive impact to the bottom line, as well as sustaining or increasing their customer base.

The nature of the reengineering effort almost mandates substantial involvement by corporate executives. This is not just the corporate sponsor of the project. Executives from all parts of the organization must provide guidance and show their support for the initiatives underway in order for project success. The vision set by the corporate officers must be represented in the business processes of the organization and the process and results measures defined to monitor and control the business. The vision must be uniformly communicated throughout all levels of the organization, and the understanding of the vision must be uniform as well. All too often, corporations define a vision for the organization and define processes and results measures that are contradictory. In a recent survey of reengineering engagements, 88 percent had moderate to heavy involvement by senior executives within the organization. Corporate officers from the CEO, CFO, COO and CIOs all see the writing on the wall that mandates the transformation of our business practices.

With the stakes being so high in today's competitive market, executives at the highest levels are rolling up their sleeves and getting involved in the projects that will sculpt the future of the organization. The reason for this is that executives are being held accountable like never before. The increased turnover in executives signifies the level of satisfaction stockholders and the board of directors have in the leaders of the world's organization. Additionally, salaries and bonuses are now directly tied to the fitness of the organization. Currently, this linkage is being strengthened to not only include short term profits but also to include the long term

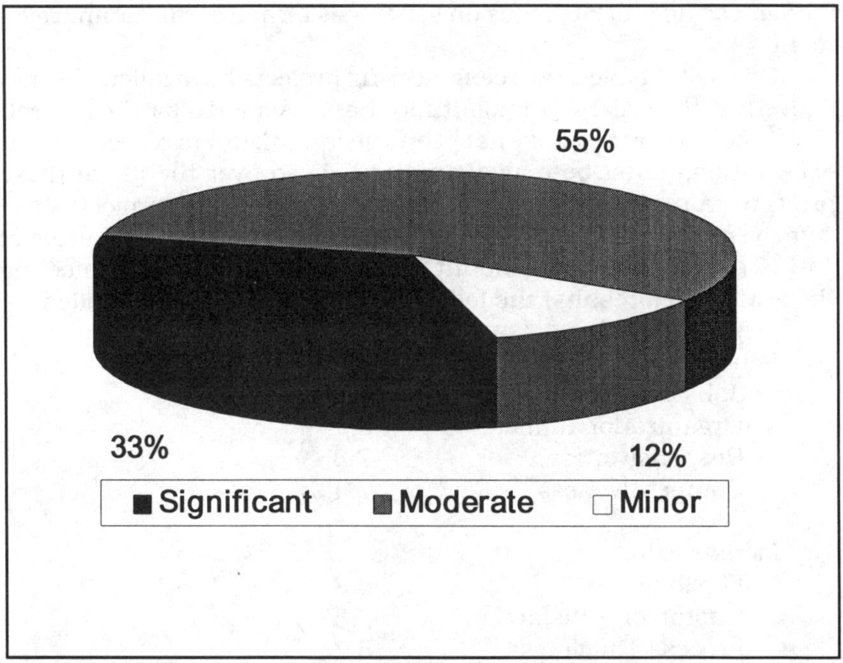

Figure 1-6 Shows the level of executive involvement in reengineering projects. None of the individuals surveyed indicated no involvement at the executive level.

success, long term growth and stability of the organization. This will instill an even greater incentive for corporate executives to rethink the way their organization does business.

Reengineering Results

Reengineering projects are not usually initiated for small growth or improvement. Rather, reengineering projects often target benefits of 10 times the improvement. In fact, one former project for an international beverage supplier was called 10X because of the anticipated benefits. The improved ability to respond to customer needs, increased ease at which business can be conducted, improved quality and timeliness of business fulfillment are all areas targeted in reengineering engagements. The results of reengineering engagements, although impressive, have often fallen short of the targets. Many results of this type of project are very difficult, if not impossible, to measure. Flexibility when dealing with customers is an example of an area difficult to measure but very essential to customer satisfaction and organizational objectives such as being perceived as easy to do business with. Intangibles and features that deal with perception and feeling about the business all serve to increase the complexity of measuring the results of reengineering. As mentioned earlier, cost is not the only factor customers look at when selecting who they wish to do business with. That is why many reengineering projects focus on softer less formal areas for improvement.

On the tangible side, reengineering projects have fallen short in delivering the orders-of-magnitude change set forth for the project. This is not to say they have not been successful, but to recognize that expectations must be realistic and managed over the life of these projects. A recent survey suggests that reengineering projects have come very close to delivering the anticipated results. On a scale of 1 to 10 (1 being the least amount of delivered results and 10 meeting the anticipated results) the following information was compiled.

Improvements in:	
Job Satisfaction	7.4
Organizational Image	8.1
Responsiveness	7.8
Competitiveness	7.4
Increases in:	
Flexibility	6.8
Customer Satisfaction	7.3
Process Timeliness	8.7
Process Effectiveness	8.4
Control & Reporting	8.1

Decreases in:

Operating Costs	7.9
Overhead	8.3
Complexity of Work	9.2
Cost of Sales	8.4
Complaints	8.2

This is not meant to imply that there have not been reengineering projects that have failed. All too often, organizations are not ready to accept the magnitude of change that reengineering brings with it. The political battles that ensue when territorial areas are invaded, coupled with the fear that runs wild through the company about massive job cuts contribute to the failures of these projects. The other significant reason for project failure deals with the reengineering team. This group must be experienced and knowledgeable in areas such as human resource management, training, information systems, business, change management and, above all, communications. The enthusiasm around reengineering has produced an outbreak of firms offering reengineering services. This outbreak is epidemic in proportion. In order for organizations to take such risks and trust, the future of their business to inexperienced firms is unthinkable, even though it has happened all too often.

What's the impact on MIS?

The changes experienced by reengineered organizations are so vast that it is inconceivable that MIS would not be effective. Increased demands on MIS driven by the business's need for information mandates changes to MIS. Fundamental changes are required for MIS to adequately serve the business unit. Changes in the areas of mission, organization, process and procedure, as well as technological change, must take place in order for corporate MIS to survive. A key indicator of business' view of internal MIS can be charted by the number of organizations who are outsourcing their MIS operations.

The outsourcing trend indicates that a business does not feel they are adequately or cost effectively served by their internal MIS department. In addition, the turnover rate of the CIO's would also serve to substantiate the displeasure businesses are feeling toward their information systems groups.

The need to reengineer MIS

Although substantial efforts have been undertaken to reengineer corporations, organizations and businesses, a critical success factor was ignored. We have completely redone the business side of the

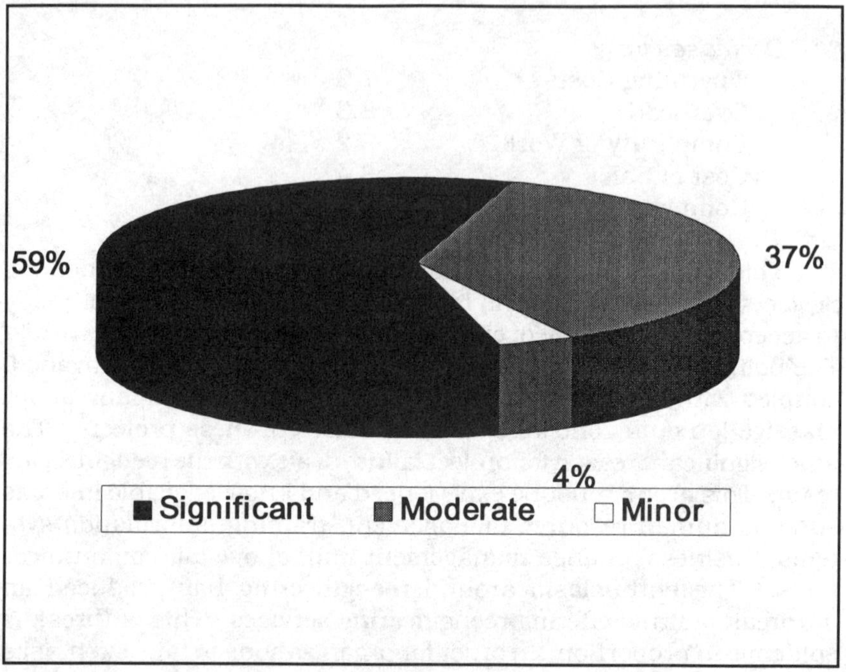

Figure 1-7 Business Reengineering has a dramatic impact on MIS. Over 50 percent of those involved in reengineering initiatives indicated the need to change MIS due to implementation of the redesigns.

house, increasing our dependence on information technology, but we have not reengineered MIS as an organization. Few executives would dispute the critical role MIS plays in business operations or the increased need for timely information and processing. We rely on this part of the organization on a day-to-day, if not minute-by-minute, basis. Yet, we have all but ignored the needs of MIS as an organization in reengineering efforts.

MIS is dealing with critical issues that have changed drastically over the last few years. The influx of new technology, the increased demands placed on MIS as a result of the global marketplace, and the increased competition which resulted in searches for ways to use MIS and information technology as a means to gain competitive advantage have served to increase the complexity and expand the role MIS plays in conducting business.

The organizational structure, skill sets, staffing levels and the internal processes of MIS require change to address the increased demands. Organizational restructuring is required for better alignment with the supporting functional business processes. Fragmented responsibilities, which have resulted as new or additional technologies were added to increase the capabilities of MIS, have left cumbersome, if not inappropriate, methods of conducting activities.

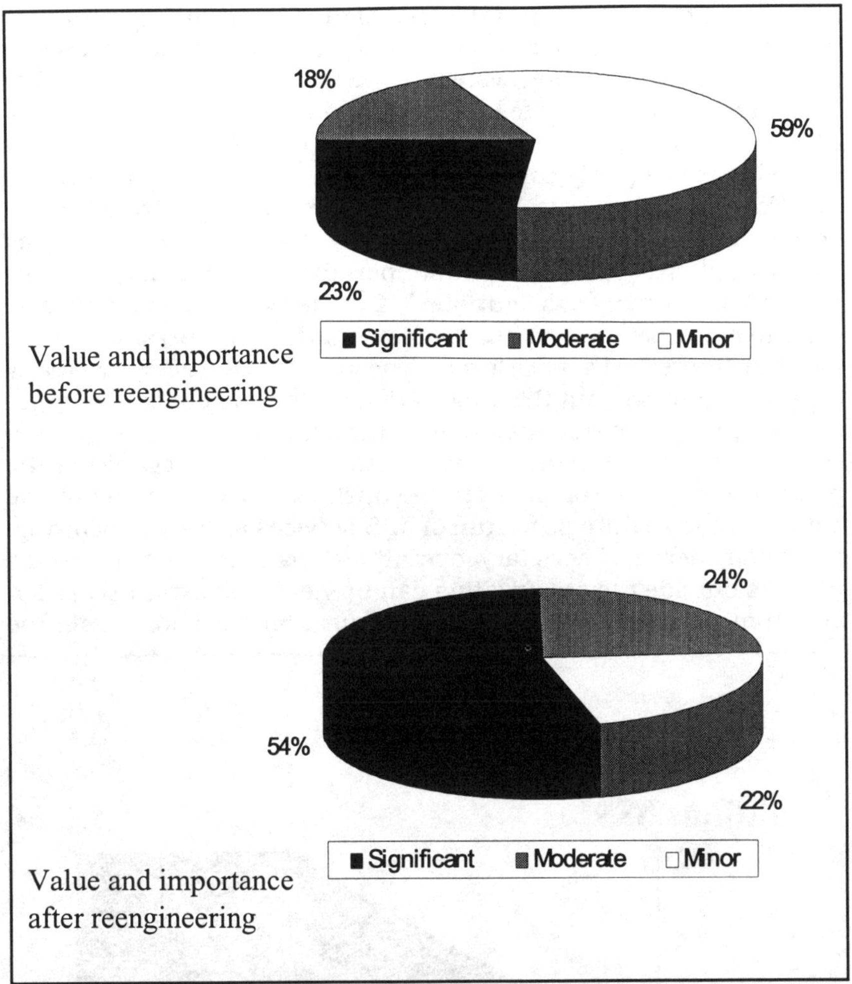

Figure 1-8 Changes to business and technological advances influence the architecture on LANs and WANs.

As the influx of new technologies increases, the ability of the staff to provide support becomes questionable. So, additional staff resources were acquired which, in many cases, formed new groups within the MIS organization. In many cases, the existing staff was not formally reskilled because of either the workload associated with the legacy systems, budget constraints or the staff not possessing the fundamental skill set necessary. Small kingdoms were built around specific technologies. Areas of technological significance changed rapidly causing constant shifts in political power within the MIS organizations. As a result, increased cost to support these systems became an issue when looking at competitive pricing of services.

Recent studies indicate that many organizations are experiencing MIS costs over three percent of gross with the average falling around two percent. At the other end of the spectrum, organizations have not invested in information technology at the levels required to sustain a viable reporting system in today's market. Figures as low as .8 percent of gross have been seen and not just in one industrial group. All these factors serve to decrease the efficiency of MIS and its ability to positively contribute to the success of the business.

Now that the costs of operating the MIS organization have become a significant hit to the bottom line, organizations are looking for the right mix of technology to support their organization. For this reason, outsourcing has flourished. Businesses look for alternative ways to decrease the cost associated with the MIS operations while requiring increased service levels. The mid- to-late 1980s saw many organizations farm out the information systems to consulting organizations and new start-ups that would take over these tasks for a contractual fee. In many cases, this was seen as a negative in the public's eye and of some risk to the business. Trusting an outside entity with the entire spectrum of MIS services as well as allowing, once considered proprietary operations, data to be handled by persons outside the organization can be viewed as extremely risky, and in many cases. actually is. However, that does not negate the

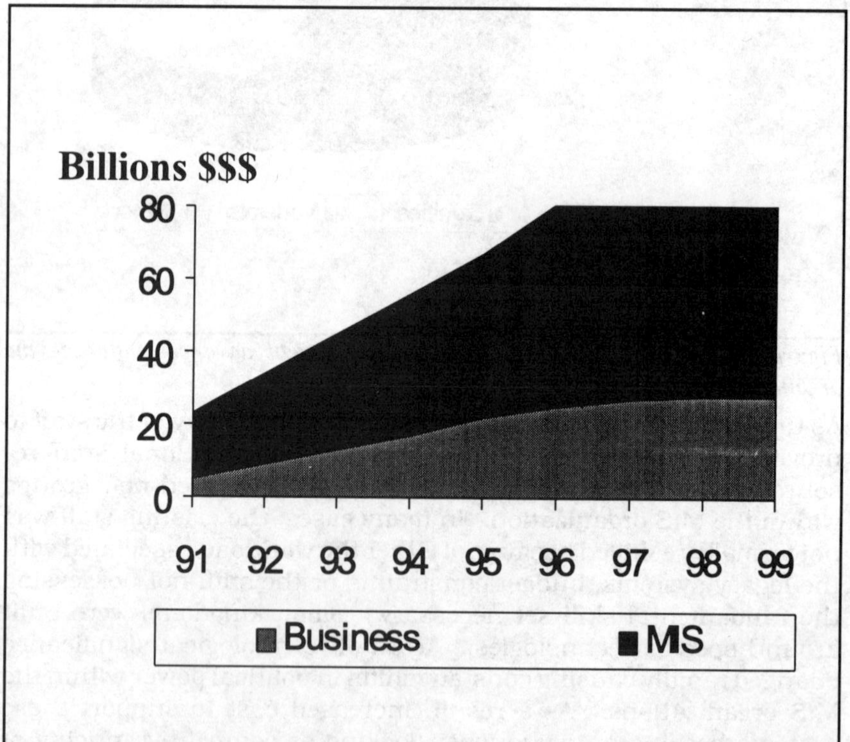

Figure 1-9 The market for reengineering MIS is about three times that of business reengineering. This multiple is expected to increase more than four times by 1997 showing clearly the reliance of business on the capabilities of information systems.

necessity for these actions in certain circumstances. Today, the focus must be on building a MIS organization that cost effectively meets the business needs in a timely fashion. To meet these requirements we must reengineer MIS and align it with the business operation.

These figures serve to further substantiate the requirement of reengineering MIS. Reengineering the business without addressing the critical needs of MIS will not permit the organization to reach their desired objectives.

Benefits of Reengineering MIS

Reengineering allows you to design your operations and processes without the baggage from the past with no preconceptions about methods and techniques. You are opening the door to do things right from the start. Additionally, you can create a work environment conducive of the overall business vision of the organization. This is a fresh start. Complete freedom is yours. The reengineering team is much like an artist with a blank canvas. The idea for the painting is in the artist's head which must be translated into an idea on the canvas. The artist's feelings and experiences are reflected the same way that the vision takes shape on the canvas.

The reengineering team should operate in the same way. It is a unified vision, influenced by the knowledge and experience of the members with each member challenging the others over key issues. The product of this free-forming environment is a set of processes that expresses the way the group desires to work and fulfill the needs of their clients, both internal and external, thus obtaining a unified vision that is aligned with the business direction.

Increased Service Levels. MIS has been seen as a provider of services to the business unit. While this is true, a much more effective approach is to organize MIS around the functional areas of the business. (This organizational structure will be discussed later.) The reengineered MIS organization will be able to respond much more rapidly and with increased accuracy to the changing needs of the business areas which they support.

Through the infusion of enabling technologies, new and unique services can be supplied to the business operations as well. Technologies such as multimedia, pen-based computing, wireless communications and ISDN will provide extensions of current capabilities that may, in some cases, provide a competitive advantage in the marketplace if applied early.

Process Timeliness. The MIS organization is under pressure of increase demands to respond to customers faster and faster.

The elimination of bottlenecks, the streamlining of business processes and the restructuring of the organization around the business functions all serve to improve upon the process timeliness seen in past years.

MIS has been known for its inability to rapidly respond to the changing business environment. The length of time for requirements analysis, design development and testing has made the applications outdated prior to their completion. Estimates as high as a million man-year backlog in MIS service validates their inability to meet the demands of our dynamic business environment. Rapid Application Development (RAD) is an approach that accelerates this process, thus allowing MIS to respond quicker to business needs.

Quality Improvement. The costs of information system errors reach far beyond the costs of repair. Errors in processes that touch the customer can be devastating. For example, a cellular phone network service provider sent late account notices out to their entire customer base. The added costs of mailing the notices, costs of man-power to answer the errored late notices, and, not to mention, the cost of the loss of customers who became irate over such a mistake far exceeded the cost to repair the software bug. This example serves to prove the far-reaching impact information systems have on our business. Designing in quality to our processes and information systems is a must as we continue our efforts for continuous self-improvement.

Cost Reduction. Increasing the efficiency of MIS improves the bottom line. The ability to shorten the development cycle of systems, reduce the number of staff required to support the business applications and reduce administrative burden are all achievable through reengineering MIS. Also, it allows businesses to react much quicker to a changing market.

Many organizations are operating on a charge-back basis. The cost of processing orders, for example, is charged back to the sales department. This approach can be an effective tool in dealing with unrealistic expectations by business units. However, the business unit does not have the ability to recoup costs for services from MIS systems that are inadequate or flawed. The charge-back system is very one-sided. New processes and result measures are clearly needed to chart the ability of MIS to respond and meet the needs of the business units in a timely fashion. The reengineering of MIS will foster such changes in measures. Also, the activities surrounding the transformation of the embedded MIS culture will serve to change the way the

MIS staff look at their work and how their work will be evaluated.

New Mission. Because of the radical change that the business environment has undergone in recent times, MIS must refocus in order to meet the needs of the business. Globalization and reengineering initiatives are forcing businesses to realign their operation with business processes. The first part of our mission should be improving MIS's ability to rapidly deliver quality systems that support the business operations and are economically developed and operated. These systems must supply increased functionality that will allow enhancements to information collection, processing, retrieval and dissemination. These added features permit better control of all processes and flexibility to make modifications as necessary throughout the business's life. Additional areas of importance include down-sizing, quality management and decentralization. New technical architectures and techniques for delivery of information systems coupled with end-user computing has allowed the MIS staffing requirements to be reduced. However, it is important to note two facts. First, an increased MIS staff may be needed for a short period of time during reengineering because of increased demands and reskilling requirements. Second, and more important, staff reduction is the politics and image. When executives within the MIS organization look at reductions in staff they translate this event to reduction in influence within the organization. This can be traced to the development of internal empires and a measures system of yesteryear that placed weight on the number of bodies you managed. The subsequent part of this issue is the overall image of the corporation of laying off workers.

Barely a day goes by that headlines in the paper publicly announce the staff reductions in organizations, and some of them are very significant. This information needs to be managed both internally and externally to minimize unfavorable press and negative impact.

Changing the basic mission of MIS will further the efforts to align business operations with MIS and technology. This alignment will provide the foundation upon which the new unified organization has been built.

Competitive Advantage. The aggressive and economical application of technology that enables businesses to provide an increased suite of services to their customers will indeed provide a competitive advantage in today's marketplace. Technological advances in the area of remote communications, portable and

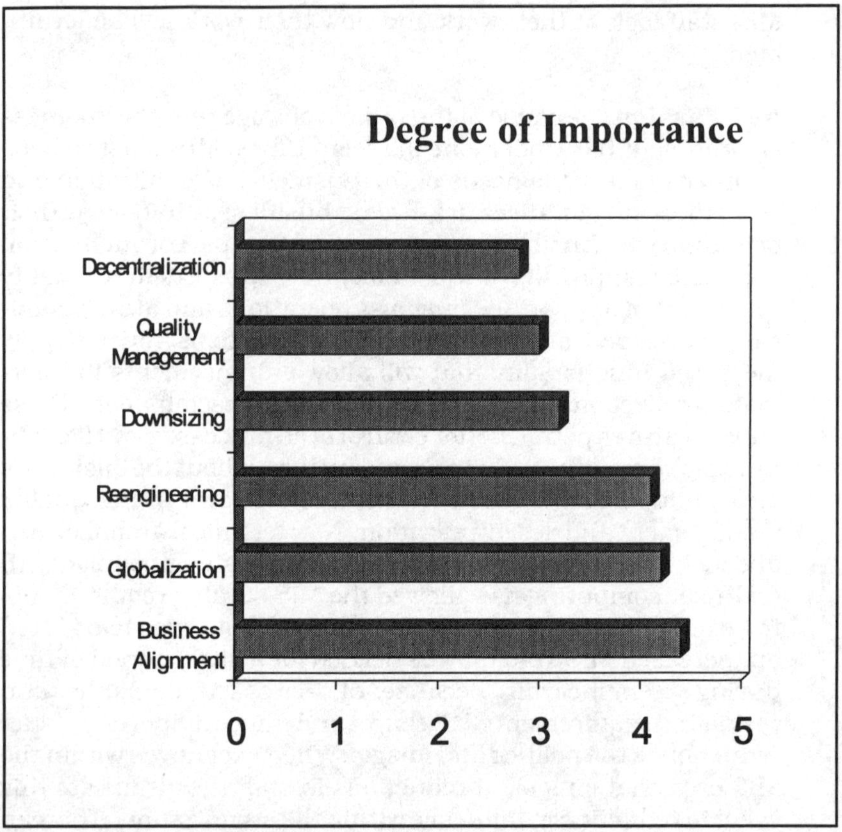

Figure 1-10 Executives rate the importance of change in MIS's mission in the top five areas. With the impact of business reengineering initiatives, MIS needs to strive to adopt the new mission.

pen-based computing increase the opportunity to collect data and process it into meaningful information. This information can then be used to more accurately forecast the market, customer needs, cash flow, etc. Improvements in technology that allow additional services—which in the past could not economically be implemented—allow progressive organizations to seize opportunities for customers to access information about their business dealings with you, and in turn promoting the vision of being a company easy to do business with. Increased levels of support and, more importantly, contributing to the success of business dealing with information will become the results of reengineering MIS.

Technology Improvements. As technology matures, we have the ability to revisit processes with increased technological abilities in mind. The ability to distribute work and processing throughout the organization not only reduces costs but also increases our ability to shorten cycle times. Providing the work force with accurate, timely information that is easy to access is critical to maximizing our through-put. Only through the exploration of emerging technologies can we remain ahead of the power curve and be competitive. However, the process for accomplishing this task is not in place in many MIS organizations today. Additionally, because of increased decentralization, telecommunications networks and long range plans are falling short of the mark when it comes to meeting the needs of the organization.

Computing Environments. The complexity of corporate computing is ever-growing. This is evidenced by the growth in the number of computing levels within organizations today. Ini-

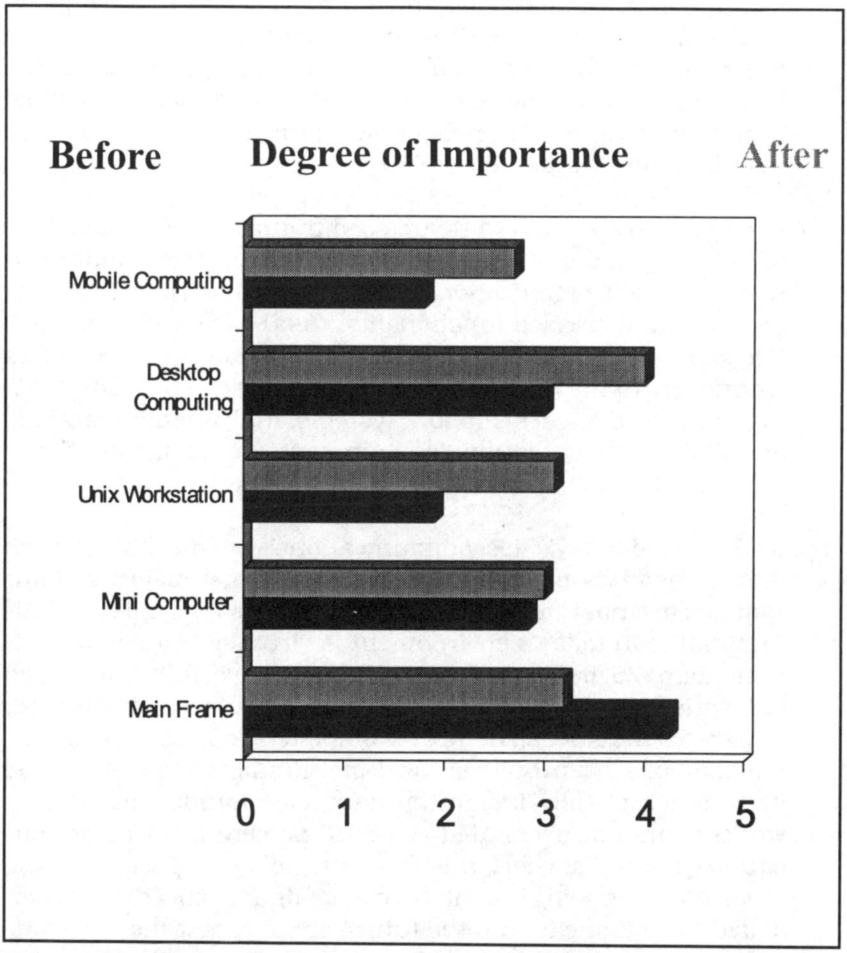

Figure 1-11 The shift of importance from the main frame to work area computing is evident in analysis of reengineering initiatives and their impact on MIS.

tially, the main frame was the only computing environment in organizations. As technology progressed, additional levels were added. Today, we have five distinctive levels of computing in most organizations.

Five Levels of Computing

1. Mainframe
2. Mini Computer
3. Workstation
4. Desktop
5. Handheld

Each of these environments brings its own set of requirements for support as well as issues surrounding incorporation into the unified structure of MIS. The role each of the computing levels has played in the past is affected by the reengineering of the business. For this reason, the overall importance has shifted from the mainframe to levels closer to the worker, the desktop, handheld and workstation.

Because of the shift to work area computing, the infrastructure of MIS must adapt. Increasing demands on telecommunications have left organizations scrambling to solve problems of growth and increased functionality. As the level of integrated telecommunications networks increase, the importance of this technology to the business will also increase. Teleconferencing, multimedia sales support systems, multimedia catalogs and distributed computing environments are all factors that will drive the demands on telecommunications.

If you look at today's telecommunications systems that focus on data transmissions, you will find that the vast majority of our systems are not integrated even at the lower levels. LAN/WAN integration in today's environment is virtually non-existent. Less than 25 percent of organizations have fully integrated enterprise wide LAN/WAN architectures in place. This further illustrates the older structure of completely centralized computing that has been built around mainframe technology. The importance of fully integrating our telecommunications networks cannot be overstated. Over 70 percent of telecommunications specialists feel this is strategically important if the organization is going to achieve their goals and objectives. When asked to look ahead into the future and forecast the reengineered architecture, the specialists saw a 180° turnaround in LAN/WAN architectures. Less than 25 percent of these systems will be host based with the vast majority moving toward an enterprise-wide view of telecommunications.

The addition of increased functions to our telecommunications networks will have far-reaching effects on the way we conduct business. One such example is teleconferencing. Today, most business leaders jump on a plane and fly to meetings. This wastes a great amount of time for our business staff. Travel time to and from the airports, waiting at the airports, flight delays and numerous other time-consuming activities around travel all

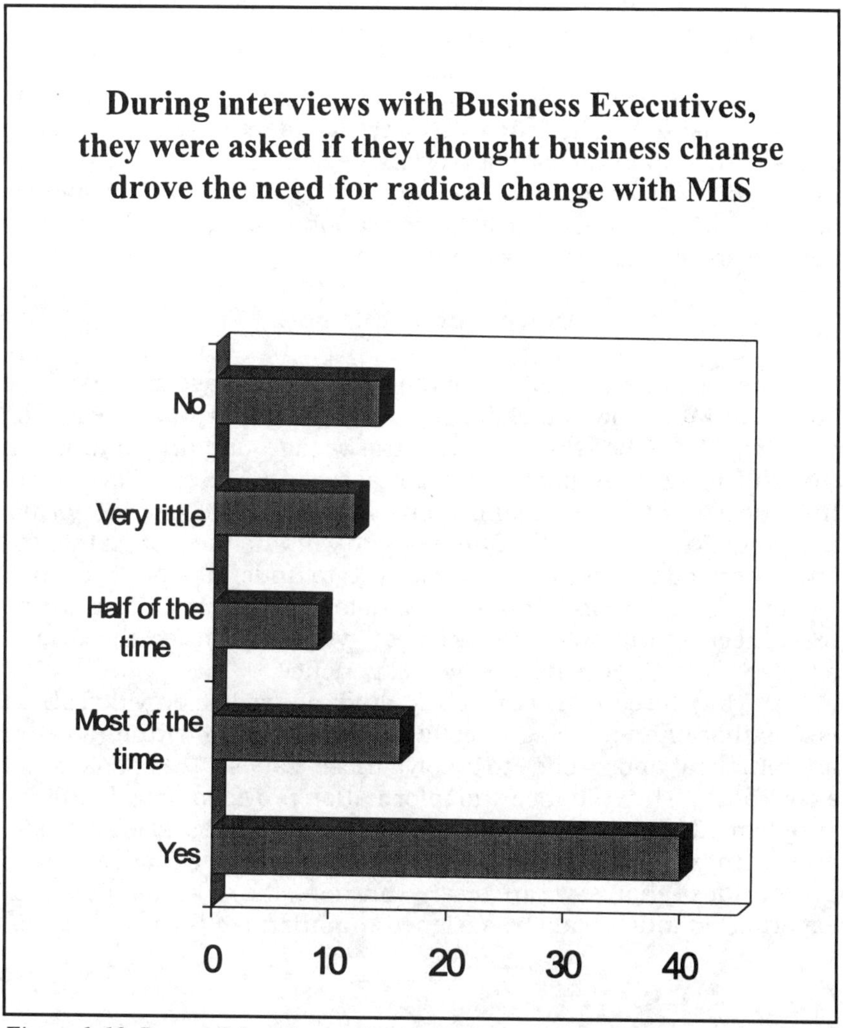

Figure 1-12 Research has shown that globalization and reengineering are two of the top challenges for business. These initiatives, more times than not, cause significant impact on MIS. Executives chart their opinions on business's impact on MIS.

serve to waste valuable time. When you add in the costs of travel, the economical way of conducting meetings is clearly teleconferencing.

Challenges to MIS. In order for MIS to increase their contribution to the business, MIS must become a full partner in business processes design, development and operation. This partnership will affect the way we address work, organize ourselves and implement sound technological solutions of value to the organization. Information system executives must adapt and recognize the technology to enable organizations to conduct business efficiently. Technology does not drive business.

Competition has forced the oil of technology to mix with the water of business. These two distinctively different disciplines, once rivals with a spotty record of working together, must now join forces to stave off our competition. The combination of strategic technology direction with strategic business operational plans provide a competitive advantage in the world market.

Objectives of this book

The reengineering efforts of the early 1990's have increased the stress on MIS. Now the challenge is to reengineer ourselves. The objective of this book is to provide the background and foundation that will allow the radical change necessary for MIS to contribute to the success of the organization. Through the use of forms, worksheets and practical examples, you will gain the insight into the reengineering process necessary for you to undertake projects such as this. In addition, through the detailed understanding of the reengineering initiatives in business, you may gauge the overall effects your MIS organization will experience.

During the course of this book, guidance will be provided about issues that often arise as a result of reengineering with innovative and practical approaches to resolve these issues. This book is not a cookbook. The guidance and information provided here should be supplemented by a project team that is experienced and knowledgeable with regard to reengineering techniques. Because of the magnitude of change we are discussing here, the risks mandate that experienced individuals be assigned to undertake these activities.

REENGINEERING

Management Information Systems

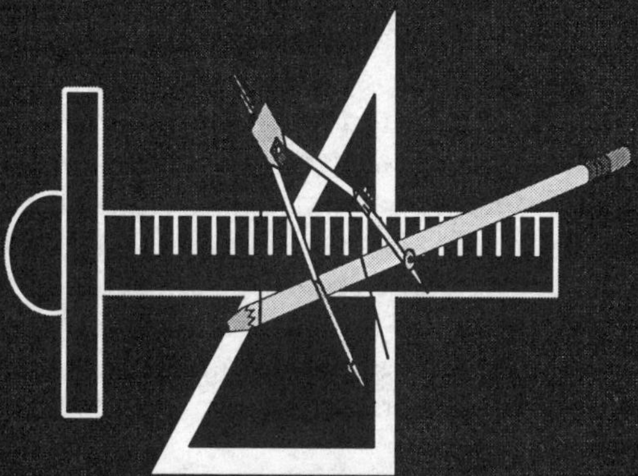

Chapter 2

Reengineering the MIS Organization

The need to improve MIS performance implies change. Reengineering the MIS organization will take the same approach as used in business reengineering. The changes brought about by the reengineering of business will be used as drivers for the redesign of MIS. Knowing what you want to become is essential before going ahead with reengineering. To bring about successful change, MIS must have a well-defined vision to provide direction and guidance. Today, in many cases, MIS is lacking a true vision. If you don't know where you want to go, any road will take you there and if you only have a general idea you will take a long time finding out your true destination. The reengineering efforts must be based on a concise vision of the future. You need to know where you want to end up before you begin the journey. The vision must position MIS as a contributor to the business. This is the underlying strategy throughout the reengineering of MIS.

Vision refers to an anticipated image of the future organization as seen in the minds of the executives. This image must be articulated and shared by all those who are participating in the reengineering efforts and charged with effecting the changes. The visions paint a shared picture of the future of the organization, establishes direction and values. Incorporated in the formulation of the vision are influencing factors such as customer, market, regulations, best practices, technology, and competition.

Vision Frame: The future MIS organization will be transparent to the operation of our core business. Built around the core business processes, the technological infrastructure will be modularly constructed to adapt to the evolution of the marketplace. MIS will equip our business process families with tools upon which they may compete from a position of strength. Information necessary for the efficient operation and control of the business will be collected, processed and stored so as to transform raw data into a business asset. These features shall be accomplished with minimal cost and maximum benefit to the business operation and our customers.

The objectives of the visioning phase need to be achieved prior to moving forward. The first objective is to script guiding principles that will drive the vision of the new organization and define all the influencing factors. Care must be taken to align the vision of the MIS organization's view and the business view of the future. Once this has been completed, you can establish a vision that looks at the future and defines how the organization would like to be viewed at that point in time. This looks at not only who the organization, business and MIS are, but defines how they want to be positioned by the values and beliefs that they feel will meet the future market needs.

The first step is to set the mission, goals and objectives on the new MIS organization in accordance with the vision. The mission statement needs to reflect the true work being accomplished by MIS. This statement should be short, no more than a half dozen sentences, and have a concise statement of what MIS is all about. This statement must be 100 percent aligned with the direction and strategies of the business. Questions answered in the mission statement are:

1. Why does MIS exist?
2. What is the scope of products and services we provide?
3. What customers do we intend to serve?

Mission Statement: Our organization will provide customers, internal and external, with a technological base required to effectively conduct business easily and from an advantageous position. We will anticipate the future needs of our customers and deliver superior capabilities through the monitoring and sound application of technology. Our efforts will be judged by our contribution toward achieving the business's critical measures of success and exceeding customer expectations.

As you can see, the mission of MIS has significantly changed from the original charter. At first, MIS merely developed and operated a facility to collect and disseminate data about the business operations. Thus the original name Data Processing (DP). This role expanded as technology provided new functionality and capabilities. DP began to process data and transform it into meaningful facts. This is how we became Information Systems (IS). In an effort to elevate the importance of information systems, the title Management Information Systems (MIS) was adopted. The MIS organization provided management the information they needed to monitor and control the organization. A new name is needed to correctly portray the new charter of the reengineered MIS organization. Information

Asset Management (IAM) reflects the "what" the organization requires of information technology today. Information is an asset when managed as a resource for efficiently and effectively conducting business. Implicit in the future vision and mission of the reengineered MIS organization is the support and contribution to business through the use of this new and valuable resource. Now that we have a vision of what MIS will become and a name that is reflective of what will be accomplished by this part of the organization, objectives for the new organization can be established.

The objectives are the guiding principles upon which the MIS organization will operate. Each of the eight focus areas identified on the disk of change have a set of principles to place some lines around the area and add structure to the areas operation. The alignment of these objectives and principles with the mission statement is a critical success factor for the reengineered MIS organization. Assistance should be sought from the core business process owners on establishing the guiding principles and placing goals to evaluate success. They know what they need and expect in terms of support from information systems. IAM is responsible for not just meeting, but exceeding their expectations. Here are some examples of objectives which have merit and may be considered in establishing objectives specific to your organizations needs.

Objectives:

1. Implement a cost-effective technology architecture that is flexible enough to rapidly adapt to the business dynamics and scaleable to expand and contract as the demand for goods and services change.

2. Develop cost-effective techniques and tools that will allow rapid response to required changes to our application portfolio.

3. Drive the best practices process models by anticipating the future information needs of the business and deliver the necessary technology and applications.

4. Manage information assets in a fashion that will provide a competitive advantage.

Goals are the milestones or significant accomplishments along the way to achieving the mission and ultimately the vision of the reengineered MIS organization. These goals must be specific, attainable, relevant and framed in a given period of time. This will allow management to measure the progress toward the future image of the reengineered MIS organization. Example goals that have been used in this process are identified next.

Goals: *Within two years MIS shall:*

Have a 70 percent reduction in time and cost to deliver new systems;

Replace all basic functions with package solutions;

Obtain 100 percent ownership of critical projects by the business-process family;

Be flexible to accommodate 80 percent of user autonomy;

Educate the business-process families about process transformation brought about through application of technology.

It is important to understand that goals are identified based on the current position of the MIS organization. Goals identified for one specific situation may have already been achieved by other organizations in the field. On the other side of this equation, some goals listed above may be very far off from the current position of another MIS organization and therefore not attainable in a reasonable period of time. Reasonable expectations must be set or the entire project will not be taken seriously and is destined for failure. This is not to say they should not be difficult to achieve.

At this point a clearly identified picture of the future organization should be in everyone's mind. This illustrates what we plan to achieve through the reengineering of MIS. Now we can concentrate on the reengineering activities required to achieve this vision. Reengineering takes a holistic approach to redefining the way we conduct business. All components that combine to make up the total organization must be incorporated in the reengineering activities. The product of these activities are the redesigns. Redesigns are newly defined processes and accompanying attributes needed to operate and conduct the business of MIS. The associated metrics controls required to monitor and manage these processes are just a few of the attributes. There are several components upon which the reengineering efforts will focus. The review and probable redesign of each component is necessary to achieve dramatic results. Addressing all of the components that make up the MIS organization will provide a holistic approach to change. Failure to address all of these areas typically result in failure or only incremental improvement in critical measures of success.

Eight Components for Reengineering

Processes	Human Resources
Measures	Organization
Values & Beliefs	Technology
Controls	Culture

These eight components are individual focus areas within the reengineering efforts for MIS. It is unlikely that any one of these areas will go untouched by the reengineering effort. The magnitude of change required of each area is dependent upon how close or far away the existing organization is in terms of the new vision. Additionally, it depends on how well aligned MIS is with the business unit. The more significant the change, the longer and more difficult the reengineering process will be, if for no other reason than to reduce risk and allow the new organization culture *and* values and beliefs to be nurtured and internalized by the staff.

Reengineering the MIS organization is a difficult and time intensive process. Very little organizational change takes place instantaneously and MIS will be no exception. The project team should plan to spend the majority of their time concentrating on the redesign of the MIS organization. Key participants in this effort will be dedicating 80 percent of their time while others will need to participate on an *as needed* basis. Reengineering starts with the perspective of a blank slate and asks, "What do you need to do to meet the needs of your customers, clients, government and the organization?" Un-hampered by the sins of the past, innovative, out-of-box thinking allows freedom of design when redefining the MIS processes, policies, procedures, etc. The design freedom translates into new approaches which offer tremendous benefits in terms of productivity, efficiency and customer satisfaction. It is not uncommon for goals as high as 10 times the profitability to be set for reengineering projects. Not surprising, recent studies have concluded that these projects, in many cases, have only come close to meeting the desired goals. Other projects have only achieved incremental improvements. With every technique comes successes and failures. All too often we become so embroiled in the reasons why we should not try such bold undertakings needed to improve our operations, we all but eliminate projects that are all but sure things when it comes to success. Inaction has its own risks and should be considered when making decisions. If you and your organization are only a little unhappy with the performance of MIS, the associated costs and the benefit MIS brings to the business, keep with what you are doing now. But as the evidence in Chapter 1 points out, our business counterparts are not at all happy about the performance of MIS, nor do they like to deal with MIS because of the attitudes of our people and we speak a technical language fraught with jargon and not well understood by the business community.

Reengineering, when done properly, will touch virtually every part of the organization and subsequently every person within the organization. In many cases, the efforts required to change the mentality of the workers dwarfs the work effort expended performing the redesigns of the MIS processes. The redesigns often meet with substantial resistance. Generally, the mentality encountered is "We always did it this way before," and "Why should we change the way we do things?" This reflects the culture currently ingrained in the current MIS organizations. Changing this attitude will indeed be challenging. Along with the new approaches and processes, new tools, techniques, methods and skill sets will all become a by-product of reengineering effort. Failure to retool our MIS shops will surely result in failure. In order to provide a framework to assess, plan and coordinate the changes that will take place as a result of reengineering, the touch points need to be identified and documented. Thus the birth of the Disk of Change (see figure 2-1). This unit of measure allows one to look at and consider all the components that make up the operating environment of MIS. When one component is disrupted due to change, the ripples expand and are felt in all the other areas represented on the disk.

During the reengineering effort it becomes necessary to look at what a change in one area will cause to others. In order to assure that all areas are considered, you must walk the parameter of the Disk of Change and explore the ripple effects. Processes are the key to reengineering. You must start with redefining the MIS processes and move the supporting components. By starting at the top and working in a clockwise motion you must visit each area and assess what concussion will be felt due to the changes brought about by the reengineering initiatives.

Scope of MIS Reengineering

Complete redesign of what we now know as MIS is required to meet the challenges of the 21st century. Being second best or status quo will no longer be acceptable. The structure of the organization is such that it is disjointed with our business counterparts. Misalignment between these two factions have lead to many autonomous work-around solutions being formulated and based on PCs or in some cases manuals, journals and logs outside the control or knowledge of the executive leaders.

Bringing the business improved information and increased functionality is the main thrust behind the new MIS organization.

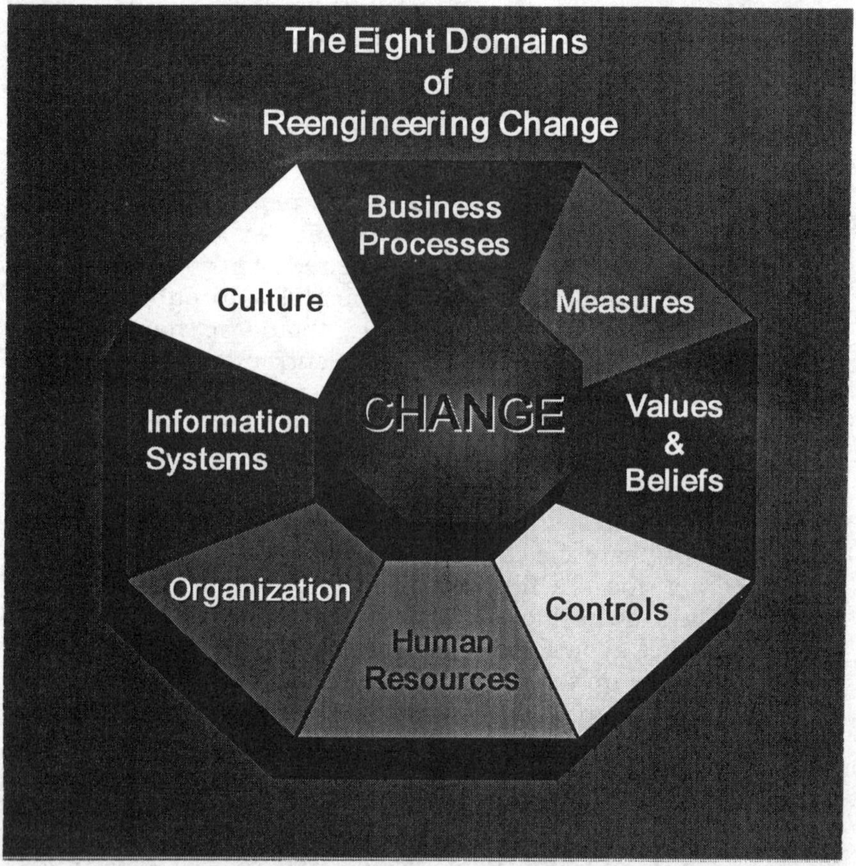

Figure 2-1 The Disk of Change depicts the areas where the ripple effect of reengineering may be felt. The touch points identified here must be considered any time you make a change to any element on this disk.

But how do we get there from here? Looking at the magnitude of the change, many CIO's would answer, "You can't." Clearly, the task is challenging, but can be achieved through proper planning and talented resources being brought to bare against the fundamental problems that exist within MIS.

In looking at the scope of Reengineering MIS let's first list all the functional areas within the sphere of a MIS organizational support of a product, manufacturer, and distributor. The following is a list of the areas which often make up the functional model for an organization as MIS relates to business.

FUNCTIONAL AREAS

* Sales
* Financial

* Manufacturing
* Management
* Marketing
* Human Resources
* Distribution
* Shipping & Receiving
* Export/Customers/International

Each of these areas have their own characteristics and needs. For this reason the MIS organization must align a portion of itself with each of these functional areas. This is necessary to fully understand the intricacies of the functional area and to become a partner with that area in the development, maintenance and support of the area's information needs. This functional area alignment will be further addressed in this section when we look at the organizational structure of MIS.

No one will dispute the importance that technology plays in almost every part of our lives. Never before have we experienced the

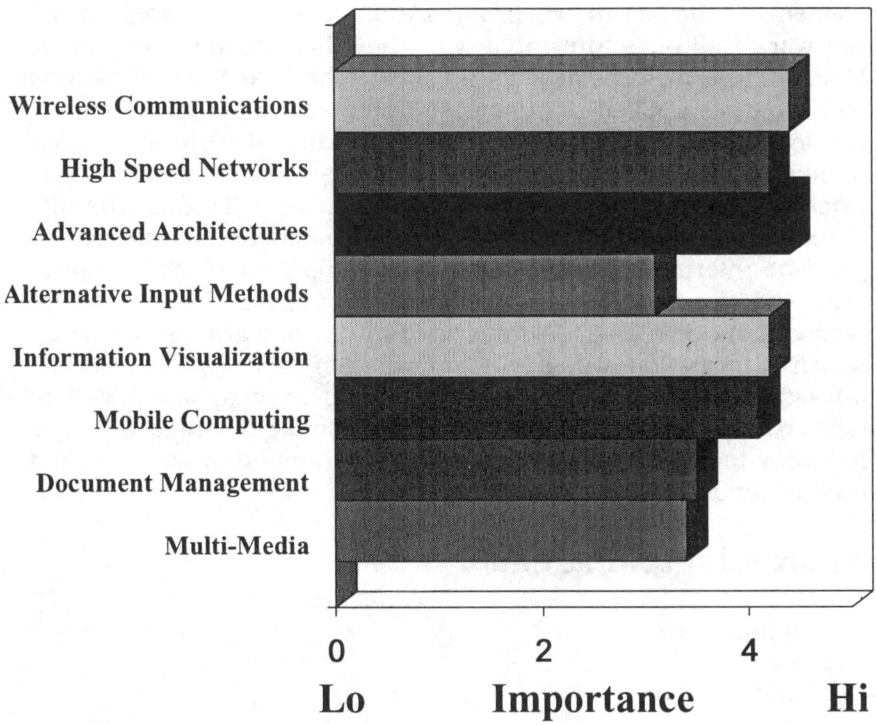

Figure 2-2 Technologies that hold the most promise for MIS in their efforts to better align themselves and meet the needs of business.

magnitude of change brought about by technology. Nor have we experienced the accelerated rate at which technological advances came into the market. This impact has been felt the strongest in the business community. The challenge of MIS is to identify technologies, both existing and emerging that will support the functional areas of business and improve the responsiveness and service levels of those areas both internally and externally. This requirement will necessitate the modification of the traditional MIS organizational structure as much as the alignment of MIS with the functional areas within the business unit. A technology model must be developed that describes the supporting technology for each functional area of business. The following is a list of technologies that hold the most promise for business process transformation.

Each functional area presents a challenge and its own special set of requirements and needs that must be satisfied by the information infrastructure. Focus groups are often spawned to address specific technical areas in order to drive the redesign to the necessary level of detail. In the event that the size of the undertaking requires multiple focus groups, particular attention must be given to cross-functional area integration and design issues. Failure to include all elements of the picture will produce a process or structure that will not work well once integrated with the other technological areas. History illustrated the need for an across-the-board view of the way technology is applied to business. Today the MIS organization is burdened with systems we give fancy names to that are inhibiting our ability to deliver technological solutions cost effectively. The enterprise-wide view of the way technology is applied will reduce the cost of maintenance and support required for business operations.

The information infrastructure is comprised of technological areas that are required to provide process support. These areas are components that must be integrated into a cohesive backbone on which information will flow. Information is an asset and the infrastructure and architectural planning is what allow MIS to deliver information at a cost that is attractive to business. The following technological areas need to be addressed in the planning and initiation of any reengineering project.

Technological Areas

* *Architecture*
  Data
  Application
  Processing
  Communications
  Technology

* *Methodology*
  Tools
  Techniques
  Approaches

Definition of the information infrastructure will require each of the technological areas above to be represented in MIS and the reengineering team. The new MIS organization is a blending of technologists from each technological area and business content analysts from the functional areas. The organizational structure of MIS is modified to leverage the strength of each area while providing additional support for the horizontal cross section of the MIS operation. This organizational structure is without question the area of greatest impact to MIS and the most difficult to change. For this reason, we will address this issue in greater detail later in this chapter. The considerations and techniques that will lead you through the numerous decisions you will make in defining your architecture will be discussed in later chapters as well.

The Reengineering MIS Project Team

The reengineering approach in and of itself will not be successful without the proper project structure. Proper selection and coordination of this team is as essential to the success of this project as the executive sponsorship mentioned earlier in this book. The roles, responsibilities and background of the individuals must be clearly defined and understood. However, all too often the responsibilities of an individual and their authority are misaligned. This misalignment will cause reengineering projects to fail. The empowerment of the reengineering team must permit decision making without the fear of consequences that often times befall individuals who are innovative and do not play the political game in today's business environment.

The reengineering project team is a diverse group of individuals that come together with a common understanding and goal. The backgrounds of these individuals are as varied as the roles and responsibilities each will play in the project. Let's take a look at the key positions of a reengineering project, their roles, responsibilities, backgrounds and the authority each possess.

Team Members

Executive Sponsor

Role: The role of the Executive Sponsor is that of the visionary. They share their views of what the

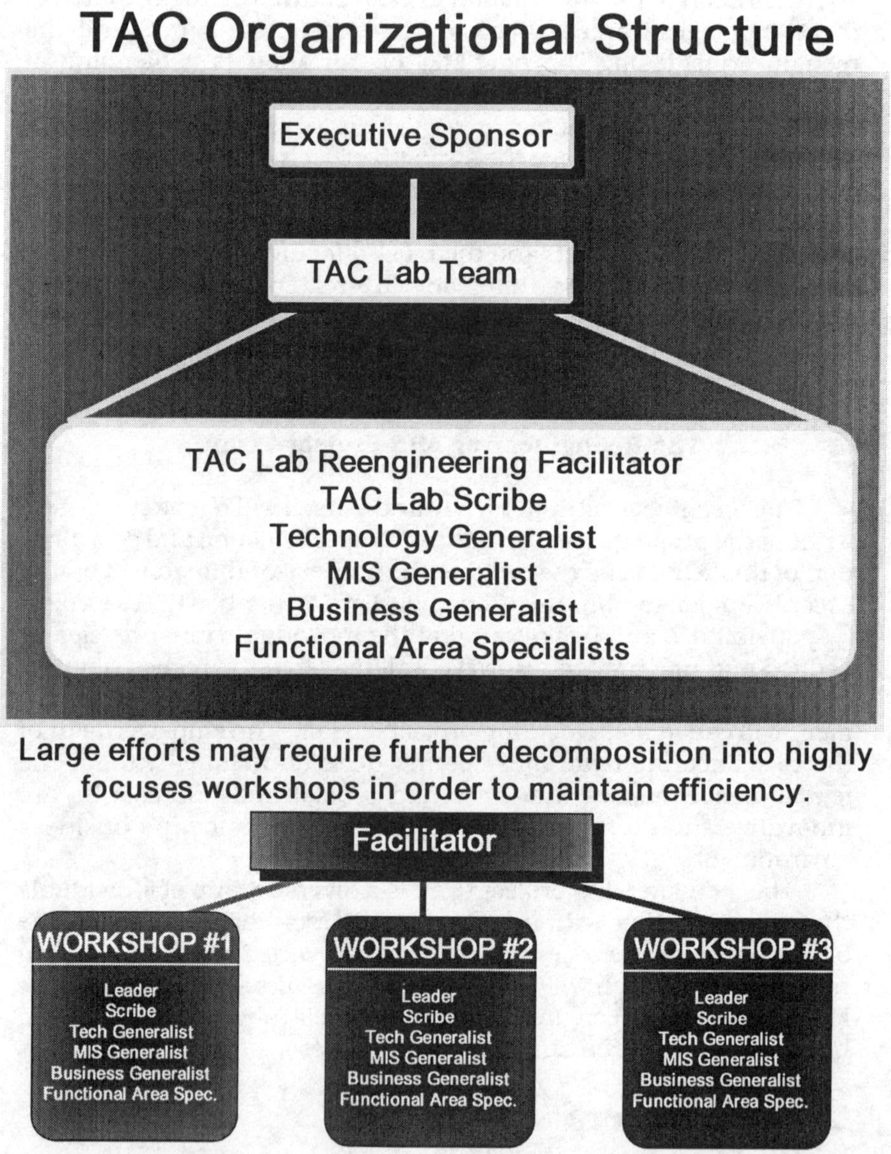

Figure 2-3 The organization of the reengineering project team. This team will evolve into the Technology Advisory Counsel and the Core Team to facilitate continuous improvement.

reengineering project will bring and the benefits that can be achieved.

Responsibility: The responsibility of the Executive Sponsor is that of an internal salesperson, referee between political camps and keeper of the purse strings.

Authority: As a general rule the Executive Sponsor must possess the clout to breakdown political and organizational walls, place demands on individuals and departments in terms of objectives and goals, and be able to get resources and financial commitments.

Background: There is no one perfect fit for an Executive Sponsor. The individual should have a business background with a high level technical understanding of what technology can bring in terms of benefits to the organization. Also, the Executive Sponsor must have an "I think I can" attitude which will light the fires of passion to excel within the reengineering project team as well as throughout the organization.

Motivation: Keeping the momentum going is critical to the success of the reengineering effort. To accomplish this, the Executive Sponsor must keep the vision of success and feeling of importance alive within the project team, upper management, as well as throughout the organization.

Reengineering Facilitator

Role: The role of the Reengineering Facilitator is that of a catalyst; one who brings about change, challenges approaches and forces the project participants to think out-of-box. One or more facilitators may be required based on the size and complexity of the undertaking.

Responsibility: The Facilitators are charged with assuring a productive environment for the project members to work. In addition, he or she must make sure that innovative problem solving is occurring and that the participants are not merely re-automate or get caught in a grid lock battle over opposing views.

Authority: Keeping with the team approach to reengineering, the Facilitator remains neutral and cannot overshadow the individual participants. However, the Facilitator does have the authority to escalate any issues or problems to the Executive Sponsor in the event they fall outside the project members sphere of influence.

Background: Key ingredients for a good Facilitator include confidence, general business knowledge, teaching experience and a personality that permits handling confrontation and constructive criticism in a tactful fashion. Individuals who conduct workshops, seminars, JAD sessions or have been trained as Facilitators should be used in this role. Due to the special skill mix required for this position, outside consultants are often used to fill this position.

Motivation: In the event an internal individual is used for this position, certain considerations must be given due to the nature of reengineering. Reengineering by nature will significantly change or eliminate many of the current jobs. For this reason, the Facilitator cannot be concerned over the loss of their position or the changes in functions their former position many undergo.

Reengineering Scribe

Role: The Reengineering Scribe is charged with the day-to-day documentation of the reengineering Team/Lab activities. This includes documenting issues, redesign activities, walk-throughs, and development of numerous deliverables/reports required during this process.

Responsibilities: The development of documentation, deliverables, reports and minutes of work sessions are the primary responsibility of the Reengineering Scribe. Presentations that depict the redesigns are also the responsibility of the Scribe. These presentations are often in a graphic format and require knowledge of one or more of the presentation graphics packages.

Authority: The Scribe is responsible for submitting the minutes and documentation to the members of the team prior to issue. They are required to ensure that all comments or concerns of the team are resolved and reflected in the final document. In addition, they are charged with the task of pursuing team members who have not contributed their comments in a timely fashion.

Background: This individual can be an administrative clerk or assistant who is good at coordinating the preparation and filing of documents. Additionally, they should be knowledgeable of the word processor and presentation graphics package of choice, plus a thorough knowledge of site specific file management and document control. Technical writers or documentation/communications specialists are excellent choices for this position.

Motivation: This individual must take pride in the punctual processing and production of documentation. This individual is measured on the timeliness and quality production of the massive amounts of reengineering documentation that are typical for these projects.

Technology Generalists

Role: The role of the Technology Generalist is to provide the reengineering project participants with a high level understanding of what technology is available, a perspective on emerging technologies, and the benefits and drawbacks of the specific technologies.

Responsibility: The Technology Generalist is responsible for ensuring that the redesigns are technically feasible and that all areas of emerging technologies that can be leverages to increased thru-put and efficiency are explored. In addition, this individual works closely with the MIS Generalist to gain an understanding of how and why the existing systems are designed and architected.

Authority: This individual has the authority to present new ideas and challenge old practices around the use of technology in the work environment. In addition, they must also have the authority to request outside sources commitment to presentation of new technologies that are appropriate to the work underway.

Background: This individual must have a technical background with a high-level view of business. With all the progress that has been made in the area of technology, this position may, out of necessity, be split up into technology tracts to assure proper coverage. It is important that the individual be up-to -date on the latest in technology. A key indication of a person such as this is one who frequently reads technology trade publications and experiments with new ideas.

Motivation: The main consideration with the motivation of the Technology Generalist is biases. Specific technology bigots cannot be permitted to participate due to the undue influence that they end up interjecting into the evaluation and visioning process. The Technology Generalist must remain neutral and each specific approach to a given technology must be evaluated solely on its merits, not personal preference.

MIS Generalists

Role: The MIS Generalists primary role is to contribute information and specific knowledge about legacy (existing) systems, processes and procedures that currently are in place within the MIS organization undergoing reengineering. This input is extremely critical when designing and developing the transitional plan. This plan is what details the steps necessary to move from the existing MIS state to the reengineered operation.

Responsibility: This individual is responsible for providing the information necessary to design the new processes and systems with temporary integration to the legacy systems. Additional responsibilities include contributing to the technical depth and breadth of knowledge within the reengineering project team. Also under this are the responsibilities of the coordination with existing MIS operations and the standards-making body of the MIS organization.

Authority: The authority of the MIS Generalist focuses on gaining access to data, systems, software and operational help from the organization. This individual must be able to commit to accomplishing activities around these areas and just do it.

Background: The MIS Generalist must be a part of the MIS organization which is undergoing reengineering. This individual must possess a detailed knowledge of the current MIS environment, organization and systems that are currently in place and the level of expertise that is within the current MIS staff.

Motivation: Because of the traumatic experience that MIS has as an organization and the individuals that make up the organization, this individual must be free from influence by personal relationships within the organization both with management and their peers. In addition, a future role for this individual must be defined prior to being placed on the team. This will go a long way to free them from inhibitions that an undefined future will bring.

Business Generalists

Role: The Business Generalist provides insight into the processes that exist within the various process families of the organization. Each segment has its own set of requirements and specific characteristics that must be understood in order for MIS to provide support. The knowledge and first-hand experience the Business Generalist possesses about the processes and functions currently in place provides MIS general perspective and valuable insight into business.

Responsibility: The Business Generalist is charged with transferring a moderate level of understanding about the business operations to the project team. This will allow the MIS Reengineering team to envision the information processing environment that must be in place to add value to the business function.

Authority: Providing the guidance surrounding business process and system support requirements, the Business Generalist establishes the baseline from which business processes and systems will be developed and supported under the new MIS. This individual must be able to select the level of information technology support, authorize the selection of enabling technologies and the application of this technology to the business.

Background: The background of this individual is the key to their ability to assure proper support of business functions by the new MIS organization. This individual must have a broad base of business experience and a thorough knowledge of how the business operates and the direction that the business is headed. This person must be able to see the benefits that the new systems will provide to the business side of the organization.

Motivation: The Business Generalist is motivated by seeing his organization, specifically the business side, able to achieve new heights in competitiveness through the proper use of information technology. This individual must express enthusiasm in this reengineering effort.

Functional Area Specialists

Role: The business functional areas previously defined in this chapter must be called upon from time to time for their insight, process knowledge and business sense. Providing support to the MIS reengineering team, these individuals work with the group on an *as needed* basis. The entire effort of Reengineering MIS may be jeopardized if the support from the business functional areas is not obtained. Additionally, this starts the buy in to the New MIS early on and reassures the business side of the house of their role in defining the support necessary for their success.

Responsibility: This individual has a dual responsibility; first to support the Reengineering Team in their efforts to design an MIS organization that supports business operations; second to the functional business area to influence the architecture and direction of the new MIS to align it with the goals, measures and objectives of the functional business area.

Authority: These individuals have the authority to present their view of the present and future functional business area operations and requirements. In addition they can evaluate the benefits of technologies that MIS is exploring in an effort to identify enabling technologies.

Background: These individuals are key functional business area users that possess full knowledge of the business operations and direction of the marketplace and the future direction of the business unit or functional area.

Motivation: The person or persons chosen to fill this role strive to get the assistance that is so badly needed to fulfill their functional areas' objectives. They must be free to express their individual opinion without ridicule from their department or supervisor as long as they fall within the general business direction.

Now the reengineering team has been identified, where do you begin the horrendous task of completely redesigning the way in which MIS operates and conducts business? The very first step in the Reengineering process is to perform self assessment. During this self assessment phase, you must gather a substantial amount of information about where the company is and where it wants to go. Reviewing the Strategic Business Plan often times brings to the front of the team's minds the objectives that the organization has set, and identifies areas where information technology can play a vital role. From here on out reengineering requires a fairly unique approach often times an approach that is foreign to most of the participants.

Approach to MIS Reengineering

Leaving the envelop in which all of us feel comfortable operating is the basic principal behind reengineering. However, first establish where the most pressing areas of change are. This provides us with a prioritized list of what we need and points to the most urgent and, given limited resources, focuses our efforts where the most gains will be achieved, and builds momentum based on these early successes. The structured frameworks used for this activity comes from a company that developed this methodology to lend a business approach to areas not traditionally considered businesses or business operations. Applied Business Intelligence recognized the benefits of using approaches pioneered for business to positively impact the functions of operations which were considered outside what people would normally think of as business. ASCERTAIN is an acronym that is used to describe the nine phases used to orchestrate change in traditional and non-traditional business-related areas. This technique was developed by Applied Business Intelligence in the early '90s and has been updated and enhanced on a regular basis. ASCERTAIN has been applied to a wide variety of organizations in private sectors, state and local government, military, as well as traditional businesses. ASCERTAIN is a structured framework used to evaluate operational support, policies, procedures and organizational operations. The method of applying this technique is based on a nine phase approach. Each phase addresses the specific information and organizational knowledge needed to support change within an organization. Within each phase of the ASCERTAIN process,

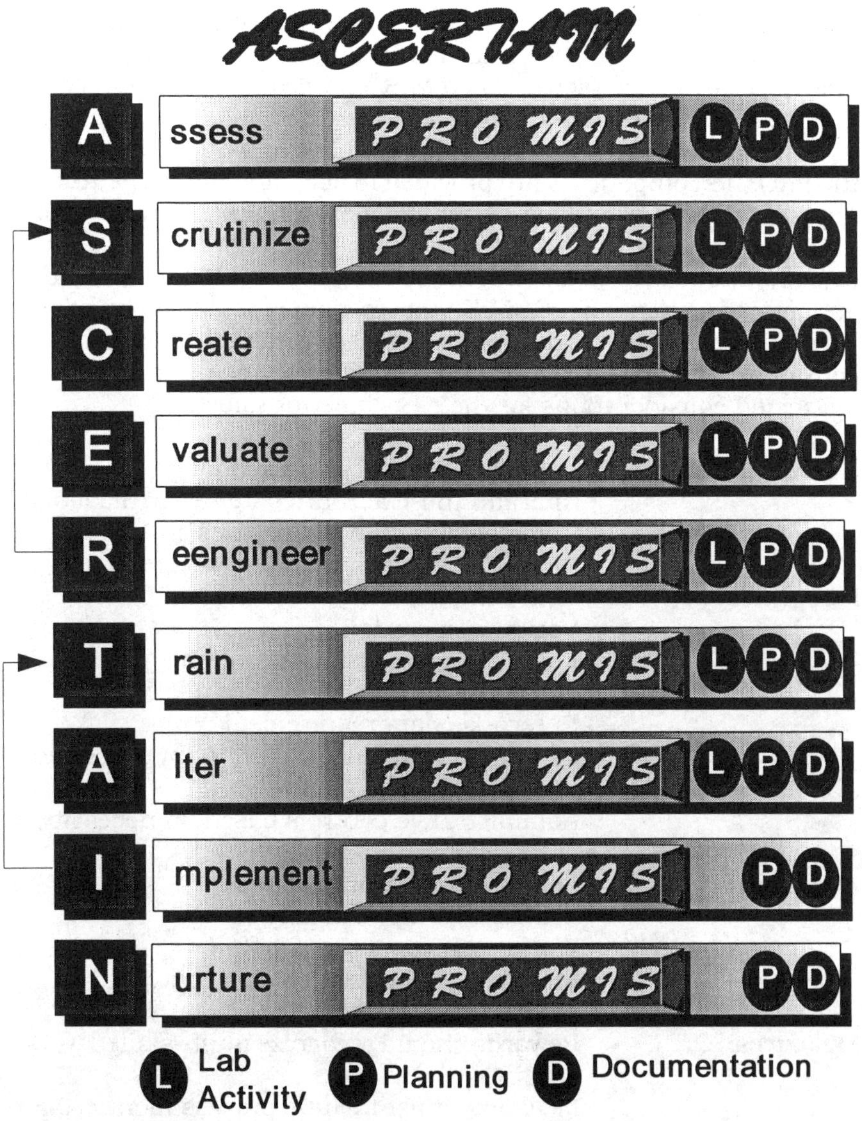

Figure 2-4 This figure depicts graphically the ASCERTAIN framework techniques used in reengineering.

various segments are included in the focus of that specific phase.

Each of the nine phases must be broken down into specific focus areas. By taking these activities to the next level of granularity, specific resources can be leveraged to address the appropriate level of detail necessary to fully understand existing functions and to design the new functions. PROMIS is an acronym used to identify the segmentation within the nine phases of the ASCERTAIN process. PROMIS looks at specific components that make up the operational organization. In an effort to maximize the benefits of reengineering

MIS, each of these segments must receive attention. Failure to investigate any one of these segments can prove to be disastrous. The structure of the reengineered MIS organization is reinforced by the specific components of PROMIS.

Design consideration that influence the way we address each of the PROMIS components are provided to elicit and stimulate thinking around how to do things better and more efficiently as well as the first question of, "Why are we doing this at all?". These design considerations fall into several functional groupings. When looking at any component of PROMIS, the reengineering team needs a checklist with these and other influences identified to validate all considerations have been made. The following are the minimum suggested considerations for the reengineering efforts.

Achievement:	Improved efficiency and economy Internal and external customer satisfaction Complete work unit based design
Integration:	Core competencies Variance operations Production-focused organization of processes, etc. Enterprise data requirement Unbiased design not constrained by old boundaries Administrative controls based on necessity
Autonomy:	Self-governing work groups Self-regulating work groups Work load balancing Intergroup coordination and control
Measures:	Rewards should recognize multi-skilled work groups Measures must include process monitoring Measures must include results monitoring Measure must include financial rewards for coaching and mentoring
Learning:	Continuous assessment must be interracial in design Change must be planned for and designed in

Including these influencing considerations in the redesign efforts of each of the PROMIS segments will increase the value of the products coming out of this reengineering effort. Note, these are the minimal criteria that need to be considered. Many other influencing

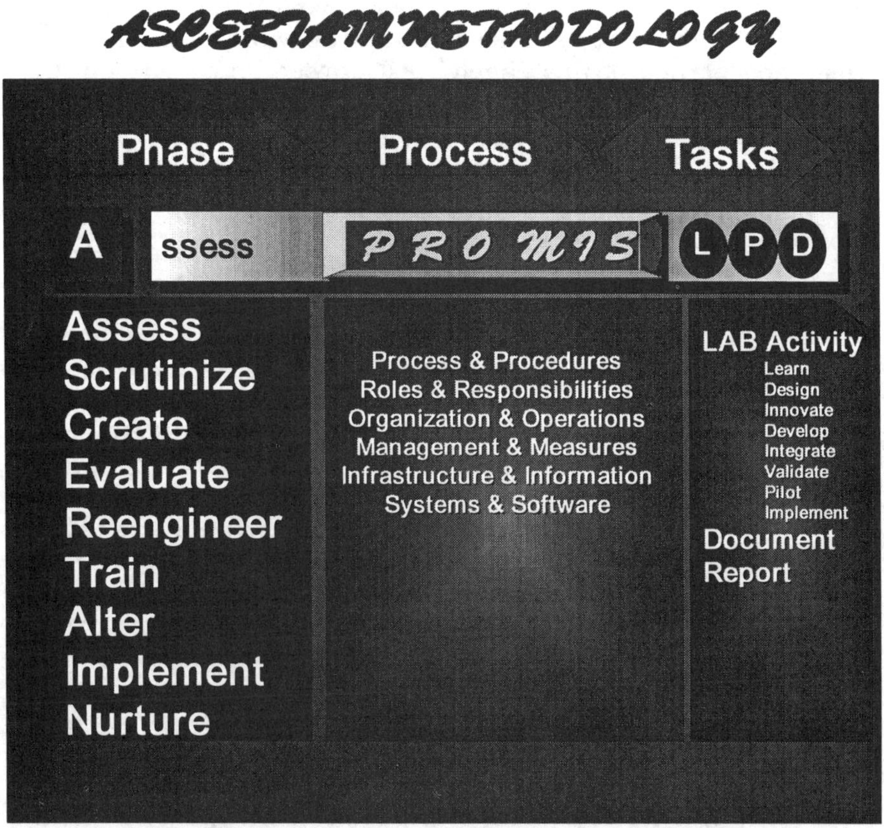

Figure 2-5 This figure represents the individual segments within each phase of the ASCERTAIN process.

factors for the specific business area must be identified in order for MIS to properly provide support.

Methodologies are not detailed formulas or recipes for success. Methodologies should be used to provide a roadmap to the journey you are undertaking. You need the option to pick the specific roads that will make up your journey. ASCERTAIN allows multiple methodologies to be incorporated within the guiding framework. This allows easy integration within organizations and decreases disruption by not forcing individuals to comply with a totally foreign approach. The path you take is as important as getting there. All too often MIS organizations get religious with regard to methodologies.

Comment How can you tell a methodologist from a terrorist? Easy, you can negotiate with a terrorist.

The use of a methodology is critical to the success of the

reengineered MIS organization. Even the methodology contained within this book needs to be tailored to your specific needs on a project by project basis. The same is true with ASCERTAIN. The following portion of this chapter will provide an overview of this technique and how it should be applied to the reengineering of MIS. This technique is enhanced by leveraging the cross-functional team and lab methodology that is presented in this book.

ASCERTAIN

Assess: This is an iterative investigation of the organization as a whole under analysis. This investigation may include the detailed documentation of these internal and external processes that impact the target organization. The product of this phase is a prioritized list of focus areas requiring change. The change that we are discussing here is not incremental in nature. To qualify magnitude of change for areas on this list one would have to establish a minimum of 40 percent in order to be a high priority focus areas. Worksheets 2-1 thru 2-8 are suggested for collection of information needed to accurately assess the current state of the MIS organization.

Below are the areas requiring investigation that follow the PROMIS philosophy. Each of these segments must be visited in order to properly paint the picture of the current state of the MIS organization. This current state picture will serve as a baseline measure to gauge the extent of the change necessary within the MIS organization.

Process & Procedures
Roles & Responsibilities
Organization & Operations
Management & Measures
Infrastructure & Information
Systems & Software

Once you have completed your assessment of the current PROMIS segments, you can start to focus on some of the more subtle areas. Often times the importance of these areas is obscure, if not addressed they can lead to disaster.

With the formal areas of MIS assessed, other areas

such as the political environment, hidden agendas and individualism (little kingdoms) must be investigated in order to provide the needed input to the impact analysis, change management and problems and issues that often arise in projects such as this. These obstacles are as important to overcome as any technical issue. Even though these areas are often referred to as soft areas, they are the most difficult to analyze and change. All too often internal staff and management is blind to many, if not all, of the issues surrounding these areas. For this reason, it is often necessary to go outside the organization in order to get a realistic and unbiased view of our internal political environment.

Scrutinize: After documenting and clearly understanding the organization under analysis, the reengineering team must sort out the political issues and biases that are always a part of organizations. Once these influencing factors have been removed, a clear and unimpaired view of the current operation can be drawn. This is important to document these findings because it now becomes the baseline to monitor and measure the changes brought about by the reengineering effort. At this point the reengineering team must challenge the current view of the way the organization operates and must ask not only, "Is this the best way to operate?"; but, "Do we need to perform these activities at all?". Always the team must strive to meet the stretch goals and aspire to become the best in its class.

Process & Procedures
Roles & Responsibilities
Organization & Operations
Management & Measures
Infrastructure & Information
Systems & Software

There is no sacred ground when it comes to reengineering. Older philosophies would endeavor to suggest, "If it is not broke, don't fix it". This is extremely outdated. This tends to bring surprise after surprise to management. Additionally, when something does break, it is always at the worst possible moment and has a substantial amount of negative impact on the organization. The new philosophy that needs to be introduced in this process is, "If it's not broke, break it, fix it and break it again". Only through the investigation and analysis of weak links in our operations can we properly position ourselves and our organizations. This has become necessary in the organizational wars between competitors in an effort to survive much less grow in today's marketplace. Only the strong or reengineered will survive.

Starting over with a clean slate is easier said than done. It is very unsettling to undergo self-examination much less the microscopic exploration of why we perform work in the fashion we do. Previous architects and management who developed the interworkings of MIS often feel ownership for their past work. Any scrutiny of past practices must be made on a professional level. Also, it must be recognized that these practices may have been state-of-the-art or even far ahead of their time when originally defined. For this reason they need to be respected and care must be taken to assure all parties that this is not an attack on the work they had previously performed.

Create: With a clear vision of what is and is not important to efficiently operate, the reengineering team sets out to create the perfect (or as close to perfect) organization and operation. The development process or methodology used to accomplish this is quite simple and easy to use. The important thing to keep in mind is that there are no sacred areas. Everything, all of our ideas, beliefs, values and methods, are free to be challenged. Out-of-box, innovative approaches are the goal of this phase in the reengineering project. The iterative lab approach detailed later in this book is an excellent methodology for conducting this phase of the ASCERTAIN process.

Once the creative problem solving has come up with the new approaches to the entire organization, clear and concise documentation which accurately depicts the new processes and structures are developed. These documents should be in as graphic a format as possible rather than text. Pictorials are much easier to understand, internalize and more importantly rationalize. Additionally, scripts that depict normal organizational operation are authored so that portrayal of these new processes can be presented to the executive sponsor of the project.

Process & Procedures
Roles & Responsibilities
Organization & Operations
Management & Measures
Infrastructure & Information
Systems & Software

All too often projects dive down into great detail at this point of the project. The goal is not to fully design the new MIS organization and operation. Rather it is to set a vision, both short- and long-term, that will become the common threads used to bind information technology and business practices into a cohesive environment. This environment must be viewed at a high level, documented and understood by all parties including executive management. A very important part of this exercise is the development of a business case for action. The business case for action identifies the benefits, both tangible and intangible, that will be weighed against the cost of pursuing the proposed vision. Recognize that this vision is high level and so are the estimates in the business case.

Comment: *Don't get caught up in the tech weeds, you'll never get out!*

Evaluate: Determine which areas require immediate attention. Identify what the current best practices are, not just within your specific field but in general. Identify the time frame within the current structure, that the technology-based software applications and operational processes were developed. Look at where you are today and where you need to be in the long run. Graphically represent the comparison. Form 2-6 will provide general guidance as to the structure and format used to make this comparison. The variance between these two measures is the gap that requires attention.

The evaluation process is meant to identify the magnitude of change required to reach your goals and objectives. With this magnitude identified, now the focus turns to identifying what benefits will be derived from closing the gap. The benefits may be tangible and intangible. The benefits should not be solely focused on head count reduction. Too often organizations revert back to head count reductions as the end all means of cutting costs. This is an outdated policy that is shortsighted. Numerous companies have found themselves in deep trouble from following this philosophy. Experienced employees are extremely valuable and important to the long term success of the organization. Positioning for the future is of top importance. Planning for long duration market trending can allow the organization to respond to the changing market quicker and more accurately and with better service. In addition, planning for expansion or new marketing thrusts will allow the MIS organization to be responsive when these needs arise. The cumulative total of the information collected in the phases completed up until now will allow the objectives and stretch goals to become more refined.

Process & Procedures
Roles & Responsibilities
Organization & Operations
Management & Measures
Infrastructure & Information
Systems & Software

The gap analysis and comparison of our contributions toward the business against the best of the best allows us to properly gauge our position. Positioning ourselves against competition will not only allow another means of substantiation for the changes identified as a part of the reengineering effort, but will also allow management to gauge the financial and increased benefits technology may be able to provide.

Reengineering: Now that we have clearly identified our targets, how will we reach these goals? The path or road ahead of us is filled with discoveries and learning that far exceeds what you would anticipate. The first step in Reengineering MIS is to focus on specific areas identified as prime candidates for change. Too often reengineering projects set out to solve the world's problems in one foul sweep. Not only does this take an extreme amount of time and money, but the complexity it adds to the process when not broken down, is extraordinary. This in many cases is what causes reengineering projects to fall short of the desired goals or even fail. Take the world of change you have identified up to this stage of the project and logically decompose the areas into small segments or labs. Each lab should require a team no larger than 10 individuals. Teams larger than 10 rapidly become inefficient, difficult to manage and historically less effective. This does not mean to imply others, outside the lab resources, cannot or should not be leveraged when the need requires. This is meant to limit the labs primary full-time participants. Each lab should be given a specific area on which to focus.

The reengineering lab must create the new approaches to completing the work identified within the scope of the lab. The reengineered views should align around the various areas identified under the auspices of PROMIS. Workshops and simulations are used to work through the complex redesign tasks. Roll playing becomes an important part of this process. By placing yourself in a different position, new and unique views and understandings surrounding PROMIS components can be discovered. A side benefit of this effort is a much broader understanding of the internals of MIS by the entire reengineering team.

Process & Procedures
Roles & Responsibilities
Organization & Operations
Management & Measures
Infrastructure & Information
Systems & Software

The resulting product needs to be formally presented to management. This presentation should

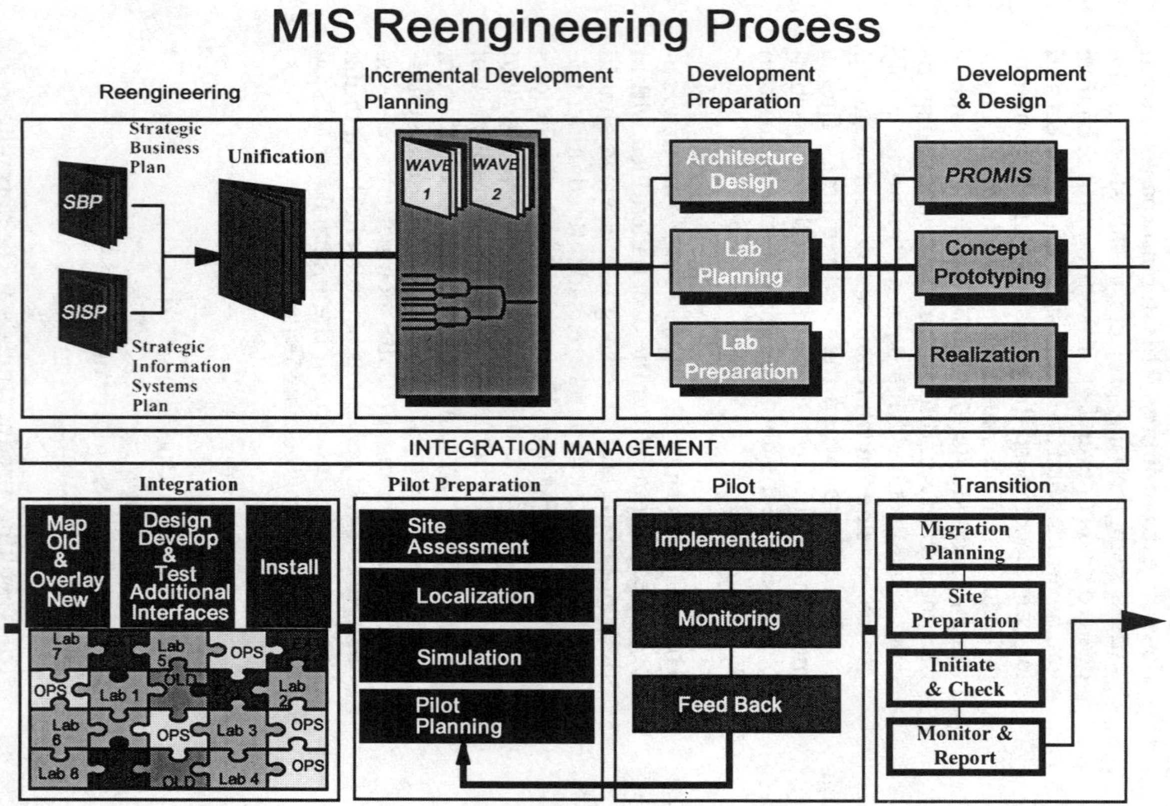

Figure 2-6 The reengineering process is represented in this graphic. Particular attention should be paid to the iterative technique used in this process.

include both high-level senior management and lower-level detailed portrayal for scrutiny and understanding by the entire reengineering team. Once again pictorial presentations are much more desirable. Documentation is required for all PROMIS components.

Train: As the organization takes on a new face, consideration must be given as to how to dress up the rest of the package. Little benefit will be gained from this effort if the staff is unable to support the new technologies employed to better support the business. Likewise, the staff must be reskilled in the area of tools and techniques that will now be used in the day to day operation of the new MIS. As well as being educated in the new culture and values the reengineered organization has adopted.

Reskillling the MIS staff is a significant challenge. This activity will be costly and require planning and time. Unfortunately, no matter how well you plan and how sound the instructional methodology, some of the staff will not make the cut. Unfortunate as this is, it is a fact that we must face and we need to be aware of this. Estimates as high as 40 percent of the MIS staff will not be able to make the cut even after reskilling. As part of planning the reskilling effort you must also plan the out-placement process and begin to put together an approach to coping with this extremely touchy issue. Keep in mind, the new MIS organization will require fewer staff so other individuals may not be required.

Process & Procedures
Roles & Responsibilities
Organization & Operations
Management & Measures
Infrastructure & Information
Systems & Software

The reskilling effort is the first step in internalizing and accepting the changes within the organization. Also this shows an interest and investment in the individuals which will serve to calm some of the fears that accompany change of this magnitude. So often skills such as team building and social skills should also be considered but are not. This is extremely important given the close ties that will be required to the business side of the organization.

Comment: MIS is filled with talented individuals. If you would look back into their past you would see they were great at math, science, and problem solving but did not get along with others. The ego often associated with MIS must go. It will inhibit our ability to become the catalyst for change within the total organization.

Alter: Probably the most difficult task in the whole reengineering effort is getting the organization as a whole to accept the changes in culture, values and beliefs that accompany these projects. Resistance to change is natural. The only way in which we have achieved success in this area is to communicate the reasons for the change in a manner that all the staff can understand and cope with. *Communicate. Communicate. Communicate.* Give the staff the true story and the entire story. Reinforce the new goals and let everyone know things will be all right. Under no circumstances should you paint a different picture than you envision. If staff reductions are going to occur, get it out on the table and deal with it. Deliver all the bad news before it leaks out.

Several vehicles have been used to successfully communicate the goals and objectives of reengineering projects as well as the impact these efforts will have on the corporate lives of all the workers. Video demonstrations, town meetings, newsletters and formal briefing sessions are all valuable assets when combating the misinformation and rumors that often accompany projects of this nature. No one mechanism will meet the entire needs of this effort and use of several of these methods are required to achieve the desired results. The more graphic the communications tool the better. One organization developed a computer game that was based around the new processes and measures. This turned into a contest to see who could score the highest. Playing the game also educated the staff in the redesigns.

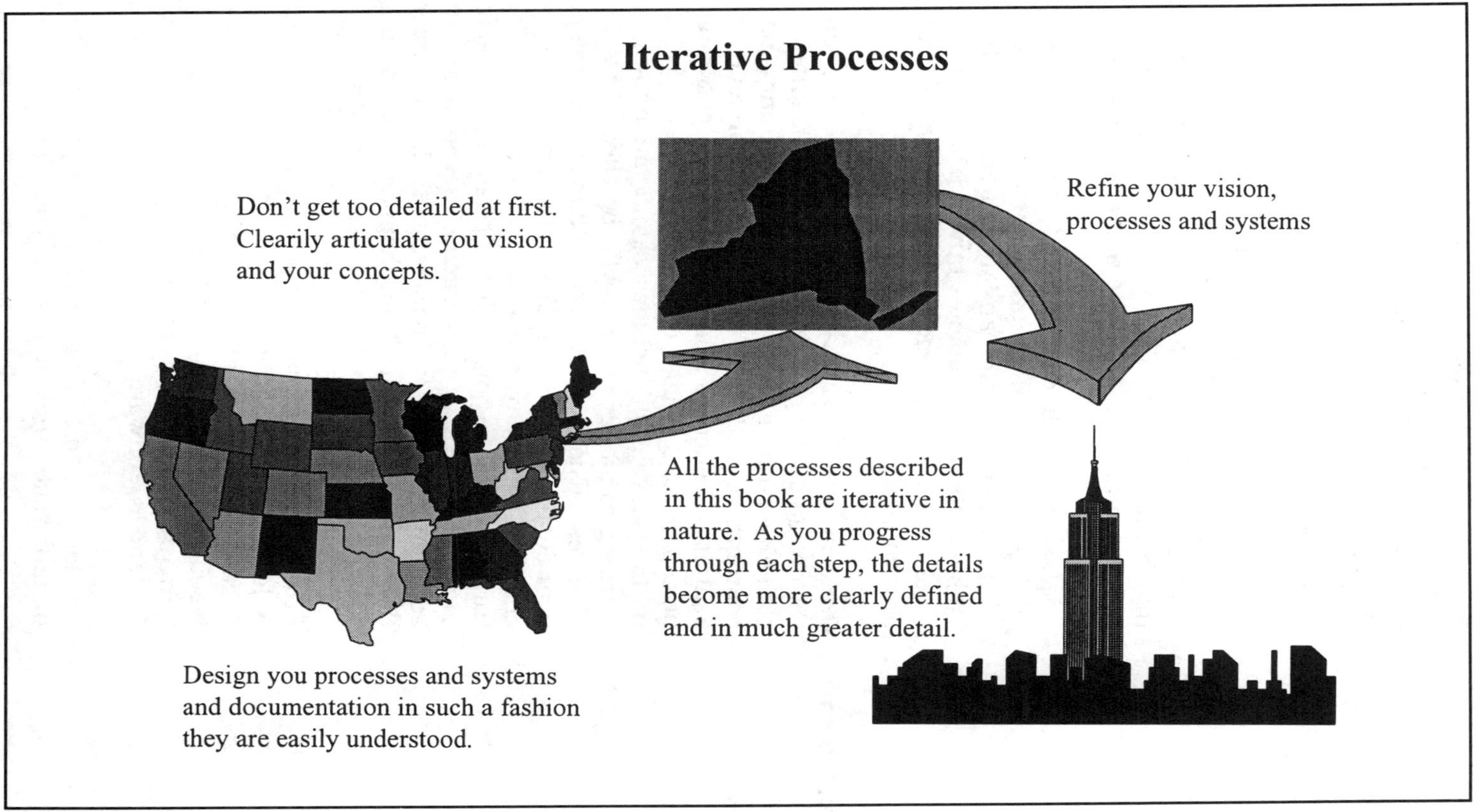
Iterative Processes
Don't get too detailed at first.
Clearily articulate you vision
and your concepts.
Refine your vision,
processes and systems
All the processes described
in this book are iterative in
nature. As you progress
through each step, the details
become more clearly defined
and in much greater detail.
Design you processes and systems
and documentation in such a fashion
they are easily understood.

Figure 2-7

Process & Procedures
Roles & Responsibilities
Organization & Operations
Management & Measures
Infrastructure & Information
Systems & Software

Failure to communicate openly and honestly will cause increased levels of anxiety and stress. This is already a stressful time. Any effort for reducing this feeling of doom will serve to ensure a smoother project and transition to the new organization.

The second method of enticing the workforce to change deals with their involvement in the design of the new organization and measurement system. This methodology promotes buy-in because of the involvement of all members and use of cross functional teams.

Implement: Designing a new organization is one thing but getting the design off the paper and into action is another. Careful planning of the transition, timing and coordination with functional business areas is essential for a successful cut-over. This activity must be coordinated. This coordination is extremely important and should include a significant amount of warning to all parties who will be effected by the changes. This is no more true than in the area of your customers. Giving them advanced warning of changes that may cause a minimal amount of turbulence in the normal flow of business will serve to smooth the way for customer acceptance. In addition, this will send a message to the customer that you are thinking about them and considering their participation in your business operation.

Process & Procedures
Roles & Responsibilities
Organization & Operations
Management & Measures
Infrastructure & Information
Systems & Software

The foundation of a smooth implementation is the planning effort that must go on. This planning effort must not only look at switching systems over, but also changing personnel and operating policies. Just as you used the Disk of Change to assess the impact of reengineering on the business, you must also use this tool to look at how to develop an implementation strategy and plan. The incremental planning and phases approaches to implementation reduce the impact and risk. Many of these efforts have experienced significant pain because they bit off more than was reasonable.

Nurture: MIS is an organization, much like business. It grows and changes over time. This is a natural process and it will continue to evolve. The natural occurrence has necessitated that we revisit the way we work and redefine these processes and architectures from scratch. In order to transition from the deeply routed organizational culture with the heavily embedded values and belief, we must cultivate the initial change and continue to foster the growth and movement toward the newly defined organization.

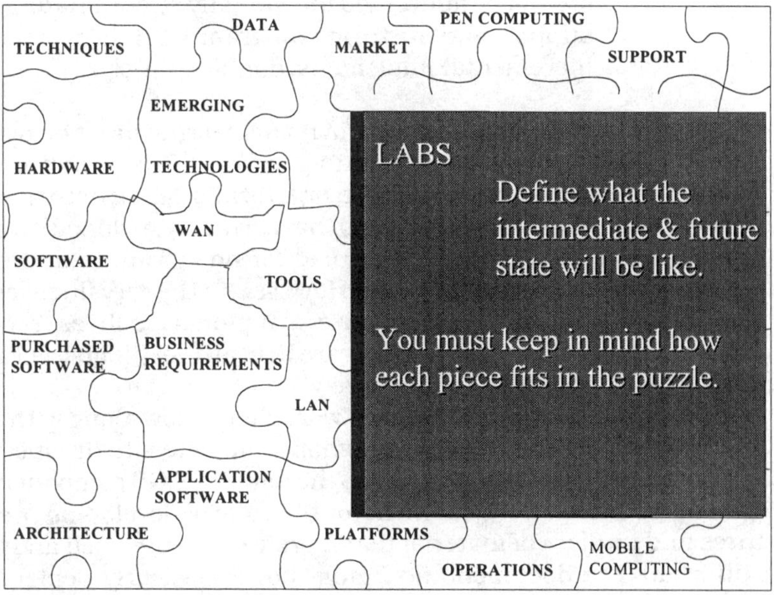

Figure 2-8 As a general guideline, the following workshops should be used as a baseline for getting started.

The growing organization will follow the path which provides the elements it needs for survival. The nurturing process must provide those elements. Elements such as rewards and measures. A sure way of ensuring failure is for management to act in the same old fashion and expect the staff to make the change first. Communications and proper measurement alignment will help nurture the personal change that must take place.

Process & Procedures
Roles & Responsibilities
Organization & Operations
Management & Measures
Infrastructure & Information
Systems & Software

Changes of this magnitude require time and assistance if they are to be internalized and made second nature. On-going support is necessary to assist the organization and the staff in continuing to grow, adapt and learn along with the reengineered MIS organization. A general plan needs to be developed for overall change. Specific components of PROMIS should be addressed individually. Coordinating the support and nurturing program with the phased or incremental implementation is a must.

Focus of the effort: The efforts of reengineering must be broad in scope with narrowly focused sub-groups. This structure is depicted in the Reengineering Team organizational structure presented earlier. Numerous projects have run into difficulty not recognizing that the area was too broad for one group to address. This is often times difficult to gauge. However, in the very first weeks of this effort monitors can recognize symptoms such as scope, expansion and contraction. Sessions are held at a very high level and numerous open issues will be boarded.

The products coming out of each workshop follow along with the PROMIS segments once the workshop completes their specific charter redesign and fully documents the new PROMIS components. Keep in mind you do not document for the sake of developing pretty pictures and binders of material that merely sit on the shelf and are not utilized. The documentation must however clearly depict the redesigns in sufficient detail so to communicate them efficiently to all parties. This documentation will be used in the communication planning function as well as the basis for educational curriculum development.

Organizational Structure

As mentioned previously, as technology was infused into the MIS organization, new departments of divisions resulted. This has left us with a fragmented operation that is difficult to control and impossible to measure. In addition to these negative attributes, the

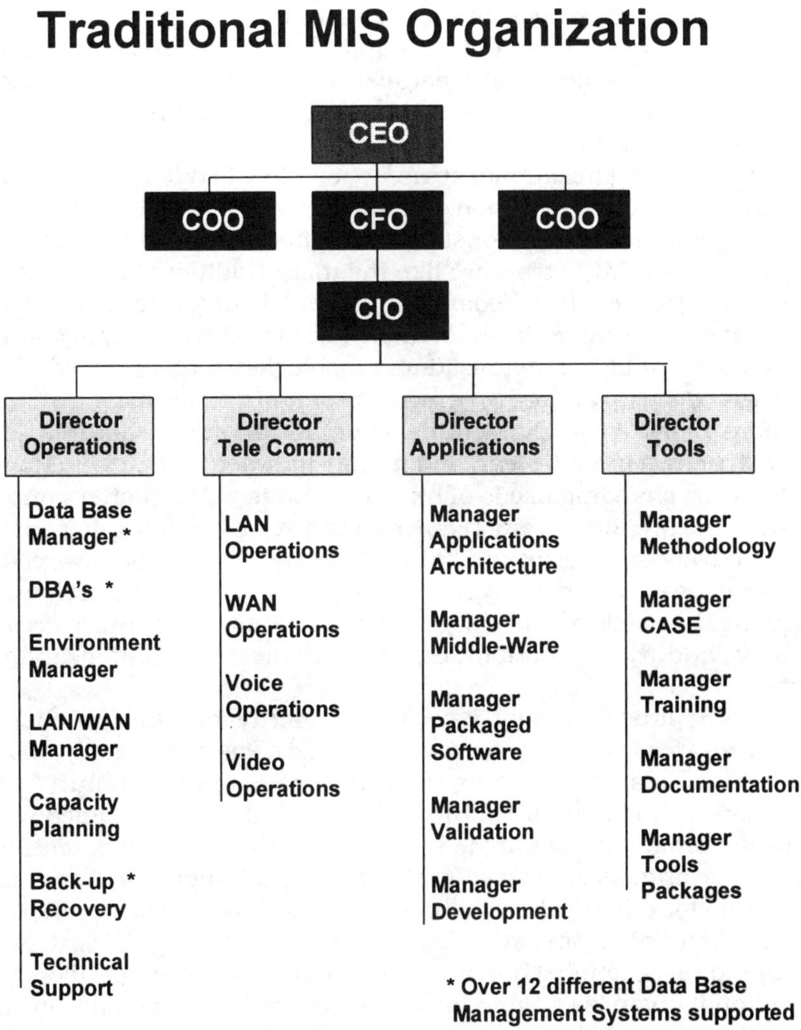

Figure 2-9 This diagram represents the MIS organizational structure of an international product manufacturer and distributor.

MIS organization was often a sore spot for functional business areas due to the added cost whether founded or unfounded. In looking at the MIS organizational structure found in most businesses today, clearly there is a need for restructuring. Let's take a look at a poor example of a MIS organization. One that is typical in today's business world. After we review the current organizational architecture, we will discuss a problem that actually arose in the course of operating.

The sheer number of departments, groups and sub-groups in this organization is evidence that the work is fragmented and a clear technological vision and strategy is either not in place or not being followed. The ability of this organization to respond rapidly to any request has been impaired. Change in this organization in its current state would be like parallel parking an oil super tanker. Sure, you can do it but it is going to take a long time and I don't know anyone who would want to.

The new organizational structure of MIS will differ slightly from organization to organization. However, the underlying structure should remain relatively constant throughout the business community. The New MIS structure like the more traditional approach is under one IS Executive. Today, traditional MIS organizational structures are primarily centralized. Centralized MIS currently accounts for 45 percent of the organizational topologies in place today. One disturbing fact is that 18 percent of organizations have no clear responsibility or clearly identifiable organizational structure. The new structure must be lean and nimble in order to rapidly respond to the ever-changing needs of business and is able to better control costs. The MIS organization currently existing has failed to control the runaway costs associated with hardware. To control these costs the new organization will control what hardware can be purchased. Meeting the needs of the business while looking at the entire picture will provide the support necessary to achieve the organizational goals.

MIS must not only have the authority but the functional business area knowledge to make informed decisions not only about hardware but all components of the information infrastructure. For this reason, the majority of the traditional MIS staff is aligned with the functional business area. The centralized control under one MIS Executive and decentralization into functional business areas only accounts for 6 percent of existing MIS organizational structures. A dramatic change from today, the concept of mini MIS groups aligned along side of functional businesses is catching on. This will allow the functional business area to have more control and influence in the application development and to determine the extent of information technology necessary to support their specific operation. Additionally, this allows the functional business areas to decide what

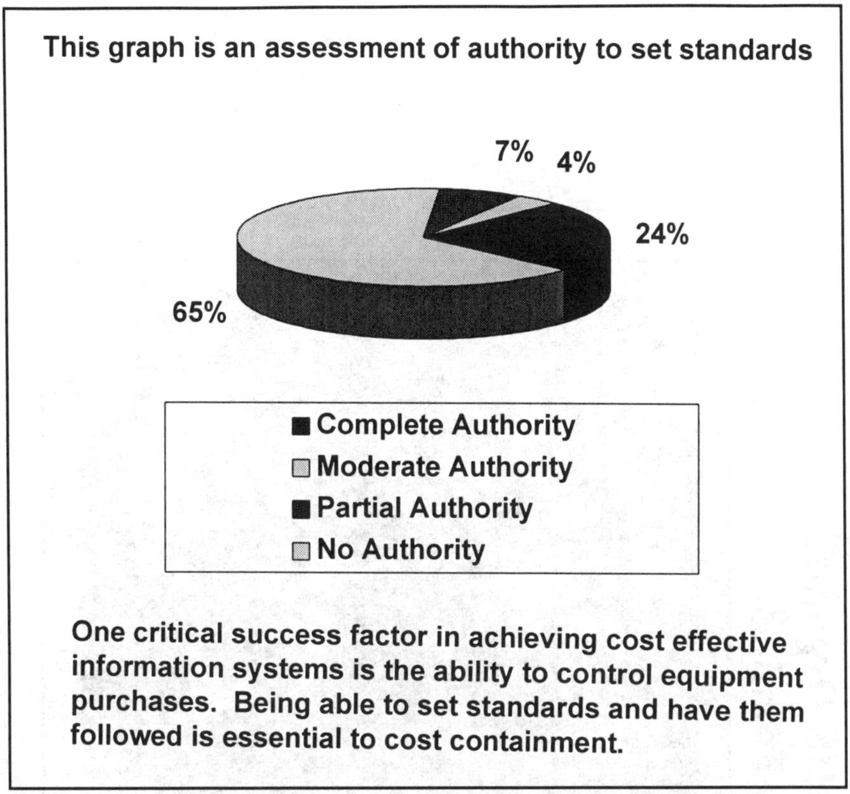

Figure 2-10 This represents the current state of MIS authority to govern purchases. Only 24% have complete authority, 4% have no say whatsoever, 7% have slight authority with 65% having a moderate amount of control over this area.

investment they wish to make in information systems as well as a sense of ownership of the systems they use.

The new MIS organization is comprised of two fundamental components—the Core Team and the Technical Advisory Counsel (TAC). These two groups are the nucleus around which the rest of MIS is built. The individual participants in these two groups must be carefully chosen and highly skilled in general business and technology. Many organizations have opted to retain outside specialists, often referred to as Subject Matter Experts (SME) to enhance the knowledge pool from which they can draw.

Core Team

This diverse group looks at business issues, problems and opportunities to identify areas where improvement can be made and is justified. In addition, they pose the question, "What would our customers, internal and external, want to do if they knew that they

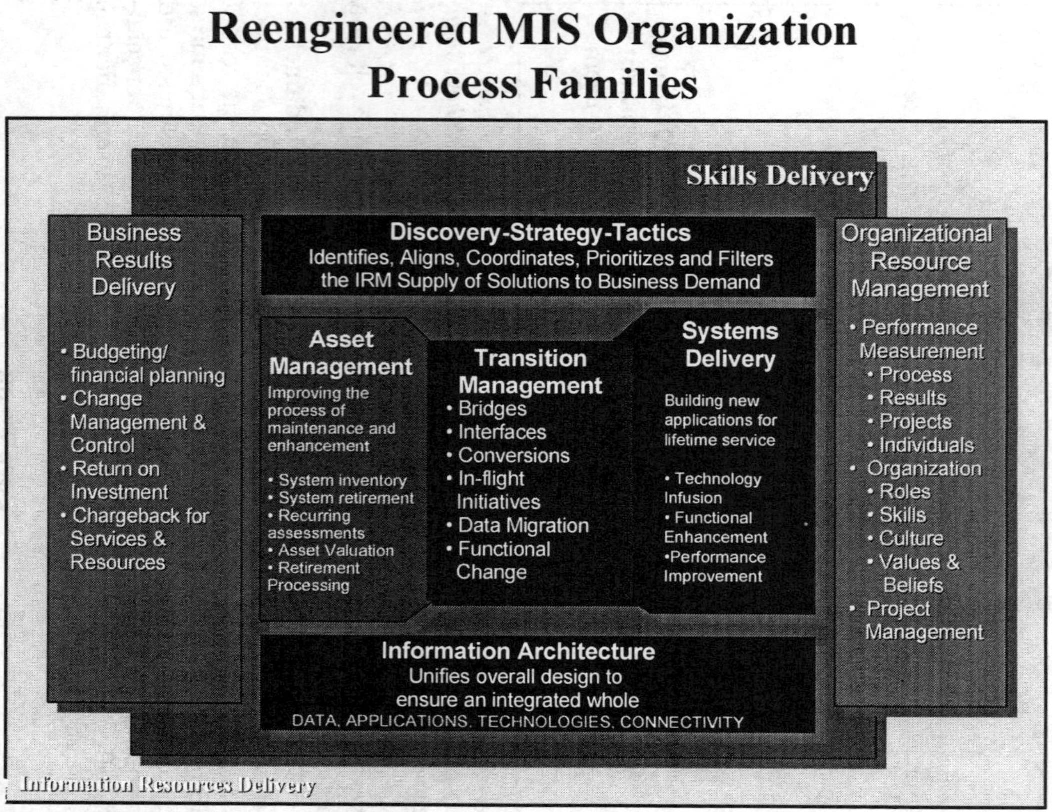

Figure 2- 11 a The new MIS Organizational Alignment Structure.

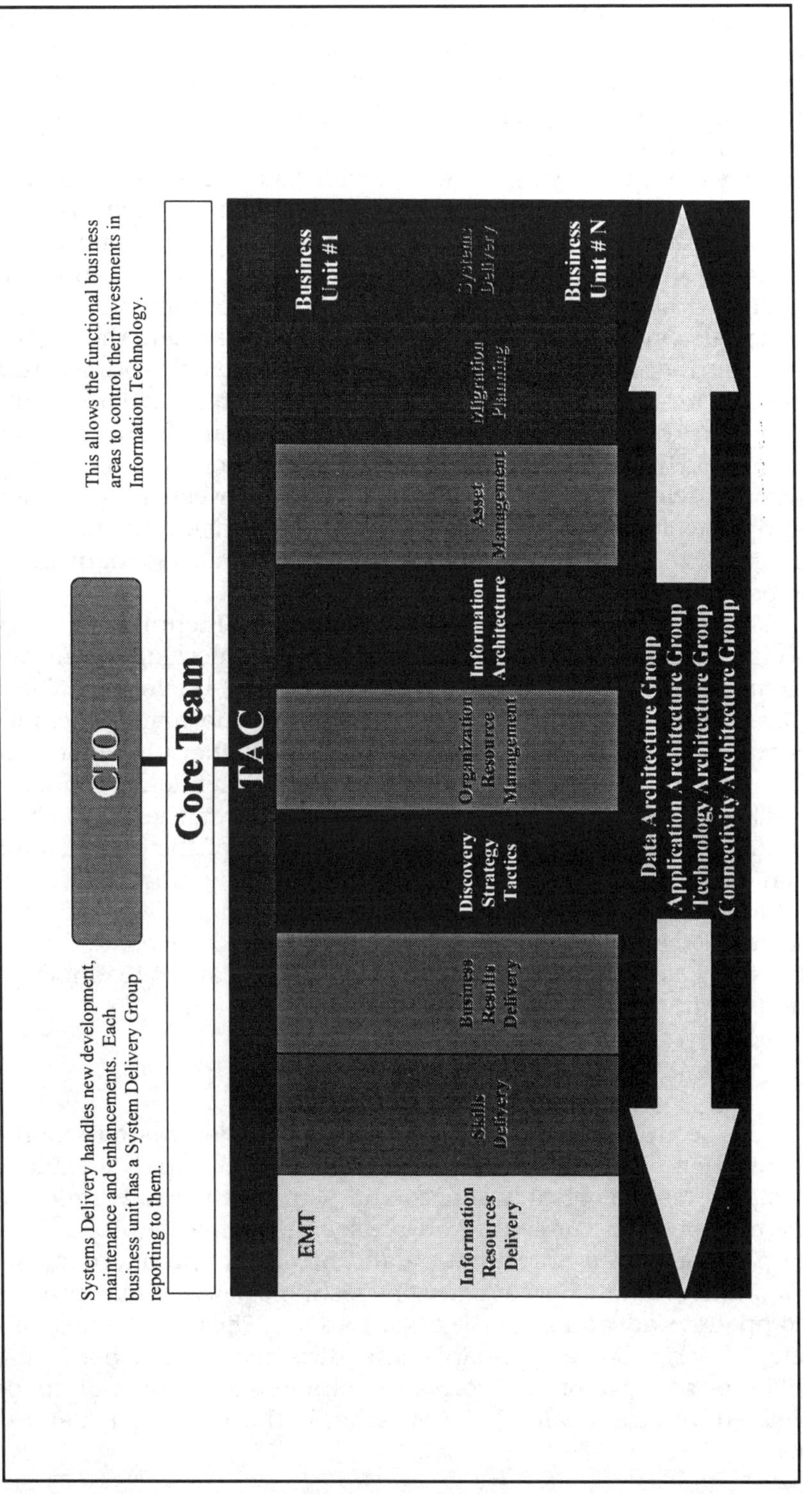
Systems Delivery handles new development, maintenance and enhancements. Each business unit has a System Delivery Group reporting to them.
CIO
This allows the functional business areas to control their investments in Information Technology.
Core Team
TAC
EMT
Information Resources Delivery
Skills Delivery
Business Results Delivery
Discovery Strategy Tactics
Organization Resource Management
Information Architecture
Asset Management
Migration Planning
Systems Delivery
Business Unit #1
Business Unit # N
Data Architecture Group
Application Architecture Group
Technology Architecture Group
Connectivity Architecture Group

Figure 2- 11 b

had the opportunity?". This does not mean to imply we have reverted back to the philosophy of "If it's not broke, don't fix it". A vigil of review and questioning is imperative to the success of not only MIS but to the entire organization. Through this self-examination, continuous learning and improvement is achieved. This achievement is what, in many cases, will provide competitive advantage in the corporation of tomorrow. The Core Team is comprised of representatives from the functional business areas (business process owners) as well as technologists. Individuals who are intimately familiar with current business and MIS operations as well as individuals who have a unique view and vision of where the organization and markets are going. Outside SMEs are used to bring in new ideas and for their knowledge about how other organizations within the industry of the business as well as external to the industry group conduct business in specific areas. Use of consultants in this fashion provides the most benefit for the dollar invested due to their broad base of experience. But —choose your consultants based on personal interviews not company profiles, responses to inquiries or company reputations.

The Core Team is heavily supported by the Technical Advisory Counsel. The TAC provides insight into new or emerging technology that may provide an advantage in conducting business. These groups are what provides the synergy between information technology and business operations. Through this collaborative effort, the alignment of MIS and business is achieved. Tremendous productivity arises from leveraging this working group. First, there is likely to be much greater support from all components of the organization when they have a hand in design and architecting the future technological superstructure upon which business will be conducted. Second, is that each individual can compensate for the others' deficiencies and serve to balance the scale of technology/ business drive.

Technology Advisory Counsel

This group charts the course for the information systems for the organization. In the past, most organizations have not been able to anticipate technological advances and plan for their integration in time to capture a competitive advantage in the marketplace. This group is comprised of technology and business practitioners who review and evaluate new or emerging technologies that may provide a competitive advantage to the organization. They are, for lack of a better description, a standards and direction setting body that functions as part of the corporate MIS organization not to be confused with the localized MIS presence at the functional business areas.

Defining a standard suite of hardware, operational support software and packaged application software allows the business to function with some degree of uniformity as well as providing a baseline for the development of functional business unit application software that will seamlessly integrate into the selected computing environment. Many organizations are spending up to 80 percent of the IS budget on maintenance due to fragmented and over expanded hardware and software suites. An example would be where Microsoft Office is the base package for all PCs and a lone group within the organization decides to use LOTUS or Dell being the PC of choice and Gateways being purchased by another group. Controlling the breadth of the hardware and software suite is essential to controlling MIS maintenance costs. As mentioned previously, the TAC has the authority to specify the hardware and software standards. Standards do not imply that deviations will not occur. However a premium charge can be assessed to the business area who has necessitated the deviation due to the increased cost of support.

Finally, the single most important responsibility of this group is the coordination of the cross functional development efforts at the functional business unit level. The overseeing of these activities will reduce the reproduction of functionality and duplication of code and effort across the functional business areas. This approach can be compared to the development and operation of individual modules that make up a fully integrated software package that will allow the business to function as a hole while allowing the individual functional business areas to operate all but independently. Thus allowing flexibility in the design and implementation of application software. However, along with this flexibility comes some restrictions. In order for this to work, formal standards for design must be established and enforced. These standards are what allows the simultaneous and independent development that is easily integrated into the overall suite of software without the costly rework that often accompanies this type of development.

Support is another function of the new corporate MIS organization. Setting up, operating and maintaining the hardware, operating systems and core group of software such as network management, data base management systems and other non application software require constant and consistent attention. For this reason these functions are retained by the new streamlined corporate MIS organization.

Outsourcing is an option for this function. The '80s saw many organizations turn to outsourcing as a mechanism of managing their MIS costs. Some of these decisions were made due to business reasons. A large one time influx of cash due to the transfer of title to the information resources often was used to drive stock prices higher. In some cases this was the basic reason for the action. In

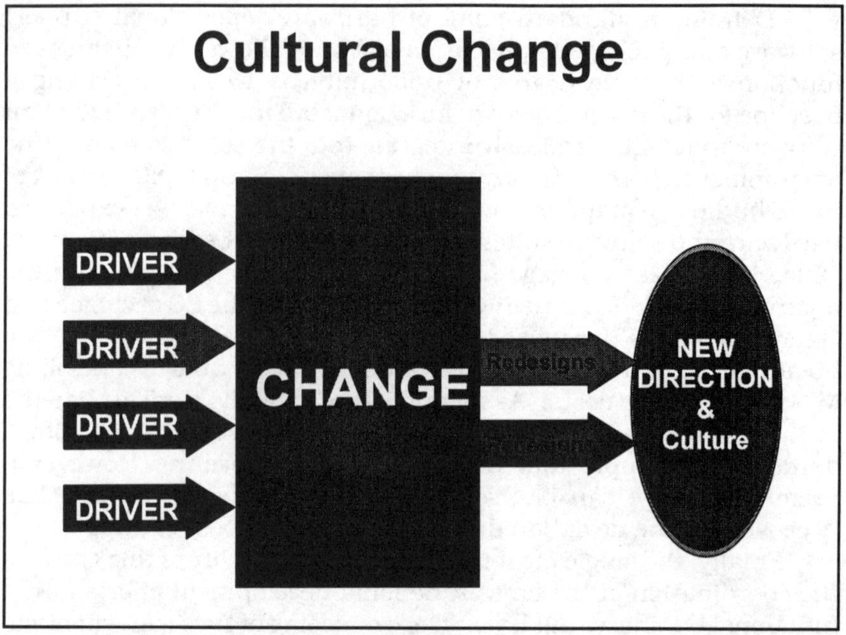

Figure 2-12 This graphic depicts the multiple drivers that directly influence the culture of an organization.

others, the business unit thought they would solve all the problems surrounding information systems. The truth of the matter is the jury is still out. Many executives would say they are receiving great operational services from their outsourcer, but they are left with outdated systems. Most of the outsourcing contracts to date do not provide incentives to increase technology, retool or redesign systems and move to more cost-effective solutions. This is where outsourcing falls short. Properly structured outsourcing can be advantageous to business. Careful design of the agreement to cover the points just presented is required. *Remember —You get what you contract for — nothing else.*

Environment Management Team

EMT serves to operate and maintain the systems and infrastructure that is defined through the collaboration of the Core Team and the TAC. The traditional glass house is managed by this group as well as the new additions which may result from changes brought about as a result of changes in the business or in the marketplace. Legacy systems may eventually be replaced. However, they must still function in order to support the business during the transition period. This period can be as short as a few months or stretch out over a decade. For this reason the size of this group is changing to respond to the retirement of subsystems under the old structure and systems.

Other areas of responsibility for the EMT include:

- Capacity planning
- Disaster planning and recovery
- Security Enterprise-wide data model
- Application maintenance
- Legacy systems evaluations, operation and maintenance
- Facility management, modifications and maintenance

Everything dealing with the day-to-day operation of the information systems in production is included in the sphere of influence given to the Environment Management Team. In the event it is determined it is more economical to outsource the operations, whether it be just legacy systems or systems operations in total, the EMT turns into purely a management organization. At which point their charter is to monitor and control the outsourcing agency and to verify the quality of the systems operations services that is provided to the functional business areas.

MIS Element

Each functional business area is supported by an MIS Element. The MIS Element is charged with the design and development of applications to the specific business processes related to the functional area. In addition, they must coordinate and work with their counterparts in the functional business area to support cross-function applications. The MIS Element within each functional business area reports to that specific area. That allows the functional business areas to decide how much they can afford or wish to invest in information technology. This provides application control with the business function where it belongs. When information systems first arrived on the scene, the business had to adapt their way of operating to fit the inflexible ways in which the systems operated. When systems evolved and began to become more limber and adaptable to the individual requirements of organizations, a lag still existed and businesses were forced to operate the way the technical personnel wanted the software to operate. Thus making their life easier. However, business revolted and began to shift the balance to business operations. This resulted in neglect to many technical issues that would cause a significant amount of pain later. With the organizational structure we are presently using, the pendulum is now centered and equilibrium has finally been attained. In addition to the control of applications and financial investment into systems, this structure provides a high degree of autonomy for the functional business areas. While some restrictions are felt by the functional business areas because of the requirement to adhere to standards, they have a much greater say in their supporting systems than in previous structures.

Reengineering the MIS Culture

Introduction

The cultural aspects are without question the hardest area to bring about change. Changes in platform, operating system or even the programming approach is much easier to foster within the workforce than changing the cultural aspects of the individuals as they relate to their jobs within the organization. The softer side of the make-up of our organizations is oftentimes based on opinion not reality. Key areas must be communicated, internalized and reinforced in order to nurture the transition from the old mind set to the new.

There are numerous driving forces behind cultural change. These forces include regulations, rules, corporate position and strategies, and power structure. Other areas include, political and cultural groups and behavioral styles. The combination of factors

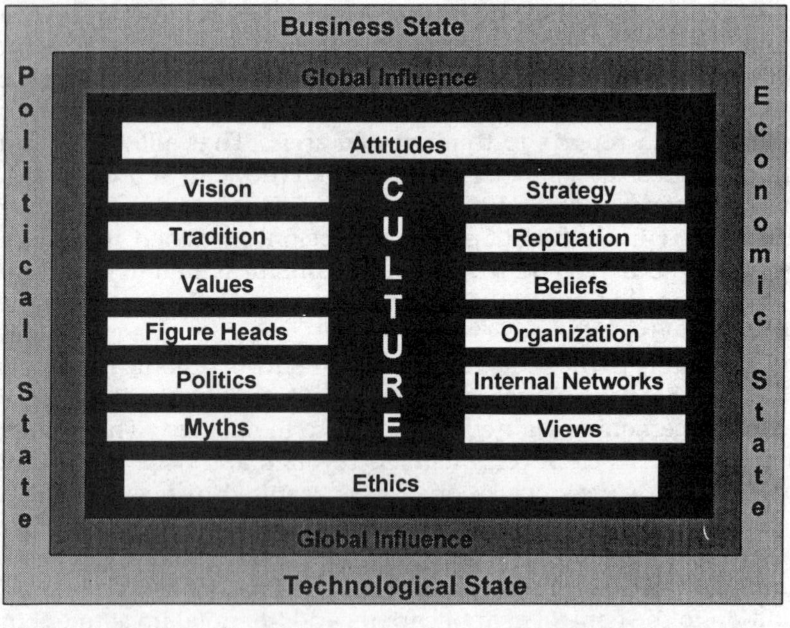

Figure 2-13 This graphic represents the topology of cultural change and factors that influence culture.

along these dimensions serve to shape and influence the way we conduct business and function internally.

In addition to the cultural change factors identified in Figure 2-13, other factors influence corporate cultures. Workforce diversity, although not directly, significantly influences almost every factor that defines our culture. The US is known as a melting pot of cultures. We have the most diverse workforce today and it pales in comparison to the projection of workforce makeup in the next century. Every person that makes up the workforce contributes to the knowledge about other places and civilizations which by its own nature will serve to shape our own future culture.

As our business climate has evolved globally so must the culture of organizations. Failure to align these two elements will serve to severely handicap the organization as they strive to compete for business in the next decade. Understanding and appreciating the differences in the cultural aspect of business along the dimensions discussed previously will promote efficient cross-cultural management important for cross-border operations.

To clarify and distinguish how the new MIS culture differs from that currently in place, we have provided a 50,000 foot view of a modified culture. In order to properly devise an internal culture, multiple factors must be considered.

NEW

1. Lead with improved reality
2. Charts own course, autonomy
3. Reveals significant difference
4. Establishes differences in believable and quantifiable ways
5. Exposes reality that may be at odds with own image then redefines themselves
6. Integrates design and process and considers all touch points
7. Depends on internal and external customer word of mouth
8. Lets service express organizational values
9. Builds trust and credibility
10. Integrated marketing and delivery of services

OLD

1. Leads with technology image
2. Focuses on competition's use of technology
3. Exaggerates trivial differences
4. Makes claims supported by contrived evidence
5. Hides reality at odds with image
6. Applies world class style
7. Depends on company sponsored communications
8. Separate marketing and delivery and does not recognize internal customers

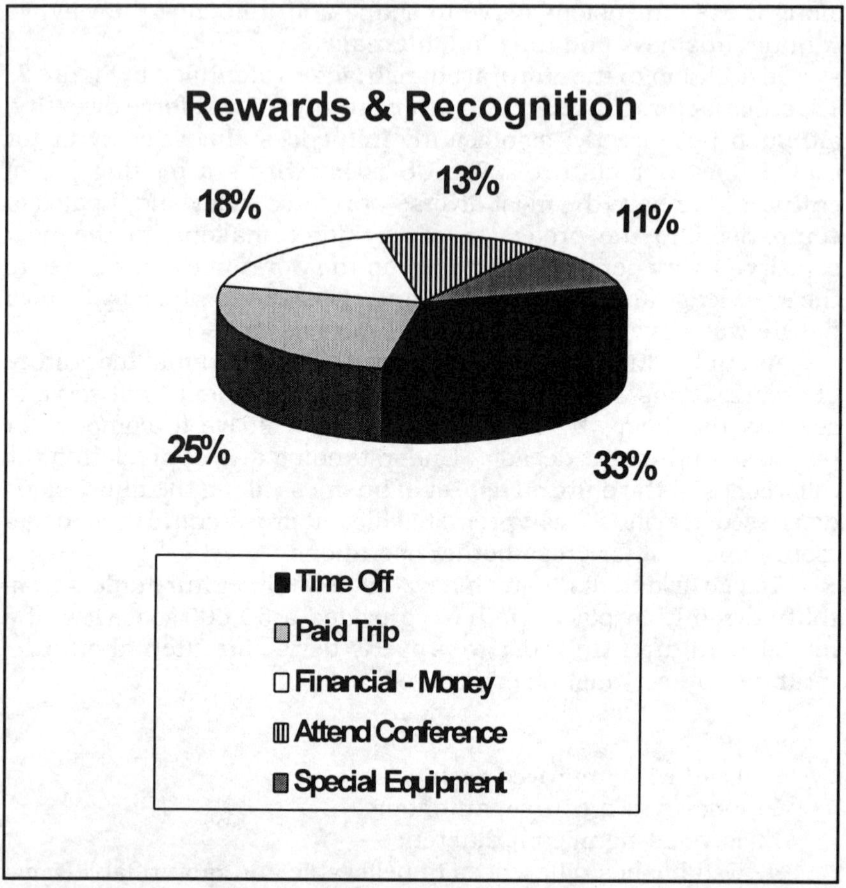

Figure 2-14 This graphic represents the response of MIS staff on what type of rewards they would prefer.

9. Strains credibility
10. Manages service with conflicting values and measures

To further understand the current MIS culture and the shortcomings that accompany it we must develop several key areas that reflect and influence our internal culture as it relates to work initiatives, not human resources. We will focus on values & beliefs, measures and rewards. All too often inconsistency in these areas lead to confusion due to conflicting messages produced by misaligned measures with rewards and other areas.

Values & Beliefs

What an organization holds in high regard influences the way individuals work within a group. The human character thrives on admiration and recognition. Therefore, we all try to do those

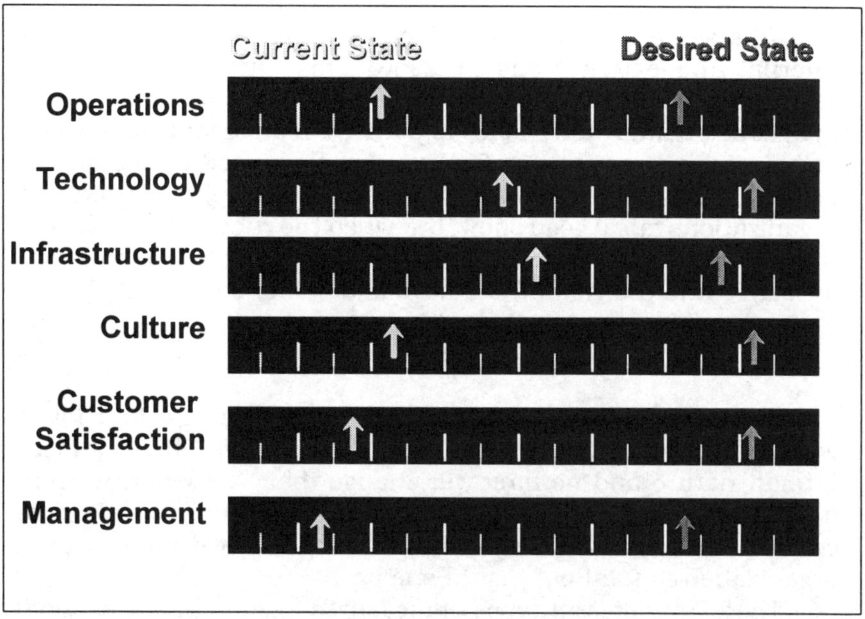

Figure 2-15 Analysis of the gap between current state and the desired state provides valuable insight into how much change needs to occur.

activities for which we will be rewarded. Values of the new MIS organization should revolve around internal and external customer satisfaction. Meeting the customer's needs in a timely fashion and contributing to the success of the customer are the primary values for which the new MIS organization will be founded.

The second area under this topic looks at what we, as an organization, believe we are. It is our image of ourselves. What we see in the mirror, so to speak. All too often in the complex and chaotic business environment outsider perceptions of us differ greatly from how we see ourselves. An important exercise to go through is to list how others perceive your MIS organization and then blindly canvas your customers for their opinions.

To obtain a complete view of your image be sure to journey into the following areas and document your findings. Startling communications and image discrepancies will provide insight to still other areas for improvement.

- How we perceive ourselves?
- How others perceive us?
- How we want others to perceive us?
- How we treat ourselves?
- How others treat us?

- How we wish to be treated?

This self-examination coupled with the objective view of our internal and external customers will help architect our future culture as it relates to values and beliefs. These two areas project the image the organization wishes to portray. If an organization wishes to be perceived as looking for honesty, they need to operate in a fashion which is perceived to support this vision. All too often organizations talk a good show, but when the rubber meets the road they take the easy way out. This is usually the reason our view of ourselves and the view others have of us differ so greatly.

Measures

People do not like to be measured. The monitoring of individual's work often sends chills up the backs of the staff. This is a fact of human nature and nothing will change that. However, we must make sure the measure systems are aligned with the values the company has and the measures look after the best interest of the organization in total not just in one part.

There are different types of measures used in business today. Two of the most common deal with the measurement of progress within a process. The second measures the outcome of work effort or processes. These are referred to as results measures. Each of these two measures serve a different purpose. While process measures allow one to track the progress of work in a given area they say nothing about the quality or quantity of the product resulting from the work. Result measures are typically qualitative and quantitative in nature.

It is critical to take a global look at the organization when developing a new measures system. The fragmented work structures that are prominent throughout business today promote conflicting measures. Conflicting measures result when the best interest of the company or organization as a whole is sacrificed in order to increase the performance as defined by the measures system for a specific area of the organization.

- How we measure ourselves?
- How others measure us?
- How we want others to measure us?
- How others treat us?
- How we wish to be treated?

Rewards

Rewards systems serve two purposes. First to serve as recognition for past performance. The second is through positive reinforce-

Benefits

1. Economic application of appropriate technologies
2. Leverage of technology for competitive advantage
3. Flexibility to rapidly change with markets/business
4. Contribution of MIS to organizational goals
5. Maximization of human resources
6. Business requirements driven and controlled
7. Continuos learning and improvement
8. An operation that supports globalization

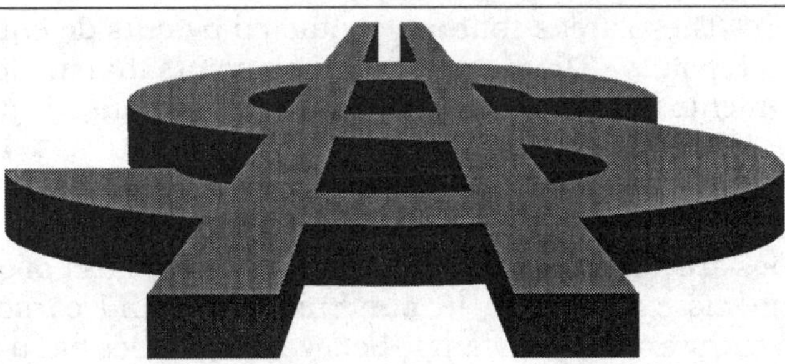

Figure 2-16 This figure represents the expected benefits from reengineering MIS.

ment to encourage future performance. Now that we have identified what is of value to the organization and how we will gauge ourselves against achieving these goals we must look at how we will reward the efforts of individual contributors to success. As a mechanism to develop a rewards system, the following information must be gathered.

- What value do we place on our work?
- What value do others place on our work?

- What value does industry place on similar work?
- What would the company lose if a resource left?

We now need to identify the various types of rewards we wish to offer as incentives for perpetuating the desired response from workers. Historically, organizations relied heavily on monetary rewards and promotions. However, in today's work environment other non-traditional ways to reward employees are growing in popularity. These non-traditional types of rewards include recognition, non-work related assignments, perks (such as trips or dinners), and benefits (such as company cars, etc...).

The objective of the rewards system is to remain competitive in the marketplace while meeting the needs of your staff. This sounds a lot easier than it actually is. Clear understanding of processes and procedures as well as the organizational structure is required to design the system. The complexity of the work we perform each day mandates a significant amount of time being spent when defining the new system. In addition, it is almost a necessity to dry run the new rewards system prior to implementation.

Impact Analysis

Any time one area of an organization is changed, the ripples can be felt by the divisions that touch or interact with the area undergoing change. The ripple effect that always accompanies change must be identified, analyzed and planned for in order to minimize the disruption. These areas that are contacted by outside entities are called touch points. There are eight touch points that are identified as the segments that are vulnerable to the ripples caused by change.

Politics

Politics are a factor that touches almost every facet of our lives. This is no more true than in our businesses and corporations. Although many executives want to believe that politics has a minimal impact on the business line, experience leads us to believe otherwise. Due to the inherent nature of reengineering, you cannot avoid entering the political waters of the organization. For this reason, executive visibility is key. The Executive Sponsor can be used as a bulldozer to knock down the political walls that have been built up within the organization. Throughout the business community invisible organizations and policy-setting bodies exist. These entities are clearly inhibiting the ability of organizations to reengineer.

The amount of politics in large or even medium-sized corporations today staggers the imagination. Failure to take the necessary precautions to safeguard oneself and the project exposes all parties to unnecessary risks.

Putting it all together

Customers and management are demanding greater levels of performance, efficiency, quality and control over the work being done by MIS. In order to meet the customers' and management's expectations, MIS professionals must strive to reskill the workforce in order to reduce the skill gap of the MIS staff. The MIS staff, as well as the organization, must be fully committed to continuous reskilling and investing long term in human resources. Those who are not able to meet the reskill challenge must be transitioned out and this too must be well planned, communicated and understood by all members of the organization. Once the MIS staff has undergone the reskilling necessary to bring them up-to-date, they must be encouraged and strive continuously to update their skills. MIS must now accept the challenge to change. They must embrace change rather than resist it. To do this they must look to the future and plan back to the present. This will enable MIS to at least stay up with the power curve, if not get ahead of it. With the ever-changing technology suite, MIS must resist the tendency to incorporate technology for technology sake. Each and every decision to change or update technology must be based on a sound business case. For this reason technology must be viewed as an enabler for business to operate in a different fashion.

In order to take full advantage of the organizations investment in technology, a technology transfer plan must be developed in order to fully realize the benefits throughout the organization. Without a plan MIS will not be efficient in the continuous improvement journey. They will choose many paths that lead to dead ends and become the cause of lost profits and revenues.

With the skills and technology in place to provide the supportive information systems required in business today, we must turn our attention to methods, tools, and techniques that will expedite our response to the needs of the user community. The migration of the tried and true methodologies to rapid application development will require total MIS buy-in. The tendency of MIS to complain about changes to the core of development coupled with adherence to outdated techniques that were designed to support what one would now consider antiquated technology by today's standards will be replaced with enthusiasm and vigor. Allowing the MIS group to explore new and innovative technology and approaches to systems development will promote the open acceptance of this move.

The new lean and mean MIS organization is positioned not only to take advantage of late breaking technology but to respond rapidly to internal and external customer needs. The business process transformation process that will accompany the reengineered MIS organization will serve our organizations like never before.

Benefits

But what is the payoff for the pain and suffering that will accompany this reengineering effort. How can MIS justify in their minds and the minds of management the journey is of worth to the entire organization. Actual benefits will vary based on how aggressively the reengineering team approaches the issues and the level of innovation applied to the resolution to current issues.

METHODOLOGY

Reengineering Management Information Systems

Chapter 3

Methodology: Approaches to Today's Systems Development

The use of systems development methodologies varies from Information Systems department to department. Every technical professional looks at the process of delivering systems a little differently, even when using the same 'methodology.' In this chapter, the current approaches or methods to developing systems will be discussed at an informational level. The primary focus of this chapter, however, will be on the self-directed team or partnership-based accelerated approach to delivering business solutions using techniques such as: vision development, right-to-left thinking, and simulation for design. Finally, this chapter includes a practitioner's field guide for one such approach. Keep in mind that the guide is an overview of one such approach, not a detailed methodology.

Introduction

A methodology gives procedural direction to its users to achieve a solution. In the case of software development, methodologies control the life cycle of a project. They describe the stages that a software system goes through from the first ideas or needs to the usage of the software in the field. Using the right methodology ensures at least the possibility for success. Using software methodologies is nothing new to the technical professional. However to the unsuspecting business user who has become a partner in this process of system development the approach may be a mystery. Most business professionals have become users of PC hardware and software, in some cases they have developed small applications themselves. This experience should make the transition to systems development partner easier for both technical and business professionals faced with creating a joint business solution. Sometimes this experience has created more resistance to the sometime long process of system development and the associated cost.

The software development approach can be formal or informal, it depends on the culture of the Information Systems organization. No one methodology is the "right" one for every development environment. For this reason an assessment of the environment is necessary before determining which methodology will work for an organization, or what modifications are needed to the current development process or the organizational structure in order for the development process to be successful. Most information systems organizations are experiencing a tug-of-war, see figure 3.1, between old development concepts and the new expectations generated by business reengineering and process improvement and other business imperatives. The questions are: Can we implement a total business solution when it's needed? Can we do it without breaking the bank? Can the current methods deliver business solutions?

As a result of investigating popular system development methodologies two primary approaches surfaced. One approach is based on technical and functional specialization and the other on reducing time. In some cases, the methodologies have tried to combine both approaches. The first approach is the development by specialist experts, that includes: waterfall and model approaches. These approaches complement the current skills of the technical professionals. These methods rely on a series of hand-offs from one skilled individual to another: business user to business analyst, business analyst to systems analyst, systems analyst to system designer, System Designer to Programmer, Programmer to System Tester, system tester to system trainer, and finally, system trainer back to business user. So, which came first; the professional skills to work with the approach or the methodology to use every skill? It really doesn't matter, the business professional is left with a process that may or may not fit the business need. Further, this approach does not cover the total business solution of process, organization,

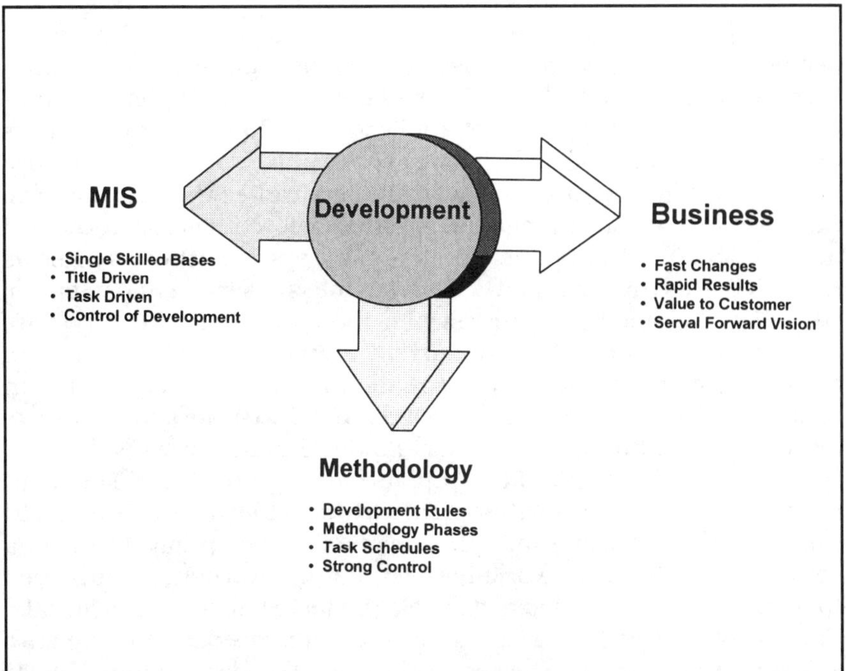

Figure 3.1 The tug-of-war between new and old concepts in development.

technology, facilities, and application.

The second primary approach is the accelerated approach that circumvents some old organizational baggage with the new approach of the technical caseworker. The caseworker is not a new idea. It has evolved from the systems engineer idea. The caseworker is a technical professional who has a combination of technical skills that include; business analysis through system implementation. The use of functional specialties and resulting IS organization barriers are minimized and the need for hand-offs is reduced.

Hand-offs

Approaches that include hand-offs allow for the use of the technical skills needed to produce an automated solution. This approach provides a structure and control of the process. It uses both the individual skills of system professionals and the structure to perform the task the same way each time the task is performed. What this process also controls and constrains is the creativity which is needed to meet new business challenges, new organizational structures, and reduced cycle time. Two such approaches are waterfall and model-based methodologies.

Waterfall Method

Waterfall methods are better known as "the next step" methods, see figure 3.2. These methods are the most common "traditional" methods of system development and delivery. The Waterfall methods break the development of applications into four major phases with hand-offs and sign-offs between each phase. These approaches give the systems organization a written guarantee that the user will not be able to easily change the solution before it can be developed and implemented. Anyone who has built systems this way knows how well this has worked. The business user, in most cases, becomes the enemy of the systems organization. This type of development has created the current animosity between the user and the systems group. It does not allow for the flexibility of human nature. Humans change their minds and learn how to do things better. This methodology does not allow for human growth or errors.

The waterfall method has a phase for requirements. The business analyst conducts this phase by working to get automated system requirements from a business user. The phase is either a series of interviews or a workshop. The use of a workshop has helped to reduce the time needed to go back and forth between individuals. The use of a workshop also reduces the time needed to make sure everyone understands the requirements. The production of large volumes of requirements adds overhead to this process. The workshop can help to reduce the amount of paper produced.

The first hand-off is to the systems analyst or system designer. This phase is known as the design phase. The business analyst gives the signed requirement to either the systems analyst or the systems designer. This depends on the functional skills and expertise available in the information systems department.

Unfortunately the system designer, who receives the requirements from the Business Analyst, has little-to-no interaction with the business users from phase one. In most cases they will contact the business analyst to interact with the user if questions about the requirements arise. This tends to happen because the System Designer either cannot communicate with the user or because the organization will not allow the communication.

User interaction and hand-offs usually change when workshops are introduced in phase one and continued into phase two. The use of workshops allows for control of the process and the interaction of technical professionals with the business users for a longer period of time. It also reduces the phase time and paper production time.

The construction phase uses the specifications developed by the designers from the business user requirements. This phase is the creative time for the technical systems developer. This phase allows for the creativity of the developer, allowing them uninterrupted time to think and work from the documentation supplied by the first phase. Here is where the technical professional tends to expand scope trying to think of all the exceptions and conditions that the user may need or want.

In most cases, however, they do not need most of the extras that are developed. Even with all the controls up to now to control the user, the technical professional expands the functions trying to create the "perfect" solution. After all, the technical professional knows more of what the business professional needs, and it is this very belief that has proven to be deadly for projects and systems organization.

Once the applications are developed the automated system is turned over for testing and quality assurance. During this phase, called integration and test, those responsible for testing check the programmers' work. Although this phase is used to control the quality of the system it tends to provide a mechanism to create competition between the developer and the tester. Unfortunately this phase, as it stands now, does not include the overall question: "Does this automated system support the needed business process and provide any return on investment?".

The implementation phase brings the automated solution back to the business user. This may be the first time that the business user gets to see the system again since the initial requirements phase some months ago. In some cases shock sets in, in some fear, and in some cases the automated functions are right on target. The questions to be asked here are: Did the approach bring the correct automated solution or the quality of the developers? Did the developers' industry knowledge create the business solution or did the requirements supplied by the business user drive the results? In some cases it is hard to tell and in some cases it doesn't matter because it all took too long.

The waterfall method has created many problems for MIS organizations. The rigid control that allowed the systems organization to produce a product has, in most cases, alienated the very business users they tried to please. Each phase allowed the requirements to get further away from the overall business solution needed. The requirements had no flexibility to keep up with the changing business needs of the user. If a manufacturing company continues to produce a best-quality product that is outdated, the result will be the same. Customers will go elsewhere for the newer products hoping to get the latest product that will meet their needs. The same is true of the product that MIS organizations provide. MIS organizations must change and diversify their approaches to meet the needs of their business partners.

Information Engineering or Model Method

CASE (Computer Aided Systems Engineering) tools and Information Engineering approaches created a new era of technology professionals. Analysts became modelers and automated processes

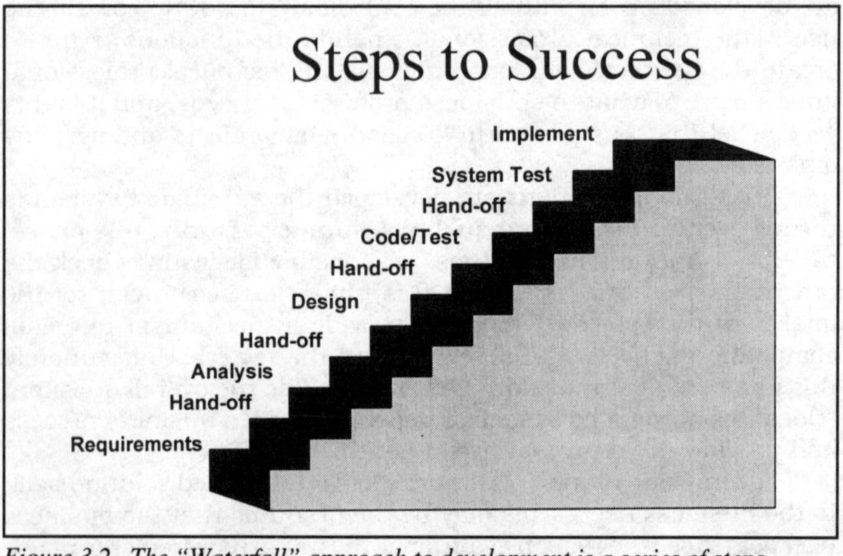

Figure 3.2 The "Waterfall" approach to development is a series of steps.

were divided into interconnecting models. Everyone was talking "CASE ease" and expecting the business community to join their enthusiasm for the new CASE tools. The flood of new models did little to insure the quality of technical professional understanding of the total business solution. The new design approach extended the analysis phase and, in some cases, projects moved to the next phase.

MIS organizations soon found that the models were only as good as the modelers. This began to impact the quality of the process and, in some cases, created a strong MIS hold on the process much like MIS DBA's (Database Administrator's) hold on enterprise information.

The process that the CASE tool was built to support began to take a back seat to the capabilities of the tool. In some organizations, the tool took on a life of its own, even overriding how the organization wanted to develop systems if they were different.

In some very extreme cases, the tools gave MIS the incorrect perception that they could dictate how the business process worked. Modelers lay victim to fitting the needs of the organization into the tool. They soon found their natural tendency for perfection impacted their ability to deliver. The perfect model seldom came, delivery time was lost due to the complexity of the tool and model.

In most Information Engineering methods the process is supported with workshops that support group requirements gathering. The workshops are used much in the same way as the waterfall method. The difference is that the modeling effort is conducted with the business partner. The work is then given to the technology group where it is business as usual. The development team goes away and emerges after the application development work is complete or nearly complete. This causes the same effects as the waterfall methods.

MIS organization's continued endeavors to find the Holy Grail in CASE tools has had, in some cases, tremendous negative impact. MIS looking for a quick fix to an old problem, bought CASE tools and were disappointed in the outcome. The "perfect" models where never produced and the learning curve was steep. The promise of generated code to reduce delivery time was a long time coming for companies using this approach. Companies became quickly disenchanted with the tools and when looking for an easier solution, only found that the next tool required more time and effort. The promises of these tools were to be realized only when the tool was used methodically and correctly; and this took time. Time, however, was the very thing that companies bought the tools to shorten.

The outcomes of the information engineering push to model and automate all elements of a systems effort fell short. MIS organizations found projects still took time and the methods did not guarantee user acceptance. The lessons learned from this approach were that most of the lost time was not a tools problem or necessarily a methodology problem but was caused by the steep learning curve of the tool and MIS continuing to move too far away from the business partner. Some Information Engineering methodologies are working to shorten the delivery times by adding a traditional rapid application approach to the process but have done little to improve the information gathering and business partner interactions.

Just-Do-It Method

The Just-Do-It method is sometimes referred to as the "quick and dirty" method. It is being used by MIS organizations as an accelerated application approach to achieve rapid results and user involvement. The process has become a common form of development in some MIS organizations across the country. This method uses different techniques from all types of approaches, one technique from structured analysis, one from Information Engineering, and some from prototyping. Each MIS organization has its own way of "getting the job done" to meet today's need for rapid results. It's no wonder that some organizations are spending large budgets to maintain current software while others do not have a clue as to how current programs actually work or how they will move the processes to new client/server environments. Are MIS organizations being forced to accept just-do-it approaches? In some cases they are, not because they have too, it's because they feel they have no other way of getting the job done.

This approach is not always quick-and-dirty, it can create a quality automated result with full user acceptance. The argument against this type of method is usually the lack of control on the part of the project manager and the fear that the quality of the application will be inconsistent. These fears do not have to undermine the approach. If the MIS professionals build quality into their work and have the required skills, this approach can and does work.

This Just-Do-It method is found when: 1) management has tried to implement structured methodologies and failed, or 2) when they have tried to implement accelerated development without understanding all the concepts and techniques, or 3) when individuals do not believe in methodologies at all. This approach tends to be practiced in smaller MIS organizations which are not bound by titles and levels. They have the flexibility to get the job done and everyone plays many roles. This approach enables the technical professional to be a caseworker.

Prototyping Method

This method creates a mechanism for getting closer to the

business partner. It sometimes shortens the overall design phase. In some cases, it becomes another bottleneck because the MIS professional cannot control the design session in order to keep the process moving. Time is sometimes lost due to premature over design or the inability to change one's mind about how something should work.

Prototype tools allow us to demonstrate different screen designs and understand more about the business process and data, more quickly. This prototyping method does not include simulation of the total business process, instead it focuses totally on the menu flow and screen information.

This method accomplishes two important interactions with the business partner. First it forces contact to identify the elements of the screen and second it allows for more interaction during development by creating a live demo system. Business partners become more involved with the application before it is implemented. This approach does save time as long as the developer can control scope creep.

Prototyping, when used along with workshops, enables the project life cycle to become even shorter for the business partner. However, for most MIS professionals, working with this process extends working hours into weeknights and weekends, not because of prototyping but because of their inability to control scope. This approach creates a struggle for the MIS professional, "do I sacrifice the business process or do I finish?".

Prototyping is commonly used to enhance both the waterfall and Information Engineering methods of application development. Prototyping used for screen design only will not ensure the overall success of the user acceptance. It is only one of the techniques that a technical professional should have in their packet for business partner success. Prototyping can be more than screen design and process mapping. It can be a mechanism for creating an interactive learning environment of simulation and total business solutions.

Accelerated Application Development

Accelerated development is nothing new to the marketplace. Large companies like DuPont have been experimenting with this type of development since the early 1980s. With the demand of the new client/server environments and business driven approaches (Business Reengineering and Business Process Improvement) accelerated development has been given a new lease on life, not unlike the renewed push for object-oriented development. Accelerated development approaches all have four main techniques as part of their process: timeboxing, workshops, prototyping, and joint business and technology teams. See figure 3.3. The approach of accelerated development has given MIS organizations the interactions with the business partners they needed and provided a mechanism to reduce development time. This method provided control for the project manager and structure for the developers. Accelerated development has become the required way to develop automated systems.

The well-known accelerated development approaches only cover the automated elements of a solution. They do not include a business case to support the effort or staff requirements to implement the developed functions. Although accelerated development approaches do enable MIS organizations to deliver faster they do not include critical business elements necessary to implement a total business solution. The time gained in the development phase in accelerated development is lost during the implementation phase, as a result of the missing business components. Taking into consideration, the total business solution will enable business results to be implemented more quickly.

Things to Think About

How fast is fast?

How fast is fast? This question should be the first question asked of the joint development team. The team should determine when the business needs the solution and what will happen to the business if the time frame cannot be met. The business time frame should drive the need for quick development results. If the organization is being redesigned, time is relevant to the amount of change required to create success and the organizations ability to change. How fast the MIS organization can develop the automated elements of the system

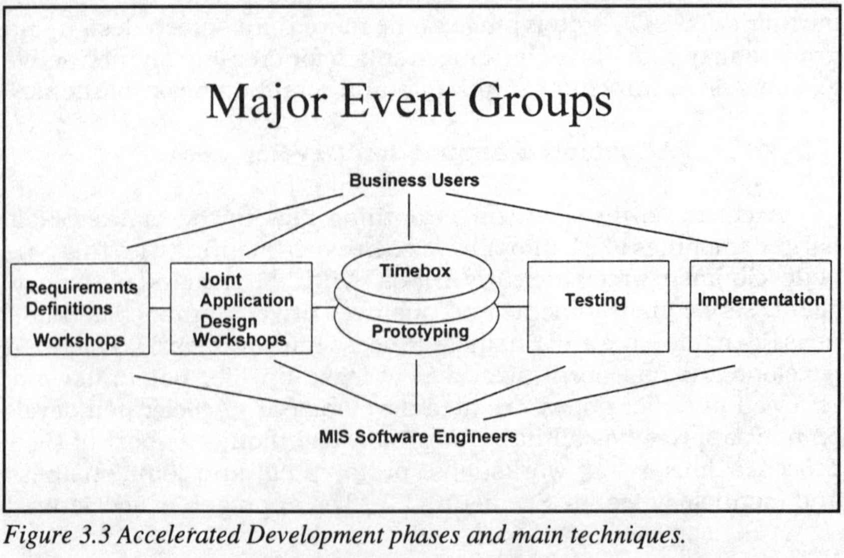

Figure 3.3 Accelerated Development phases and main techniques.

may become a non-issue if the organization is not ready to change the way it does business.

If the current accelerated application development concepts and techniques are used during the development of automated solutions, functions will be delivered much sooner than when using other methods. The development speed will be determined after the design phase is completed and the timeboxes estimated. Scope control will play an important role in delivering within the timebox.

Only the team can determine how fast is fast. Remember, results can be achieved faster by using joint analysis and design techniques. If workshops are used, productivity is improved over the traditional use of interviews. If this is still not fast enough, expand the use of prototyping for simulating and testing. See figure 3.4.

Why use a methodology?

The question being asked is: If applications can be delivered without methodologies, why use a methodology and doesn't it slow the development down? In order to understand the need for methodologies the objectives should be known. The objective of every methodology is to create a road map that will support the MIS professional with tasks that can be followed to ensure consistent success of development efforts. However, methodologies alone can not ensure success for today's development efforts. The dimensions of application development have changed. The requirements are broader and the time pressures are greater. The rules of the game have changed, business no longer waits for rigid MIS structure to achieve results. MIS professionals at all levels are required to interact with business partners. Business analysts are no longer the priminary contact with the business environment.

Until the new partnership is formed and the joint development practices have been fully understood, a road map will be necessary for success of this new organizational structure. A well understood methodology will support the activities for teams to understand and meet milestones when implementing business solutions. The methodology alone will not guarantee improved system development time or better partner interactions. It will however, ensure that the team is playing the same game with the same understanding of the activities needed to implement total business solutions. The approach or methodology is only one of the tools needed for implementing total business solutions.

What Expectations have Technological Organizations Created for System Delivery?

MIS organizations have set themselves up for hard times when using accelerated development approaches. One of the largest

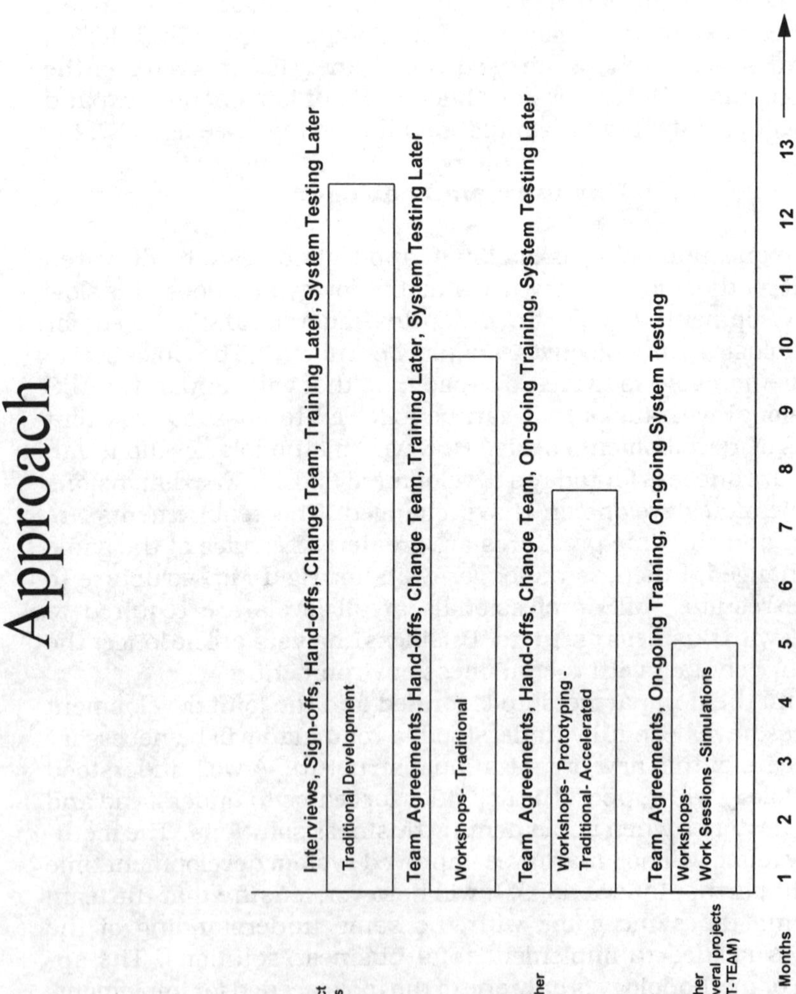

Figure 3.4 Productivity gains through the use of different techniques.

obstacles to overcome is business's expectation. The current business user expects to be delivered an automated system with the bells and whistles. This is typically the trade-off for the overruns. Accelerated development tries to deliver business priorities or baseline functions first. This may or may not include any bells and whistles.

MIS professionals have dedicated careers to making sure that delivered functions are everything that the users may need and, in most cases, more. Even with this approach, history has shown that most systems developed and delivered, encounter change requests after only two weeks of usage. This indicates that the time to deliver may not be the only problem and that no matter how much time is spent in achieving "every" possible requirement the system will never have all the "right" components. There are several factors at work here; one is the learning curve of mastering the mechanics; the second is the expectations of the user; and finally the third is the learning through doing that happens after the automated solution is in the hands of the business user daily. The affect of this is the increased need of the MIS professional to create the "perfect" system, which will never happen. This exception has hindered MIS organizations in their ability to implement more accelerated approaches and control scope. MIS organizations have created this problem. They have set the users' expectations so high that the user now expects systems that have "perfect" functionality with all the bells and whistles.

Looking at Accelerated Development in a Non-Traditional Way

Today's accelerated development needs to be viewed as non-traditional. The approach of accelerated development will be a "holistic" approach to achieving business results using technology to enable the automated components of the solutions. This approach will assume that the organization is committed to self-directed team work and joint commitments to reaching a total business solution together. The accelerated development approach today is more than workshops, screen prototyping, and the use of timeboxing. The approach involves performing work differently, creating a new radical idea about system development, developing a new mind-set in team work, and approaching information gathering differently. This approach will be different from how the MIS organizations understand the process of developing and implementing automated solutions. This approach involves a total commitment with business professionals to understand the vision needed to enable a solution. This accelerated process will tear down the internal technology walls and replace them with more skills and more business understanding. The very existence of MIS organizations depends on their ability to change the focus and become business centered.

Understanding the Concepts of Accelerated Business Solutions

An organization's ability to manage the scope of accelerated development lies in three main areas: 1) educating the business as to the impact of accelerated development, 2) understanding the learning process for each team member, and 3) learning to negotiate a "win-win" timebox to produce a total business solution which includes process, people, automation, space, and business results.

What the New Team Needs to Know

Understanding Expectations

Expectation management has to be a key principle of the accelerated team development. This is not a new principle. However, it is a critical success factor (CSF) to team-based development. Expectations are often misunderstood or down played when starting an accelerated project. There are two sets of expectations that need to be looked at. One is the organization's expectation of accelerated development. Today's media has set expectations for all types of accelerated development efforts by placing unrealistic expectations on the process's ability to solve all problems and still delivery quickly. The expectation of how quickly this team can deliver a business solution should be stated as soon as possible. Remember, how fast is fast should be applied to this expectation. Today's organizations have missed the small print about right team skills, right tools, management support, and flexible scope. Teams find themselves fighting the never-ending battle of meeting those expectations, failure after failure. Don't let this happen.

The second is that MIS organizations need to understand that they have set an expectation that they can deliver automated systems that are "perfect" and the expectation is that they can deliver this in a shorter time frame. If a team works together for some time and spends time planning the approach to the team effort, they can achieve the level of fully functional (bells and whistles) in half the time. However, in most cases this will not happen the first time developing a total solution together. In some cases this will not happen even the second time. Don't give up. Create a new expectation that will focus on the organization's business and use the 80/20 percent rule to deliver value based on business priorities. This expectation should include a development process that is continuous. This will allow for process improvements that are on-going. No business process should be allowed to become stagnant or outdated.

Dealing with Scope Management

Scope can be managed in several ways. Scope management through controlled swapping is one of the best means of achieving business results. Function swapping is when scope which has less business priorty is swapped with higher business priorities. Function swapping and the use of timeboxing can also be used to limit the amount of scope creeping that a team will experience in an accelerated development effort.

Function swapping is then a mechanism for handling changes of functions that are discovered during the development process. It allows for the trading of discovered functions for previously identified priorities. The functions that are swapped are then placed on an enhancement list for the next timebox. If continuous improvement becomes a way of life for the organization this will not create a problem. The timebox priority management process is based on individual functions that are ranked by the business value they deliver. The functions with the highest business value are completed first.

The 80/20 Concept

Timeboxing is one of the techniques used to create a sense of urgency within the team. This urgency helps to keep the focus. Another technique in keeping the team moving is the use of the 80/20 rule. The 80/20 rule is an important concept used in accomplishing team efforts within a set timebox. This use of the rule states that 80 percent of the functionality can be developed in 20 percent of the time. The remaining 20 percent is what tends to take projects into years of development and overruns. The use of this rule will allow the team to get past the "perfect" stages and question whether the remaining 20 percent brings business value. This rule allows for the first 80 percent of information to be addressed quickly and keeps the team moving.

The Concept of Levels of Learning

Levels-of-learning is a concept based on an individual's ability to learn and the different learning stages that an individual goes through during the accelerated team development approach. What is known is that humans learn by gradually exploring and trying new things. If this is truly understood, the accelerated team can apply this knowledge to the approach of accelerated team development. This knowledge can help the team to control scope. The team can control the amount of change by balancing the timebox of each activity in the accelerated process.

If level one has to do with the business requiring or introducing a change, this is what I need. The next level will include design of the requirements, this is what it looks like. The next level is how it works and the last level is I need a little change here or there. Compare this example to the purchasing of a software package for the PC. First the identification of the package and its functions. The individual is happy with the software purchase. Second is the installation of the package on the PC. The individual is learning to use the software. Third the individual is learning to use the speed keys. Finally, the individual starts to find problems or limitations with the software. Why does this happen? For the understanding of levels-of-learning this is a normal human learning cycle. The accelerated development approach creates an even faster learning cycle. It allows for the second and third levels to be accelerated by the use of visioning and simulations.

Techniques used to control learning during prototyping include taking a horizontal slice of the process not a vertical slice, not expanding the sub-timeboxes, and not spending too much time in any one timebox. Once the team has this horizontal view of the results and has set business priorities, controlling the learning becomes focused on the priorities at hand. If the team allows the human learning level to go beyond a short timebox, the human learning patterns will take over. Once individuals understand what they are doing in the automated solution they will start to ask for the remaining 20 percent of functionality not always required for the business solution.

No member of the team sets out to expand the scope; it becomes easier to ask for other things as the learning process is increased. It's this 20% additional functionality that will cause expanded scope and create stress for the whole team. Use timeboxing to help control this. See figure 3.5 levels of learning.

Level 3, I need something more.
Level 2, I am testing my research.
Level 1, I am researching my needs and what will satisfy them.
Level 0, I have a need.

Workshops/Work Sessions/Labs

The use of workshops are nothing new to the systems individual and in some organizations the use of workshops has become the only way to start a project off. Workshops have improved the partnership of business and system individuals in the development of automated solutions. They have shortened the system development life cycle while creating productivity for all involved.

If organizations use workshops alone, they need to start looking

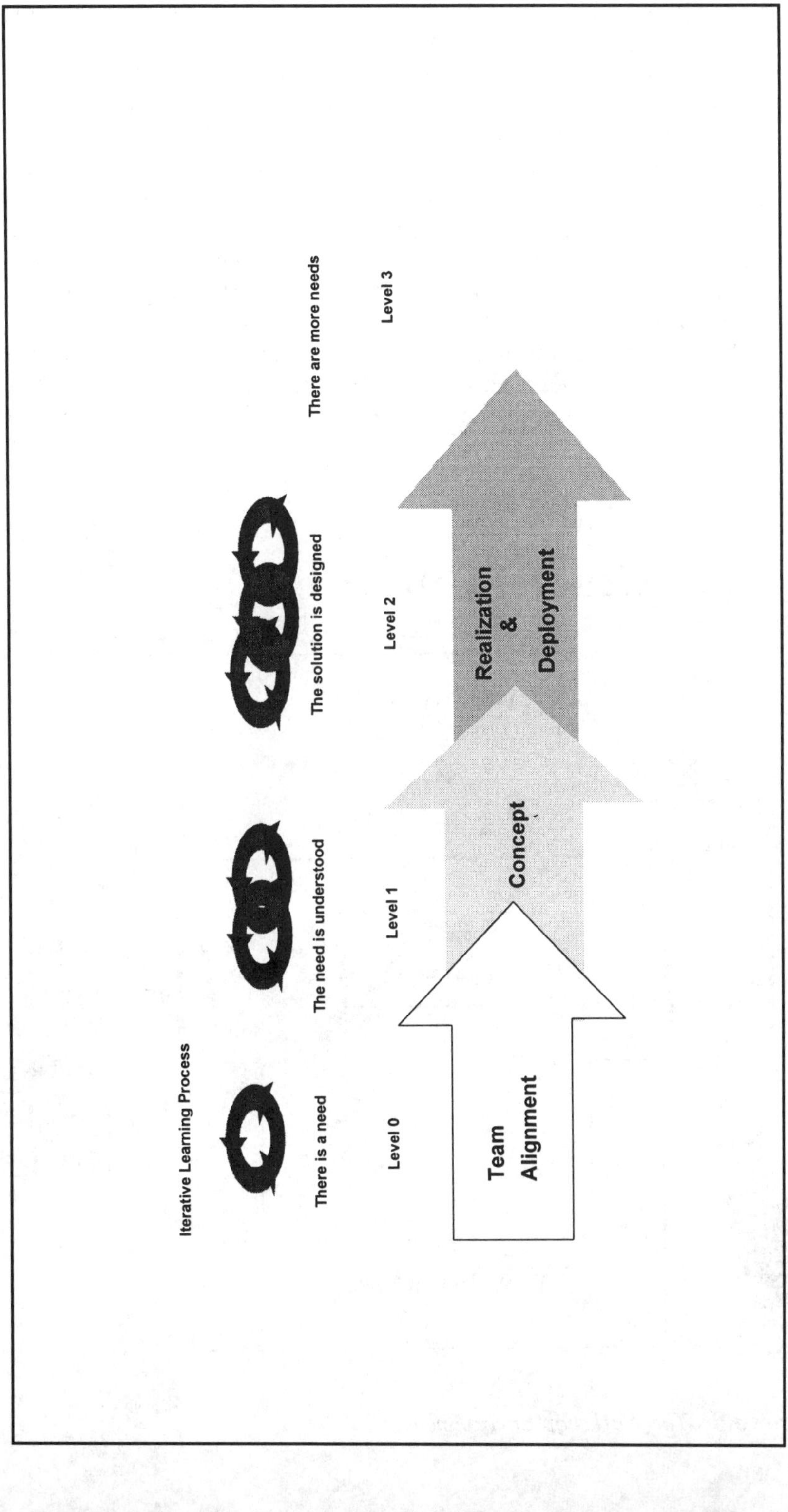

Figure 3.5 The levels of learning within the Accelerated team development approach.

at the implementaion of work sessions and labs in the development method. In the accelerated team development approach the power of self-directed teams with the new implementation of labs or work sessions create a unified business approach improving team dynamics and overall productivity.

A work session is similar to the workshop. The key difference is the role of the facilitator. In the case of the work sessions the facilitator may be part of the team. They have the job of getting everyone involved in the activity and interacting with team members. The team member who is facilitating is using techniques such as brainstorming, displayed thinking, and small group.

The lab environment brings the new organization together to create a joint business solution. The lab is a work space that supports large and small teams. The lab allows for creativity and

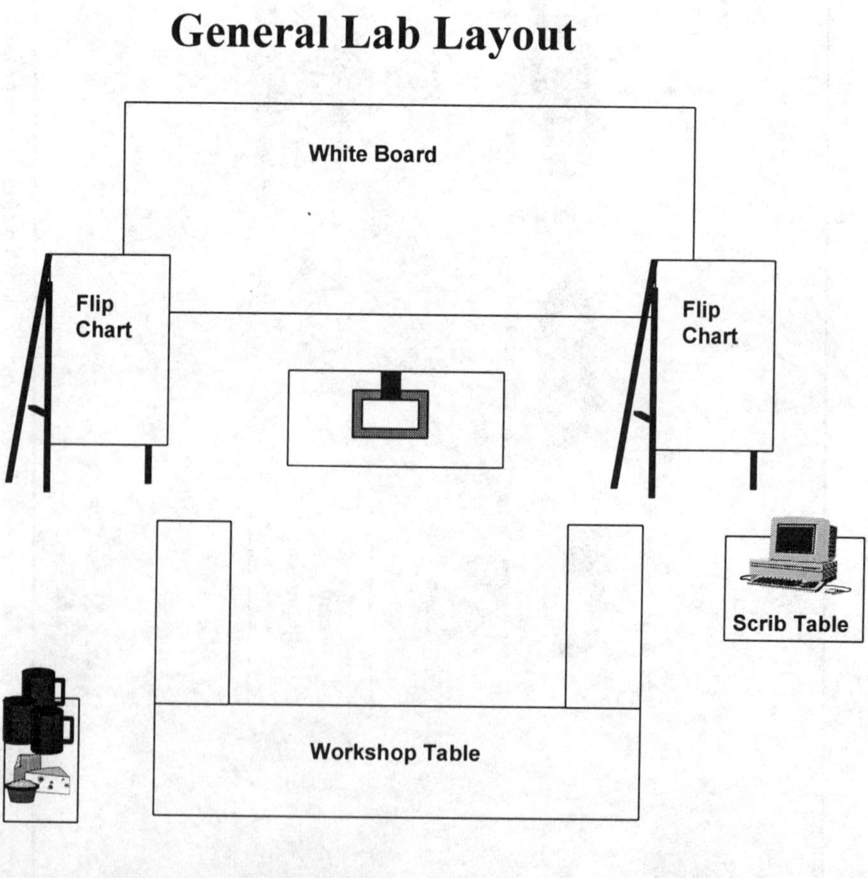

Figure 3.6 The Workshop Environment

simulations not bound by rigid methods. It is a safe place for creating total business vision and solutions. It becomes the center for open communications.

The Role of Workshops

The role of the workshop has been expanded to include almost everything from executive visioning to designing of technology models. Workshops do improve team dynamics and awareness of the task before a group of individuals. The physical layout of the room enables the facilitator to hold the participant's attention and supports group consensus on workshop topics. See figure 3.6. In accelerated team development, the workshop is used for executive interactions only.

The Role of Work Sessions

The role of the work session is similar to the workshop. The work session is used as a hands-on, working session. The room is designed to support community groupings and team sharing. Work sessions are used for requirement's design, prototyping and simulations. The physical layout of the room is similar to a lab environment. See figure 3.7. The attention is placed on the work session activities not the facilitator.

The Role of the Lab

The role of the lab is to bring together the new team in a physical space that they will share during the design and development process of the accelerated team approach. The environment of the lab is fast-paced, exciting, and dynamic; a place for the team to deliver results quickly. The lab facilities should closely resemble the targeted business environment or future office. This will allow for early simulations of the new business results. The lab should also have a work session space. The lab enviroment should promote teamwork and reduce team stress. The space should have the required equipment for development, displayed resource material, and have community space as well as individual work space. See figure 3.8.

Training the Team

Reskilling the new team is important to the success of each new development process. Reskilling can be accomplished through formal classroom, self-paced CBT courses, and on the job, just-in-time methods. One experience with an accelerated approach does not make an expert. The continued advancement of new skills

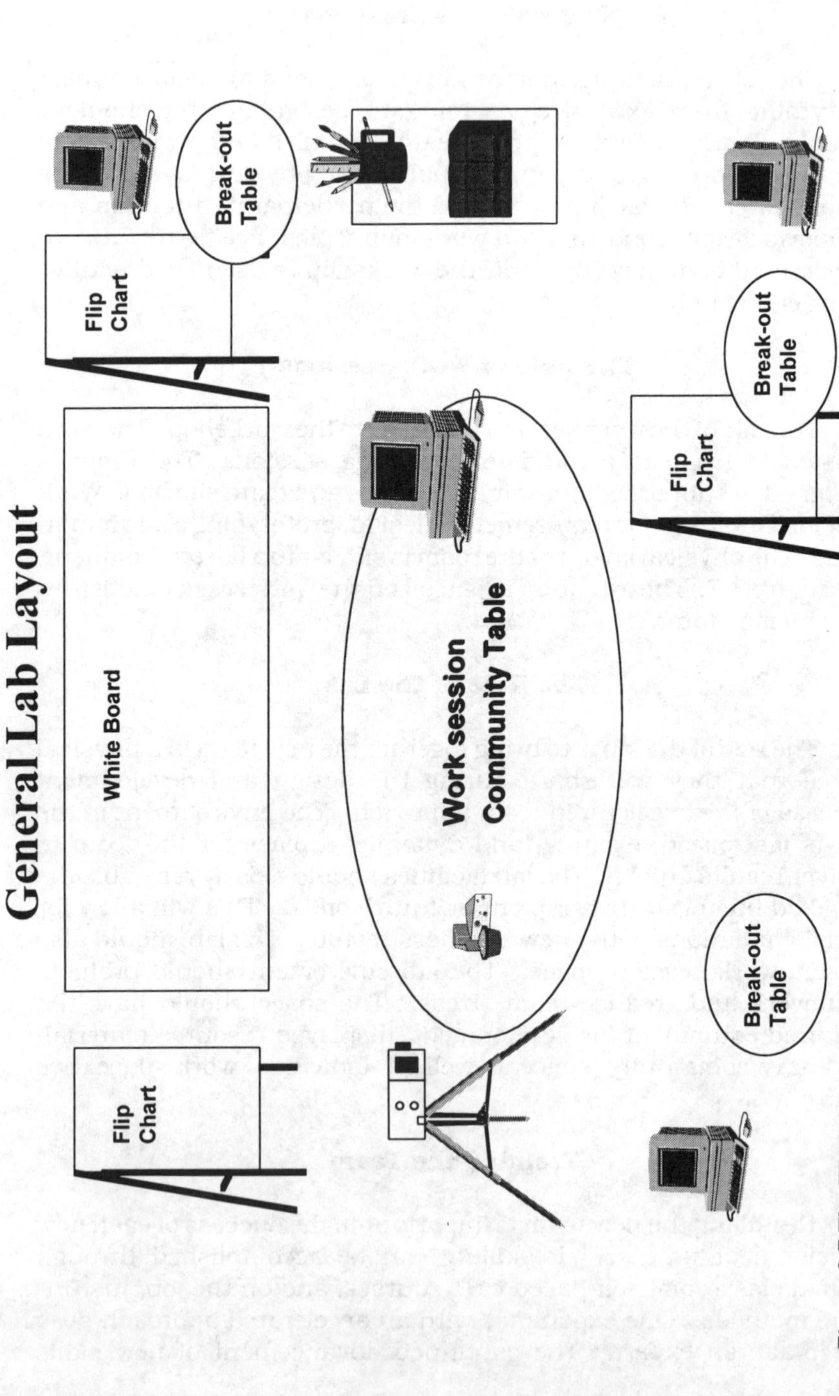

Figure 3.7 The Work Session Environment.

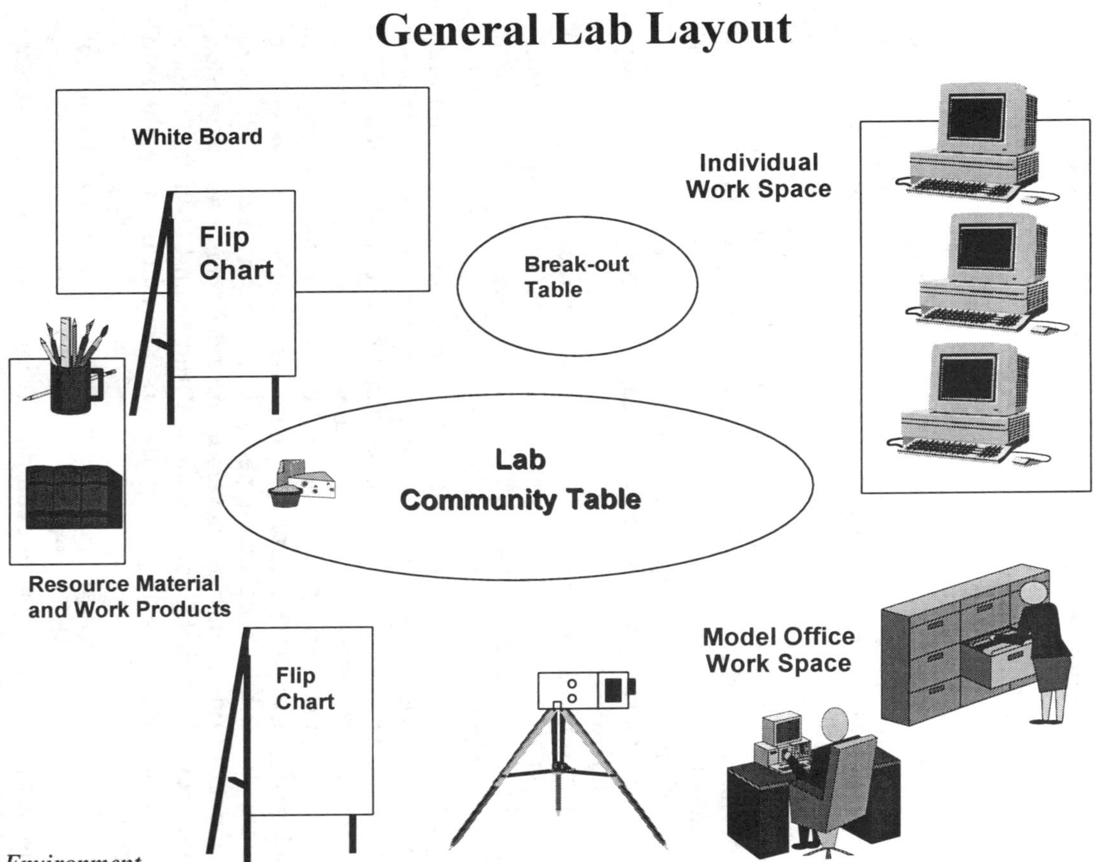

Figure 3.8 The Lab Environment.

should be included in the new accelerated team approach for the organization. There is no training that takes the place of a committed team and a united goal.

A Field Guide for Creating the New Reengineered Environment for Accelerated Team Development

Organizations intending to adopt a new development strategy must focus on three main elements: 1) the incorporation of MIS professionals with business professionals to develop an accelerated team development environment; 2) the activities needed to assess the current skills and the creation of a strategy for reskilling; 3) the development of a new approach to accelerated development which allows for flexibility and creativity.

One such approach to accelerated team development is described in the following pages. This approach coupled with the other information in this book should create a starting point for the needed changes to the MIS organization and its approach to systems development. The approach attempts to create flexibility and creativity for the new organization engaged in accelerated joint team development.

When reengineering the technical environment an accelerated development path for the future is a requirement of the organization. Currently, technology controls how aggressive the development process can be when creating an automated system. In the future, technology will be flexible and "smart." If MIS professionals continue to allow for rigid techniques in the development process, business will go on without them. Off-the-shelf software and multimedia CDs are easy to get and the demand for this level of creativity is growing.

A few key assumptions should be understood about the team before trying to use this appraoch. One assumption is that reskilling of the team has been completed. The second is that all team members understand key development needs such as integration and testing. Third, team dynamics and team-based facilitation techniques are known. Finally the organization has already been restructured.

The approach that is offered in this section is a collection of continued interactive activities where the MIS professional is already part of the business community and works for the business solutions and goals.

Background about the Process

There are three iterative activities in the approach described in this chapter. They are: Team Alignment; Concept Development; Realization and Deployment. See figure 3.9 for the activities of the accelerated approach.

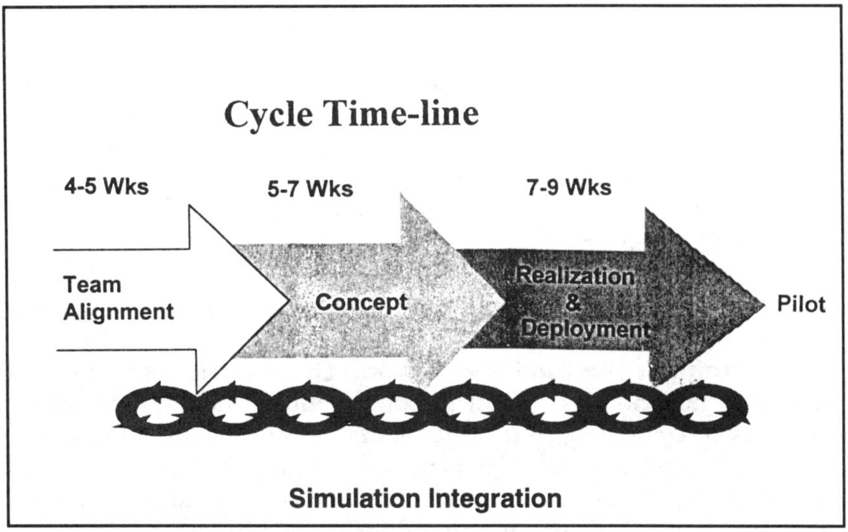

Figure 3.9 The Activities of the Accelerated Approach.

- Team Alignment includes the activities of team charting, the creation of the business mission and the strategy for design.
- Concept Development is the activity of identifying, designing, building and simulating the business solution.
- Realization and Deployment are the modification of the design solution to the objective, the completing the objectives, and preparation of implementing the new business process in the environment.

Each set of activities are designed to create a continuous environment for the business solution to be tried and understood by the implementing team. This process should change over time to reflect the new learning of the team working with this framework.

Accelerated Team Development Activities

Team Alignment

Team Alignment is the first set of activities the team performs to prepare for concept building. The team focuses on the relevant business problem or problems to be solved. The team clearly states the business objectives to achieve and the business results needed. The objectives should be declarations of business targets and priorities, not design features. The universal understanding of the business objectives is critical to the success of the effort. Scope is directly dependent upon the objectives and should be set accordingly to achieve these objectives. The use of active play and video taping will enhance the team's understanding of the objectives.

Alignment Activities

• ***Align the vision and scope of the business process.*** Establish the business justification and case for action for this team effort. The case for action or business case is critical to the success and direction for the results. The required business results must be known and the proper expectations for these results must be established when creating the priorities, the business scope, the objectives, and the measurement categories for the effort. This can be accomplished by either workshop, work session or lab utilizing facilitation techniques.

• ***Establish the Business Vision.*** Develop the vision for this effort and describe the vision in compelling terms. Use business concepts and modeling techniques to develop the visual understanding of the new process. Identify the principles that define the guidelines for the business vision and the considerations that the team must consider when expanding or modifying the business process. Note all assumptions, risks, and possible issues that are identified at this point. Identify possible impacts to the customer base or other work teams within or outside of the organization. Build the vision by using creative modeling techniques. This includes the use of magazines, clay, color markers, and construction paper. Creative ideas can become clear with the use of models and pictures. See figure 3.10.

• ***Identify the total staffing needs of the effort.*** The core team should be established from the business areas if possible. Identify any additional experts in related subject matter from both industry and technology-related areas.

• ***Get the facilities ready and put the team together.*** Purchase and set up any facility's requirements identified to support the effort. This includes setting up the workshop, work session or the creating of the model lab. This setup would also include the technical equipment to design and implement the new business process.

• ***Conduct Team-Building Exercises.*** The objective of team building is to create a common understanding of the characteristics of effective teams. Even though the individuals on this team should be working together already, improving team bonding and welcoming new members is always important to the accelerated approach. Team members define working principles and identify any barriers to the success of the team and effort. The barriers include work barriers to the team and the effort. Once the barriers are identified, solutions are created to proactively solve problems.

Team Building Activities

Develop team awareness:

Talk to the team about the importance of having and under-

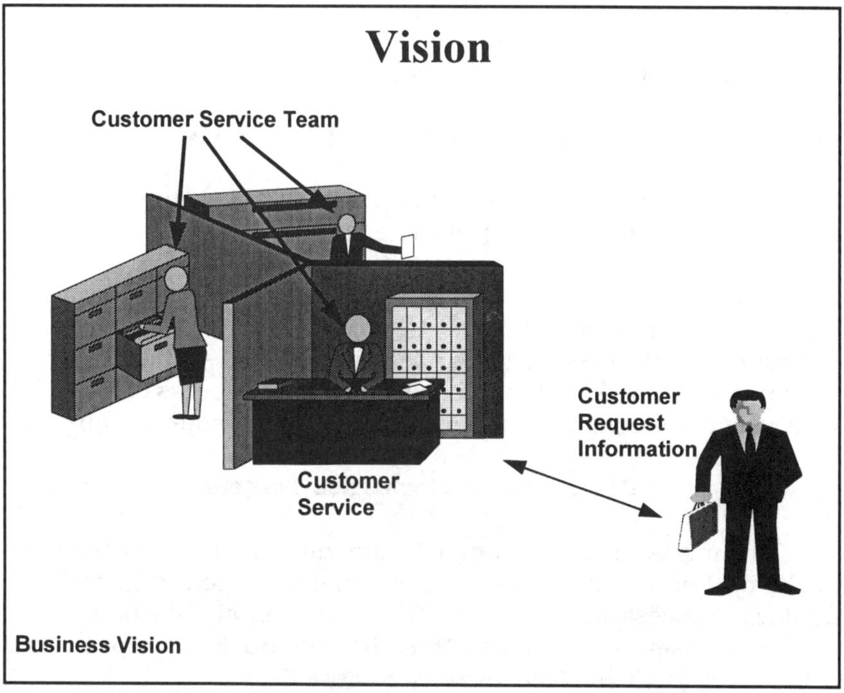

Figure 3.10 Redesigned Office Process.

standing the following:

- Clear goals
- Defined roles
- Effective communication
- Mutual respect
- Well-defined decision process
- Balanced participation
- Team awareness of the approach to be used for this effort working
- Understanding of the new tools or improvements to the overall effort

Develop a Team Mission Statement

The purpose of the team mission statement is to build consensus as to the team's goals and objectives for this effort.

Activity:

Introduce the team members if any new members have joined the team.

- Explain the roles and team responsibilities.
- Develop the overall mission statement of this team against the objectives of the business requirements.

- Identify any problems in accomplishing the objectives.
- Identify solutions to solving the problems.
- Post the statement where everyone can see it.

Develop Team Operating Principles

The purpose of this sub-activity is to establish the guidelines that will govern the behavior of the team.

Activities:
- Review guidelines for balance.
- Establish guidelines for team operations.
- Identify values and beliefs that will ensure the success of the effort.
- Identify items and events that might cause the effort to fail.

Review the Performance Targets

This review creates a common understanding of the objectives of the design and develops the performance targets that the new business process must satisfy. These targets should be used to influence design decisions so that the new business process will achieve the business objectives. See figure 3.11.

Activities:

Take each business objective or initiative and identify the performance targets that must be met. Identify the targets in terms of improvement measurements for the business process.

Building the Structure for the New Business Process

The initial activity for building the new business process is the left-to-right decomposition chart. This chart is a combination of decomposition using process flows and process mapping. Once the process is defined, identify where the process is being performed, by whom, and how long to complete the process. Use role playing to simulate the new process. This simulation will allow for the identification of exceptions to the process. Video taping can also be used to help with the analysis of the process after the simulation.

Activities:

The team should strictly enforce timeboxing methods to maximize work. They should follow these steps during this activity.

- As a group, the team should create a one-level process chart.
- Working left to right, one horizontal level at a time, the process should be charted.
- Continue the decomposition until the low-level business processes

Process	Time		Cost		Capital		Business Value	
	Current	Future	Current	Future	Current	Future	Current	Future

Figure 3.11 Business Performance Target Worksheet.

have been reached.

- Identify any integration points between the business processes. This includes possible hand-offs to other business process areas. Identify integration points by determining the triggers and results for each identified process.
- Identify the location where the process will be performed.
- Identify the time requirements for each process. At this point check the performance targets.
- Identify the need for technology, management measurement, reporting and distribution, and audit and controls.
- Once the team is comfortable with the technique of horizontal decomposition, sub-teams should be formed. Each sub-team should be composed of cross-functional team members (content expert, technologist and H/R) .
- Set rigid timeboxing rules and have each sub-team independently and concurrently further decompose the process.
- At the end of a timeboxing session, have all the sub-teams report their work to the whole group. Have the team simulate the total process and tape the activity. At this time a record of all issues should be formally entered in an automated Issue Tracking Log.
- Iteratively repeat the steps until the process is fully defined.
- After the flows are completed ask the following questions:

■ What are the business process rules?

- How will this process support the business objectives?
- Will this process meet the performance targets?
- Do I have to wait for information or another individual?
- What are the assumptions of the process?
- Who does the process effect?
- Who do I work with?
- Can I build this?
- Do I buy this?
- Can I modify anything I currently have to make this work?

Develop a Graphical Depiction of the Process

Build the conceptual model of the process that was defined. The purpose is to create a mechanism for communication of the new process. See figure 3.12.

Activities:
- Create a graphical depiction of business process scope.
- Create a graphical depiction of technical scope.

Develop the Testing Strategy for this Effort

Define the methods employed to test the various business and application components of the designed process. In addition, the Testing Strategy will define the policies and procedures to be followed for each level of testing. The complete testing plan is developed during Concept Development. Testing and validation are part of several different activities.

Figure 3.12 Conceptual Office Model.

Activities:

- Define the procedures used to test all business and software that has been modified or is a new development. The plan should have information about business process validation, technical testing (unit/string/performance), and integration simulation testing.

Concept Development Activity

This activity will build on the conceptual vision of the new business process and provide the team with a proof-of-concept simulation. It also clarifies the operational steps of the process both manual and automated. Concept Development will identify and describe requirements for staffing, management systems, facilities and locations, technology, and new value structures needed to make the process successful. Think of all the activities that take place when creating a new business. What are processes that take place the first day of operation. They are called the dimensions for business operations. When building the new process consider each dimension as they impact the company's ability to operate. Develop the Design of the Business Solution.

Mapping the Process Solution

The purpose of mapping the process is to work out the starting point of the design solution. A detailed understanding of the process steps is necessary to optimize the process design, enable system construction, and facilitate the development of roles and related management systems. This activity can be combined with the simulation. Assign a team member to document the map as the simulation progresses. If video taping was used during the simulation, productivity can be improved by reviewing the tape and documenting the results.

Activities:

- Identify all roles that perform the process and list them vertically as row headings. Create a role for the computerized functions.
- Map out the discrete tasks within the process. Place the tasks in their appropriate sequence, paying attention to interdependencies.
- Add a timeline to the column headings reflecting elapsed time.
- Identify key inputs and outputs of work process.
- Identify decision points and wait stages.
- Identify other interaction points between workers, operations, customers, and suppliers.
- Identify new process steps (if this is a redesign).
- Identify process relationships and dependencies.
- Identify technical enablers and integration points.

• Identify skills needed to perform the job.

Develop the Process Logic

Develop process model for more detailed process flows. This sub-activity will include manual and automated logic. The manual logic will be used for testing business operational procedures. The automated logic will be used for script development. Developing the process logic includes a prototyping procedure that gathers information in a three-phased approach. The first pass will collect data that will be needed by the business solution. As this information is being gathered, the various models and prototypes are being developed. This process is iterative in nature. The process should be focused on answering questions and assessing the impact of the answers to the business process and touring around the business dimensions. Do not focus on the design of the automated screens at this point. The screen designs will develop over the second and third prototyping pass. Using a good prototyping tool is the fastest way to gather information that will be used in the automated process.

First Pass Activities and Information:

Break the group into small teams to work on a major business flow. After the sub-teams have gathered the information, they meet as a full team. Start the process by answering questions about the information that is used in this process. Record the information and its uses to create models. Models are a way of recording knowledge not for controlling the approach. Models are created after the activity is complete or during the activity. Check the models for possible problems. The questions to ask in the first pass include:

- What is the information I need to work with?
- Are all the information needs covered?
- Do I have any bridges and conversions?
- Do I understand the relationships between the data and the process?
- Do I know who initiates, changes, reads and deletes the data?
- Who owns the data?
- What are the values of the data?
- Does my data flow follow my process flow?
- What are the acceptable ranges of the data?
- What makes this screen, report, or form acceptable?
- Is the team still within scope?
- Does the team have any static tables to define?
- Are there definitions for all the data items?

After completing the small group prototype work sessions get together as a large group to simulate the whole process and identify issues, assumptions, and risk. Assign a team member to research each issue and assumption, assign a response date.

Model Building

Break the team into content expert areas in order to complete information requirements.

Business Models:
- Process Descriptions
- Business Process Model
- Process Mapping
- Business Rules

Staffing Models :
- Staffing/Location Model

Technology Models :
- Data Model
- Volumes and Retention
- Data Definitions
- Data Access Model
- CRUD Matrix

Second Pass Information

The second pass will provide the format for gathering additional information relating to the business process—what information is used with what process and in what order. Use the following questions to gather information:

- What is the flow of information based on the business process?
- Who will use the information and how will they use the information?
- Have the data conversion needs been identified?
- Do we know what data needs to be audited?
- Do we know who can use the data?
- Do we know how long we want the data around?
- Have we identified any bridges to other systems or integration points to other functions?
- Do we understand how much data needs to be stored?
- What does the business professional need to know in order to use the automated process?
- What are the job skills required in order to work with this information and process?
- What are the exceptions or other needs for this information?

- What are the principles, constraints, and assumptions associated with the process?
- How are we going to solve any business issues or changes in the use of the information?
- Do we have any new facility requirements?

Once again, when the sub-teams have completed the prototyping work session they get back together as a large group to simulate the whole process and identify issues, assumptions, and risk. This process is the same as pass one.

Model Building

Break the team into content expert areas in order to complete the information requirements based on their area of expertise.

Business Models :
- Updated Process Descriptions
- Business Process Descriptions

Staffing Models :
- Skills Requirements
- Compensation Descriptions
- Training Descriptions

Technology Models :
- Key Performance Factors
- Application Process Definitions

Facilities Models :
- Paper Layout of Facilities

Third Pass Information

This pass allows the team to work with "what-ifs" and simulate through the day-in-the-life of the business professional. The team runs through the process and links the performance to the original targets. Consideration is given to system down time, start of day procedures, and end of cycle processing and reviews. The questions to answer follow: ** *This third pass should be an integrated simulation conducted with all sub teams. The model office should be used or the real environment.*

- Do we understand the design rules derived from the business process and business rules?
- Will the automated technical design support the business needs for performance and availability?

- Does the team know the support functions for the technical process? What happens when the system goes down?
- Will the technical design fit the architecture?
- Does the design meet the development environment standards?
- Do I know all my integration points?
  - Who do I report to?
  - Who do I work with?
  - What are my work hours?
  - What skills do I need?
  - Who will I interact with and when?
  - Will my coworkers resist the changes?
- Can I map what we have done back to the business case?
- How do I know this is going to work?

Building and Completing the Models

Business Models:
- Test Script Simulation Models
- Update changes to all business models

Staffing Models:
- Training Models
- Compensation Model
- Management Responsibilities Model
- Management Styles Model

Technology Models :
- Object Models
- Application Models
- Interface Model
- Conversion Models

The Function of Building Models

Creating models is a mechanism to study the information gathered at the work session and should be used as a process for cross checking the information and structuring the technical enabling solution. Models include business and technical. Models do not drive the approach, the team activities do.

Analysis of the information collected in the three passes:
The purpose is to analyze the information and complete the staffing, technology, and communication models.

Business Rules Model :
- Review all noted Business Process Rules during the development

of the design prototype.
- Note the dependencies between the rules and the designed Business Process flows.
- Confirm that the goals and business rules for the effort will be met by the process.
- Note any issues, assumptions, or risks associated with the implementation of the designs.
- Assign issues to be resolved, keep a list of whom the issue is assigned to, and the date by which the issue is to be resolved.
- Verify all assumptions before moving on to the next activity.

Staffing Requirements Model:
- Identify the events and activities associated with each job.
- Determine the number of transactions expected for each day.
- Establish the work time per transaction.
- Multiply the number of transactions per day times the work time per transaction.
- Determine the number of full-time-equivalents (FTEs) required for the job.
- Link the job to the process location.
- Determine the additional part-time employees required for the job.
- Identify employee transition needs.
- Determine the performance measures to be associated with each task.
- Identify the skills that will be needed to conduct the specific tasks.
- Determine the training that will be associated with the tasks.
- Develop a new job profile if needed.
- Validate organizational structure.
- Diagram the organization for the jobs identified.
- Describe the reporting relationships.
- Describe the span of control associated with the organization design.
- Determine the issues that will be associated with the new organization.

Business Scripts or Procedures:

The scripts will include both manual and automated procedures. The scripts will include such information as: what the individual needs to think, as well as what the individual needs to have at hand in order to do the job. See figure 3.13.

A business script needs to include:
1. What the activity is called,
2. Who is doing the activity and where,
3. What is the activity process,
4. What is done (complete forms, use technology) and how is it done,
5. Any time requirements,
6. Information coming into the process and going out of the process.

Business Scripts

Process Name:____________________
Staffing:__________________________
Estimated Work Time:__________
Equipment Used:_________________
Performance Required:__________

Departments to Interface With:

Process Steps:

1 .
2 .
3 .
4 .
5 .
6 .
7 .
8 .
9 .
10 .
11 .

Figure 3.13 Business Scripts Worksheet.

Develop the Automated Scripts

Automated scripts are written for each automated process in the solution. The process flow can be used for screen flows and screen logic. A high level script should be created for the logic that controls objects or denotes the structure for the application. As part of the prototype design, document automated logic, which must be consistent with the business description and prototype design. Create scripts for interfaces, bridges, and conversions based on the entry points into the process and database requirements. The scripts should be easy to read and concise. If necessary, diagrams should be drawn to depict complex relationships and/or requirements. Actual screen prints with prototype information should be included with the script. See figure 3.14.

An automated script needs to include:

1. General description of the process,
2. Names of screens or objects defined by this process and functions,
3. Security definition and rules for users, screens and screen modes,
4. The source (manual or automated) of all information required to support this process,
5. All programs, data, bridges, interfaces, or conversions used by this process,
6. Data that is accessed by this process and the access path used or expected ,

System Scripts

Application Name:______________ Interfaces:
Functions:______________
Estimated Performance:________
Equipment Used:____________ Databases:
Description:______________

Logic Steps:
1 .
2 .
3 .
4 .
5 .
6 .
7 .
8 .
9 .
10 .
11 .

Figure 3.14 System Scripts Worksheet.

7. Description of each button on the screens,
8. Description of the field validation requirements ,
9. Description of all list boxes on the screens,
10. Description of each menu used by the screens,
11. Identification of help functions.

Job Profile Description

The profile descriptions identify the responsibilities and skill requirements associated with new jobs or jobs impacted by the new business process. These profiles should be revisited and clarified during this activity. See figure 3.15.

Activities:
- Identify a job title from the company's list, if one does not exist, create one.
- Detail what has changed from the current job description to the new job skills required. If a new description is needed, complete a new company job description form.
- Indicate position requirements based on accountability. Position requirements are the minimum requirements for acceptable performance on the job. They describe what an individual must have in order to be considered for the position.
- Determine the work group structure.

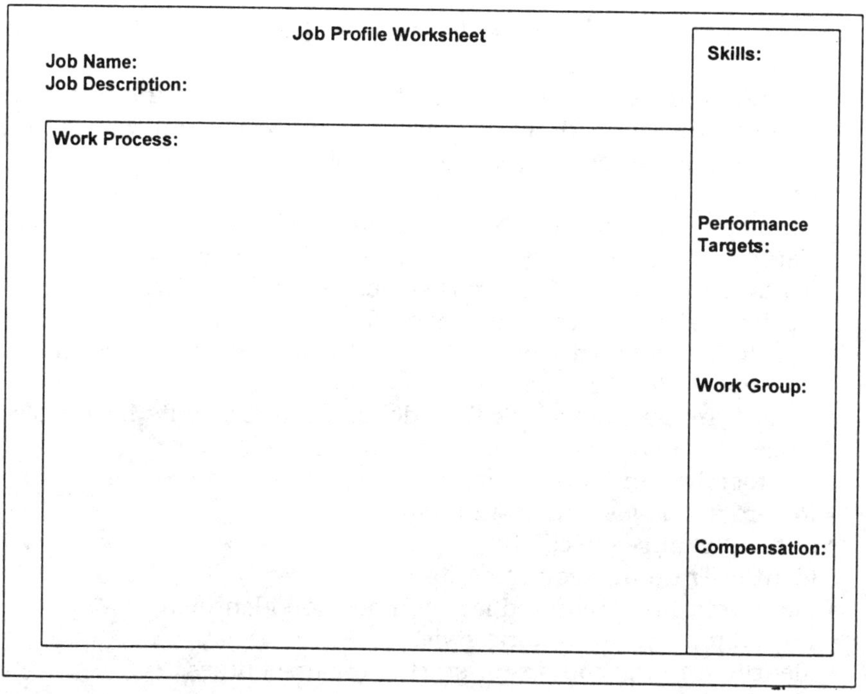

Figure 3.15 Job Profile Worksheet.

- Determine if an individual is a member of a team and list the team members' position names.
- Determine the job classification and compensation type.

Determine Compensation Plans for Job

Identify methods for rewarding and motivating individual behaviors as they relate to the new process. This information will be used to design compensation plans.

- Review the tasks and measures identified on Job Profile.
- Review the business maps.
- Define process measurement procedure.
- Monitor and diagnose problems in the process or business system.
- Identify key process measures indicating success of the process in time, cost, and quality.
- Identify all possible negative results which could occur from the process.
- Identify all possible causes for each negative result.
- Create Control System Plan.
- Respond to problems with modifications to process or business system.
- Add audit process, as necessary.

Review the Architecture

The necessary technical architecture to support the new process must be reviewed. The review looks at the current system and validates integration points and data points.

- Develop the architecture options and variables.
- Verify with the Architecture team that the architectural components (applications, data, infrastructure, and technical) expected will be available at the implemented site.
- Conduct a detailed technical walk through work session of the Concept Prototype.
- Walk through the technical model and requirements for consistence.
- Put together an architecture plan.
- Record all issues and assumptions.
- Note all changes needed.
- Identify Training Requirements.
- Identify training required for each new job identified.
- Determine type of training style.
- Identify training courses or start to create courses.
- Plan training for pilot.

Getting Ready for Realization

- Create a physical data model.
- Document primary key for each entity.
- Review foreign keys.
- Document physical data design.
- Create a first-cut physical database.

Realization

The Realization phase includes developing the process models of the business vision into the production ready business process, application and deployment-ready changes to the business environment. In traditional development methodologies this is the construction phase. Some building of the business process is aready underway at this point.

Activities:
- Develop the working prototype from the design prototypes.
- Develop screens, reports, and forms.
- Design batch and background programs and common modules.
- Develop program code.
- Develop interfaces.
- Develop data conversions.

- Document module interfaces.
- Document calling parameters for each module in a Parameter Data Definition.
- Document module logic.
- Develop test cases.
- Test the development programs.
- Document the test results.
- Review and Update Subsystem Documentation.
- Develop training materials.
- Complete staffing plan.
- Simulate and validate all functions.

Specifications for the staffing plan:
- Create a list of positions that are currently involved in the business process.
- Determine current staffing levels for those positions
- Create a list of positions that will exist as a result of the new process.
- Identify staff that will migrate from a current position into a new position.
- Identify positions that still need to be filled and extra positions after the migration.
- Determine the total number of current employees and total number of future employees involved in this process.

Specify functional requirements for some complex functions:
- Build the complex business algorithms and document their complexities.
- Build the business algorithms from the concepts identified during concept design.
- Build conversion programs.
- Update test scripts.
- Update the data models based on the changes made during simulation (the purpose of this task is to keep the logical and physical entity model up-to-date with changes, additions, and deletions as discovered).

Don't forget operations(PC/Mainframe):
- Create operational procedures based on the standards for:
  - Inputs into the process
  - The flow of the process
  - The expected results
  - Special restart and recovery procedures
  - Special security requirements
  - Information retention requirements
- Operational Procedures should be created for batch jobs, back-up, recovery, archiving, and JCL.

Facts about Testing:

- Technical team members are responsible for testing developed programers code or scripts. Business team members are responsible for testing the business process and training material.
- The team should develop a list of all screens and objects that require testing. Create a testing matrix that will link the schedule with testing and assign responsibilities for testing.

Business process testing:

- Walk through the business process definitions.
- Test the performance targets through simulation.
- Use the facilities model to test performance and space requirements.
- Identify problems in hand-offs and interactions with other business process areas.
- Review the results.
- Document the results.

Technical testing:

- Identify data interactions and flows.
- Develop test data from sample data identified during design prototyping.
- Develop test scripts and cases.
- Execute unit and string testing.
- Execute cycle testing.
- Execute performance testing.
- Review the results.
- Application testing is composed of three main tasks:
  - Simulation testing: Referred to as a day in the life of a business professional.
  - Business cycle testing: A business cycle is defined as a given period of time such as day-end, week-end, period-end, quarterly and year-end processing.
  - Business Performance Testing: This testing evaluates the process to ensure usability of the functionality across the application

Simulation/Prototype Reviews and Validations:

- Review working prototype and cover the following items:
  - Review the prototype set, business process flow, and narratives for the review.
  - Review the change log for associated entries.
  - Review fixes from the previous prototype review.
  - Review the Test Problem Report Log.
  - Simulate through the prototype set utilizing the business scripts and test cases.
  - Document all raised issues into the issue log and bugs noted during prototyping to the change log (Note: Only changes that

have a high priority should be addressed).
- Debrief changes, bugs, and issues with the whole lab team.

After each Simulation Development Activity:
- Review all subsystem flow diagrams and definitions to other systems of other business processes.
- Develop and test the logic for the next set of functions.
- Design the logic flow for the interfaces, bridges, and conversions for the next set of functions.
- Update system process scripts for interfaces, bridges, and conversions (with any changes identified).
- Develop the Test Scripts Case.
- Test the developed logic and data transfer by file if communications link is not available.
- Test the developed logic interface with subsystem or other lab processes.
- Update Test Problem Report Log if needed.
- Communicate the list of interfaces and issues to the integration manager.
- Perform some program and database optimizations based on performance results.
- In optimizing the data design, use the following steps:
  - Define indexes and foreign keys
  - Partition large tables
  - Move history into a separate table
  - Optimize small table access
  - Avoid small table locking spots
  - Define owner static attributes in a member table
  - Define member summaries, counts, or flags in the owner table
  - Denormalize finite repeating groups
  - Cluster related entities
  - Merge one-to-one relationships
  - Re-evaluate data sharing
- Have the business professionals validate performance.

Deployment Sub-activity

The deployment phase is the final integration of the business process. It is the time in which the pilot is being prepared for the new process and the work group structure is being formed. This phase is the gateway to the pilot.

Activities:
- Collect Barriers/Resistance Factors to the new changes from the pilot area. Have select individuals review information on barriers and resistance factors, as well as any new barrier information

coming out of current efforts. Brainstorm solutions/interventions that may be used prior to or at implementation of business processes. Record all information coming from the brainstorming.
- Complete all descriptions of performance changes across all levels of the Business Process Dimensions for input into pilot stakeholder change interventions. Document the information and develop a change management plan.
- Complete any programming and testing that could not be completed until now. Make sure that the programs are integrated with the work already completed. Re-test all functions to ensure that the applications are still working.
- Complete any organizational structure changes that accurately represent and support the new business processes.
- Complete all data conversions and test the results.
- Install security on the application.
- Finish all operational procedures and test.
- Demonstrate the functionally to the pilot area if it's different than the current work area.
- Complete all business scripts and training materials.
- Review all performance targets.
- Move the production system to the business area and retest.
- Complete Pilot Preparation.
- Install and test all new hardware and communications software
- Install and test all PC support software.
- All training schedules and materials should be ready for the pilot.
- If the current facilities need structural changes they must be completed before the hardware and software is installed.

Conduct Integration Tests

Integration testing should start as soon as any programs are operational and should continue after programs have been unit tested. As additional pieces of the system are coded, test the new pieces with the existing pieces.

Evaluate Prototype for Technical Performance

The purpose of this task is to evaluate the prototype by benchmarking the performance of critical business functions.

- Build and benchmark performance critical functions first. For critical system processes where performance is anticipated to be at the boundary of acceptable service, conduct informal benchmarks as soon as a running program is available.
- Concentrate this effort on:
  - Processes with high transaction volumes
  - Processes with complex data access requirements

- ■ Processes with critical response time requirements
- ■ Batch processes with complex data access requirements and fixed-time windows.
- Document findings from performance evaluation.
- Keep performance modeling findings and benchmark results as Test Results.

Simulation Integration

Simulation Integration is not a phase but a continuous activity to integrate the evolving business process with all its dimensions. This activity combines role playing for analysis and provides a format for visual understanding of the integration of the new process to the total business environment. It allows for trying new ideas and understanding the impact of these ideas on the design. This is a powerful activity for the integration of several team efforts. This process should be used throughout the approach. The larger the effort the greater the need for this activity.

Activities:

- Reserve a regular half-day every two weeks in which all team members focus on integration testing. Provide some level of planning for these sessions to help maintain focus and to ensure that all areas are tested.
- Conduct an integrated team review.
- Validate the concept and ensure the quality of the design. This will provide a mechanism for each team to understand the latest design revisions.
- Review any design refinements or completed documentation.
- Validate the design changes. Any inconsistencies or concerns about the design should be raised.
- Record all issues, assumptions, and integration points.
- Note all changes needed or make changes at the review.

How to run the Simulation

A sample approach for review would be to:

- State the objectives of the review (The day in the life of.......) or (A Customer Inquiry)
- Set the stage for the review using information from the process flows
- Describe any issues and assumptions identified during the design process. Simulate or walk through the business process asking questions and solving issues and assumptions.
- Raise and respond to *what-if* questions about the process during the review.

- Document all issues, assumptions, and risks identified during the simulation.
- Tape the session if possible to review later.

Pilot Planning

Pilot planning is a process to clarify how the new process will be implemented and where. If the MIS organization is aligned with the business, the implementation should be easy unless the business solution is to be implemented in multiple sites. The plan includes detailing the pilot requirements and the requisite implementation activities for each process. Pilot planning should be worked into the activities of each major accelerated team development activity.

Activities:

Identify long lead time pilot site implications early in the development process. These items should take the form of:

- Facility preparation
- Asset improvements
- Staffing adjustments
- Information technology improvements
- Data conversion procedures
- Technology changes
- Identification of communication needs
- Development of a communications feedback process
- Creation of the pilot implementation plan

Where to Go from Here

As awareness of accelerated development approaches and the power of self-directed teams are understood, use the process of continuous improvement to create the accelerated approach that works best in the new organization. There are many ways to implement the new organization's approach to total business solutions. However, similar to redesigning today's business, a few key concepts should be deployed to facilitate the success of the team and business results.

❒ Break down walls between business application and technology.
❒ Consider the results and priorities .
❒ Creativity beats the competition.
❒ Create a series of small successes that provide business value.
❒ Develop a continuous improvement plan.
❒ Don't be bound by old ideas.

Following these simple ideas will keep technical skills in demand and create an atmosphere of professionals working for the growth of the organization.

ARCHITECTURE

Reengineering Management Information Systems

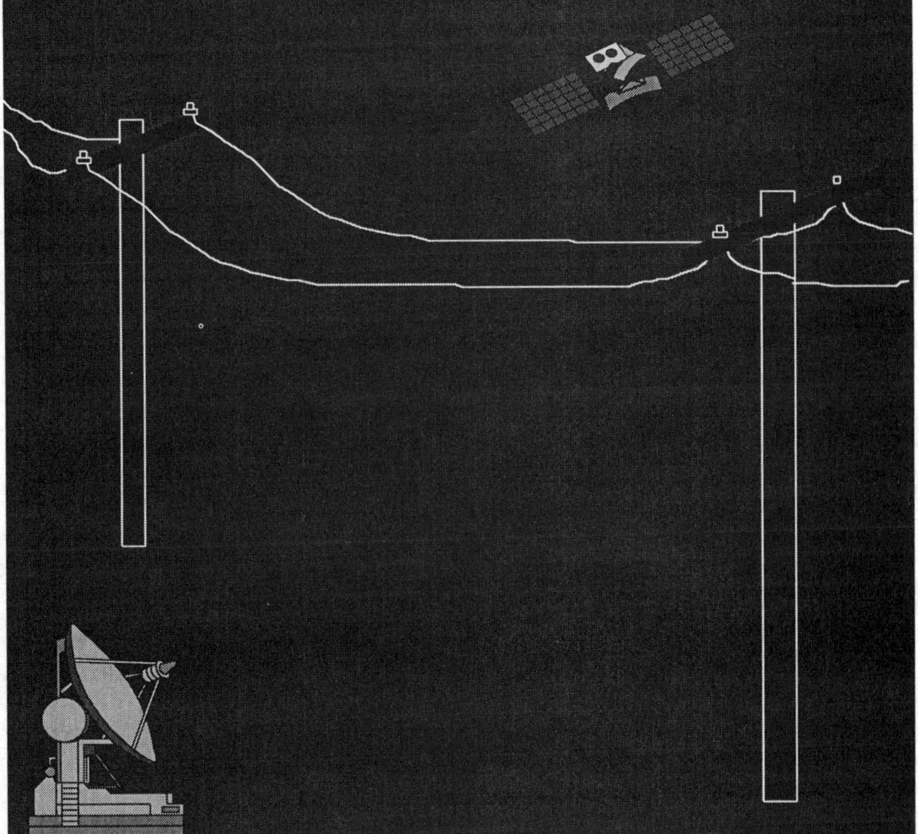

Chapter 4

Comprehensive Technical Architecture

Reengineering success depends on MIS having an infrastructure and an organization capable of supporting reengineering development and the redesigned business processes. One way to satisfy these dependencies is to develop a Comprehensive Technical Architecture. The principle difference between a normal MIS architecture and the Comprehensive Technical Architecture is the inclusion of answers to the question "How?" as well as answers to the question "What?" For example, the Comprehensive Technical Architecture's Process Architecture describes how the MIS organization will work to accomplish their reengineering project responsibilities. This chapter will describe the components of a Comprehensive Technical Architecture and how to develop one. It will also describe the roles and responsibilities of the architects and their relationship to the reengineering labs. Chapter 5—*Reengineering Integration* will expand on the integration roles and responsibilities of the architects and Chapter 8—*Organizational Change* will describe developing an MIS organization capable of supporting reengineering.

To realize the benefits of reengineering fully, enterprises must aggressively employ information technology. A tenet of reengineering is that the new processes are new capabilities afforded, in most cases, as a result of new technology. The innovative use of information technology is fundamental to successful reengineering. For the first time in history, information technology is the enabler to improve the business in a real and measurable way. Figure 4-1 indicates the impact information technology can have on the enterprise in the short-, medium-, and long-term. The enterprise will use information technology to make money, not just to count money.

MIS organizations have a tremendous opportunity. The technology MIS now controls will be the enabler of change in the enterprise, but MIS must change itself and choose to be a change agent for the enterprise. MIS must deliver flexible, technical functionality in an uncertain and changing environment to support changes in the business. Given this requirement to change and the desire of most enterprises to continue to rely on their existing, internal MIS resources, the greatest challenge MIS must really face is to change. The change will include organizational change, changes in techniques, changes in ways of relating to and working with business partners, and, finally, technological changes.

Figure 4-2 highlights reengineering-enabling technologies that enterprises have successfully used to achieve the dramatic

Short-Term	Access to information Business-oriented solutions Improved application interface "Simple" integration Improved Productivity Easier application development
Medium-Term	Better integration Workflow computing capabilities Improved vendor management Improved MIS resource usage Improved integration among dissimilar architectures
Long-Term	Flexibility Speed Quality Innovation Cross-functional cooperation Rapid changeability New technology adaptability

Source: Clelland Johnson

Figure 4-1 Reengineering Benefits from Information Technology.

- Graphical Interfaces to applications
- Standard information access, e.g., Structured Query Language (SQL)
- Interoperability and Open systems
- Application development products designed for client/server applications
- Application development products designed for accelerated applications development
- Pen, hand-held, and other portable computers
- Knowledge-based and Executive Information Systems (EIS)
- VSAT, ISDN, Cellular modems, Radio frequency LANs, FDDI, ATM, SMDS, and Cell or Frame relay
- Networking, interconnectivity, and Network computing
- Distributed Relational Database Management Systems (RDBMS)
- Common Application Program Interfaces (API)
- Middleware components
- Object Oriented Design and Programming
- Workflow and Groupware Computing
- Multimedia, Interactive videodisk, and Optical storage
- Standard operating system interfaces and features, e.g., POSIX, UNIX, OSF/1, etc.

Source: Clelland Johnson

Figure 4-2 Information Technologies for Implementing Business Reengineering.

reengineering results. World-class MIS organizations will employ these technologies to meet the same attributes of nimbleness, speed, compression, flexibility, quality, and innovation that are required for reengineering business processes as described in Figure 4-3. An enterprise embarking on a reengineering journey can use the list in Figure 4-2 to assess if their MIS organization can support them. If MIS cannot, they can use this list as the guide for reengineering MIS to be able to support the business, or for selecting an alternative to

Nimbleness	Easy to change Easy to implement
Speed	Faster development time Faster business partner training time Faster access to information
Compression	Lower cost environment Lower cost of development and training Higher-IQ environment
Flexibility	Easily integrated across computing and database environments More connectivity options More technology-literate environment
Quality	Improved reliability and availability Faster access to more information
Innovation	User-centric and technology rich Flexible, fast, and easy to change

Source: Clelland Johnson

Figure 4-3 Achieving Reengineering Critical Success Factors with Information Technology.

the internal MIS organization.

Readying the MIS organization to support reengineering is critical to the success of any reengineering effort. Some organizations will not even undertake reengineering the business until they have reengineered MIS. It is common, however, for MIS to become involved in the reengineering effort as more of an afterthought. This results in MIS being behind in preparing for reengineering and can sometimes position MIS to be an impediment to achieving the reengineering objectives. Another related risk is the timeframe expectation set by the reengineering project team for achieving the business value suggested by the business cases.

To be ready to support reengineering labs and reengineered business processes in the necessary timeframe, an enterprise must start to change MIS concurrently with starting the business reengineering activity. The two organizing principles for the change that MIS must master to be successful in supporting their enterprise's reengineering efforts are:

- Developing a Comprehensive Technical Architecture that is a foundation for the technological innovation required for business process reengineering, and
- Organizing MIS appropriately to support the reengineering labs, the new business environment, and new changing requirements. Chapter 8—Organizational Change discusses the organizational aspects of reengineering MIS.

The Comprehensive Technical Architecture

The key to preparing MIS for reengineering is development of a Comprehensive Technical Architecture that will enable the MIS organization to support the reengineering labs to accomplish the objectives of the reengineering effort. Indeed, industry watcher, Gartner Group has confirmed this condition:

> "Without a client/server applications architecture and system development methodology, merely selecting client/server tools will result in minimal and isolated successes (0.8 probability)." Applications Development & Management Strategies, SPA-480-815, Gartner Group, Inc., Stamford, Connecticut, 1993.

> "If an organization has not assembled the appropriate I/T infrastructure, BPR efforts will bog down or fail (0.8 probability)." Industry Service, K-955-950, Gartner Group, Inc., Stamford, Connecticut, 1993.

The Comprehensive Technical Architecture is the broad description of the rules and implementation aspects of the infrastructure that will support the reengineering vision through information technology. Figure 4-4 depicts a Comprehensive Technical Architecture as five balanced parts that form a bridge connecting business imperatives to the product of the MIS organization. These parts are the Process Architecture, the Information Architecture, the Applications Architecture, the Applications Development Environment Architecture, and the Technology Infrastructure Architecture.

The Process Architecture described in Figure 4-5 defines how MIS will translate business vision into application systems and data stores, i.e., the techniques for implementing the business process reengineering vision. The Information Architecture described in Figure 4-6 is the definition of data, data stores, database management systems, and data distribution schemes. The Applications Architecture described in Figure 4-7 is the "picture album" of how legacy and new application systems fit together over time and the definition of tools used to accomplish integration among them. The Applications Development Environment Architecture described in Figure 4-8 is the collection of tools for building new applications. Finally, the Technology Infrastructure Architecture described in Figure 4-9 is the definition of hardware platforms, operating systems, and interconnectivity networks, as well as, any unique technologies required to achieve the business vision.

Also, there is a time-sensitive nature to Applications, Information, and Technology Infrastructure Architectures. First, there is the current architecture representing the legacy systems environment

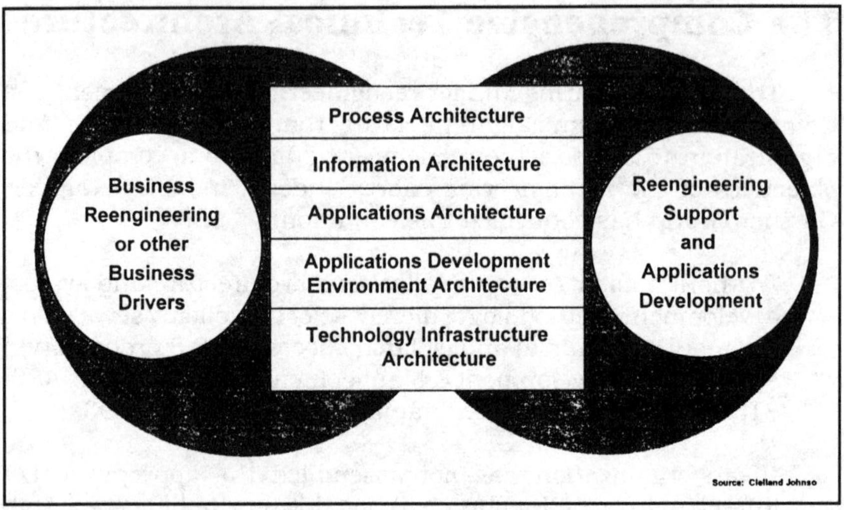

Figure 4-4 The Comprehensive Technical Architecture

- ❑ Methodologies and Processes
- ❑ Quality Management
- ❑ Reengineering Lab Techniques
- ❑ Design and Development Techniques
- ❑ I/T Integration
- ❑ MIS Assessment Skills
- ❑ MIS Reskilling and Retooling
- ❑ MIS Communications and Change Management Programs
- ❑ Training and Coaching
- ❑ Issues Management
- ❑ Scope Management
- ❑ Change Control

Source: Clelland Johnson

Figure 4-5 Components of the Process Architecture.

- ❑ Information Policies
- ❑ Information Access
- ❑ DBMS Technology
- ❑ Data Distribution
- ❑ Data Conversions
- ❑ Logical Data Modeling
- ❑ Database Performance Engineering
- ❑ Logical and Physical Database Design
- ❑ Data Bridges

Source: Clelland Johnson

Figure 4-6 Components of the Information Architecture.

- ❑ Architecture "Picture Album"
- ❑ Application Integration
- ❑ Legacy System Integration
- ❑ Application Bridges
- ❑ Legacy System Retirement

Source: Clelland Johnsor

Figure 4-7 Components of the Application Architecture.

- ❑ CASE Tools
- ❑ Software and Database Version Control
- ❑ Programming Tools
- ❑ Software Distribution
- ❑ ADE Installation, Configuration, and Integration
- ❑ Common Objects and "Middleware" Design, Development, Integration, and Management ADE
- ❑ Applications Development Standards and Guidelines
- ❑ Process Management Tools

Source: Clelland Johnsor

Figure 4-8 Components of the Applications Development Environment Architecture.

- ❑ Platform and Operating Environment
- ❑ Connectivity and Networking
- ❑ Systems and Network Management
- ❑ Operations Management
- ❑ Performance Management
- ❑ Unique Technologies
- ❑ I/T Integration Management

Source: Clelland Johnson

Figure 4-9 Components of the Technology Infrastructure Architecture.

and the starting point for any new architectural direction. Next, there is the target, or end-state architecture that is the ultimate architectural vision as understood, now. Finally, there are the interim architectures that describe the changes to the architectures that will occur as a result of migrating from the current architecture to the target architecture. These interim architectures for Applications, Information, and Technology Infrastructure are in the architectural "picture album" mentioned earlier.

The ultimate objective of the Comprehensive Technical Architecture is to give MIS a framework within which to prepare for whatever changes the business dictates. That may mean, not being locked into a single vendor, style of computing, or technology; or it may mean using only those vendor's products supplied through a specific business alliance. In any event, it means developing a framework based on principles driven by business decisions.

Some architectural principles, rules, and "lessons learned" include:

- Architectural rule # 1 is accommodation, including accommodation of legacy systems, new systems, unique technologies, and unique products.
- Architecture defines interfaces, not products. These interfaces are the "white space" between other information technology components. These interfaces include operating system functions, application program interfaces (APIs), information access mechanisms, and communications interconnectivity.
- MIS should not implement any information technology just for the technology's sake. Furthermore, MIS should encourage technology-literate business partners to avoid this trap, too. Along similar lines, MIS should not implement any information technology without looking at the underlying business processes to see if they need work first.
- MIS should not be intimidated by current vendors. Likewise, MIS should not become so locked into a technology, a vendor, or a product suite that they are constrained from doing what's right to support the business.
- MIS should avoid "analysis paralysis" in tool evaluation or any other decision-making.

Each part of the Comprehensive Technical Architecture is equally necessary and equally important to all other parts. So, an architecture that emphasizes one part over the others is not a truly balanced architecture and is therefore flawed. For example, an architecture may be technically elegant, e. g., the latest and greatest GUI client/server, RDBMS system around, but not implementable because it does not take into account MIS' capabilities. Conversely, it may be implementable, but not address the business requirements, or provide adequate flexibility to change in the future, e. g., a traditional monolithic mainframe system.

The Comprehensive Technical Architecture will enable innovation. It will allow MIS to introduce new technology to solve business problems and to support reengineering. Besides the specific relationship between reengineering and architecture, there are numerous other benefits to developing a business-focused Comprehensive Technical Architecture. Briefly, they are:

- Faster development and delivery times.
- Definition and use of common business information by multiple business applications.
- Greater business partner and MIS productivity.
- Improved quality for business processes and MIS deliverables.
- Reduced rework for MIS.
- Reduced technology costs through volume discounts and standard products.
- More focused MIS training and less retraining.
- Reduced product "customization" cost and time.
- Reduced risk of MIS schedule slippage.
- Reduced cost of changing or adding new technologies.

The first step in developing a Comprehensive Technical Architecture is to define what is and what is not important to the enterprise. This will influence the degree of importance and the balance placed on a particular architecture. The architecture teams discover this by answering certain business questions. To make sound architectural decisions, an enterprise must determine:

- The timeframe for implementation.
- The acceptable degree of business and technical risk.
- The technical competency of the MIS organization.
- The degree of vendor independence or dependence desired.

This exercise will always include the MIS organization, but it is the business process owners whose answers are most important. Answers to these questions will force the architecture to emphasize one or more attributes: the business process, the system's performance, operations efficiency, a business relationship with a vendor, technical elegance, or implementation timeframe. The answers to these questions could lead an MIS organization to decide, for example, that:

- Better application interfaces make systems easier to use and faster to learn.

- Common application program interfaces (APIs) make applications faster to develop.
- Standard communications architectures, like TCP/IP and OSI, and a standard information access mechanism, like SQL, make information and services easier to get.
- Standard operating system interfaces make application programs portable.

There are typically three impediments to success when developing Comprehensive Technical Architectures, but by adhering to certain critical success factors for Comprehensive Technical Architecture development outlined in Figure 4-10, enterprises enhance their chances for success. The impediments to developing a successful Comprehensive Technical Architecture are:

1. Not understanding the nuances of the architecture development process. Asking questions like:

    - What are the activities and their sequence?
    - Who should be involved and when?
    - How will we avoid or resolve technical issues and avoid "analysis paralysis?"

    An even more dangerous manifestation is the habit some techni-

- ❑ Management endorsement is required for the investment to develop the architectures and to enforce its use in all development projects.
- ❑ A focused effort is needed to accomplish developing the architectures in the near-term before other projects using potentially opposing architectures are started.
- ❑ Additional I/T expertise is needed to determine the correct choices for the various segments of the architectures.
- ❑ Typical architecture work done to date focuses on platform, operating system, and network product selections, but the architecture must cover additional areas, such as MIS processes, information, applications integration, and applications development environment.
- ❑ The architectures must address the migration of legacy systems critical to the enterprise's operation. However, these systems are probably based on technology and tools disparate from any of the recommended architecture components.
- ❑ After developing the architecture, a good communications plan is needed to orient the organization, within and outside MIS, in the new architecture.

Source: Clelland Johnson

Figure 4-10 Critical Success Factors for Comprehensive Technical Architecture Development.

cians have of "developing architecture by reading magazines." This is characterized by proposing architectural solutions that are the "latest and greatest" vendor promises, but are not used in production anywhere.

2. An inability to get business partners involved in the process, both—early in the process and throughout the process. This is necessary to ensure the Comprehensive Technical Architecture provides the right foundation to support the business now and in the future.

3. An inability to gain acceptance for the results of the architecture project, both within and outside MIS. The whole point of developing an architecture is to provide a framework within which work will be done, providing the rules necessary to achieve consistency and ensure integration.

Approach to Developing a Comprehensive Technical Architecture

One successful workplan for building a Comprehensive Technical Architecture follows and is summarized in Figures 4-11a and 4-11b. This workplan will need to be modified to satisfy the specific needs of any MIS organization attempting to undertake development of a Comprehensive Technical Architecture. The changes will be based on the business imperatives forcing the undertaking, the MIS organization's starting point, and its capabilities.

Develop Context for Project

- *Enlist Management Support for Process:*
It is extremely important that a project of this nature have the full endorsement of management, certainly MIS management, but also management outside MIS. Without such support all activities are undertaken at risk. Management commitment is required to ensure the results of the analysis will serve the enterprise in the future. This commitment will also ensure comprehensiveness of the architecture for satisfying business requirements. Finally, this commitment will ensure adherence to the architecture when new applications are planned (whether MIS or business units plan and develop them).

- *Identify Architecture Teams:*
To define the best future architecture, teams of specialists must be formed to focus on different architecture areas. These teams will

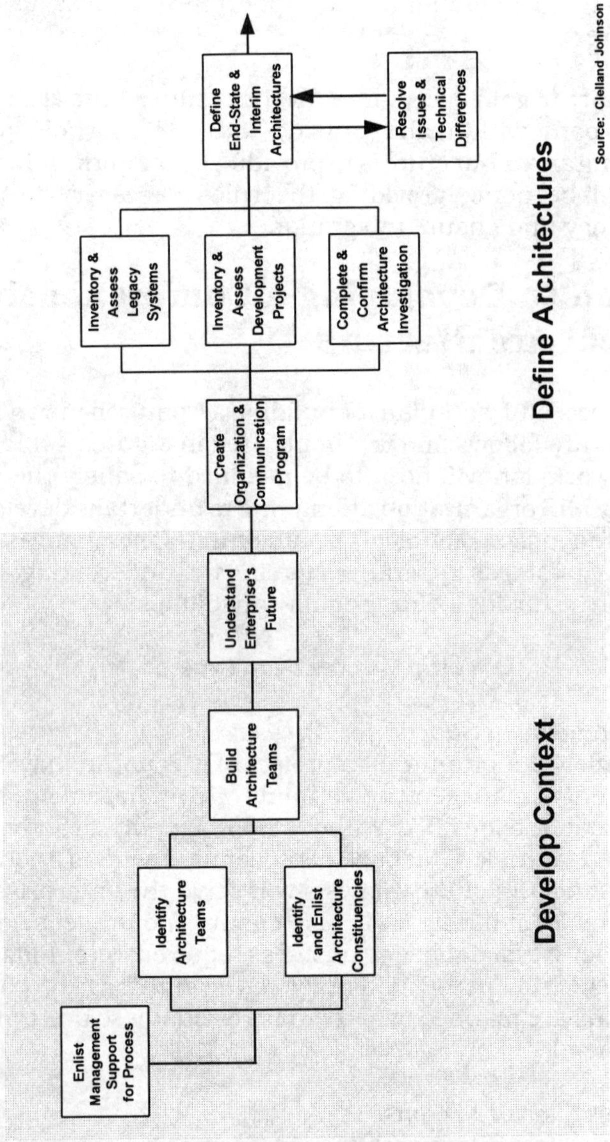

Figure 4-11a Comprehensive Technical Architecture Development Process

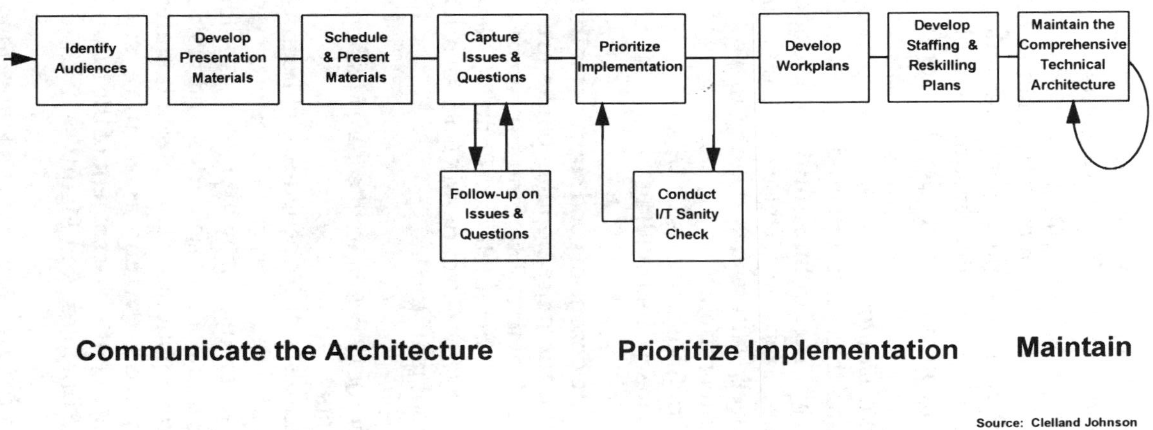

Figure 4-11b Comprehensive Technical Architecture Development Process (cont.)

begin a structured process to set architectural direction, define architectural components, and communicate the architectural plans to management. Some members of the architecture teams will probably not be MIS staff, but rather technology-literate business partners.

- *Identify Architecture Constituencies and Involve Them in the Process:*
  There are a number of constituencies that will be affected by any findings of the architecture teams, e.g., those who design, develop, and implement new applications within and outside MIS, and those in MIS who implement and maintain the various architectures. These interested parties will ultimately determine the success or failure of the architecture and its implementation. As a result, they must be involved in its development.

- *Team Building:*
  To foster the maximum productivity and insure a common goal and objective, the architectural teams should engage in several team building exercises. These exercises will prepare the teams to deal effectively with issues relating to:
    - Integration
    - Communications
    - Consensus building

  There are dozens of good sources for these team building exercises. Some of the more popular books are *Games Trainers Play*, *More Games Trainers Play*, and *Still More Games Trainers Play* all by Edward E. Scannell and John W. Newstrom (McGraw-Hill) and Workplay by Carmine M. Consalvo (Organizational Design and Development, Inc.).

- *Review or Develop Architecture Mission, Principles, Objectives, and Benefits:*
  The teams will investigate architectural alternatives and match them with the enterprise's mission and objectives. An architecture mission statement will provide a guiding direction for both the initial architecture definition and maintenance of future architectural components. This mission statement must agree with the enterprise's current and future statements of direction and management's assessment of the future. One example of Architectural Principles is in Figure 4-12.

- *Understand the Enterprise's Future (and the Resulting Architectural Implications):*
  The architecture has no purpose if not to support the business.

- Results Drive All Decisions and Plans
- Business Processes Drive Results
- Standardize Whenever Possible
- Simple Processes with Complex Tasks
- The Only Customers That Count are External Customers
- No Process Design is Static
- All Systems Have a Common Look and Feel
- All New Business Processes and Systems are Developed Fast

Source: Clelland Johnson

Figure 4-12 Architectural Principles.

Therefore, the requirements for the Comprehensive Technical Architecture derive ultimately from the current and future plans of the business. Part of setting the context within which the architecture must operate is to understand the current and future business environment. MIS should already be well aware of the historic and current business environments, but may be less well aware of the future business environment. During this activity, the architecture teams must establish a working relationship with the appropriate business executives, discuss and understand their visions of the future, and identify any architectural implications of those visions. To add value to the process and to make this expenditure of the business executives' time worthwhile, the architecture teams should also provide recommendations to the business executives regarding technologies that may enhance their visions of the future. In this way MIS can add value to the reengineering initiative. The more credibility MIS can achieve now, the more likely they are to be considered a partner in future business decision making.

- *Collect Architecture Work Done* :
In many cases, there is significant architectural work that has already been done. This work cannot be discounted. So, it must be reviewed and evaluated considering the new business requirements. This is an activity requiring extreme diplomacy. The architecture teams do not want to accept prior work without applying the business needs filter to it, but they also do not want to ignore prior work. In the initial phases of the project the

architecture teams must review the documentation and presentations concerning prior work and evaluate its current state and its applicability.

Define Architectures

- *Develop Architecture Organization and Communication Mechanisms:*

The MIS staff responsible for implementing and maintaining the architectures will be identified by defining the various roles and responsibilities required for developing, maintaining, and communicating the architecture. While these can be part-time assignments, the responsibilities must be assigned to individuals who can be held accountable for them. These roles include the Chief Architect, the Process Architect, the Information Architect, the Applications Development Environment Architect, and the Technology Infrastructure Architect. Each position is briefly described, below:

- The Chief Architect is responsible for the overall direction and management of the architecture and ensuring that the changes made to the architecture adhere to the mission statement. Also, the Chief Architect is the technical "decision-maker of last resort."
- The Process Architect is responsible for defining the techniques (methodology) that will be used, for ensuring the overall quality of the products created, for ensuring testing plans are developed and executed, and for preparing and delivering process and applications development training to the reengineering labs on a just-in-time basis.
- The Information Architect is responsible for defining information management policies, logical data modeling, data distribution and conversion strategies, database management system evaluations and implementations, and ensuring satisfactory database performance.
- The Applications Architect is responsible for ensuring the smooth integration of applications that must coexist. The Applications Architect is also responsible for defining and, over time, maintaining Applications Architecture diagrams of new and legacy systems. This requires understanding legacy system functionality, process flow, and integration points and developing and maintaining the vision of functionality, process flow, and integration among new systems and between new and legacy systems. Finally, the Applications Architect is a participant in evaluation of methodologies and applications development tools to ensure consistency with the Applications Architecture.
- The Applications Development Environment Architect is respon-

sible for defining and maintaining a tool set containing the components necessary to support new applications development and the maintenance of all current applications, for setting up the applications development environment, identifying common applications development objects, and for integrating applications development tools with other tools and with the new applications building processes. The Applications Development Environment Architect must also provide the appropriate development environment training for the reengineering labs. Finally, and most importantly, the Applications Development Environment Architect is responsible for defining and managing the development activities that build the common applications development environment component within the organizing principles of selected methodologies and tools.
- The Technology Infrastructure Architect is responsible for defining the production infrastructure components necessary to support all production systems, including newly developed applications, i.e., hardware platforms, operating systems, LAN and WAN architectures, and overall systems management architecture. The Technology Infrastructure Architect will also develop plans for migrating from one architectural component to another.

- *Inventory and Assess Legacy Systems:*
To continue with the specification of the Comprehensive Technical Architecture, it is important to understand the current legacy system environment fully. This includes:
  - Types of applications
  - Application production environments
  - Ages of applications
  - Methods of development
  - Technologies used
  - Interfaces among applications

By fully understanding these items, the architecture teams can assess the impact of the current architecture on the choices to be made in defining the new Comprehensive Technical Architecture. There are many current interfaces and instances of data sharing that can place constraints on architectural choices. A complete inventory of legacy systems can provide the necessary overview of these interfaces and interactions. The architecture teams will also be able to assess the maintainability of these legacy systems and, perhaps, identify candidates for redesign and redevelopment. This would only occur where the age or maintainability warrant this effort. It is important to note that all redesign and redevelopment must make economic sense.

MIS Activity	Business Process Affected	Is this MIS Activity on the Critical Path?	Expected Functionality Fit (%)	Expected Timeframe Fit (Date)	Logistical Overlap with Other Activities	Estimate to Complete (Workdays)	Alternatives to Current MIS Activity	Estimated Costs of Alternatives	Business Process Owner Preference

Source: Clelland Johnso

Figure 4-13 MIS In-Flight Activities Template

MIS Activity	Business Process Affected	Is this MIS Activity on the Critical Path?	Expected Functionality Fit (%)	Expected Timeframe Fit (Date)	Logistical Overlap with Other Activities	Estimate to Complete (Workdays)	Alternatives to Current MIS Activity	Estimated Costs of Alternatives	Business Process Owner Preference
MIS identifies development, production, and other activities that may impact their reengineering activities. These could include acquisition or development of applications or functions, migration of existing applications, or other changes. Emphasis should be placed on efforts that are on the reengineering critical path or that will consume large amounts of MIS resource.	For each MIS activity, indicate the business process or function that will be affected.	If the MIS activity is on the reengineering critical path, note this here. These MIS activities may need to be accelerated, but in any event, one or more contingency plans must be identified.	For each MIS activity, indicate how closely the result is expected to fit with the functional requirements of the redesigned business process.	For each MIS activity, indicate how closely the result is expected to fit with the timeframe requirements of the redesigned business process.	For each MIS activity, indicate how closely it is expected to overlap with other significant process changes.	For each MIS activity, indicate the current estimate for completion of the activity assuming the existing scope of functionality.	If the MIS activity is necessary for the successful implementation of the redesigned business process, and if the functionality fit, timeframe fit, or estimate to complete is out of line with the requirements of the redesigned business process, indicate alternatives to the current MIS activity.	If any alternatives are identified, indicate as closely as possible, the costs associated with the alternative. If precise costs are not available, indicate what assumptions were used to estimate the costs provided here.	For each MIS activity, the Business Process Owner should (based on the redesigned business process requirements and MIS's findings) indicate whether the MIS activity should be accelerated, terminated, or allowed to run its current course.

Source: Clelland Johnso

Figure 4-14 MIS In-Flight Activities Template Description

- *Inventory and Assess MIS Projects:*
  The architecture teams will look at the current portfolio of all in-progress MIS projects. For those nearing completion, they must evaluate their architectural components and assess the impact, if any, on future architectural choices. For those that are just beginning, the Chief Architect will determine if the project should adhere to the new architecture or perpetuate the old architecture. One tool for collecting this information is the In-Flight MIS Activities Template depicted in Figures 4-13 and 4-14.
  All in-flight MIS activities will have something to offer the architecture definition process. They all reflect the latest thinking within the enterprise concerning ideas and implementations for system design and construction.
  Because it is important that the enterprise standardize on methods and tools early, to get the full advantage from a new architecture definition, the focus will be to incorporate, where possible, the new architecture without increasing costs or deferring needed functionality.

- *Define End State and Interim Architectures:*
  "Architecture" covers a lot of territory. It includes the Process Architecture of how systems are built, the Information Architecture of data, data stores, database management systems, and data distribution schemes, the Applications Architecture of legacy and new application systems, the Applications Development Environment Architecture of techniques and tools for building new applications, and, finally, the Technology Infrastructure Architecture of hardware platforms, operating systems, and interconnectivity networks. Also, there is a time-sensitive nature to architecture. There is the current architecture which is the environment in which legacy systems exist and the starting point for any new architectural direction. There is the target, or end-state, architecture which is the ultimate architectural vision as understood, now. And, there are the interim architectures which describe the changes to the architecture that will occur as a result of migrating from the current architecture to the target architecture.

- *Assess the Feasibility of Architectural Direction with the Marketplace:*
  Given the time constraints and the scope of the evaluation activities for a Comprehensive Technical Architecture to support reengineering, the architecture teams will have to select the best product set without the luxury of a long evaluation process. Therefore, another means of validating the selection must be used. This method is the market validation of architectural direction. It includes finding sites that use the planned architectural compo-

nents, qualifying the sites against certain criteria, such as time in production, size of implementation, etc., and determining, through surveys, the pros and cons of the proposed architectural direction.

- *Review Development Philosophy, Approach, and Methodology:* Before tool choices can be made an overall philosophy of the types of development must be created. This philosophy will lead to an approach and methodology for development that further limits tool choices. This limitation is necessary to put some borders around the tool arena quickly. Without these limitations the array of tool possibilities would be vast, and reviewing them would be extremely time-consuming. By limiting the choices here the architecture teams can concentrate on those tools that best fit the candidate development environment.

- *Identify and Recommend Alternate Development Approaches:* Upon review of the applications development approach and methodologies, the team may discover that these approaches are inconsistent with the applications development capabilities demanded by the business partners or the Technology Infrastructure or Applications Architectures that will be part of the target architecture. If this occurs, the team must assess, as part of the Process Architecture definition, the techniques and methodology used to develop new applications systems.

- *Identify Functions (Application Services, Utilities, Common Objects, etc.) to be included:* For the architectures to deliver on the promise of decreasing applications development time and improving maintainability, they must define a framework for reusability. Within this framework are application processes that are common and used by multiple applications systems such as utility functions and common application development objects. Part of the architecture project is to identify these, prioritize them, and include them in the workplan for implementation of the architectures.

- *Resolve Issues and Technical Differences:* In any effort of this nature there will be widely disparate views on many of the issues being considered. The architecture being defined is new and often enters some new areas of discussion, not considered previously. A process needs to be defined that can help resolve these potential conflicts.

  Certainly, the position of Chief Architect would be one focal point for issue resolution. This team member must make sure the architecture being defined meets the needs of the enterprise in its current state and is capable of expanding to meet the needs of the end state. As a result, this team member must have broad knowledge and experience, and the respect of both the business process owners and the rest of the MIS organization. This responsibility should not be given to the most senior technician in MIS unless they have demonstrated the necessary business acumen. In many cases, no suitable candidate can be found in MIS and this role is assigned to an external resource such as a consultant.

Issues within the architecture teams themselves will usually be resolved by discussion and consensus building. These issues will often center on philosophical subjects but can also focus on technical criteria as well. Issues between the architecture teams and other organizations within the enterprise present a more difficult resolution path. These issues are often political and usually based on personal experiences of those involved and protection of past decisions. The Chief Architect becomes an important player in the resolution of these issues because they usually are not simple *black* and *white* decisions.

In any case, a certain set of issues may remain unresolved at the end of the architecture definition process. This does not make the architecture any less usable but only indicates that additional definition and study may be required before the architecture is complete. These issues can be either major or minor. Major issues will most often require a high-level management review and approval before work can continue. Minor issues can usually be solved by a joint meeting among the disagreeing parties. In some cases, management involvement may be necessary to make certain that this process is completed promptly.

Communicate the Architecture

Once the architecture is defined and documented, it is necessary to communicate it to the right audience. Since this Comprehensive Technical Architecture will be new to many it will be necessary to present it at several levels. Summaries will be needed for management and business partners, detailed presentations and training sessions will be needed for those who will be using technology to solve business problems. With the proper presentation and management commitment, a consensus can be forged and the new architecture can be used.

- *Identify Audiences:*
There will be several audiences who may receive information about the architecture. Presentations need to be tailored to each audi-

ence to communicate those elements that are most important to them. Management and business partners need to understand:

- What a Comprehensive Technical Architecture is
- Who uses the architecture
- What it means to them
- What are its strengths
- What are its limitations

Those involved with implementation of technology need to understand:

- What a Comprehensive Technical Architecture is
- How it is used
- What are its strengths and weaknesses
- How will it be changed and maintained
- How the components fit together

- *Develop Presentation Materials:*
  The Comprehensive Technical Architecture can best be communicated through a combination of informal and formal presentations. Examples should be used where possible to communicate how things will work. Presentation materials can include:

  - Presentation Slides and Scripts
  - Video tape
  - PC demos
  - Handouts
  - Guidebooks

- *Schedule and Present:*
  These presentations need to be scheduled during the final stages of architectural definition. It is important to present the architecture soon after it is complete. An ongoing schedule of presentations will be necessary to make sure that everyone has had an opportunity to learn about and understand the new architecture.

- *Capture Issues and Questions:*
  During these presentations many questions will be raised concerning choices made and philosophies adopted. It is important that those presenting be fully schooled in the issues surrounding the architecture and be able to answer most of the likely questions. Issues will be raised, as well. These must be captured for later review and response.

- *Follow-up on Issues and Questions:*
  During each session those in attendance must be made to feel that

they are a part of the architecture process. Questions and issues should be welcomed, and participants must be promised a response to all open issues and questions raised.
All open issues should be addressed in a timely and straightforward manner. These issues and questions should be communicated to all who participated in the architecture presentation.

Plan Implementation

- *Prioritize:*
  Because the Comprehensive Technical Architecture is defined based on the requirements of the business, the initial implementation sequence of the architecture components will be dictated by the business value expected from each component. After the initial implementation sequence is developed, technical dependencies are applied to the sequence to develop the ideal implementation sequence. It is from the ideal implementation sequence that the detail workplans are developed.

- *I/T Sanity Check:*
  The I/T Sanity Check confirms the I/T requirements and implications of redesigned business processes and identifies and schedules the interdependencies between the reengineering effort and its I/T components. There are primarily two aspects that are evaluated:

  Technology availability —Assuming the desired capability is within the realm of feasibility, this is usually not a problem. Problems arise only if the technology is completely inconsistent with the current technology architecture and there is no way to integrate the new with the old, or MIS was reticent to change direction to support the business.

  MIS capacity —Assuming a compelling business case exists, MIS must be prepared to support the desired technology changes, applications development, pilot, and rollout in the timeframe required by the business cases. For many MIS organizations, this will be a defining moment when they realize they cannot support their business partners adequately. At this point the reengineering executive sponsor and the Chief Information Officer must make a decision about who will provide the I/T components to the reengineering project and if it is the MIS organization, how they will do it.

- *Develop Workplans:*
  Detailed workplans will be developed to accomplish the ideal

implementation sequence for the architectural components. These workplans will be developed using a project management tool to ensure they can be tracked and reported against. The workplans will include the activities and tasks to achieve the desired result and the work effort and skills required to carry out the work. It has been our experience that there will be so much implementation work to be done that management must reevaluate the implementation sequence and reschedule some of the work effort to develop a final workplan that fits both available time and budget.

- *Develop Staffing Plan for Implementation:*
  When the final workplan is complete, resources will be identified and scheduled against work activities. This will result in a staffing plan for the implementation period. It will also identify any staffing or skills shortfalls and the impact of them.

- *Develop Staff Reskilling Plan:*
  Two reskilling plans that will be required. One will address any shortfalls in the resources and skills required to implement the architecture components and the other will prepare the reengineering lab staff to develop applications that will exist in the new architecture using the new Process Architecture techniques and the new Applications Development Environment tools.

Maintain the Comprehensive Technical Architecture

Many technical architectures have been developed over time just to sit on shelves. For an architecture to be useful it must be current; therefore, a process must be instituted to maintain the architecture over time. This is accomplished through review and update sessions periodically (usually annually) and when business imperatives dictate the need. At both of these junctures, the entire Comprehensive Technical Architecture should be reviewed considering the current short- and medium-term business and MIS plans. Also, a market assessment should be conducted to "reality check" the architectural directions. Additionally, when business imperatives dictate a significant change in the enterprise's directions that will lead to new development activities, the specific tools for applications development should be reviewed to determine their continued appropriateness.

Tactical Activities Supporting Reengineering Labs

Along with development of the Comprehensive Technical Architecture, there are activities that must be completed to support the reengineering labs. Since this work load is likely to be overwhelming, they are prioritized according to the phases of the reengineering lab they support. Also, because they span all architectures in the Comprehensive Technical Architecture, they are organized by architecture.

In some reengineering projects, these are referred to as I/T Critical Programs because they are necessary for the reengineering activity to be successful. In many cases, these are long lead time items, such as infrastructure replacement, or MIS staff reskilling or retooling. The need for these critical programs typically results from the MIS organization's not being able to invest in the right technical infrastructure or skill improvements to make MIS ready for reengineering. This is the most obvious result of reduced MIS budgets, out-of-control maintenance loads, and in a few cases, lack of foresight.

Process Architecture

- *Assess and Orient MIS Staff:*

  This gets immediately to the core of MIS' participation in the reengineering effort and understanding their ability to accomplish the stretch goals that reengineering requires. This is also the critical point for many in MIS who cannot or will not make the change. Gartner Group, a firm specializing in information technology industry analysis, states, in their September 1992 Strategies for Building Client/Server & Other Next Generation Applications, that only "five percent of the average IS staff [can] master the intricacies of client/server today (0.8 probability); this will increase to 15 percent by 1997 (0.7 probability)." While Gartner says no more than 15 percent of MIS staff will be able to make the change, our experience suggests that 20 percent to 25 percent will be superstars and only 20 percent to 25 percent cannot or will not survive.

  The orientation presents the need for the reengineering project indicating what pain the enterprise is facing and why such radical change is necessary. This will be translated into implications and pain the MIS organization will face, and ultimately into implications and pain for individuals in MIS. This personalization of the message is critical to get the support for the program that is necessary for its success. This is the most brutal part of the entire process, but doing it and doing it honestly is also the most necessary.

  The assessment will cover several areas including willingness to change, technical skills, experience with new systems creation and rollout, closeness to business partners, etc.

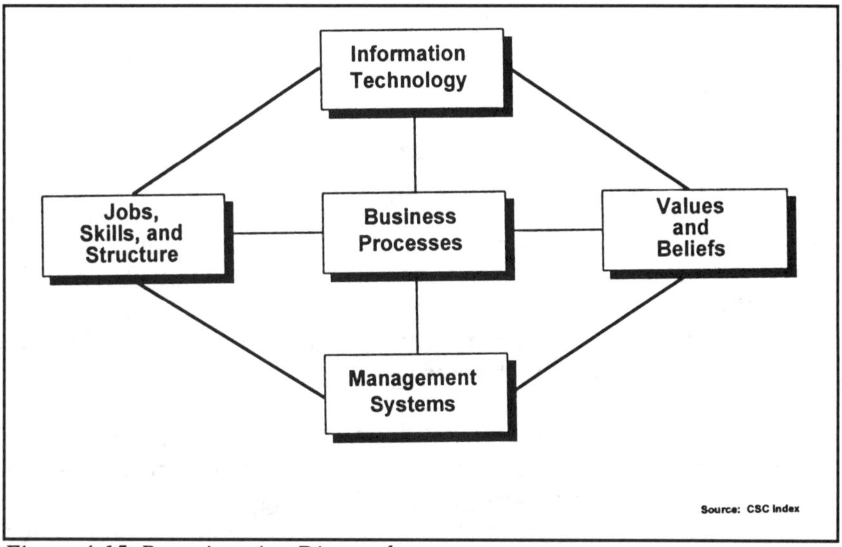

Figure 4-15 Reengineering Diamond

- *Assess MIS Procedures*
  Reengineering involves building holistic solutions that include information technology, jobs, skills, and structures, management systems, and values and beliefs in equilibrium with each other and with the underlying business process as depicted in Figure 4-15. This is a very different model from the traditional myopic view presented in "waterfall" methodologies which only address the I/T point of the diamond and which assume completed user requirements that will not change during the two years required to develop the system. Many MIS organizations are already starting to move to new processes and this assessment will indicate where on the spectrum the organization is.

- *Develop Reengineering Lab Process Training Material:*
  Both MIS participants in the reengineering labs and MIS support staff need a detailed understanding of the reengineering process. This training is developed to include an initial summary of the process and just-in-time (JIT) training on the specifics and details of the process. JIT training has proven to be the most effective for reengineering labs because it ensures currency and consistency of procedures and it enables introduction of "best practices" into the process as they are discovered.

- *Develop Methodology for Accelerated Training Development:*
  As part of the holistic approach to solution development, training for the business partners who will ultimately use the new business process must be developed during the reengineering lab. Since the

lab timeframe is so short, traditional training methodologies cannot be used successfully and a methodology that enables creation of materials fast is necessary.

- *Conduct Initial Release Planning and Roadmap Development:* One of the biggest mistakes reengineering efforts make is emphasizing the notion of empowered teams designing and implementing new business processes and producing deliverables as a series of small successes without emphasizing the very real need to coordinate the various work streams by providing precise scope statements and the context into which the deliverables will work. This is discussed further in Chapter 5 — Reengineering Integration.

- *Identify and Train Coaches and Start Coaching Process:* The centerpiece of successful reengineering integration is the process of interventions in the reengineering labs by coaches and Subject Matter Experts (SMEs). The earlier the coaches and SMEs can be identified and acclimated to their roles in reengineering support, the faster they will be able to carry out their responsibilities and the less likely that a reengineering effort will go astray.

Information Architecture

- *Define or Review Enterprise Data Model:* As with all architectures, a description of the existing baseline must be developed (if it does not already exist) and must be reviewed when planning the vision of the Information Architecture.

- *Define or Review Business Process and Lab Data Models:* To ensure integration of data definitions across reengineering labs, each lab starts with a set of data definitions or slice of the Entity Relationship Model (ERM) that relates to the scope of their lab. This is strictly a starting position, much like the existing baseline architectures. It is the point of departure for the business process owner to define the information requirements for the business process. It can also be used by the lab team and legacy system SMEs to determine where information may be pulled from.

- *Associate Data-Related Business Rules to Data Models* : Since the center of the reengineering diamond is the business process, the information requirements and resulting data models are based on rules of the business process.

- *Design Database and Data Distribution Strategies:* One of the typical technological improvements that result from reengineering is the ability for more business partners to get access to more of the information they need to execute the new business processes. This means the information needs of the redesigned business processes must be restated as requirements for access to information and placement of information. This will result in logical designs and first-cut physical designs for databases. Furthermore, if information will be distributed, the mechanisms for ensuring data integrity and currency must be defined early in the process so any custom mechanisms can be built and implemented.

Applications Architecture

- *Review Legacy Applications Architecture:*
  Unless one knows where one is, one cannot use a map to get to some place else. The same is true for an MIS organization undertaking significant change. Without a baseline of the applications architecture, MIS cannot plan how applications integration will be accomplished over time. This activity, then, is the review, or creation and review, of the Applications Architecture of the legacy environment.

Applications Development Environment Architecture

The applications development environment is a technology that is essential for building systems that can be integrated. Since one of the promises of new age development is the ability to build systems faster and less expensively, developers must be ready to respond to business partners when business imperatives dictate. Developers cannot go through an architecture, technology, or product evaluation process every time they build a new system. Likewise, neither developers nor business partners can afford to go through a reskilling effort for a new architecture with every new system.

- *Define Common Look and Feel for Custom-Developed Applications, Packages, and Help Facilities:*
  An objective of next generation systems is consistency across applications for both custom-developed and package solutions. Part of this consistency is providing consistent help across all applications. Setting or validating the standards and guidelines for common look and feel is instrumental to this.

- *Review Current Application Development Environment:*
  As with all the architectures, before determining the future course, the architecture teams must evaluate the existing baseline. In this case, that includes all applications building tools (GUI developers, compilers, debuggers, object libraries, etc.) and applications man-

agement tools (version control tools, distribution mechanisms, etc.). The existing baseline must be documented and reviewed for consistency with the future Applications Development Environment Architecture.

Due to the aggressive timeframe for reengineering and reengineering the MIS organization, an unconventional technique for tools selection is required. The accelerated approach to evaluating and selecting I/T tools, including Applications Development Environment, is to identify the top two or three contenders in any given category (by researching Datapro, Auerbach, *et al.*) that fit in the overall technical architecture, then just pick one that seems to be superior to its peers (based on company reputation, support capability, or some other business measure, not on a matrix of functions and features.) Then, use the time that would have otherwise been absorbed by "analysis paralysis" to try to disprove the selection. In any event, the total time spent on tool selection should be one-to-two weeks, maximum.

- *Design Reengineering Lab Environment and Build Reengineering Labs:*
  Before a reengineering lab can convene, the physical space in which the business processes will be redesigned and solutions built must be designed and constructed. For a more detailed description of the physical space, see Chapter 6—Retooling.

- *Identify, Design, and Start Building Common Objects and Middleware:*
  There is no silver bullet for developing applications in the reengineering environment. Tools are not seamless and access to databases and legacy systems will be different in each legacy environment and in each MIS organization. As a result, there will be a significant investment in so-called middleware, the software that provides a sense of seamlessness for the developers in the reengineering labs. Some middleware may be commercially available, but even with commercially available software, significant work will be done in customization. If no suitable middleware suite can be found, it will all need to be custom-built.

- *Develop Tool Training Material:*
  Once the Applications Development Environment is determined, the reengineering labs are designed, and the middleware is developed, training materials for the technical coaches, SMEs, and lab technologists must be developed. Since it is not likely that all these components will be set in concrete before the beginning of the reengineering labs, this training development will be an on-going process.

Technology Infrastructure Architecture

- *Review Technology Requirements of the Redesigns:*
The initial business process redesigns should include Business Systems Implications (BSI) templates for all points of the business process reengineering diamond. The BSI - I/T templates and their use is discussed in detail in Chapter 5 — Reengineering Integration. Review the completed BSI - I/T templates to determine the types of information technology changes that may be required. Also, if the I/T Sanity Check has been completed, even more information will be available for this review.

- *Review Hardware Platforms and Operating Systems:*
As with the applications architecture above, a technology infrastructure architecture that represents the current legacy environment must be reviewed, or created and reviewed, to serve as a baseline for future architectural planning.

- *Determine Migration Impact:*
If a significant change in hardware platform, operating system, Database Management System (DBMS), or network infrastructure is required to support business process reengineering, then additional impact analysis must be done to prepare for the implementation of new technologies.

All Architectures

- Define Enterprise Technology Infrastructure Architecture Roadmap.
- Develop New Architecture Implementation Planning.
- Execute New Architecture Implementation Plan.
- Develop New Architecture Rollout Procedures.

Just as the reengineering effort has a roadmap that describes what will be developed and when, the Comprehensive Technical Architecture will require a plan for implementing the new architectural components.

Prior to Working Prototype

Process Architecture

- *Indoctrinate MIS Staff:*
All MIS staff involved in the reengineering effort (both in the reengineering labs and supporting the reengineering labs from

MIS) will require indoctrination and training on the reengineering process (business process redesign, reengineering lab, lab support functions, quality assurance process, etc.)

- *Conduct Detail Training:*
  For each reengineering role, provide detail training for MIS staff responsible for carrying out those roles. This includes lab participants, coaches, SMEs, and other MIS support staff, e.g., reengineering help desk, etc.

- *Develop Pilot Planning Procedures*

- *Develop Rollout Planning Process:*
  Planning for the pilot test and rollout is customized to the release plans developed for the reengineering project. The activities occurring in pilot and rollout are designed during the reengineering lab and the process and methodology for creating these are developed based on the release plans.

Information Architecture

- *Define Application Development Rules for Information Access*

- *Define Data Conversion Strategy and Application Development Rules for Construction and Usage*

- *Develop Information Access Standards*

- *Develop Backup Strategy and Rules:*
  Just as Applications Development Environment usage rules and guidance are defined and used by the reengineering lab teams for creating applications, rules and guidance for information access are necessary.

- *Develop DBMS Benchmark Tests and Stress Test DBMSs:*
  Since the new model for accelerated tools selection is to pick one then try to disprove the selection, benchmarks must be created to ensure the selected product will be successful when used and rolled out.

- *Develop Information Policies*

- *Implement Information Ownership Policies:*
  Reengineering provides MIS with an opportunity to reassign information ownership to its rightful owner, the business process owner. MIS can move back into its role of information steward,

providing safekeeping for the corporate asset, information.

This is a radical change of responsibilities for the business process owner, but it is one that must occur. One way to achieve this is to remind the business process owner that before information was automated and put into computer files and databases - when it was still kept on paper and in his staff's heads, it was the business process owner, not MIS who owned the responsibility for defining and maintaining the information. Information integration is too important and too political an issue to continue to be left to the MIS organization. It must be addressed by the owners of the business processes involved in defining and using the information.

- *Develop Data Distribution Strategy*

- *Develop Data Distribution Tools*

- *Implement Data Distribution Strategy*
- *Develop Platform-to-Platform Data Transfer Process and Tools*
One of the promises of next generation applications like those that will result from the reengineering labs is better, faster access to more, better information. If the redesigns require this, data distribution must be incorporated in the set of common capabilities provided by infrastructure to the reengineering labs.

- *Develop Database Operations Tools and Procedures*
There are operational aspects of database management that are often overlooked in a network computing implementation. Because the new database may not be on a traditional mainframe computer, new procedures for managing the information resource must be developed and incorporated in with other MIS operations procedures.

Applications Architecture

- *Develop Legacy-to-New Architecture Interconnect:*
Legacy systems are a fact of life in almost all reengineering projects. New applications will have to get information from them or pass requests to them. In any event a standard way of connecting to legacy systems must be designed before the first reengineering lab needs to access a legacy system. This is another task that should probably be supported primarily by MIS staff who are SMEs to the reengineering lab and who act as subcontractors to the lab for construction of these bridges.

- *Develop a Plan For Retiring Legacy Applications:*
  While legacy systems are a fact of life in almost all reengineering projects, every effort should be made to remove them from the production environment as quickly as possible. This will create a production environment that is easier to maintain and will speed the migration of the MIS staff from legacy-focused to reengineering-focused.

Applications Development Environment Architecture

- *Develop Software Distribution Strategy and Tools:*
  Whether data distribution is included in the architecture or not, systems and applications software will have to be distributed. This will be true even if all workstations and servers are located in the same building, but what is more likely will be the need to distribute software to computing platforms remote from any central site.

- *Identify Common Objects Development Approach and Inventory Mechanism:*
  Prepare to support the reengineering labs by forming a team of developers to define, design, build, and manage any modules or elements that will be shared among multiple reengineering labs.

- *Develop API Standards and Application Development Rules for API Usage*

- *Define Application Development Rules for Network API Usage*

- *Define Application Development Rules for Program Modularity*

- *Define Application Bridge Strategy and Application Development Rules for Bridge Construction and Usage*

- *Define Application Development Rules for Security*

- *Define Application Development Rules for Error Processing*

- *Implement and Integrate Applications Development Environment Architecture*

- *Develop Network API and Application Messaging Strategy and Standards*

  Prepare to give the reengineering labs some context within which to conduct their applications design and development by providing guidelines and rules for usage of the Applications Development Environment infrastructure. One result of the iterative nature of reengineering lab application development is creation of systems holistically, from concept design to functionality. This results in systems that are superior, from the business partner's perspective, to traditionally developed systems, but systems that are not complete from a traditional systems perspective. These rules describe how the reengineering lab-developed systems will be supplemented (and by whom) to incorporate these necessary functions.

A hint: There is a very delicate balance between the speed and creativity of the reengineering lab process and the rigor required for production-ready applications systems. The most successful model has this armor plating performed by SMEs as part of the reengineering lab activity.

- *Build Common Look and Feel Components*

- *Build Common Help Facility Components*

  Just like all other common objects, the Applications Development Environment team must construct the common look and feel components that the reengineering labs will use for their applications systems.

Technology Infrastructure Architecture

- *Define Restart and Recovery Strategy and Rules*

- *Develop Security Strategy:*
  Just as Applications Development Environment and database usage rules and guidance are defined and used by the reengineering lab teams for creating applications, rules and guidance for utility functions are necessary.

- *Develop Distributed Computing Strategy*

- *Develop Systems Management Strategy*

- *Develop New Architecture Administration Strategy and Tools*

- *Develop Network Management Strategy*

- *Develop Network Addressing Scheme*

- *Develop or Acquire Security Server*

- *Develop Implementation Plan for Systems Management*

  To manage a network of distributed clients and servers in the infancy of network computing, MIS must design and implement appropriate controls to ensure the reliability of the entire technology infrastructure. This is an often overlooked infrastructure area because of several common misconceptions: network computing and client/server systems include mainframe-style utilities and controls, or "it's just a network of PCs, it does not really need management controls," or "that's all the user's responsibility." This is a real problem in most next generation implementations because it is not addressed early enough to be effective in the reengineering pilot and rollout timeframes.

- *Design/Build Field Simulation and Testing Lab:*
  Even though reengineering labs produce business solutions, this is still an applications development project. As such, the I/T point of the diamond still must be integrated with legacy and other new systems and the programs must be tested. This points to the need for a systems test function to ensure this functional correctness and integration.

  Additionally, since this is a holistic view of business process change, the other points of the diamond must be tested before pilot test and rollout, too. This points to the need for a testing facility that is more than just traditional systems test. The Field Simulation Lab (FSL) is a facility that reengineering lab teams come to with their redesigned business processes, completed I/T systems, completed change management programs and training materials, redesigned organization structures and management systems. In the FSL, reengineering lab teams are able to test their work before going to pilot test with real business partners. They are also able to test the integration of their work with that of other reengineering labs and the legacy environment.

- *Develop Operations Tools and Procedures:*
  There are operational aspects of non-mainframe implementations that must be custom-built, or at the very least custom-integrated by MIS. These must be developed and incorporated in with other MIS operations procedures.

On-Going Activities

Process Architecture

- *Continually Refine the Reengineering Lab Process*
  The reengineering process, just like any other business process, is subject to continuous improvement through lessons learned, best practices, and infusions of new techniques and technologies. A key role of the Process Architect is the continued evolution of the reengineering process.

- *Lab Support - Process and Methodology Coaching*

- *Deliver Reengineering Lab Process Training*
  Process Coaches are the primary links between the staff in the reengineering labs and the outside world of the rest of the reengineering project and support organizations. They provide almost constant just-in-time training on the process and improvements to the process. In addition, they provide more formal training to the labs and to those outside the lab in the process.

- *Coordinate On-going MIS Training:*
  As part of the role as trainer in the processes used by the reengineering labs, and keeper of the reengineering lab process itself, the Process Architect must ensure any other training activities in the MIS organization are consistent with the reengineering lab process and its associated training.

Information Architecture

- *Prepare and Maintain Enterprise Entity Relationship Model (ERM)*

- *Maintain Information Catalog*

- *On-Going Information Management, Data and Database Strategy:*
  In addition to the physical data stores, the Information Architect maintains the definitions of information and means for accessing information. Part of this responsibility is to ensure the Information Architecture continues to evolve to support the business partners through the use of technological innovations in the management of information.

- *Build Database Environment:*
  The principle responsibility of the Information Architect is to ensure that the physical representation of the enterprise's informa-

tion is maintained in a safe, reliable information store.

- *Conduct Information Access, Information Management, and Database Training*

- *Lab Support - Data Analysis/Database Design*

- *Lab Support - Enterprise Data Model*

- *Lab Support - Data Conversions:*
  The reengineering labs must rely on the Information Architect to provide the necessary information to support the new business processes. In addition to providing the information and access to it, the Information Architect must work closely with the reengineering labs to understand their information requirements, and how those requirements affect other reengineering labs.

Applications Architecture

- *Maintain the "picture book" of Architectural Diagrams:*

  Maintaining the architectural diagrams will be a daunting task, especially if the reengineering project will require numerous waves of change. For every architecture and for the integrated picture including all architectures and all legacy environments, the diagrams that describe the then-current state for any given moment in the project must be maintained.

Applications Development Environment Architecture

- *Develop Common Objects:*
  Throughout the reengineering project reengineering labs and technical coaches will identify new common objects that must be developed, tested, and integrated with the existing set of common objects and middleware.

- *Refine Application Development Environment*

- *Refine Application Development Rules*

- *Lab Support - Application Development Tools*

- *Conduct Tool Training:*
  Throughout the reengineering project as teams develop best prac-

tices and as technology enhancements are introduced into the reengineering environment, the rules developers use will change to reflect the new reality. These changes must continue to be documented and training, probably just-in-time, will need to be developed and provided to reengineering labs.

- *Lab Support - Armor Plating:*
  Enhancing the products developed by reengineering labs and making them production ready will be an on-going task. Each new application must adhere to the architectural rules and be a well-behaved citizen in the environment. Making these necessary changes will probably not be done in the reengineering labs due to time constraints, but these changes must be made prior to pilot and rollout.
- *Develop Strategy for Application Integration*

- *Customize Application Integration Tools:*
  Applications integration, both among new applications and between new and legacy applications, will be critical to the success of the new applications. A strategy for ensuring applications integration and any tools or middleware components necessary for applications integration must be designed, developed, tested, and made available to the reengineering labs and the armor plating teams.

Technology Infrastructure Architecture

- *Design, Acquire, and Install Technology Infrastructure Components*

- *Architecture Integration*
  There are numerous components that comprise the Technology Infrastructure. It falls to the Technology Infrastructure Architect to ensure the integration of these various elements.

- *On-Going Technology Infrastructure Architecture Strategy*

- *Review Technology Infrastructure Capacity for New Business Processes*

- *Continued Evaluation of Emerging Technologies:*
  In addition to ensuring the integration of the existing technology infrastructure, the Technology Infrastructure Architect must ensure the technology infrastructure will support the requirements of the enterprise in the future. Likewise, as new technologies enter the market that may make further redesigns of business processes possible, the Technology Infrastructure Architect must investigate and be prepared to counsel business process owners on their

applicability.

- *Conduct Architecture and Technology Training*

- *Lab Support - New Architecture for New Business Processes*

- *Lab Support - Unique Technologies*

- *Lab Support - Package Evaluations*

- *Lab Support - Enterprise Technology Infrastructure Architecture*

- *Lab Support - Application Bridges:*
  As with other architects, the Technology Infrastructure Architect is responsible to the reengineering labs to provide whatever information is required to make them successful using the technology infrastructure to develop and roll out their new redesigned business process.

Comprehensive Technical Architecture Summary

So, to summarize:

- In most cases, the technology infrastructure must change to support the redesigned business processes.
- MIS productivity must improve to keep pace with the timeframes required for reengineering.
- MIS' focus must shift to be more supportive of and collaborative with the business.
- Information integration must improve to give business process owners the amount, type, currency, and granularity of information they need when, where, and how they need it — this requires the owner of the business process to become the information owner for that process.

The best way to accomplish these is by developing a Comprehensive Technical Architecture that includes MIS Processes, Information, Applications, Applications Development Environment, and Technology Infrastructure. This will require either significant reskilling of the existing MIS staff or retooling MIS by supplementing or replacing it with staff already knowledgeable in the technologies, tools, and techniques required to support reengineering.

This will also require funding; and it will not be cheap. It probably will not be funded by stopping other MIS activities, such as maintenance on systems that will be replaced, investments in technologies not destined for the future environment, etc. Granted, over time, some additional MIS funding will be available from these sources, but it will not be enough and it will not be immediate enough. So, MIS will require significant investment and the investment in MIS to support reengineering will be greater if these types of investments have not been made continuously over time.

Bibliography

Gartner Group, Inc., "Applications Development & Management Strategies," SPA-480-815, Stamford, Connecticut, 1993.

Gartner Group, Inc., "Industry Service," K-955-950, Stamford, Connecticut, 1993.

Gartner Group, Inc., Strategies for Building Client/Server & Other Next Generation Applications, Stamford, Connecticut, September, 1992.

INTEGRATION

Reengineering Management Information Systems

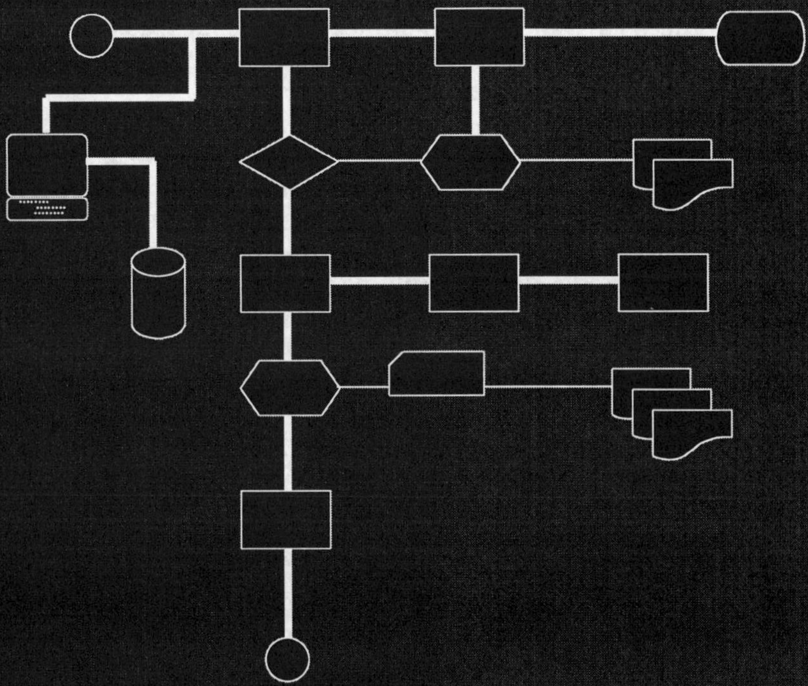

Chapter 5

Reengineering Integration

Integration, or rather the lack of integration, is the bane of reengineering efforts. Integration is an activity that must begin when the reengineering management team begins the effort and it must be a focus of a senior leader of the reengineering project. There must be an anticipation of the types of integration needs that the team will encounter for all points of the reengineering diamond and among all the participants in the reengineering effort, process families, labs, and support organizations. Also, integration management must be a formal process that includes identification of issues, assumptions, integration points, and risks, assessment, assignment, resolution, communication, and adherence.

Historically, applications development coordination has resulted from using "waterfall" development methodologies that enforce functional silos, longer development times, throwing deliverables "over the wall," and sign-offs. These characteristics have ensured a certain degree of coordination among the business partners requesting a system, the developers building it, and any other MIS staff supporting it. On the other hand, these development life cycles have also ensured finger-pointing, long systems development timeframes, and delays between design and delivery resulting in systems not satisfying business requirements.

Reengineering requires an holistic perspective using techniques and technologies that allow teams to build systems faster that are closer to the real needs of the business partners requesting them. This holistic approach is exponentially more complex from both technical and coordination perspectives. We call the coordination process required to manage this more complex approach reengineering integration. As an indication of the relative importance of reengineering integration supporting this holistic approach, Figure 5-1 which summarizes a survey of the extended management team of one recent reengineering project indicates integration among processes and among reengineering labs as the most critical "reengineering hot spot".

The key idea in reengineering integration is in the term "holistic." According to Dirk Gently, the private detective and philosopher created by Douglas Adams, "the term 'holistic' refers to my conviction that what we are concerned with here is the fundamental interconnectedness of all things... The connections between causes and effects are often much more subtle and complex than we, with

A survey of the extended management team of one large reengineering effort identified these Reengineering Hot Spots:

1.	Integration among processes and among labs	12
2.	Scope creep	11
3.	Change Management in pilot areas	9
4.	Changes in schedules and deliverables	8
5.	Inadequacy of decision-making (not made or made in a vacuum)	6
6.	Danger of working in Lab "silos"	6
7.	Timing and Responsibility of Bridges and Conversions	6
8.	Acceptance of new processes in field	6
9.	Data Integration and Integrity Issues	5
10.	I/T Architecture - By Wave	5
11.	Systems Test Entry Criteria	4
12.	Inability for MIS to keep up with the pace	4
13.	No time for pilot and rollout planning	3
14.	Unclear responsibility for I/T deliverables	2
15.	H/R understaffed	2
16.	Quality of project management above process families	2
17.	Right SME in Lab at the right time	1
18.	Understanding technical architecture by Lab	1
19.	Personal sacrifice and imbalance	1
20.	Business risk in pilot areas	1

Source: CSC Consulting

Figure 5-1 Reengineering Hot Spots.

our rough and ready understanding of the physical world, might naturally suppose..."

Dirk's definition is probably more inter-galactic than a reengineering team will encounter, but it is essentially correct. Reengineering integration is the fundamental interconnectedness of all things and it is critical to successful reengineering efforts. The activities that make up reengineering integration include:

- Coordination among points of the reengineering diamond as depicted in Figure 5-2.
- Coordination among all reengineering labs and among all business process families.
- Coordination between reengineering labs and all critical and supporting programs.
- Coordination between new I/T and legacy I/T components.
- Coordination of all of these aspects over time.

Reengineering integration incorporates a number of new ideas to the program management activity. While these ideas are just common sense, they are themselves integrated and institutionalized here, as part of reengineering integration as depicted in Figure 5-3. These "new" ideas also include several new ways of looking at systems development more holistically. Reengineering Integration is based on using:

- *Release Planning:*

  Release Planning provides a framework and project management

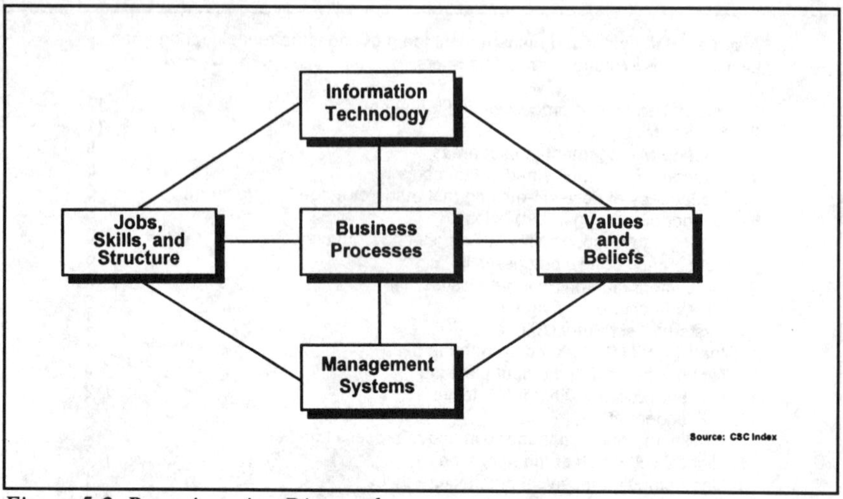

Figure 5-2 Reengineering Diamond.

context for the entire reengineering effort. It is an iterative planning process that begins with prioritizing the reengineering initiatives based on an assessment of business value for all the reengineering initiatives. After prioritizing to create the most value in the shortest timeframe, the plan is compared to the constraints of the organization's ability to rollout the necessary changes in the desired timeframe. This cycle continues until the organization determines the optimum balance of value, timeframe, and cost.

- *Business Systems Implications (BSI):*
  Business systems implications describe the impact of the redesigned business process on each point of the diamond: jobs, skills, and structures, management systems, information technology, and values and beliefs. They are created by the reengineering teams with the participation of the constituencies that will be affected by the new business processes.

- *Sanity Checks:*
  One of the first modifications to the release plan comes from a series of sanity checks. Sanity checks for information technology (I/T) and human resources (H/R) apply constraints against the initial, business value-based release plan to derive a realistic, implementable release plan.

- *Critical Programs:*
  Less than half the work in a reengineering project is done in the reengineering labs. The rest, the critical programs, represents work necessary to provide the foundation for successful reengineering. This work is usually concentrated on human relations, change management, and information technology. The

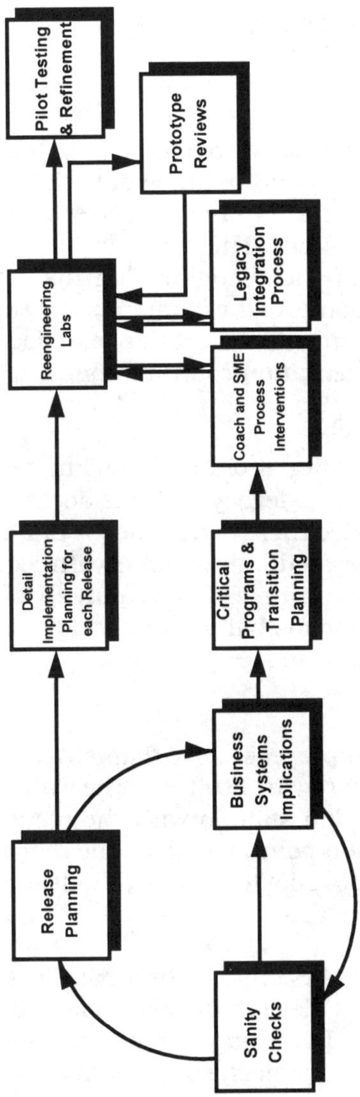

Source: Clelland Johnson

Figure 5-3 Reengineering Integration Process

breadth of the critical programs becomes evident during the Sanity Checks.

- *Coaches, Subject Matter Experts (SMEs), and Interventions:* Once the release plan is completed and the reengineering labs begin, several organizational and operational constructs are used to ensure consistency, quality, and integration among all reengineering labs and between reengineering labs and the rest of the organization. These are implemented through a series of interventions by process coaches, technical coaches, and various subject matter experts (SMEs).

- *Integration Processes:* Because of the speed of activity in reengineering labs and in the supporting critical programs and because of the short timeframe for pilot testing and rollout, a more creative and even more rigorous integration process is required. These Integration Processes are focused on each point of the reengineering diamond and the interconnections among points of the diamond. They are organized to include issues management, integration management, scope coordination, and implementation coordination.

- *Legacy Integration Process:* Since reengineering is looking at old problems in new ways, and since MIS' typical approach to legacy systems access is to replace the legacy system, and since there is no time for unnecessary MIS activity (nor will it be tolerated), integration with legacy systems and legacy data is even more critical. This requires a formal process and defined roles and responsibilities to provide the necessary information in a timely fashion.

- *Flow-Through Staffing:* Reengineering integration processes are diametrically opposed to traditional MIS habit of "throwing stuff over the wall." As a result, part of the reengineering lab staff go with the reengineering lab products at every transition point, i.e., from the reengineering lab to the field simulation lab, to pilot testing, to rollout support, to help desk, and to maintenance labs.

A reengineering-ready MIS organization can be successful in reengineering integration by "delegating out" some ordinarily internal management processes. For example, reengineering integration implies this is a reengineering project, so the ultimate responsibility for delivery of the business case lies with the project sponsor. Reengineering integration, therefore, assumes:

- Active involvement of the executive sponsor of the reengineering effort. In fact, ensuring the sponsor takes responsibility to make the decisions and break the ties that will occur between teams.
- An established overall reengineering project management resource with tools for project tracking, budget management, issue identification, and staff planning.
- Formal coordination points at many levels within the reengineering effort, e.g., among business process family leaders, among I/T Integration Managers, among H/R Integration Managers, among lab leaders, among Lab I/T Leaders, among H/R SMEs, among all I/T SMEs, among architectures, etc. These will probably take the form of Integration Days.
- Informal communications and coordination at all these levels, too.
- Existence of baselines and preparation of an end-state and interim-state architectures for process, information, applications, applications development environment, and technology infrastructure. It should be obvious, but an integrator must know what exists before integrating anything else with it.

Release Planning

A release consists of a coordinated set of redesigned business processes and their associated jobs, skills, and structures, management systems, values and beliefs, and information technology. While they may be coordinated by business process, function, employee population, information technology, etc., what makes them a release is more a matter of timeframe than anything else. Ideally, they are also coordinated from a business value point of view, but because the planning effort must occur prior to starting reengineering labs in order to master the timeframe, resource, and long lead time items necessary for pilot test and rollout, management may decide to implement some changes to receive their benefit before implementing the optimal package of changes. As a result, the components that make up a release may or may not affect the same areas of the business, the same employee populations, the same customers, or the same physical locations.

The objective of release planning is to develop a realistic plan that will enable the reengineering project to deliver the greatest amount of value to the enterprise the fastest. The release plan will initially be a high-level, but ultimately, a detailed plan for the entire reengineering activity. It will include all the business processes to be redesigned, when, at what cost, and resulting in what business value. Release planning must be clear and explicit and must happen early. The reengineering labs must be managed according to what is expected from the Release (right-to-left thinking). Releases must be defined clearly for all points of the reengineering diamond so everything will be ready at delivery time.

The basic building blocks of the release plan are business cases which are developed for each business process being considered for redesign and the completed end-state designs. The business case includes:

- *Business Context:*
  The case for action (why it is imperative to redesign the process), the future vision (what the process will look like), and the business objectives (a description of the end-state with stretch goals).

- *Benefits Realization Schedule:*
  The expected business value in terms of time, cost, quality, or capital utilization benefits prepared in a time-phased representation of the results, along with the estimated costs and timeframes for implementing the changes for all points of the reengineering diamond.

- *Business Release Overview:*
  A description of major reengineering program releases including release schedule details.

The completed end-state design is simply a representation of the reengineering design team's vision that can be articulated. It is, at least at a high-level, a single integrated end-state design that must be specified and communicated before reengineering labs begin. As planning becomes more detailed, this end-state design will be supplemented with interim-state designs that describe the visions of the future that will be in place as reengineering labs complete their development phase and move into pilot and rollout. Also, the reengineering labs must be held to their interim- and end-state designs.

This will begin to ensure integration before reengineering labs even begin. It will also mitigate the situation in which reengineering labs take advantage of their new freedom to expand their scope or to create solutions that are not architecturally feasible given the end-state design. By the way, this is the second most important hot spot identified in Figure 5-1.

Now, this is not intended to imply that the end-state designs should not be revisited based on the evolution of the rest of the reengineering effort. Whenever a new business process is identified for reengineering, or when a new reengineering lab starts there is the opportunity for the review of the end-state, but this should be exercised with extreme caution. A project team can implement a principle of continuous improvement, but if the end-state changes too radically, the business case and timeframes must also be revisited. This decision should be made by the reengineering project sponsor with the full knowledge of the impact of making the changes.

Release planning, done correctly, optimizes the delivery of the highest priority results against the difficulty of implementing technical and organizational change initiatives. This results in improved return on investment and immediate solutions to most critical business problems.

If multiple integrated releases, sometimes referred to as waves of change, are planned for implementation, some guiding construct must be in place to ensure coordination and integration among the releases. This is usually accomplished by assigning a senior leader the responsibility for each wave of change. This wave manager is responsible for the content of the wave, its pilot deployment, and any refinement of the wave's content in pilot. As a result of this last responsibility, the wave manager is also responsible for ensuring the wave's content is integrated with any future waves or releases. The mechanism for collecting and assimilating this release information is the Release Profile Form, Figure 5-4, and basic release information questions, like these:

- How many releases do you expect?
- What is the business urgency of each release?
- What is the anticipated frequency of action within a release?
- What infrastructure and utility functions do you expect to be needed to support release development and to support the business process on-going? (Infrastructure and utility functions include

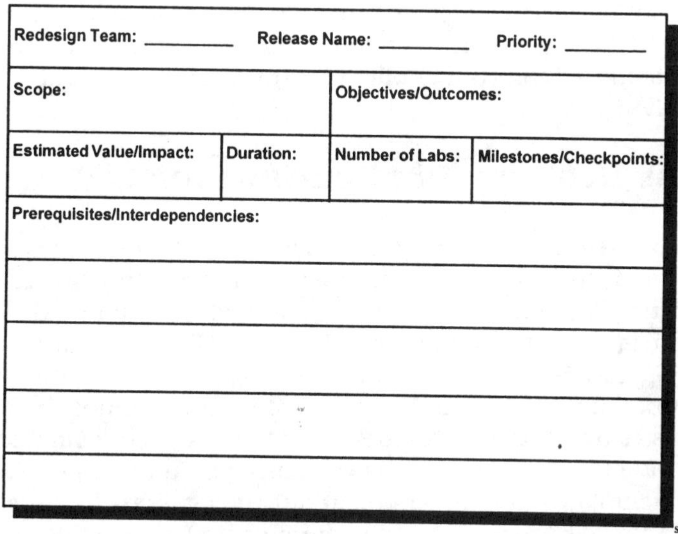
Redesign Team: ________ Release Name: ________ Priority: ________

Scope: | Objectives/Outcomes:

Estimated Value/Impact: | Duration: | Number of Labs: | Milestones/Checkpoints:

Prerequisites/Interdependencies:

Source: Clelland Johnson

Figure 5-4 Release Profile Form.

networks, databases, application-to-application communications, type of user interface, etc.)
- Are there any dependencies or interfaces to other reengineering redesigns within or outside this release?
- Describe any interfaces to other organizations - internal or external.
- Do you anticipate any special lab equipment to be required?
- Who are the stakeholders of the existing and new business processes?
- What are your concerns and expectations about migration from the current to the new business process?
- Where and how do you plan to conduct pilot testing and refinement?

Besides ensuring a greater degree of integration as a result of complete planning, the plan will provide a significant foundation for the total organizational change program required to implement the new business processes successfully. For example, to gain greater acceptance of the new redesigned business processes and other associated changes, the pilot sites should be active participants in the reengineering labs that will define these new business processes.

Even though the pilot sites will be instrumental in developing the new business processes, the end-state business process must be applicable enterprise-wide, and not just for the particular pilot sites. Finally, the pilot sites must buy into the reengineering process early in the effort because they will be asked to make a significant investment in terms of staffing and willingness to attempt the changes necessary to test the new business processes.

On the up side, accomplishing this means the reengineering activity will have a real business unit owner and will not be perceived to be "something new from corporate." This will make acceptance easier and it will give the reengineering organizational change organizers some willing staff to pilot test the change and communications activities with.

Business Systems Implications for I/T

As a part of the business process redesign, the business systems implications of the new process are identified for each point of the reengineering diamond. For the I/T point of the diamond, this information is collected using the BSI - I/T Process Summary, Figures 5-5a and 5-5b, and the BSI - I/T Detail Process, Figures 5-6a and 5-6b, templates. This BSI - I/T information about the new processes is also compared with the current MIS work by completing the MIS In-Flight Activities Template, Figures 5-7a and 5-7b.

These templates and questions about the general characteristics of the business are used to get as much detail as possible about the new processes. This information will enable MIS to provide

Process	From	To	I/T Implications

Source: Clelland Johnson

Figure 5-5a BSI/I/T Process Summary.

Process	From	To	I/T Implications
The process or identifier for the process.	An indication that this is a new process, or a description of the current state or the current way of executing the process. For a reengineering project this will probably indicate the many departments and hand-offs involved in completing the task.	A brief summary of the new process description including the what, who, where, and how.	The implications, strictly from an information technology point of view, of the new process or the changes to the process implied in this new process description. This could indicate the need for a new information management structure that allows access to more information by more business partners from more locations, or it could indicate the need for direct computer-to-computer connections between the enterprise and its suppliers, customers, or even competitors, etc.

Source: Clelland Johnson

Figure 5-5b BSI-I/T Process Summary Description.

Release Name:____________ Process Name:_____________

Functions	Business Partners	Unique Technologies	Information Requirements

Source: Clelland Johnson

Figure 5-6a BSI-I/T Detail Process Template.

Release Name:____________ **Process Name:**____________

Functions	Business Partners	Unique Technologies	Information Requirements
By process or release, indicate the functions, activities, or tasks that are to be performed. This should include I/T and non-I/T functions. This information will be used for release planning and to develop estimates for application development.	By function, indicate who (what jobs) are the performers of the function. Also, if possible indicate where the function will be performed (what type of locations), how many of such sites there are expected to be, and how many business partners are expected to perform the function in each site.	By function, indicate what new (to the enterprise, to the process, or to the industry) technologies have been, or are being considered to support the business partner in the execution of the function. If a technology has been considered and excluded, briefly describe the evaluation criteria used to exclude it. On the other hand, if specific technologies have not been identified, describe the requirements of the unique technology that will provide the greatest degree of support to the business partner.	By function, indicate the information that is required by the business partner to execute the function. Indicate whether or not the information currently exists. If so, indicate where the information exists or is created. If not, indicate where the information will come from. Indicate whether the information is source information or derived information. Also, indicate any information that is created during the execution of this function. Indicate the subsequent uses of the information and any time dependencies. If possible supply the following for information about data elements identified: Will the information element be summarized? What are the retention requirements? What are the requirements for security, integrity, and concurrency? What is the number of records locally and system-wide?

Figure 5-6b BSI-I/T Detail Process Template Description.

Reengineering Team or Business Function: ______________________

MIS Activity	Business Process Affected	Is this MIS Activity on the Critical Path?	Expected Functionality Fit (%)	Expected Timeframe Fit (Date)	Logistical Overlap with Other Activities	Estimate to Complete (Workdays)	Alternatives to Current MIS Activity	Estimated Costs of Alternatives	Business Process Owner Preference

Source: Clelland Johnson

Figure 5-7a MIS In-Flight Activities Template.

technological innovation and to prepare to support the reengineering implementation effort. Typical questions to determine the general characteristics of the processes are:

- What are the characteristics of the business process that will influence the Comprehensive Technical Architecture?
- Location Questions:
  - At what types of facilities will the process be performed (e.g., warehouse, manufacturing plant, etc.)?
  - Within a facility, where will the process be performed (e.g., loading dock, office environment, etc.)?
  - Will the process be performed while the business partner is mobile (e.g., customer site, truck-based, walk-around, etc.)?

Reengineering Team or Business Function: ____________

MIS Activity	Business Process Affected	Is this MIS Activity on the Critical Path?	Expected Functionality Fit (%)	Expected Timeframe Fit (Date)	Logistical Overlap with Other Activities	Estimate to Complete (Workdays)	Alternatives to Current MIS Activity	Estimated Costs of Alternatives	Business Process Owner Preference
MIS identifies development, production, and other activities that may impact their reengineering activities. These could include acquisition or development of applications or functions, migration of existing applications, or other changes. Emphasis should be placed on efforts that are on the reengineering critical path or that will consume large amounts of MIS resource.	For each MIS activity, indicate the business process or function that will be affected.	If the MIS activity is on the reengineering critical path, note this here. These MIS activities may need to be accelerated, but in any event, one or more contingency plans must be identified.	For each MIS activity, indicate how closely the result is expected to fit with the functional requirements of the redesigned business process.	For each MIS activity, indicate how closely the result is expected to fit with the timeframe requirements of the redesigned business process.	For each MIS activity, indicate how closely it is expected to overlap with other significant process changes.	For each MIS activity, indicate the current estimate for completion of the activity assuming the existing scope of functionality.	If the MIS activity is necessary for the successful implementation of the redesigned business process, and if the functionality fit, timeframe fit, or estimate to complete is out of line with the requirements of the redesigned business process, indicate alternatives to the current MIS activity.	If any alternatives are identified, indicate as closely as possible, the costs associated with the alternative. If precise costs are not available, indicate what assumptions were used to estimate the costs provided here.	For each MIS activity, the Business Process Owner should (based on the redesigned business process requirements and MIS's findings) indicate whether the MIS activity should be accelerated, terminated, or allowed to run its current course.

Figure 5-7b MIS In-Flight Activities Template Description.

- Business Partner Questions:
  - How many business partners will be carrying out the process at each site?
  - How many business partners will be carrying out the process concurrently?
  - Will the process be performed regularly by non-employees at external locations (e.g., customer or supplier-performed process, distributor-performed sub-process, etc.)?

- Business Process-Unique Technologies Questions:
  - Are there any technologies that are required to support this process that are new to the enterprise?
  - Have the reengineering teams identified any new or unique technologies (e.g., hand-held terminals, pen-based computers, bar code writers and scanners, document scanners, optical storage, robotic and process control equipment, intercompany communications (EDI or EFT), geographic information systems, integrated voice/data, multimedia, hypertext, hypermedia, radio frequency communications, etc.)?

- *Information Requirements Questions:*
  - What are the information requirements to support the business process?

- *Information Sources:*
  - Where does the information come from?
  - Where does the required information currently exist?
  - Where do we expect the information to exist in future?
  - Where (i.e., by whom or by what process) is the information created?
  - Is the information considered source information or derived (computed) information?

- *Information Business Rules:*
  - What are the business rules for the information?
  - What are the triggers that create the information?
  - Who can access the information? Who can change it?
  - Who "owns" the information?
  - Who can change the definitions of the information?
  - What dependencies exist among different items of information?
  - What information relationships exist that have an impact on this information?
  - What are the security requirements for the information?

- *Information Statistics:*

Reengineering Team:________________

Application System Name	Business Criticality (High or Low)	System Origin (P, MP, CI, CE, S)	System Feeds		Application and Data Environment	Technical Condition (High or Low)	Business Functionality (High or Low)
			From	To			

Source: Clelland Johnson

Figure 5-8a Current Applications Assessment Template.

Reengineering Team:________________

Application System Name	Business Criticality (High or Low)	System Origin (P, MP, CI, CE, S)	System Feeds		Application and Data Environment	Technical Condition (High or Low)	Business Functionality (High or Low)
			From	To			
The commonly-recognizable (business and MIS) name by which the application system is know.	An assessment of the relative importance of the functionality to the business.	**P = Package.** Commercial off-the-shelf (COTS) software. **MP = Modified Package.** Package software that has been customized more than 20%. **CI = Custom-Internal.** Custom-developed software that was built by MIS. **CE = Custom-External.** Custom software developed by an outside contractor. **S = Service Bureau.** Functionality provided by a service bureau.	The names of origin and target application systems, outside entities, or business documents that interact with this application system. This should also include whether the interaction is **A = Automated** or **M = Manual.**		The computing hardware, operating system, database, and applications development environments for the application system, e.g. mainframe-MVS-VSAM-COBOL or Intel server-NTAS-SQLServer-Visual C++.	An assessment of the degree of ease with which the application system is maintained, the currency of the hardware, software, database, or networking environments, and the degree and ease of integration with other application systems.	An assessment of how well the current application system satisfies the requirements of the business business partners and how well the system supports the business process.

Source: Clelland Johnson

Figure 5-8b Current Applications Assessment Template Description.

- What are the estimated volumes for the information?
- What are the storage and retention requirements for the information?
- What is the frequency of access to the information?

• *Application Requirements Questions:*
-What are the specific applications that currently support the process and what are the relative conditions of the applications in three important dimensions: business criticality (how much does the business rely on the system), business functionality (how well does the current system satisfy the business users of the system), and technical condition (how easy is the system to maintain, update, integrate, etc.)? Figures 5-8a and 5-8b, Current Applications Assessment Templates can be used to guide this information collection activity.
- Is there a preference for a package solution or custom application development?
- Are there any preferred packages or vendors?
- Are there any unique application processing requirements, e.g., real time processing, on-line transaction processing (OLTP), etc.?
- What are the requirements concerning business partner mobility and use of information technology for the business process?

• *Platform and Infrastructure Requirements Questions:*
- Are there any requirements for platform and infrastructure (hardware, operating system software, utility software, database management system software, connectivity, etc.)?
- Have any other requirements (information, application, location, etc.) forced platform or infrastructure choices?
- Are there any reengineering team preferences for any platform or infrastructure components?

The completed Release Profile Forms, Release Planning results, release and process questions, and BSI - I/T templates are the primary sources of information for the I/T Sanity Check.

Sanity Checks

H/R and I/T Sanity Checks are a dialogue between the reengineering team and the enterprise's support organizations, H/R and MIS. They are necessary because accommodating the radical change required for reengineering involves certain long lead time activities and resources which must be understood, planned for, and scheduled as far in advance as possible. Some of these are, for example, making significant changes to the I/T infrastructure, managing labor relations involving union workers, identifying and reassigning participants for the business process redesign and reengineering labs, everything to do with change programs, and anything that requires relying on a resource from outside the enterprise. These long lead time items typically fall into three areas: human resources, change management, and information technology.

Many times, these Sanity Checks will result in changes to the Release Plan to accommodate long lead time predecessor activities that were unknown to the reengineering team. It is at this point that MIS and the H/R organizations can be perceived to be impediments to the business change process. So the assessments must be done as quickly and impartially as possible and the information provided must be as detailed and substantiated as possible.

While it may not seem an obvious part of reengineering MIS, a high degree of emphasis must be placed on human resources and organizational change during release planning, both for the enterprise and for MIS. An assessment must be conducted to determine the ability of the organization to accept the changes in the timeframe required by the business cases. This assessment, called the H/R Sanity Check, looks at the prospective recipients of the changes, their ability to internalize the change in the timeframe, the cost to conduct the communications programs and training necessary to get the changes accepted, any institutional obstruction considerations such as union shops accepting changes, etc. Chapter 8 — Organizational Change details the impact of reengineering-related change on the MIS organization.

A critical and often overlooked part of business release planning that is most important to MIS is assessing the cost and timeframe for preparing the I/T infrastructure to support a reengineering solution. This includes not only development, testing, and rollout, but also readying MIS to support reengineering: technology infrastructure changes required to support the redesigned business processes, implementing new technologies, techniques, and tools in MIS, reskilling or retooling the MIS organization, upgrading legacy systems to support changes resulting from the new processes, and integrating and testing the deliverables for all points of the reengineering diamond. Besides the outright cost and timeframe required for these activities, there may be insufficient resources in the MIS organization to accomplish the needed work in the timeframe, in which case an assessment of costs and timeframe to acquire supplemental resources must be included.

The I/T Sanity Check, uncovers risks in two areas: technology availability and MIS capacity availability. Technology availability is usually not a problem assuming the desired capability is within the realm of feasibility. A problem could arise if the technology is completely inconsistent with the current technology architecture and there was no way to integrate the new with the legacy, or if MIS was reluctant to change direction to support the business. The second test, however, MIS capacity to support the reengineering project in the timeframe required by the business cases usually is a problem and is much harder to address.

Description of the I/T Sanity Check Process

The I/T Sanity Check is conducted to confirm the I/T requirements and implications of a business process redesign and identify and schedule the interdependencies between the business process redesign effort and its I/T components. The types of information required for the assessment are the initial release plan schedules and interdependencies among reengineering lab teams, the MIS and I/T Critical Programs schedules and interdependencies among MIS activities, the Comprehensive Technical Architecture, and an analysis of the current state of MIS. The I/T Sanity Check results in a consolidated schedule of all reengineering activities, including MIS and I/T Critical Programs.

The participants in the I/T Sanity Check are the reengineering executive sponsor, the reengineering governance structure, the business process owner, the MIS participants in reengineering labs, the Chief Architect, and the CIO. The CIO's participation assumes the CIO is committed to the reengineering effort, knows the capabilities of the MIS organization, and can commit to the support and timeframe. Otherwise, the CIO must be supported by additional MIS staff: the MIS directors, the MIS and I/T Critical Programs management, the architecture teams, and any other reengineering support staff in MIS.

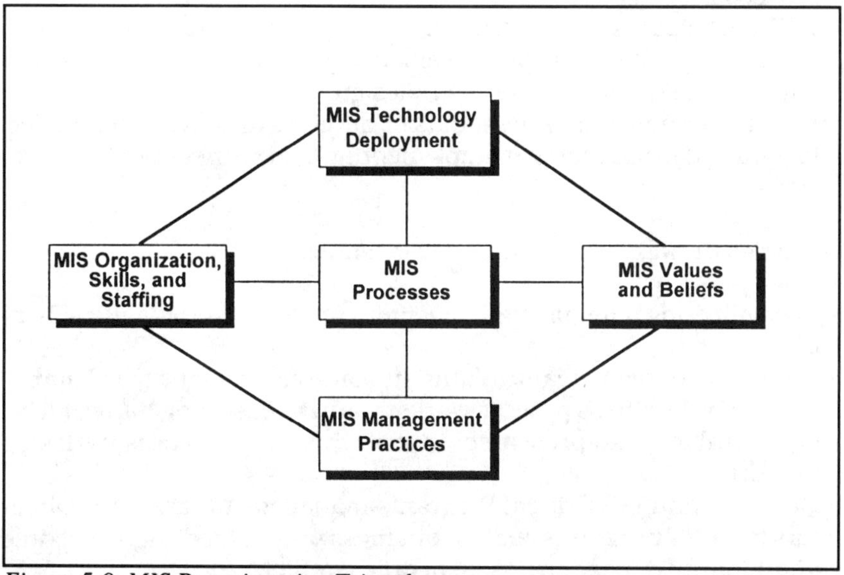

Figure 5-9 MIS Reengineering Triangle.

Question: What are the three biggest challenges your organization has had to deal with in its reengineering efforts? (Please be specific and rank in order with 1 being the biggest challenge.)

1.	Change Management	31.5%
2.	Communication	21.1%
3.	People management	9.0%
4.	Defining objectives	8.2%
5.	Other	6.5%
6.	Existing thinking	6.5%
7.	Implementation	4.3%
8.	Realizing benefits	2.5%
9.	Time management	2.2%
10.	Financing	2.2%
11.	Prioritization	1.8%
12.	Coordinating multiple units	1.4%
13.	Technical implementation	1.4%
14.	Methodology	1.1%

Source: CSC Index

Figure 5-10 Reengineering Challenges.

Activities before the Sanity Check meeting:

- Reengineering team identifies expected I/T implications using BSI - I/T templates.
- MIS participants review current MIS activities using MIS In-Flight Activities templates.
- MIS participants identify I/T Critical Programs affecting the business process redesigns.
- MIS participants understand or develop aggressive schedules, including dependencies for implementing those I/T programs that support the business process redesign.
- Reengineering team understands or develops aggressive schedules, including dependencies for implementing the business process redesigns.

Activities during the Sanity Check meeting:

- Reengineering team presents business process redesign and schedule.
- Architecture teams capture and in some cases identify I/T implications by business process workstream, release, or whatever level of granularity is presented in the business process redesign schedule.
- CIO, MIS and I/T Critical Programs management, and MIS Directors map I/T programs against business process redesign schedule and identify dependencies, schedule conflicts, etc.
- All participants look for creative ways to manipulate schedules to

achieve reengineering results without compromising the ability to implement the necessary MIS and I/T Critical Programs.

MIS and I/T Critical Programs

Reengineering will require Critical Programs in many support organizations in the enterprise. Some of the more common include Executive Team, Human Resources (H/R), and MIS.

As far as the MIS organization is concerned there are two very different types of critical programs, I/T Critical Programs and MIS

I/T Critical Programs

Infrastructure Projects:

Project Description	Sponsor	Beneficiaries
Evaluate/Select Hardware Platform(s)	MIS	MIS
Evaluate/Select Operating System Software (for each platform, as necessary)	MIS	MIS
Evaluate/Develop Distributed Computing Strategy	MIS	MIS
Evaluate/Develop Software and Data Distribution Strategy and Tools	MIS	MIS
Develop Strategy for Application Messaging and Evaluate RPCs and/or Message Queuing Tools	MIS	MIS
Evaluate/Select Database Management System (DBMS) Software (for each platform, as necessary)	MIS	MIS
Define Common Tables and Data Entities	Project Team #1	Reengineering Teams
Evaluate/Develop Distributed Data Architecture Strategy, Tools, and Procedures	MIS	MIS
Review Network Capacity Plan and Assess Ability to Accommodate New Requirements	MIS	Reengineering Teams
Design and Install New Network Components and Facilities, as necessary	MIS	Reengineering Teams
Evaluate/Develop LAN Administration Strategy and Tools	MIS	Reengineering Teams
Evaluate/Design Security Strategy and Server/Tools	MIS	MIS
Develop Security Server/Tools	MIS	MIS
Build "Data Warehouse"	MIS	Reengineering Teams
Review Hardware Capacity (by location) and Assess Ability to Accommodate New Requirements and Design for New Requirements	MIS	MIS
Acquire and Install New Hardware Components, as necessary	MIS	Reengineering Teams
Develop Internet Addressing Scheme for TCP/IP and LAN Networks and Register With the Internet	MIS	MIS
Develop LAN-to-HP Integration and Interconnectivity Strategy	MIS	MIS
Develop Network Management Strategy and Evaluate Tools	MIS	MIS
Evaluate/Develop Data Directory Strategy and Tools	MIS	MIS
Design and Build Integration Testing Lab	MIS	Lab Teams
Develop LAN Rollout Procedure and Identify LAN Installation Vendor	MIS	Reengineering Teams
Build Time-Phased Roadmap of Technology Infrastructure	MIS	MIS
Assess Current Application Development Environment for each Application Type, Platform, and DBMS (as necessary)	MIS	Lab Teams
Refine Application Development Environment for each Application Type, Platform, and DBMS (as necessary)	MIS	Lab Teams
Evaluate/Design Mechanism for Moving, Summarizing, and Archiving Detail Transaction Data Between the Location and the Area	MIS	MIS
Develop Backup/Recovery Strategy and Evaluate Tools for Area	MIS	MIS
Design and Build Technology for Integrating "Mobile" Data	MIS	MIS
Define Strategy and Evaluate Tools for Distributing the Data Model and Data Type Information	MIS	Lab Teams
Develop and Agree Data/Information Policies and Develop Management Procedures and Tools to Ensure Adherence	MIS	MIS
Continued Removal of Location HPs (in support of Area Settlement)	MIS	Project Team #2

Source: Clelland Johnson

Figure 5-11a I/T Critical Programs.

I/T Critical Programs

Lab Support Activities:

Project Description	Sponsor	Beneficiaries
On-going Pilot Test Planning	MIS	Reengineering Teams
On-going Rollout Planning	MIS	Reengineering Teams
Lab Support - Tools	MIS	Lab Teams
Lab Support - Process	MIS	Lab Teams
Lab Support - Database	MIS	Lab Teams
Lab Support - Network (LAN)	MIS	Lab Teams
Lab Support - Network (Capacity)	MIS	Lab Teams
Lab Support - Platform (Capacity)	MIS	Lab Teams
Lab Support - Platform (New Requirements)	MIS	Lab Teams
Lab Support - General Architecture	MIS	Lab Teams
Lab Support - Armor Plating	MIS	Lab Teams
Lab Support - Bridge and Conversion Planning/Consulting	MIS	Lab Teams
Support I/T Integration Across Labs Within a 10X Team	MIS	Reengineering Teams
Take Responsibility for I/T Integration Across 10X Teams	MIS	Reengineering Teams
Lab Support - Unique Technologies	MIS	Reengineering Teams
Lab Support - Shared Technologies	MIS	Reengineering Teams
Develop Tools and I/T Methodology Training Materials for New Lab Team Training (Methodology and Tools (Toolbook, Gupta, Speedware, Visual Basic))	MIS	Lab Teams
Conduct Tools and I/T Methodology Training for New Lab Teams	MIS	Lab Teams
Software Package Research Support	MIS	Lab Teams
Develop Business Process and I/T Training in conjunction with Other Training to Support 10X Pilots and Rollouts	MIS	Reengineering Teams
Operation of Integration Lab	MIS	Lab Teams

Source: Clelland Johnson

Figure 5-11b I/T Critical Programs.

I/T Critical Programs

Programming Standards Development:

Project Description	Sponsor	Beneficiaries
Develop Application Development Rules for Common Look and Feel	MIS	Lab Teams
Develop Application Development Rules for Restart and Recovery	MIS	Lab Teams
Develop Application Development Rules for Security	MIS	Lab Teams
Develop Application Development Rules for Common Help Facilities	MIS	Lab Teams
Evaluate/Develop Application Program Interface (API) Standards	MIS	MIS
Develop Application Development Rules for Application Program Interface (API) Usage	MIS	Lab Teams
Evaluate/Develop Network API Standards	MIS	MIS
Develop Application Development Rules for Network API Usage	MIS	Lab Teams
Evaluate/Develop Structured Query Language (SQL) Standards	MIS	MIS
Develop Application Development Rules for SQL Usage	MIS	Lab Teams
Develop Application Development Rules for Program Modularity	MIS	Lab Teams
Develop Application Development Rules for Error Processing	MIS	Lab Teams
Define Common Modules and Shell Programs Including Rules, Cataloging, and Access	MIS	Lab Teams
Develop Common Modules and Shell Programs	MIS	Lab Teams
Define and Maintain the Application Architecture Diagram	MIS	Lab Teams

Source: Clelland Johnson

Figure 5-11c

Critical Programs. I/T Critical Programs are those necessary to prepare the technology infrastructure, create the architectures described in the Comprehensive Technical Architecture, and prepare for pilot and rollout implementations. It is usually not too hard to identify and get funding for I/T Critical Programs, because they

I/T Critical Programs		
Shared and Unique Technologies Projects:		
Project Description	**Sponsor**	**Beneficiaries**
Develop EDI/EFT Strategy and Support Development of EDI and EFT Functionality for Labs	Project Team #2	Reengineering Teams
Evaluate MICR Printing	Project Team #3	Reengineering Teams
Evaluate Bar Code Writing, Scanning, and Reading	Project Team #4	Reengineering Teams
Evaluate Document Scanning and Optical Character Recognition (OCR) Technology	Project Team #2	Reengineering Teams
Evaluate Facsimile Server	Project Team #3	Project Team #3
Develop Electronic Mail Strategy and Evaluate Package(s) and Administration Tools and Support Labs' Use of the Technology	MIS	Reengineering Teams
Develop Electronic Forms Strategy and Evaluate Tools and Support Labs' Use of the Technology	MIS	Reengineering Teams
Investigate Knowledge-Based Technology	Project Team #2	Reengineering Teams
Develop Strategy for Customer and Supplier Access to Company Systems	Project Team #4	Reengineering Teams
Develop Strategy for Debit Cards	Project Team #2	Project Team #2
Evaluate Self-Diagnosing and Self-Reporting Vending Machine Technologies	Project Team #4	Project Team #4
Evaluate Hand-Held Computing Technology	MIS	Reengineering Teams
Identify Redeployment Opportunities for of Existing Hand-Held Computers	Project Team #2	Reengineering Teams
Design and Build Customer Service/Telephone Selling Center	MIS	Reengineering Teams
Investigate Imaging and Optical Storage Technology	Project Team #2	Reengineering Teams
Investigate Mobile Communications Technologies	Project Team #2	Reengineering Teams
Develop E-mail to Hand-Held Computer Interface/Gateway	Project Team #2	Reengineering Teams
Continued Evaluation of Emerging Technologies	MIS	Reengineering Teams
Investigate Converting packages to Another UNIX Platform and Running as a Regional or Central Application	MIS	Project Team #4

Source: Clelland Johnson

Figure 5-11d

represent more tangible, vendor-provided, product purchases.

If one applied the reengineering diamond to the MIS organization as in Fig 5-9, one would get a sense fcr MIS Critical Programs. MIS Critical Programs refer to all other points of the reengineering diamond except the information technology point, i.e., MIS processes, MIS jobs, skills, and structures, MIS management systems, and MIS values and beliefs. They are those programs that are required to affect changes in the MIS organization. They are people-oriented, not technology-oriented.

While it is often more difficult to convince management of the need and funding for MIS Critical Programs, these are the most crucial for successful MIS support of reengineering. Indeed, Figure 5-10 indicates that change management, communication, and people management are the three biggest problems faced by organizations undertaking reengineering (according to a 1991 CSC Index survey of MIS executives involved in reengineering). The fact is, technical implementation is way down the list with only 1.4 percent of the MIS

Executives indicating that it is a reengineering challenge. Since, the real challenges are in the areas of change, communication, people, and management, it is in these areas where some, perhaps most, Critical Programs must focus. Chapter 8 — Organizational Change provides more detailed information on this topic.

I/T Critical Programs are those more focused on creating the technology infrastructure for the development and production environments. Figures 5-11a through 5-11d present an example of I/T Critical Programs. These are taken from a recent reengineering engagement.

Interventions, Coaches, and SMEs

One of our key findings from reengineering implementation projects is that reengineering labs, if not implemented properly, can easily take on lives of their own and the lab teams, themselves become insular and develop functional silos. This can be just as detrimental to the overall reengineering project as the functional silos in the enterprise that reengineering is supposed to eliminate. In fact, this condition is intolerable especially due to the requirement for adherence to the end-state design. One successful solution to ensure this does not happen is a program of interventions in the reengineering labs by Coaches and SMEs.

Management's emphasis in a reengineering project is on dates and deliveries, and not necessarily on detail content. This means that testing is sometimes haphazard, integration points are sometimes not considered, issues are sometimes assumed to be resolved when they are not, or legacy integration is sometimes ignored. All of these opportunities give further reasons to support the need for Coach and SME interventions as part of reengineering integration.

This means, by the way, that interventions and outside reviews with Coaches, SMEs or the project sponsor cannot just be "show and tell" presentations, but must include the meat of the redesigns. They must be open, honest exchanges, particularly as relates to schedules, deliverables, scope management, and integration.

Coaches are a team of specialists who support multiple reengineering labs in developing high quality, consistent deliverables through coaching and training in the reengineering lab process, and through continuing to enhance the reengineering process. Coaches specialize by point of the diamond and they are assigned to Process Families. There are Process Coaches who specialize in the reengineering process. There are Technical Coaches who specialize in various aspects of the information technology. Finally, there are H/R and Organizational Change Coaches who specialize in the issues related to changing the organization.

Their mission is to provide on-site, front-line support in the areas of reengineering process and technology and to act as initial liaison between the reengineering labs and project management or MIS organizations. These Process and Technical Coaches will have frequent interaction with the reengineering lab teams. From an MIS perspective, the key MIS resources supporting the reengineering labs are the Process and Technical Coaches.

Process Coaches

If there are multiple business processes being reengineered concurrently, Process Coaches are assigned to a process family. Once initiated, the role never expires because reengineering leads to continuous improvements to the process and new best practices. The Process Coach becomes part of the management team for the process family, along with lab leaders, I/T integration manager, process family leader, H/R integration manager. The Process Coach roams among reengineering labs. Each Process Coach can support initially, a maximum of two reengineering labs, increasing to four as successive iterations of reengineering labs are conducted with experienced teams. The kinds of support provided by the Process Coach includes:

- Coaching (training, demonstrating, and facilitating) on the reengineering lab process.
- Monitoring changes to reengineering lab scope and helping to assess impact (business value, staffing, schedule) of those changes.
- Facilitating prototype reviews and quality assurance (QA) reviews.
- Monitoring and supporting the use of the reengineering process.
- Identifying and resolving issues among labs.
- Identifying resource requirements for labs.

Integration, scope management, resource management, quality management, and other project management issues are resolved by meetings with other Process Coaches to ensure consistency and identification of enhancements to the reengineering process.

Technical Coaches

If there are multiple process families, Technical Coaches are assigned to a process family based on the level of support required, i.e., the amount of I/T in the redesigned business process. Technical Coaches also roam among reengineering labs. Each Technical Coach can support a maximum of five labs, but the reengineering labs must be staggered such that during high I/T usage, e.g., I/T and H/R Setup phase, the Technical Coach is available 100 percent to support the reengineering lab in that phase. The Technical Coaches' responsibilities include:

- Demonstrating and training lab technologists on use of applications development environment tools and common objects.
- Participating in prototype reviews as technical reviewer, i.e., code reviews, stored procedure reviews, etc.
- Identifying and prioritizing MIS support requirements.
- Acting as liaison to the architecture teams.
- Helping create reengineering lab deliverables, in emergencies.

In addition, the Technical Coach meets with other Technical Coaches to ensure consistency, to identify technical integration issues, and to share best practices from all labs.

While reengineering lab teams are always responsible for the quality and consistency of their deliverables, these Coaches will be responsible for ensuring the quality and consistency of reengineering lab deliverables among lab teams and among process families. This is an awesome responsibility and very hard work. Therefore, Coaches support the lab teams but do not supplement lab staffing. They provide expert guidance and assistance in the reengineering process and will ensure a level of quality and consistency required to make reengineering successful. Their counsel must be sought after by all lab teams and their advice must be adhered to.

Subject Matter Experts

There are Subject Matter Experts (SMEs) to address all points of the reengineering diamond. Business process redesign SMEs, Human Resources SMEs, Organizational Change SMEs, and various I/T SMEs. SMEs participate in reengineering labs as required during creation of deliverables requiring a high degree of expertise. For example H/R SMEs would support a reengineering lab developing job descriptions and compensation programs for a new business process. Types of I/T SMEs include:

- Data Analyst SMEs
- Database Design SMEs
- Testing SMEs
- Networking Specialist SMEs
- Legacy Access SMEs
- Operating System SMEs
- Unique Technology SMEs
- Data Center Operations SMEs
- Software Package or Product SMEs
- Common Object SMEs

- ❑ Collect and Review all Architectural Documentation
- ❑ Schedule initial meeting with redesign teams
  - Review work and decisions to date
  - Understand technology requirements, drivers, and decisions
  - Identify any new technology enablers or drivers
  - Develop high-level technical architecture to support redesigned business processes
  - Perform gap analysis against current technical architecture
- ❑ Create applications development standards
  - Interface standards for business partner, application, information, and connectivity
  - Application development techniques and design guides for GUI, database calls, naming conventions, design guidelines, etc.
  - Packaging or armor plating standards for security, production operations, data replication, etc.
  - Estimating standards
  - Mechanism for evolving standards
- ❑ Develop and compile an Architecture Packet for the lab's use
  - To ensure correctness of the technologies used to implement the business reengineering solution
  - To identify and use any shared or unique technologies correctly
  - To ensure that a suite of common objects exists that are satisfactory for the reengineering labs' tasks and ensure their correct usage

Source: Clelland Johnson

Figure 5-12 Architecture Team Responsibilities to Reengineering Labs.

Architecture Team Involvement in Reengineering Labs

In addition to the Coaches and SMEs, all the architects (Chief Architect, Process Architect, Information Architect, Applications Architect, Applications Development Environment Architect, and Technology Infrastructure Architect) are considered SMEs and participate in certain interventions. An example of the types of activities performed by the architects and the architecture teams in supporting the reengineering labs is presented in Figures 5-12 and 5-13.

Interventions

In the context of reengineering integration, these interventions include broader coverage than is normal in a traditional MIS applications development scenario. The interventions include eight primary areas:

- Reengineering process coordination
- Lab and Critical Programs scope coordination
- Technology usage coordination
- Integration management
- Issues management
- Implementation coordination
- Work product quality assurance
- Business results achievement

Reengineering Process Coordination

Process coordination in this case refers to the reengineering process, not to business processes nor to I/T processes. Everyone

- ❑ Architecture Team Pre-Lab Activities
  - BSI - I/T Review
  - Data Model Review
  - Review Existing Technical Architecture
  - Identify and Incorporate Unique Technologies
  - Develop Target Technical Architecture
  - Identify Bridge Requirements that are not application specific
  - Develop Architecture Cost Estimates
  - Provide input to Release Plans
  - Create plans for I/T Critical programs
  - Identify and Reconcile I/T Overlaps
- ❑ Architecture Team Lab Planning and Concept Prototyping Activities
  - Apply Architecture Principles to Release Plans to determine:
    - Platform
    - Application Architecture (style of computing)
    - Data Architecture
    - Networking Architecture
  - Determine Standards for Release:
    - Development
    - Interfaces
    - Packaging
  - Design Detailed Technical Architecture:
    - Where is the data and on what?
    - What and where is the application processor?
    - Who and where are the business partners?
    - What unique technologies are needed?
    - What is the impact on the shared technologies, e.g., the network?
    - What legacy application bridges are needed?
    - What technology-induced architectural bridges, links, and interconnections are needed?
  - Identify MIS staff and skills for the lab support team
  - Prepare to design the physical data view:
    - Understand the logical view
    - Understand the logical design
    - Plan the development database
  - Design and prepare the lab facility
- ❑ Architecture Team Lab and "Build" Prototyping Activities
  - Prepare prototype database
  - Populate pilot database
  - Integration testing
  - Build lab and support
  - Support application developers in building bridges (these are the responsibility of the reengineering labs because they are the result of non-technical business rule changes.)

Source: Clelland Johnson

Figure 5-13 Representative Workplan for Architecture Team Involvement in Reengineering Labs.

is responsible for ensuring the reengineering process is understood, accepted, and followed. Discrete process coordination tasks include:

- Using the reengineering methodology, including its business process redesign, human resource, change management, and I/T components, consistently among reengineering labs—which is another way of saying, knowing what to do, how and when to do it, what work products to create, and how and when to create, review, and disseminate them.
- Planning the activities, schedules, resource requirements, and interventions for the reengineering labs.
- Ensuring the reengineering labs keep focused on their scope targets and lab objectives.
- Ensuring reengineering labs are on schedule.

Technology Usage Coordination

Because reengineering is, by definition, possible as a result of information technology, technology usage in the reengineering lab is critical to the success of the reengineering effort. Also, because technology has not yet progressed to the point of complete unfailing interchangeability among dissimilar technologies, attention must be paid to ensuring the reengineering labs' use of technologies is coordinated. It should be obvious, but this will ensure the feasibility of the redesigned business process. This is not to say that the reengineering lab will be limited in the technology choices they are allowed to make, it only means that those decisions must be taken with complete knowledge of their impact on cost, schedule, and interoperability.

Integration Management

The interventions are the project management team's means of direct access to the lab teams; therefore, the Coaches and SMEs have a key responsibility in the area of integration management. They can ask probing questions about the redesigns, schedules, scopes, and the activities the lab team are doing to identify overlaps and gaps to bring to the attention of project management.

Issues Management

Likewise, the Coaches and SMEs are in a particularly good position to identify other issues and raise them to the project management team, the process family management team, or the appropriate support organization for resolution.

Implementation Coordination

After the lab teams complete their work, test it, integrate it, and migrate it to the integration and systems testing facility, the release is compiled from all the products from all the lab teams for the release. Implementation coordination takes on three major responsibilities:

- Scheduling and content of the work products going into the release
- Preparing the pilot or rollout target for the delivery of the release
- Preparing the rest of the organization to support the rollout process and the new business processes once they are in place

Work Product Quality Assurance

Just because systems development is faster and less structured in a reengineering project than it is in traditional applications development does not mean that quality is less important. In fact, due to the pace and the impact of a reengineering project, quality is even more important. In addition, the quality of all lab team products, not just I/T deliverables must be ensured. This set of interventions allow the appropriate SMEs to evaluate and support the lab team in creating work products with the quality built in, not tacked on.

Business Results Achievement

The lab team and lab leader are ultimately responsible for the achievement of business results described in the business cases not just for work products. Due to the importance of this emphasis on results, the business partners, project sponsors, Coaches and SMEs will, throughout the lab event, provide the lab team opportunities to demonstrate and validate the expected results.

The interventions are, for the most part, scheduled in the reengineering lab workplan, but there are also times when the lab team needs immediate help and the appropriate SME responds. Approximately 75 percent of interventions should be scheduled ones and only 25 percent responses to emergencies. The scheduled interventions follow the reengineering lab methodology.

The interventions schedule will vary by project. It is based on the methodology used, the degree of reengineering experience of the lab team, the speed and aggressiveness of the schedule, etc. These interventions can take a number of forms: facilitated working sessions, prototype reviews, just-in-time training sessions, technical or functional SME support, specific work product reviews, requested process or technical support, assistance in creating specific work products, integration activities (architectural, legacy systems, between labs, etc.), formal QA reviews. One example of a lab methodology and associated interventions is described here and in Figures 5-14 through 5-20.

Lab Readiness (Figures 5-14a and 5-14b)

Lab readiness is the preliminary activity undertaken by the lab leader, the I/T leader, and the H/R leader with the process family leader, or whoever is setting direction for the lab team. The Process Coach, Technical Coach, Data Analyst SME, and Testing SME also participate in some of the Lab Readiness sessions. These activities occur before the reengineering lab starts and they ensure the team understands their role, scope, schedule, and available resources in the overall reengineering effort, and that the team is assembled, trained, and in agreement about their scope and objectives. The work techniques include facilitated work sessions, review sessions,

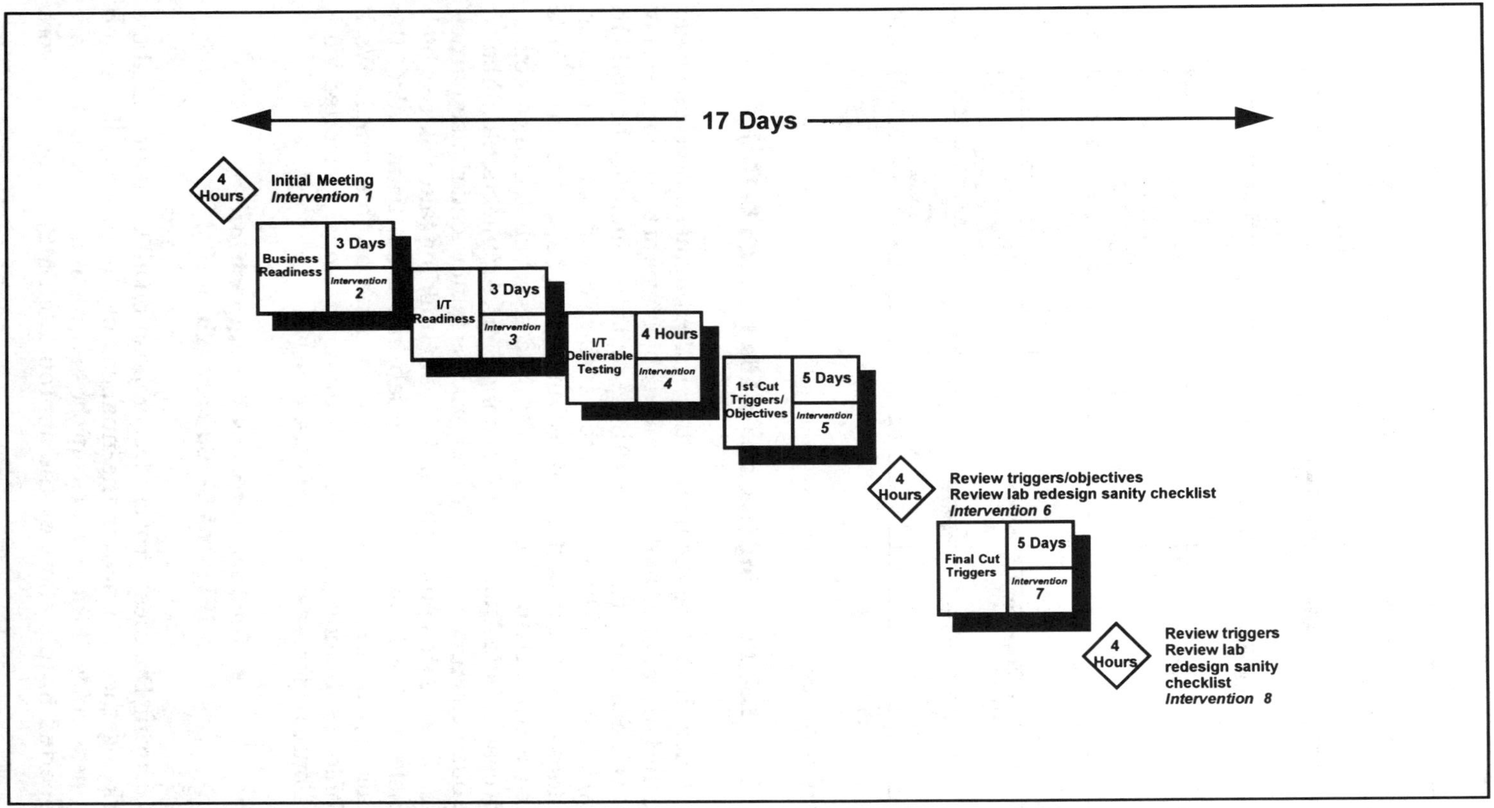

Figure 5-14a Interventions for Lab Readiness.

Interventions and Participants Lab Readiness				
Intervention	**Activity Description**	**Intervention Type**	**Intervention Duration (Days)**	**Participants**
1	Initial Meeting	Work Session	1/2	Lab Leader I/T Leader Process Coach (L) Technical Coach
2	Business Readiness	Work Session - Iterative	3	Lab Leader I/T Leader Process Coach (L) H/R SME
3	I/T Readiness	Work Session - Iterative	3	Lab Leader I/T Leader Technical Coach (L) Data Analyst SME
4	I/T Deliverables/Testing	Work Session	1/2	Lab Leader I/T Leader Process Coach Technical Coach (L) Data Analyst SME System Test Coordinator
5	1st Cut Triggers/Objectives	Work Product Review	1/2	Lab Leader I/T Leader Process Coach (L) Technical Coach
6	Final Cut Deliverables Complete	Work Product Review	1/2	Lab Leader I/T Leader Process Coach (L) Technical Coach
7	QA Review Checkpoint on tool training	QA Review	1/2	Lab Leader I/T Leader Process Coach (L) Technical Coach

Source: Clelland Johnson

Figure 5-14b

and QA reviews.

Lab Planning (Figures 5-15a through 5-15c)

Once there is agreement between the business process owner and the lab leader as to the scope and objectives of the reengineering lab, Lab Planning can begin. These activities include the full lab team (all of the full-time lab members: the lab leader, the I/T leader, business content experts, and technologists) as well as any SMEs that are expected to support the lab: process coach, technical coach, H/R coach, Data Analyst SME, Testing SME, Architects, etc. Finally, the business process owner and process family leader also participate. During this phase the initial team building takes place which transforms the individuals in the lab into a lab team. Also, the detailed planning of the lab event is done at this time. Work techniques include just-in-time training sessions, facilitated work sessions, review sessions, and QA reviews.

Business Process Decomposition (Figures 5-16a through 5-16c)

During Business Process Decomposition all lab team members work together to uncover the nuances of the process flows and business rules of the business process being redesigned. They are supported in this effort by the appropriate SMEs to get the work

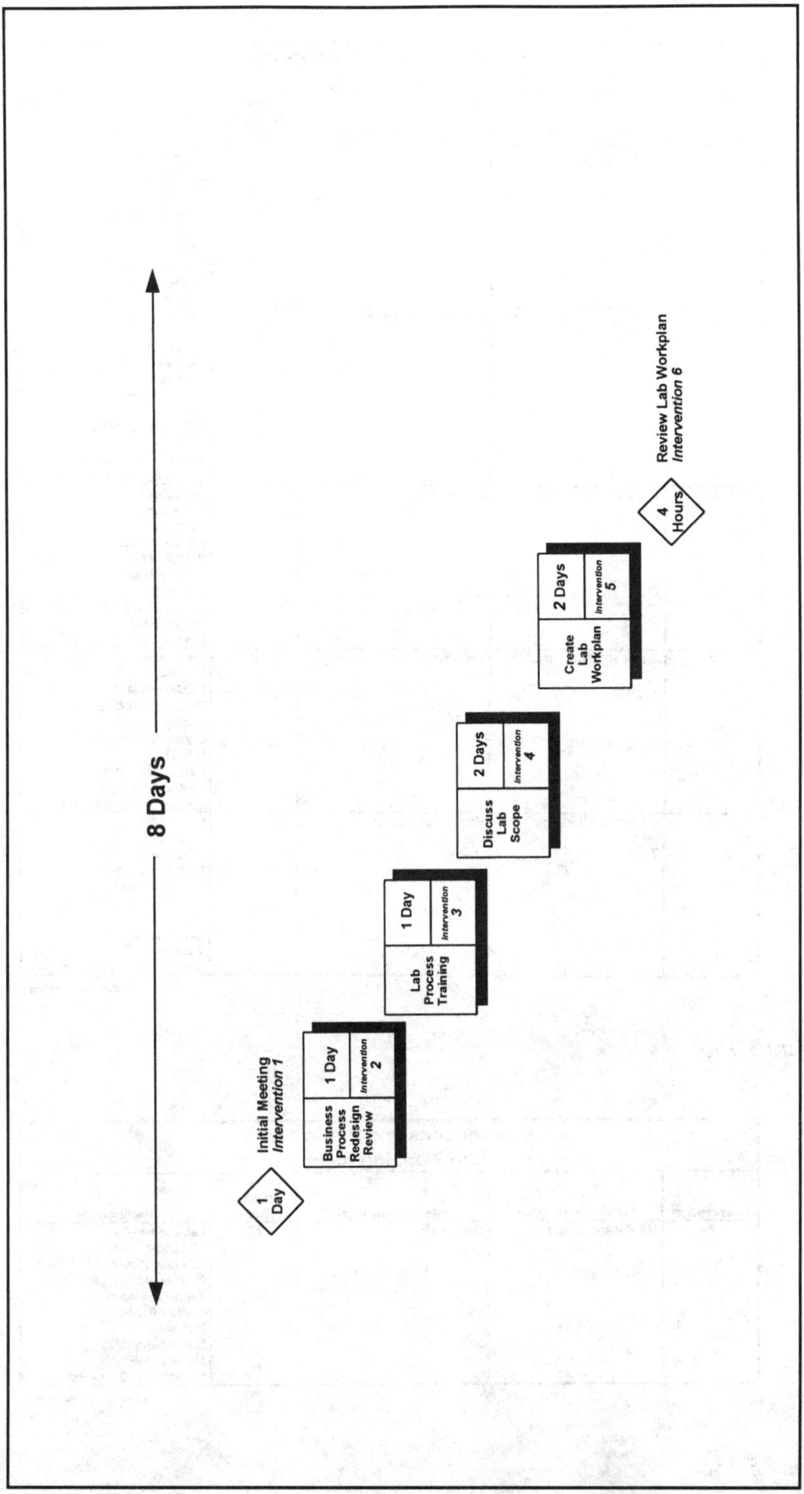

Figure 5-15a Interventions for Lab Planning

Interventions and Participants Lab Planning				
Intervention	Activity Description	Intervention Type	Intervention Duration (Days)	Participants
1	Initial Meeting	Work Session	1	Lab Leader (L) I/T Leader I/T Generalist Process Coach Technical Coach Content Expert H/R SME Data Analyst SME Testing SME System Test Coordinator
2	Business Process Redesign	Work Product Review	1	Lab Leader (L) I/T Leader I/T Generalist Process Coach (L) Technical Coach Content Expert H/R SME Data Analyst SME Testing SME System Test Coordinator I/T Integration Manager
3	Training-Lab Process	JIT coaching	1	Lab Leader I/T Leader I/T Generalist Process Coach (L) Technical Coach Content Expert H/R SME Data Analyst SME Testing SME System Test Coordinator
4	Discuss/Refine Lab Scope	Work Session	2	Lab Leader I/T Leader I/T Generalist Process Coach (L) Technical Coach Content Expert H/R SME Data Analyst SME Testing SME System Test Coordinator
5	Create Lab Workplan	Work Session	2	Lab Leader I/T Leader I/T Generalist Process Coach (L) Technical Coach Content Expert H/R SME Data Analyst SME Testing SME System Test Coordinator

Source: Clelland Johnson

Figure 5-15b

Interventions and Participants Lab Planning (cont.)				
Intervention	Activity Description	Intervention Type	Intervention Duration (Days)	Participants
6	QA Review Checkpoint	QA Review	1/2	Lab Leader I/T Leader I/T Generalist Process Coach (L) Technical Coach Content Expert H/R SME Data Analyst SME Testing SME System Test Coordinator

Source: Clelland Johnson

Figure 5-15c

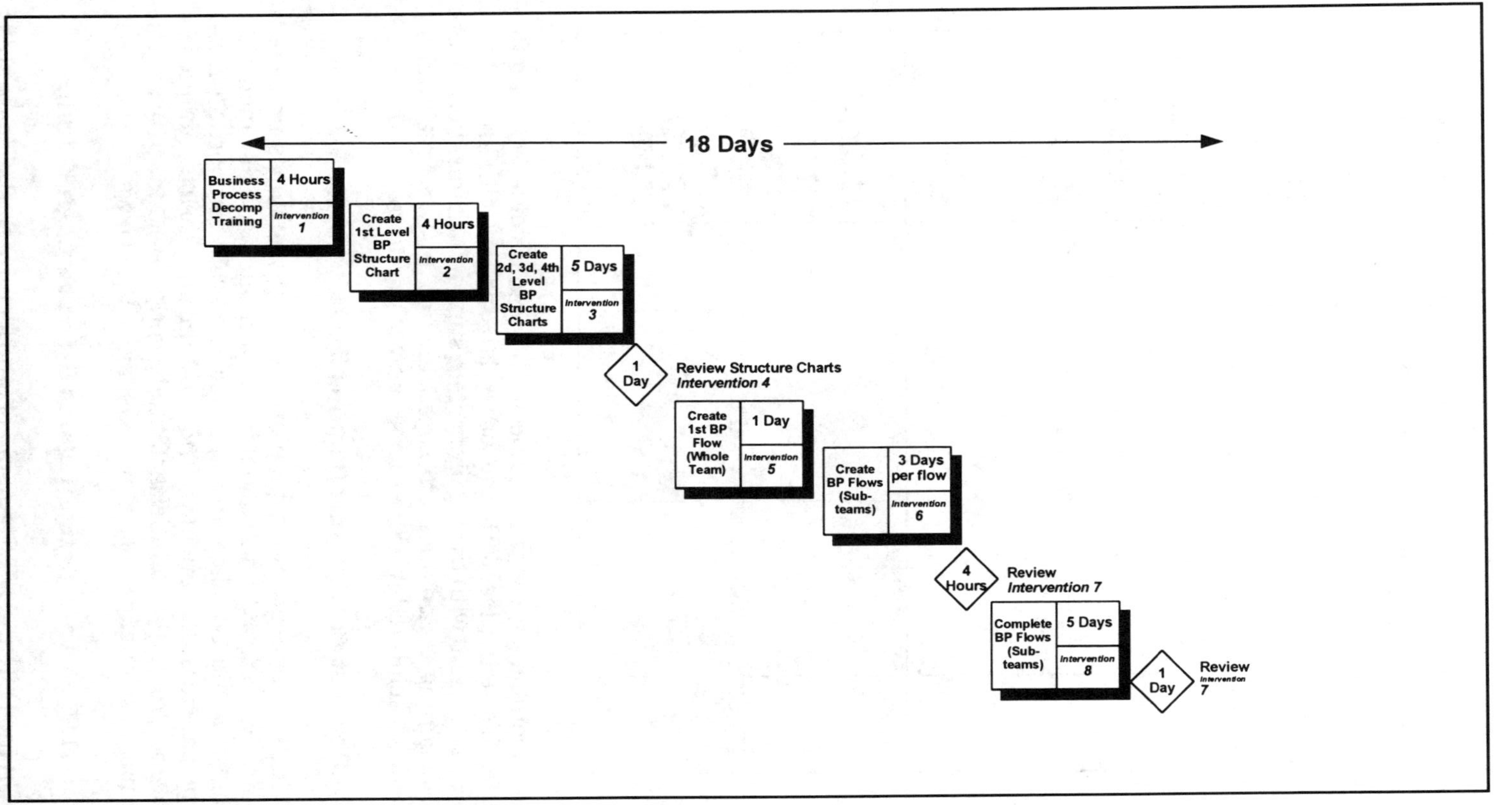

Figure 5-16a Interventions for Business Process Decomposition

Interventions and Participants Business Process Decomposition				
Intervention	**Activity Description**	**Intervention Type**	**Intervention Duration (Days)**	**Participants**
1	JIT Coaching on Business Decomposition	JIT Coaching	1/2	Lab Leader I/T Leader I/T Generalist Process Coach (L) Technical Coach Content Expert H/R SME Data Analyst SME Testing SME System Test Coordinator
2	Business Structure Chart 1st level	Work Session	1/2	Lab Leader I/T Leader I/T Generalist Process Coach (L) Technical Coach Content Expert H/R SME Data Analyst SME Testing SME System Test Coordinator
3	Business Structure Chart remaining levels	Work Session - Iterative	10	Lab Leader (L) I/T Leader I/T Generalist Process Coach (L) Technical Coach Content Expert H/R SME Data Analyst SME Testing SME System Test Coordinator
4	QA Review Checkpoint	QA Review	1	Lab Leader I/T Leader I/T Generalist Process Coach (L) Technical Coach Content Expert H/R SME Data Analyst SME Testing SME System Test Coordinator
5	Business Process Flow (1st chart)	Work Session	1	Lab Leader I/T Leader I/T Generalist Process Coach (L) Technical Coach Content Expert H/R SME Data Analyst SME Testing SME System Test Coordinator

Source: Clelland Johnson

Figure 5-16b

done, document the work, and begin the process of integrating this lab team's activities with the other lab teams, with the release coordinator, and with the legacy system support organization. Work and coaching techniques employed include just-in-time training sessions, facilitated work sessions, and QA reviews.

Concept Prototyping (Figures 5-17a through 5-17c)

In the Concept Prototype phase, the new business process is iteratively designed and validated. Again, all lab team members, along with the Coaches and appropriate SMEs supporting them, participate in these activities. The coaching and work techniques for Concept Prototype include facilitated work sessions, just-in-time training sessions, prototype reviews, and QA reviews.

H/R and I/T Setup (Figures 5-18a through 5-18d)

In the H/R and I/T Setup phase, the focus of the lab team shifts

Interventions and Participants Business Process Decomposition (cont.)				
Intervention	Activity Description	Intervention Type	Intervention Duration (Days)	Participants
6	Business Process Flow (break out)	Work Session	5	Lab Leader I/T Leader I/T Generalist Process Coach (L) Technical Coach Content Expert H/R SME Data Analyst SME Testing SME System Test Coordinator
7	QA Review Checkpoint	QA Review	1/2	Lab Leader I/T Leader I/T Generalist Process Coach (L) Technical Coach Content Expert H/R SME Data Analyst SME Testing SME System Test Coordinator
8	Final Sub-team Completion of Business Process Flows	Work Product Review	5	Lab Leader I/T Leader I/T Generalist Process Coach (L) Technical Coach Content Expert H/R SME Data Analyst SME Testing SME System Test Coordinator
9	QA Review Checkpoint	QA Review	1	Lab Leader I/T Leader I/T Generalist Process Coach (L) Technical Coach Content Expert H/R SME Testing SME System Test Coordinator

Source: Clelland Johnson

Figure 5-16c

from the business process design to the infrastructure work required before starting construction of the production systems that will follow in the Working Prototype phase. For this phase, the entire lab team and the necessary SMEs continue to work to create lab deliverables, but the work techniques are different. For H/R and I/T Setup, the work includes just-in-time training sessions, facilitated work sessions, QA reviews, and sub-team or independent work.

Working Prototyping (Figures 5-19a through 5-19f)

In the Working Prototype phase, the new business process is finished, all construction is done, and all work for all points of the diamond is completed and tested. This phase continues to involve all lab team members, the Coaches, and a number of the appropriate SMEs. Because of the construction nature of the Working Prototype phase, work is completed in sub-team or independent work, facilitated work sessions, just-in-time training sessions, prototype reviews, and QA reviews.

Integration and Systems Test (Figures 5-20a through 5-20c)

In the Integration and Systems Test phase, the lab team's work products are integrated with the work products from other lab teams and the new whole is tested. This will generally result in additional

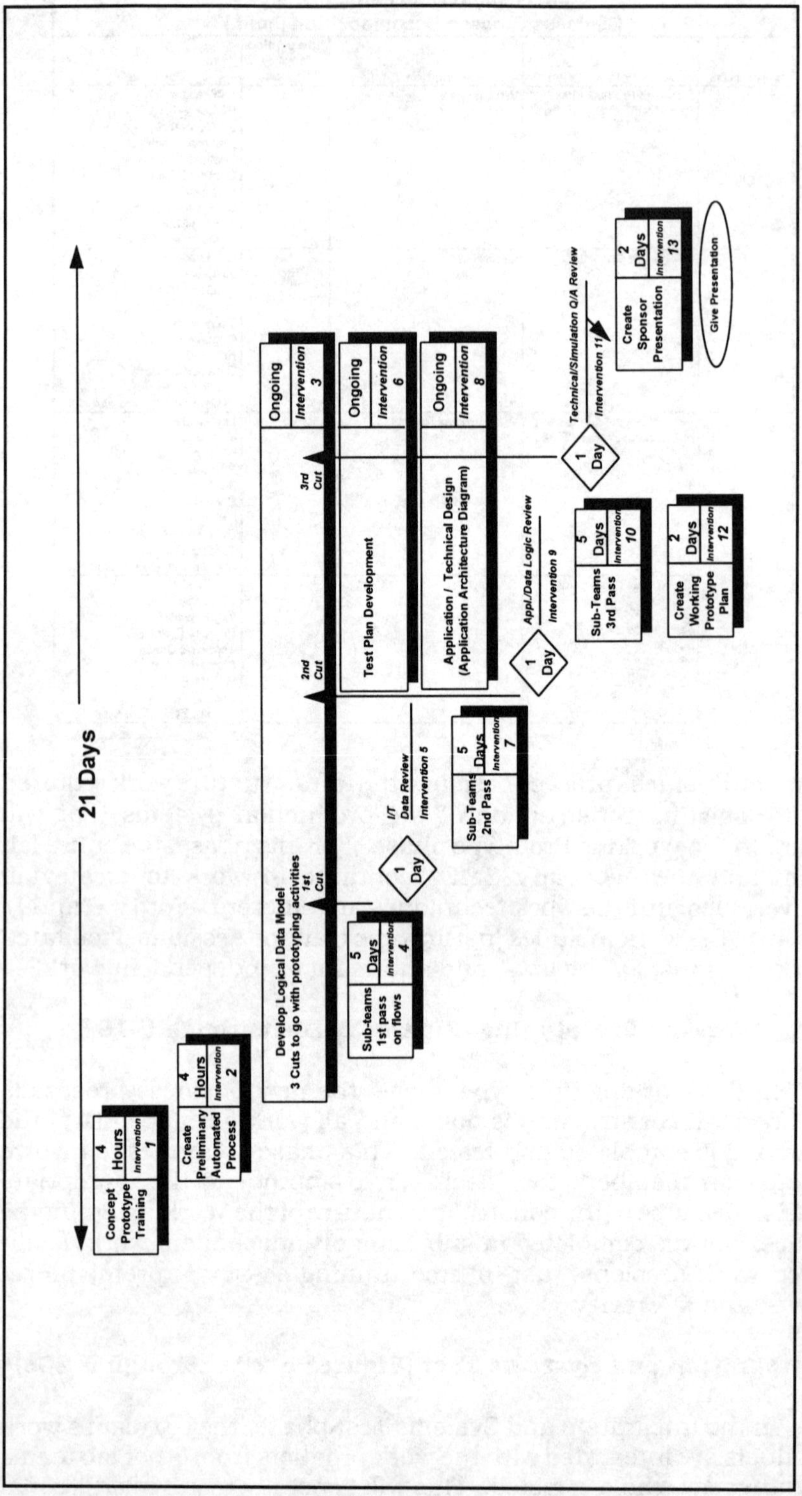

Figure 5-17a Interventions for Concept Prototypes

Interventions and Participants Concept Prototype				
Intervention	**Activity Description**	**Intervention Type**	**Intervention Duration (Days)**	**Participants**
1	JIT Coaching on Concept Prototype	JIT Coaching	1/2	Lab Leader I/T Leader I/T Generalist Process Coach (L) Technical Coach Content Expert H/R SME Testing SME System Test Coordinator
2	Development of 1st Automated Process	Work Session	1/2	Lab Leader I/T Leader I/T Generalist Process Coach (L) Technical Coach Content Expert H/R SME Data Analyst SME Testing SME System Test Coordinator
3	Sub-Team 1st Pass on Concept Prototype	Work Session	5	Lab Leader I/T Leader I/T Generalist Process Coach (L) Technical Coach Content Expert H/R SME Data Analyst SME Testing SME System Test Coordinator
4	I/T & Data Review (1st cut)	Work Product Review	1	Lab Leader I/T Leader I/T Generalist Process Coach (L) Technical Coach Content Expert H/R SME Data Analyst SME Testing SME System Test Coordinator
5	Sub-Team 2nd Pass on Concept Prototype	Work Session	5	Lab Leader I/T Leader I/T Generalist Process Coach (L) Technical Coach Content Expert H/R SME Data Analyst SME Testing SME System Test Coordinator
6	Review application data logic	Work Product Review	1	Lab Leader I/T Leader I/T Generalist Process Coach (L) Technical Coach Data Analyst SME I/T Integration Manager

Source: Clelland Johnson

Figure 5-17b

Interventions and Participants Concept Prototype (cont.)				
Intervention	**Activity Description**	**Intervention Type**	**Intervention Duration (Days)**	**Participants**
7	Sub-Team 3rd Pass on Concept Prototype	Work Session	5	Lab Leader I/T Leader I/T Generalist Process Coach (L) Technical Coach Content Expert H/R SME Data Analyst SME Testing SME System Test Coordinator
8	QA Review Checkpoint	QA Review	1	

Source: Clelland Johnson

Figure 5-17c

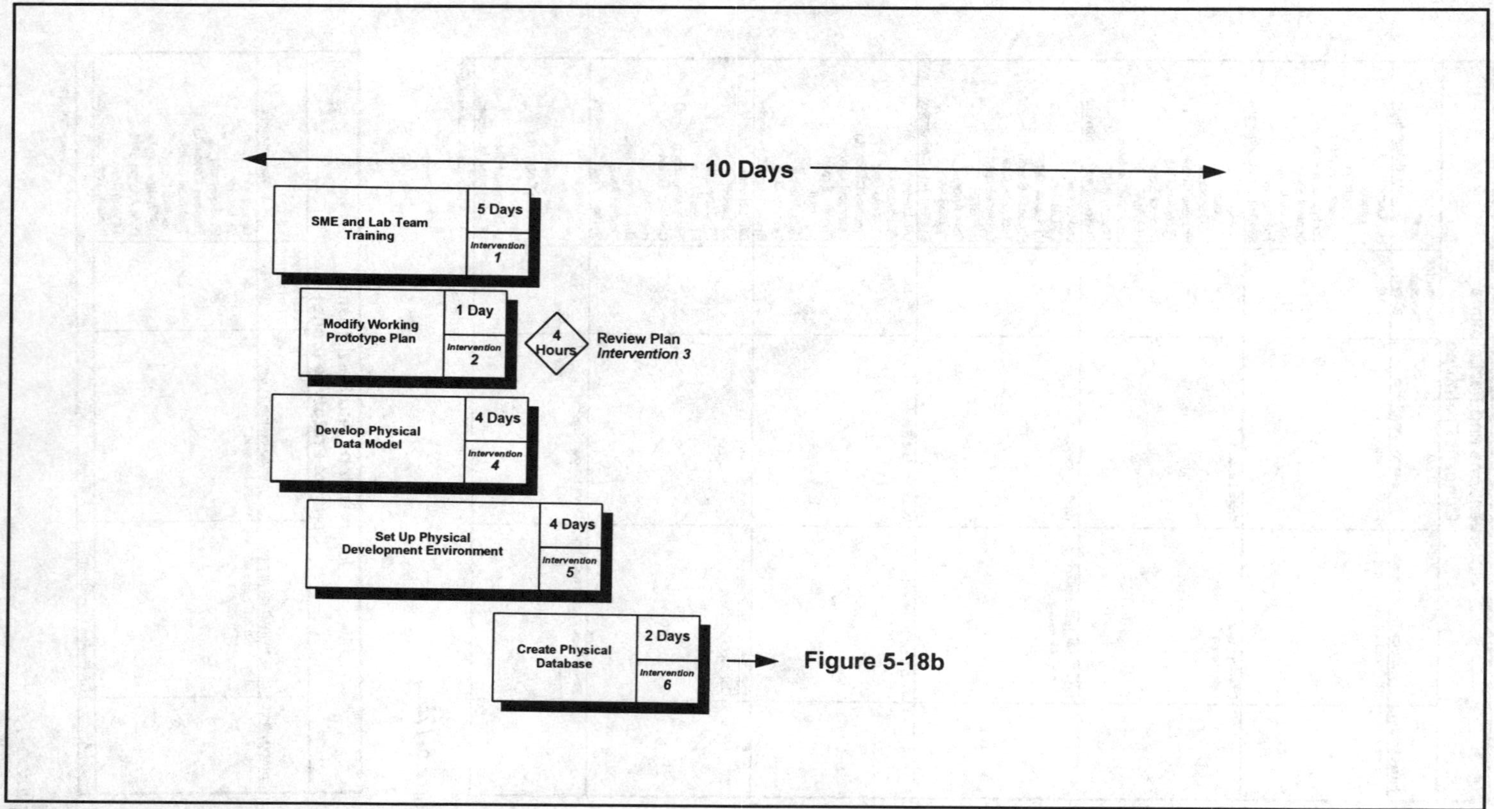

Figure 5-18a Interventions for H/R and I/T Setup.

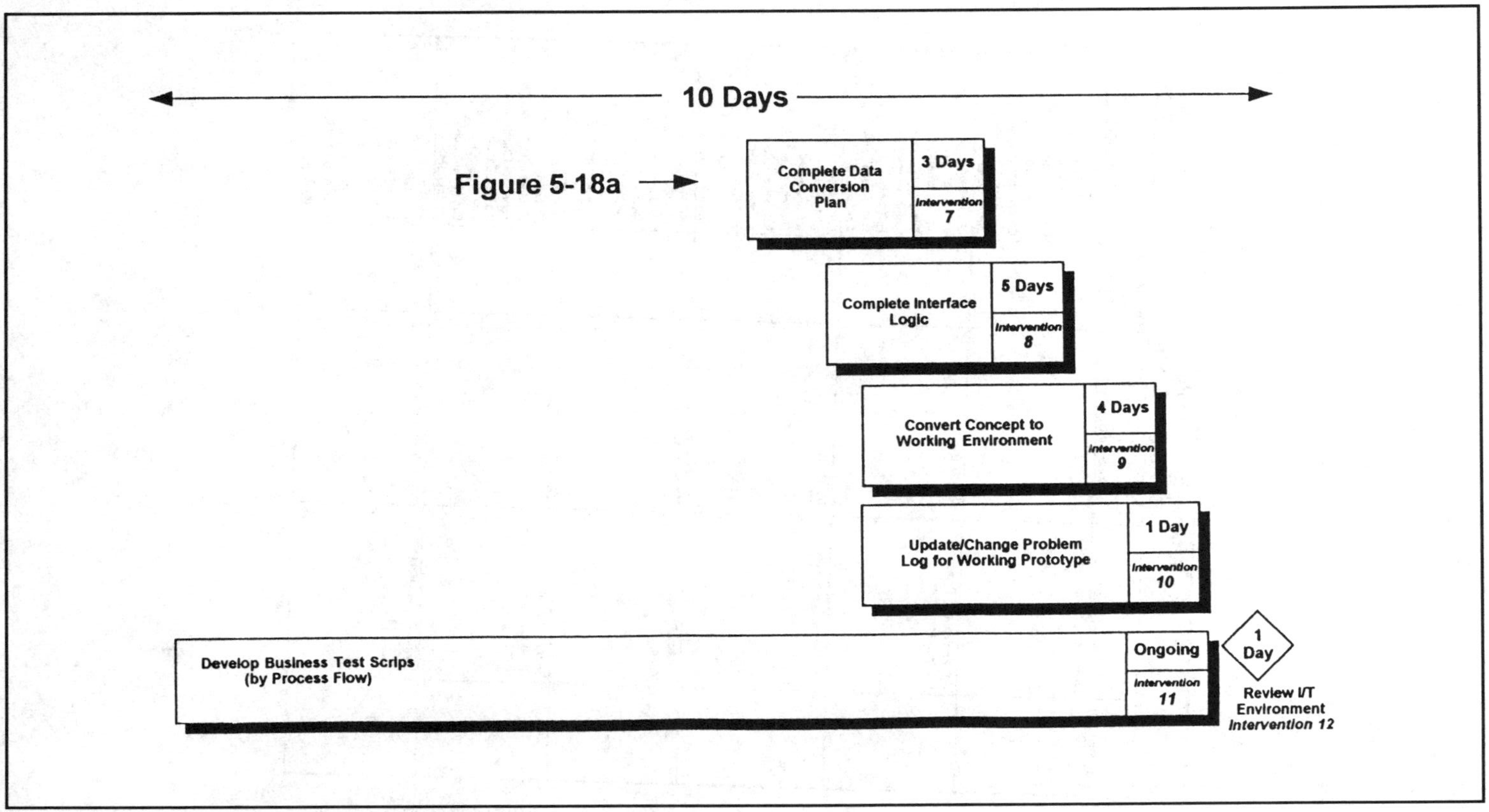

Figure 5-18b Interventions for H/R and I/T Setup (cont.).

Interventions and Participants H/R and I/T Setup				
Intervention	Activity Description	Intervention Type	Intervention Duration (Days)	Participants
1	SME Training For The Lab	JIT Coaching	5	Lab Leader I/T Leader I/T Generalist Process Coach Technical Coach (L) Content Expert H/R SME Data Analyst SME
2	Create Working Prototype Development Plan	Work Session	1	Lab Leader I/T Leader I/T Generalist Technical Coach (L) Content Expert H/R SME Data Analyst SME Testing SME
3	QA Review Checkpoint	QA Review	1/2	Lab Leader I/T Leader I/T Generalist Process Coach (L) Technical Coach Content Expert H/R SME Data Analyst SME Testing SME
4	Develop Physical Data Model	Work Product Review	4	Lab Leader I/T Leader I/T Generalist Technical Coach Content Expert H/R SME (L) Data Analyst SME Testing SME
5	Setup Physical Development Environment	Work Product Review	4	Lab Leader I/T Leader I/T Generalist Technical Coach Content Expert H/R SME (L) Data Analyst SME Testing SME
6	Create The Physical Database	Work Product Review	2	Lab Leader I/T Leader I/T Generalist Technical Coach Content Expert H/R SME (L) Data Analyst SME Testing SME

Source: Clelland Johnson

Figure 5-18c

Interventions and Participants H/R and I/T Setup (cont.)				
Intervention	**Activity Description**	**Intervention Type**	**Intervention Duration (Days)**	**Participants**
7	Complete The Data Conversion Plan	Work Product Review	3	Lab Leader I/T Leader I/T Generalist Technical Coach Content Expert H/R SME Data Analyst SME (L) Testing SME
8	Complete Interface/Bridge Development Logic	Work Product Review	5	Lab Leader I/T Leader I/T Generalist Technical Coach Content Expert H/R SME Data Analyst SME Testing SME System Test Coordinator (L)
9	Convert the Concept Prototype Environment	Work Product Review	4	Lab Leader I/T Leader (L) I/T Generalist Technical Coach Content Expert H/R SME Data Analyst SME Testing SME
10	Prepare Change Log For Working Prototype	Work Product Review	1	Lab Leader I/T Leader (L) I/T Generalist Technical Coach Content Expert H/R SME Data Analyst SME Testing SME
11	QA Review Checkpoint	QA Review	1	Lab Leader I/T Leader I/T Generalist Process Coach (L) Technical Coach Content Expert H/R SME Data Analyst SME Testing SME

Source: Clelland Johnson

Figure 5-18d

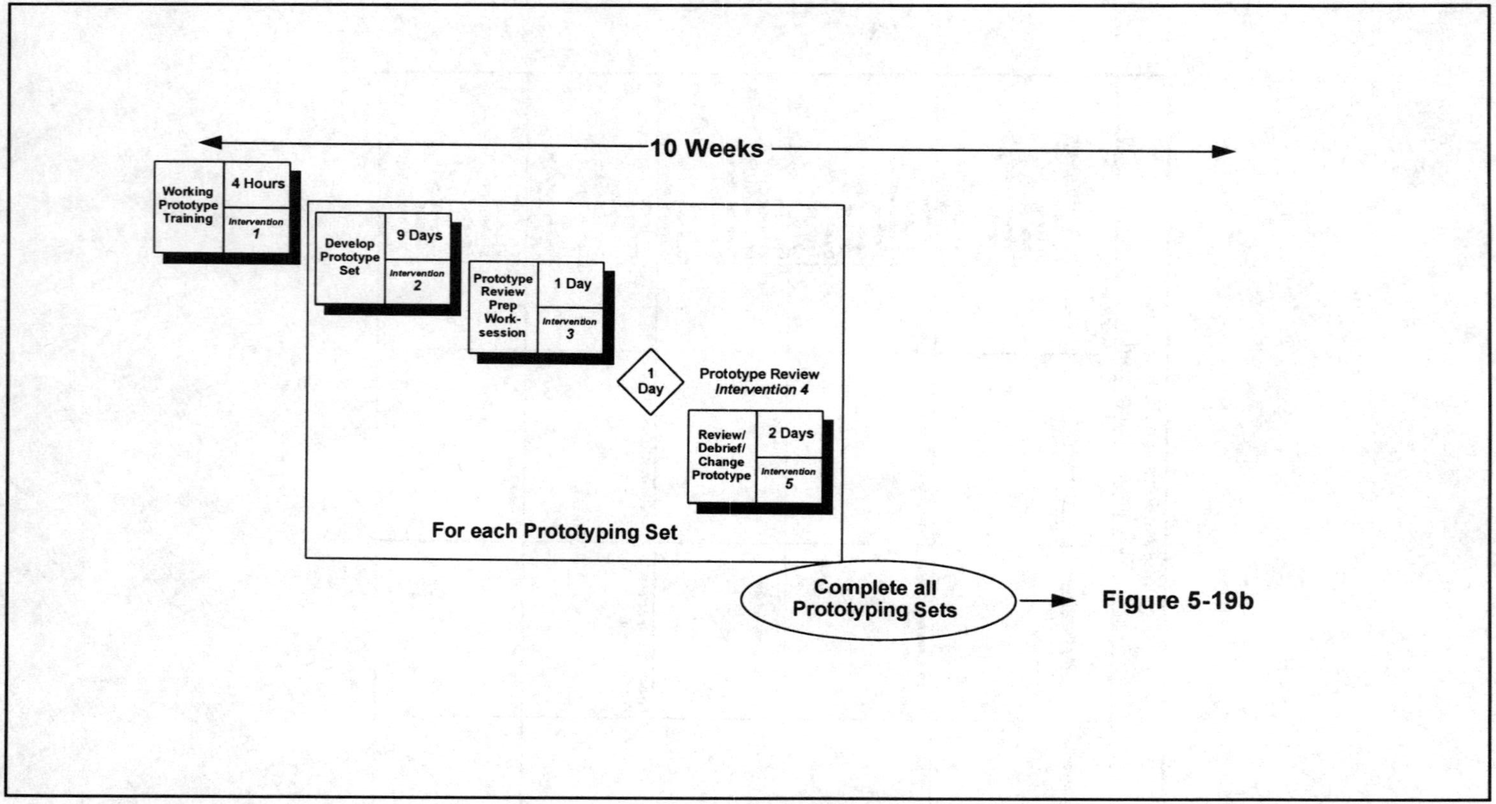

Figure 5-19a Interventions for Working Prototype.

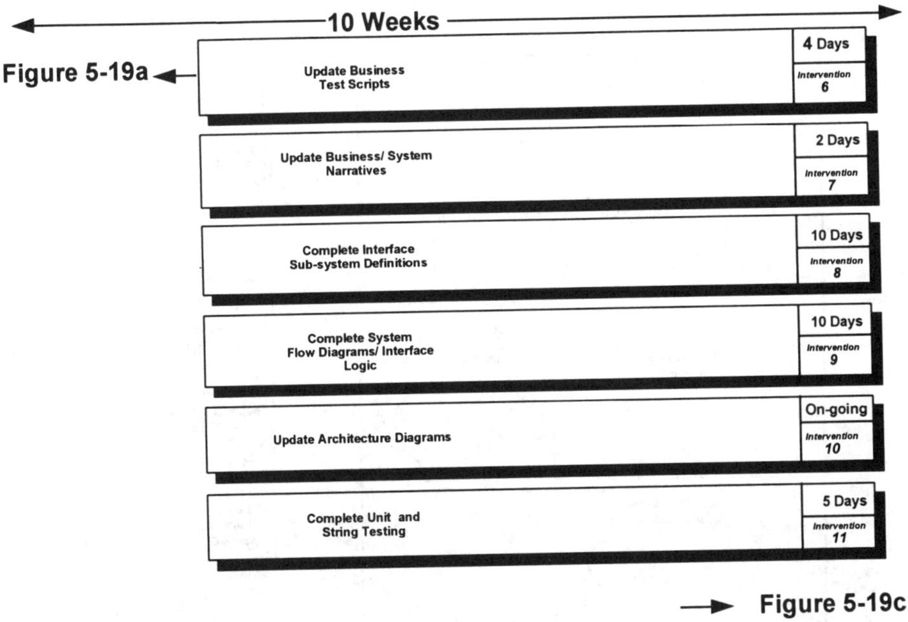

Figure 5-19b Interventions for Working Prototype (cont.).

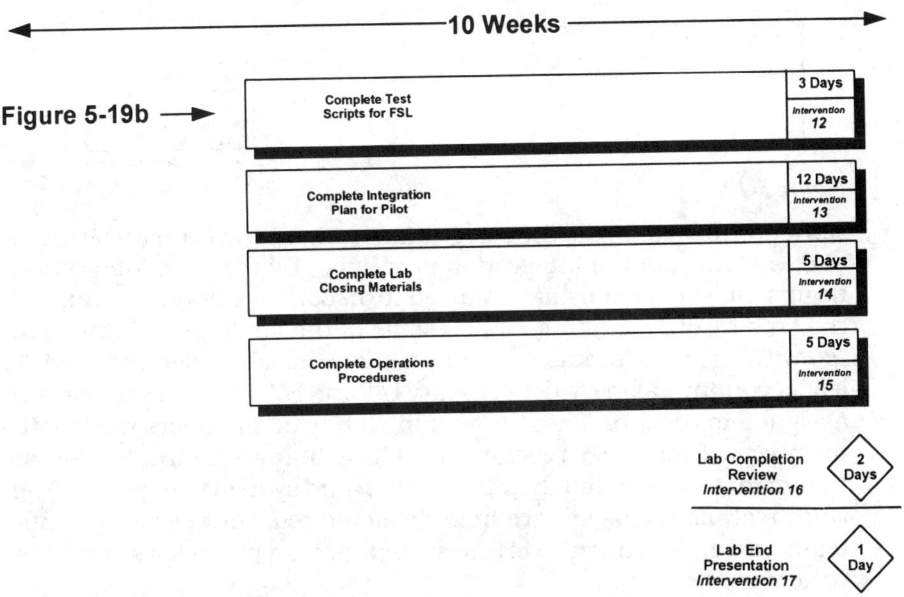

Figure 5-19c Interventions for Working Prototype (cont.).

Interventions and Participants Working Prototype				
Intervention	Activity Description	Intervention Type	Intervention Duration (Days)	Participants
1	Provide Working Prototype Training	JIT coaching	1/2	Lab Leader I/T Leader I/T Generalist Process Coach (L) Technical Coach Content Expert H/R SME Data Analyst SME Testing SME
2	Develop 1st Prototype Sets For Review	Work Product Review	9	Lab Leader I/T Leader I/T Generalist Process Coach (L) Technical Coach Content Expert H/R SME Data Analyst SME Testing SME
3	Prototype Review Preparations	Work Session	1	Lab Leader I/T Leader I/T Generalist Technical Coach (L) Content Expert H/R SME Data Analyst SME Testing SME
4	1st Working Prototype Business Partner and Quality Review	Work Product Review	1	Lab Leader I/T Leader I/T Generalist Process Coach (L) Technical Coach Content Expert H/R SME Data Analyst SME Testing SME
5	Prototype Review Debriefing & Changes	Work Session	2	Lab Leader I/T Leader I/T Generalist Technical Coach (L) Content Expert H/R SME Data Analyst SME Testing SME
2	Develop 2nd Prototype Sets For Review	Work Product Review	9	Lab Leader I/T Leader I/T Generalist Technical Coach (L) Content Expert H/R SME Data Analyst SME Testing SME

Source: Clelland Johnson

Figure 5-19d

work products to make the integration work, so the primary outputs of this phase are the integration products. By the time integration begins, most lab teams have started to disband; however, because of the flow-through staffing model, some of the lab team continues to "go with the lab's product." In particular, the lab leader and the I/T leader continue along with necessary I/T and H/R specialists who are assigned to the lab. These remaining lab team members work with members of the other reengineering labs that are in integration at that point to sort out all their integration and system test issues. The work techniques used here include facilitated work sessions, subteam and independent work sessions, prototype reviews, and QA reviews.

Coincident with these interventions being conducted by SMEs, the SMEs are concurrently carrying out a series of activities that

Interventions and Participants Working Prototype (cont.)				
Intervention	**Activity Description**	**Intervention Type**	**Intervention Duration (Days)**	**Participants**
3	Prototype Review Preparations	Work Session	1	Lab Leader I/T Leader (L) I/T Generalist Technical Coach Content Expert H/R SME Data Analyst SME Testing SME
4	2nd Working Prototype Business Partner and Quality Review	Work Product Review	1	Lab Leader I/T Leader (L) I/T Generalist Technical Coach Content Expert H/R SME Data Analyst SME Testing SME
5	Prototype Review Debriefing & Changes	Work Session	2	Lab Leader (L) I/T Leader I/T Generalist Technical Coach Content Expert H/R SME Data Analyst SME Testing SME
2	Develop 3rd Prototype Sets For Review	Work Product Review	9	Lab Leader I/T Leader (L) I/T Generalist Technical Coach Content Expert H/R SME Data Analyst SME Testing SME
3	Prototype Review Preparations	Work Session	1	Lab Leader (L) I/T Leader (L) I/T Generalist Technical Coach Content Expert H/R SME Data Analyst SME Testing SME
4	3rd Working Prototype Business Partner and Quality Review	Work Product Review	1	Lab Leader (L) I/T Leader I/T Generalist Technical Coach Content Expert H/R SME Data Analyst SME Testing SME
5	Prototype Review Debriefing & Changes	Work Session	2	Lab Leader (L) I/T Leader (L) I/T Generalist Technical Coach Content Expert H/R SME Data Analyst SME Testing SME

Source: Clelland Johnson

Figure 5-19e

ensure coordination and integration among reengineering labs, among business process families, and between reengineering labs and support organizations: MIS, H/R, et al.

I/T Integration Manager and the I/T Integration Process

One premise of successful I/T integration is that business process redesigns are sufficiently detailed to ensure there are no overlaps or gaps between process families nor between labs. This will

Interventions and Participants Working Prototype (cont.)				
Intervention	Activity Description	Intervention Type	Intervention Duration (Days)	Participants
6	Business Test Script Development	Work Product Review	4	Lab Leader (L) I/T Leader I/T Generalist Technical Coach Content Expert H/R SME Data Analyst SME Testing SME
7	System & Business Narrative Updates	Work Product Review	2	Lab Leader I/T Leader (L) I/T Generalist Technical Coach Content Expert H/R SME Data Analyst SME Testing SME
8	Complete Interface Subsystem Definitions	Work Product Review	10	Lab Leader I/T Leader (L) I/T Generalist Technical Coach Content Expert H/R SME Data Analyst SME Testing SME
9	Complete System Flow Dialogues and Interface Logic	Work Product Review	10	Lab Leader I/T Leader (L) I/T Generalist Technical Coach Content Expert H/R SME Data Analyst SME Testing SME
10	Update Architecture Diagram	Work Product Review	30	Lab Leader I/T Leader (L) I/T Generalist Technical Coach Content Expert H/R SME Data Analyst SME Testing SME
11	Lab Unit, String, and System Testing	Work Product Review	5	Lab Leader I/T Leader I/T Generalist Technical Coach Content Expert H/R SME Data Analyst SME Testing SME

Source: Clelland Johnson

Figure 5-19e (contd)

produce the other advantage that the redesigns will be detailed enough for the reengineering labs to understand their scopes and create their deliverables for all points of the diamond. Likewise, process and system narratives must be detailed enough for training programs to be developed. And, working prototype H/R deliverables, such as end-state organizational structures and compensation plans must be detailed enough for the organizational change program for the pilot sites to be completed.

I/T Integration within the context of reengineering integration is the on-going conversation between the labs, process family management teams, MIS and I/T Critical Programs management, architecture teams, and reengineering project management team. It is used to provide the reengineering labs with context and standards for their work and to integrate and optimize the deliverables of the reengineering labs and the MIS organizations providing support or infrastructure for the reengineering labs.

Interventions and Participants Working Prototype (cont.)				
Intervention	Activity Description	Intervention Type	Intervention Duration (Days)	Participants
12	Test Scripts For the Integration and System Test	Work Product Review	3	Lab Leader I/T Leader I/T Generalist Technical Coach Content Expert H/R SME Data Analyst SME Testing SME System Test Coordinator (L)
13	Integration Plan For Applications, Data, and Subsystems For Pilot Test	Work Product Review	12	Lab Leader I/T Leader I/T Generalist Technical Coach Content Expert H/R SME Data Analyst SME Testing SME I/T Integration Manager (L)
14	Lab Closing Materials	Work Product Review	5	Lab Leader (L) I/T Leader I/T Generalist Technical Coach Content Expert H/R SME Data Analyst SME Testing SME
15	Operational Procedures	Work Product Review	5	Lab Leader I/T Leader (L) I/T Generalist Technical Coach Content Expert H/R SME Data Analyst SME Testing SME
16	QA Review Checkpoint	QA Review	2	Lab Leader I/T Leader I/T Generalist Process Coach (L) Technical Coach Content Expert H/R SME Data Analyst SME Testing SME
17	End Of Lab Presentation	Work Session	1	Lab Leader (L) I/T Leader I/T Generalist Technical Coach Content Expert H/R SME Data Analyst SME Testing SME

Source: Clelland Johnson

Figure 5-19f

There are a number of new roles required for I/T integration. These roles are interrelated as depicted in Figure 5-21. This is one example of these roles and their responsibilities:

- Lab Technologist
- Process Family Data Analyst and Database SMEs
- I/T Integration Manager
- Other SMEs
- Architects (Chief Architect, Process Architect, Information Architect, Applications Architect, Applications Development Environment Architect, and Process Family Architect)

Lab Technologist

The lab technologist is the MIS staff member assigned to the lab to create the majority of the I/T lab products. As a result of hands-

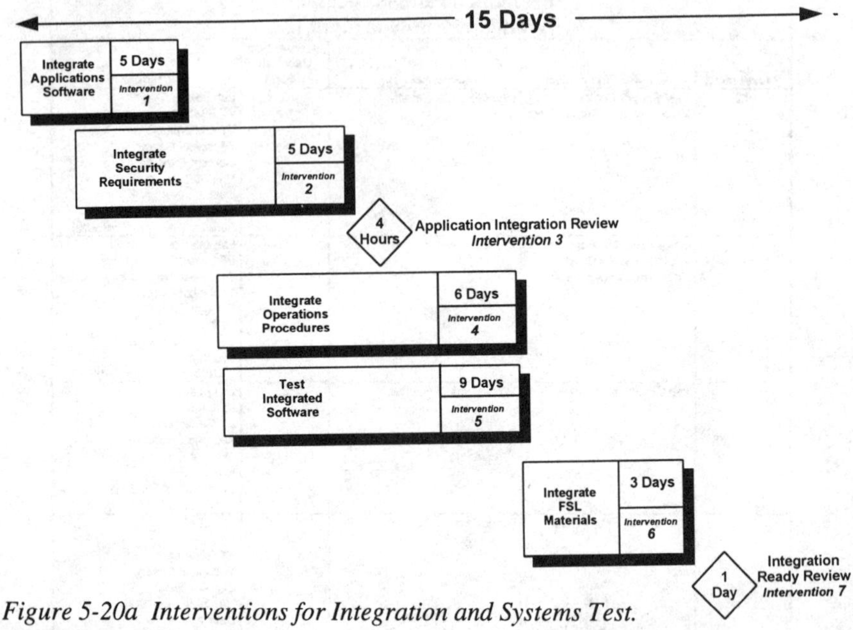

Figure 5-20a Interventions for Integration and Systems Test.

on knowledge of the I/T activities and deliverables, the technologist is in the best position to manage I/T integration issues in the lab. The I/T integration responsibilities of the lab technologist include:

- Continuously identify integration issues, assumptions, and risks, particularly focusing on triggers and outcomes that extend outside the lab and on interfaces, interdependencies, and overlaps.
- Raise integration issues, assumptions, and risks to the process family I/T integration manager, appropriate SMEs and Coaches, and the process family management team, as necessary.
- Review and update integration management tools as requested by SMEs and Coaches, e.g., CRUD matrices, applications architecture diagrams, etc.
- Design and create interfaces to other reengineering lab applications and to legacy systems (in conjunction with the appropriate technologists from other reengineering labs or the appropriate Legacy SMEs).

Process Family Data Analyst SME and Database SME

The Process Family Data Analyst and Database SMEs are responsible for the logical and physical designs, respectively, of the databases needed for the lab. They are also responsible to ensure that these logical and physical designs are consistent with the enterprise's overall logical and physical database designs and that

Interventions and Participants Integration and Systems Testing				
Intervention	Activity Description	Intervention Type	Intervention Duration (Days)	Participants
1	Integration Of Process Work Session	Work Session	5	Lab Leader I/T Leader (L) I/T Generalist Process Coach Technical Coach Content Expert H/R SME Data Analyst SME Testing SME I/T Integration Manager (L)
2	Security Integration Work Session	Work Session	3	Lab Leader I/T Leader (L) I/T Generalist Process Coach Technical Coach Content Expert H/R SME Data Analyst SME Testing SME I/T Integration Manager (L)
3	QA Review Checkpoint	QA Review	1/2	Lab Leader I/T Leader (L) I/T Generalist Process Coach (L) Technical Coach Content Expert H/R SME Data Analyst SME Testing SME I/T Integration Manager (L)
4	Integrate Operational Procedures Work Session	Work Session	6	Lab Leader I/T Leader (L) I/T Generalist Process Coach Technical Coach Content Expert H/R SME Data Analyst SME Testing SME I/T Integration Manager (L)
5	Test Integrated Software	Work Product Review	9	Lab Leader I/T Leader (L) I/T Generalist Process Coach Technical Coach Content Expert H/R SME Data Analyst SME Testing SME I/T Integration Manager (L)

Source: Clelland Johnson

Figure 5-20b

Interventions and Participants Integration and Systems Testing (cont.)				
Intervention	Activity Description	Intervention Type	Intervention Duration (Days)	Participants
6	Consolidate Integration and System Testing Materials Work Session	Work Session	3	Lab Leader I/T Leader (L) I/T Generalist Process Coach Technical Coach Content Expert H/R SME Data Analyst SME Testing SME I/T Integration Manager (L)
7	QA Review Checkpoint – Integration Ready	QA Review	1	Lab Leader I/T Leader I/T Generalist Process Coach (L) Technical Coach Content Expert H/R SME Data Analyst SME Testing SME I/T Integration Manager (L)

Source: Clelland Johnson

Figure 5-20c

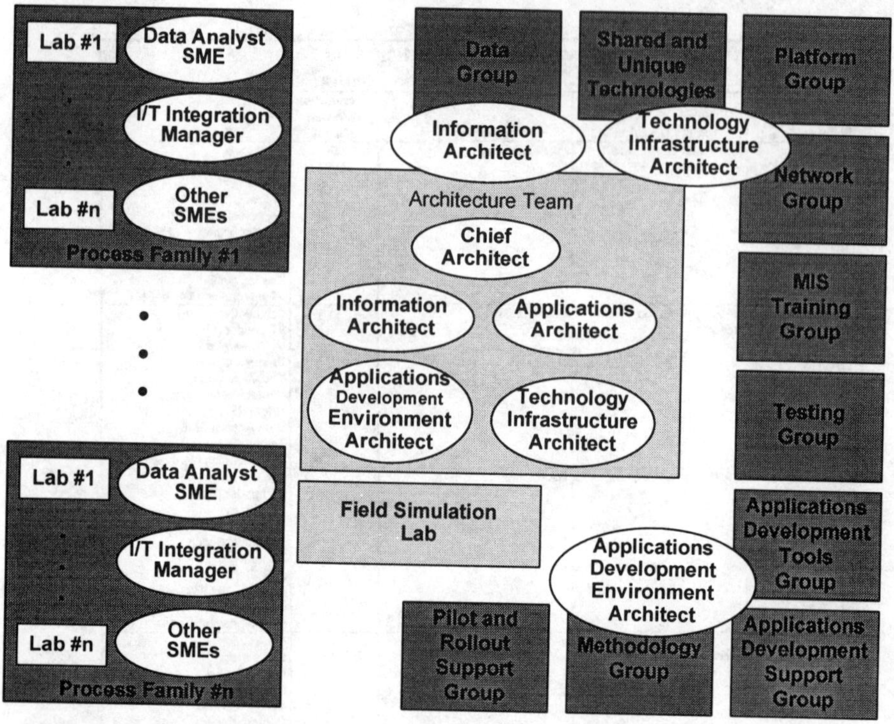

Figure 5-21 Integration Process Roles

gaps or overlaps between the reengineering labs in the SME's process family and other reengineering labs or legacy systems are identified and appropriately managed. The specific responsibilities of these SMEs related to the I/T integration process include:

- Identify and raise data integration issues, assumptions, and risks within and among process families.
- Present and explain enterprise-wide logical database and physical database context and how the lab's work is related to it.
- Support the Lab Technologists who are developing lab logical and physical database designs and identify gaps and overlaps with other reengineering labs and with legacy systems.

I/T Integration Manager

The I/T Integration Manager is the member of the process family management team who is ultimately responsible for all I/T work products from all the reengineering labs in the process family and is the direct link between Lab Technologists and the MIS organization. The role ranges from coach/mentor, to planner, to worker. The specific responsibilities related to I/T integration include:

- Identify, assess, and resolve I/T integration issues, assumptions,

and risks within the process family.
- Identify and raise I/T integration issues, assumptions, and risks among process families and between the process family and I/T Critical Programs.
- Plan lab events, integration testing, and I/T requirements over time, and ensure completion.
- Ensure reengineering lab work is consistent with the MIS architectural direction, or that the MIS architecture is modified to accommodate process family requirements.
- Ensure test, target, and production environments are prepared to provide the appropriate capability in the appropriate timeframe.
- Update and maintain release plans, and other integration management tools for all process family systems, databases, locations, pilot tests, and rollouts.
- Participate in all prototype reviews within the process family to identify gaps and overlaps among the lab teams within the process family.
- Develop, in conjunction with the lab leader, the training program to enable the technologists in the lab to work effectively with the appropriate software and hardware tools and technology intended for lab use.
- Assist the lab leader in planning and intermittent resource scheduling of I/T resources in the reengineering lab, i.e., SMEs.
- Meet regularly with representatives from other lab teams to discuss and resolve inter-reengineering lab and inter-process family issues.
- Coordinate the needs of the lab team with the overall plans and direction of MIS.

Architects

The architecture teams, including the Chief Architect, Process Architect, Information Architect, Applications Architect, Applications Development Environment Architect, and Technology Infrastructure Architect and the MIS resources they control or influence have integration responsibilities, as well. These include:

- Identify a single team responsible for defining, evolving, and communicating an enterprise architectural vision that includes the migration from the existing architecture.
- Ensure I/T architectural decisions take into account all architectural components.
- Eliminate confusion and wasted time spent searching for and assigning the right MIS resources to resolve issues.
- Ensure process family I/T issues are raised, resolved, and integrated with issues raised by other process families.

Along with these general responsibilities, each architect has other responsibilities for I/T integration:

The Chief Architect's I/T integration responsibilities include:

- Arbitrate and resolve I/T integration issues, assumptions, and risks with the I/T Integration Managers, Inter-Process Integration Managers, and architecture teams.
- Arbitrate and resolve architectural issues and decisions among process, information, applications, applications development environment, and infrastructure architectures.
- Be on the look out for integration issues, assumptions, and risks within a process family, among process families, and between a process family and I/T Critical Programs.
- Provide support to the reengineering labs by providing an overall architecture that accommodates lab requirements, providing consulting on the use of the architectures and other technologies.
- Identify architectural changes required to support the reengineering effort.

The responsibilities of the Information Architect include:

- Create, evolve, and maintain the data distribution strategy, the overall data architecture for new and legacy systems, and information policies.
- With the Applications Development Environment Architect, define components of the applications development environment (applications development tools, techniques, methodologies, standards, rules, and guidelines) that apply to information management and access.
- Be on the look out for integration issues, assumptions, and risks within a process family, among process families, and between a process family and I/T Critical Programs.
- With the I/T Integration Managers, Data Analyst SMEs, and Database SMEs resolve logical and physical data integration issues.

The I/T integration responsibilities assigned to the Applications Architect include:

- Define and maintain the applications architecture of new and legacy systems.
- Understand application system process flows and functionality, and identify integration opportunities, assumptions, issues, and risks for all new and legacy systems.
- Be on the look out for integration issues, assumptions, and risks within a process family, among process families, and between a process family and I/T Critical Programs.
- Provide support to reengineering labs in developing bridge and conversion routines.

The I/T integration responsibilities for the Applications Development Environment Architect include:

- Define the applications development environment of applications develop tools, techniques, standards, rules, and guidelines.
- Define common objects and middleware for use during applications development.
- Be on the look out for integration issues, assumptions, and risks within a process family, among process families, and between a process family and I/T Critical Programs.

The I/T integration responsibilities for the Technology Infrastructure Architect include:

- Create, evolve, and maintain the overall technology infrastructure architecture (hardware platforms, operating systems, systems software, utility software, and networking) for new and legacy systems.
- With the Application Development Environment Architect, define components of the applications development environment (applications development tools, techniques, methodologies, standards, rules, and guidelines) that apply to application program interfaces (APIs), application messaging, and process-to-process communications.
- Be on the look out for integration issues, assumptions, and risks within a process family, among process families, and between a process family and I/T Critical Programs.
- Provide support to reengineering labs by providing a technology infrastructure architecture that accommodates lab requirements, provide consulting on the use of the infrastructure portions of the applications development environment, understand the technology requirements of the labs, introduce new technologies into reengineering designs, and provide Technology SMEs to consult on shared and unique technologies.

With these I/T integration roles and responsibilities defined, the next step is to create a process and system of formal and informal communications that those responsible for integration can use to ensure issues are identified and resolved. One example of these communication processes is:

- Reengineering lab team members, including lab leader, lab I/T leader, and technologists, communicate primarily with their process family I/T integration manager, Data Analyst SME, Database SME, Process Coach, and Technical Coach through ad hoc meetings and communications and during scheduled interventions.
- I/T integration managers communicate with architects and I/T

integration managers from other process families through informal communications and during Integration Days. I/T integration days are for I/T integration managers, inter-process integration managers, architecture teams, and other SMEs, as needed.
- Data Analyst SMEs, Database SMEs, Process Coaches, Technical Coaches, and all other SMEs communicate with their counterparts in other process families informally and at regularly scheduled (weekly or more frequent) team meetings of SMEs or Coaches, e.g., data group meetings.

Integration Processes

Every reengineering project must have an established overall reengineering project management resource with tools for project tracking, budget management, issue identification, and staffing planning. The project management team will be concerned with a number of aspects of the overall reengineering effort. In particular, they will be held responsible for ensuring that the business case achievement including benefits stream, timeframe, and estimated costs, are monitored and reported to the reengineering sponsor and the managers of the various reengineering teams. To accomplish this, the team uses traditional project management tools and techniques and focuses on risk management, issues management, integration management, scope management, implementation coordination, and outcome (or work product) quality assurance.

Issues Management

Issues will arise on every project and because reengineering is so large, so fast, and so cross-functional, issues on reengineering projects are more numerous, more complex, and (potentially) more deadly than on other projects. For purposes of this discussion, issues management includes:

- Capturing issues and assumptions that come up in the reengineering labs.
- Capturing issues and assumptions that come up apart from reengineering labs that affect the labs' scopes, schedules, resources, or integration points.
- Raising, consolidating, and resolving issues promptly to minimize the impact on reengineering labs' schedules and scopes.
- Ensuring issues do not fall through the cracks.
- Ensuring participation and agreement of correct decision-makers in issue resolution.

Issues can be resolved within the reengineering lab, within the business process family, between the reengineering lab and a support organization, or at a higher level, i.e., the reengineering sponsor. As a result, issues must be captured, assigned, tracked, and, ultimately, resolved to the satisfaction of all parties concerned.

The process for issues management begins with the lab team faithfully identifying and capturing all issues, assigning the issue to someone for resolution with a date when resolution is required, and following up to ensure the issue is resolved when needed. Since some issues (mostly integration and scope issues) must be resolved outside the reengineering lab, these issues may be assigned to a SME or to the lab leader for resolution. In these cases, the SME or lab leader is responsible for understanding the issue, knowing the ramifications for the lab team of the possible resolutions of the issue, and knowing with whom the issue must be resolved. They then take the issue to resolve with the outside party and report to the lab team at the agreed time.

Depending on the size of the reengineering implementation effort, an automated tool for capturing and tracking issues may be used. In fact, in all but the smallest efforts, the number of issues that cannot be resolved within the reengineering lab and the number of integration points are such that some form of automation is demanded. This could take the form of a spreadsheet or a database system, but, in any event, it must be tracked and managed, and that means this is not an optional exercise for the reengineering lab and SMEs, and it means that some amount of human resource is required to keep abreast of all the issues, their due dates, and their resolutions, and to communicate the resolutions to all parties affected by the decisions.

Integration Management

Integration Management refers to the coordination and interplay among all the business processes that are being redesigned as part of the reengineering project and between new redesigned business processes and existing, or legacy, business processes. Integration management is discussed previously in I/T integration management and includes:

- Ensuring scope integration among reengineering processes, and among reengineering labs.
- Ensuring technology usage integration for shared and unique technologies among reengineering labs.
- Ensuring new applications fit in the applications architecture and are properly integrated with other reengineering labs' applications, by release.
- Ensuring new applications are properly integrated with legacy applications, by release.
- Ensuring content of releases is coordinated among reengineering

labs and between reengineering labs and legacy applications support.

Integration Days are the primary mechanism for ensuring integration of various content points and schedules. These are necessary meetings for every level in a reengineering project. They include all integration meetings including those used to resolve issues among process family leaders all the way to those used to resolve issues among groups of content experts and SMEs. Potentially, a project could have Integration Days for all of these principle areas of integration:

- Integration among the reengineering lab's business process redesign and all other business processes whether they are being redesigned or not.
- Integration among the H/R changes that will result from the reengineering lab's business process redesign and other H/R changes planned for the current or a future release, e.g., it would be unfortunate if the employee population expected to carry out the redesigned business process was redesigned out of existence by another reengineering lab.
- Integration among the applications to be created by the reengineering lab and the applications being created by all other reengineering labs for this release, the applications being created by reengineering labs for future releases, the applications being created independently of the reengineering effort.
- Integration among the applications to be created by the reengineering lab and the "then current" state of all legacy applications affected by this application. It is also instrumental to know the future plans for all affected legacy applications to ensure the long-term viability of the redesigned business process.

Scope Management

Reengineering lab scope must be managed very tightly against the end-state and interim-state designs, the overall schedule, and the process families' objectives. Reengineering labs are there to create the deliverables that will enable the business process redesign for all points of the reengineering diamond, not to redesign the redesign. Scope management includes:

- Ensuring that the reengineering lab has a definite scope that is agreed to by the lab leader, the lab team members, the process family leader, other reengineering labs, release coordinators, and the reengineering project sponsor.
- Identifying and coordinating the trade-offs among reengineering labs for changes in scope.

Implementation Coordination

"Enterprise" implementation integration needs to be owned by someone for all points of the diamond and with sufficient resources to accomplish the task. Responsibilities included in implementation coordination are:

- Identifying, early in the reengineering process, the long lead time items required for implementation in the pilot test sites.
- Maintaining a constant focus on the implementability of the reengineering solution.
- Selecting, or recommending, sites for pilot testing the reengineering solution.

Implementation Coordination is accomplished by integrating the planning activities for three project time slices: implementation at the end of construction of working prototype, pilot implementation, and rollout implementation. For implementation at the end of construction, the planning activities include:

- Development and maintenance of integrated roadmap
- End-state vision and interim-state integrated pictures among processes and for all points of the diamond
- Final integration of operational releases for all points of the diamond
- Final integration and testing of training, by release and by stakeholder
- System testing of all systems and all integrations among new and legacy
- Design of pilot monitoring and measuring mechanisms
- Change control decisions while release is in pilot

Planning activities related to pilot implementation include:

- Pilot site assessment
- Pilot site preparation for all points of the diamond
- Organizational change and communications programs for pilot sites.
- Pilot launch and monitoring
- Help Desk support for pilot sites

Planning activities for rollout implementation include:

- Development and updates to the reengineering business cases
- Organizational change and communications programs for national

rollout
- Labor contracts and H/R readiness
- End-state I/T architectures
- Rollout schedules and resource planning
- On-going MIS and Help Desk support

Legacy Integration Process

Legacy integration is one of the most perilous problems to be tackled in the reengineering effort. Every enterprise has manual or automated processes and systems that will not go away just because reengineering is happening. Often times the Strategic Information Asset Management Process Model is used to assess and gather information necessary for legacy integration, replacement and management (Figure 5-22). As a result, the reengineering teams' designs and work products will have to be integrated with whatever legacy systems exist. Here is one successful approach to legacy integration.

The initial step is to identify the requirements for the information as depicted in Figure 5-23. First, the requesting lab technologist defines, in as much detail as possible, the data element requirements, including the description of the data element, the business rules for the data element, the frequency and currency of the data element, and the timeframe in which the data element is required.

Next, the requesting Data Analyst SME determines the source of the required data element. The options could include:

- In the requesting lab
- In the requesting Process Family
- In another Process Family (relational database)
- In another Process Family (non-relational database or package software)
- In a legacy system
- A new data element

If the source is the requesting lab or process family, Figure 5-24, the requesting lab leader confirms the requirements (schedule and definition) for the data element with the process family Data Analyst SME and if necessary the sourcing lab leader.

Next, the sourcing lab leader determines, with the requesting lab leader and the process family Data Analyst SME, whether the requirements for the data element will be satisfied by the sourcing lab. If not, the lab leader negotiates the definition of the data element. The lab leader determines, with the requesting lab leader and the process family Data Analyst SME, the scheduled availability for the data element. If the sourcing lab's schedule does not match the requesting lab's schedule, the lab leader negotiates the schedule.

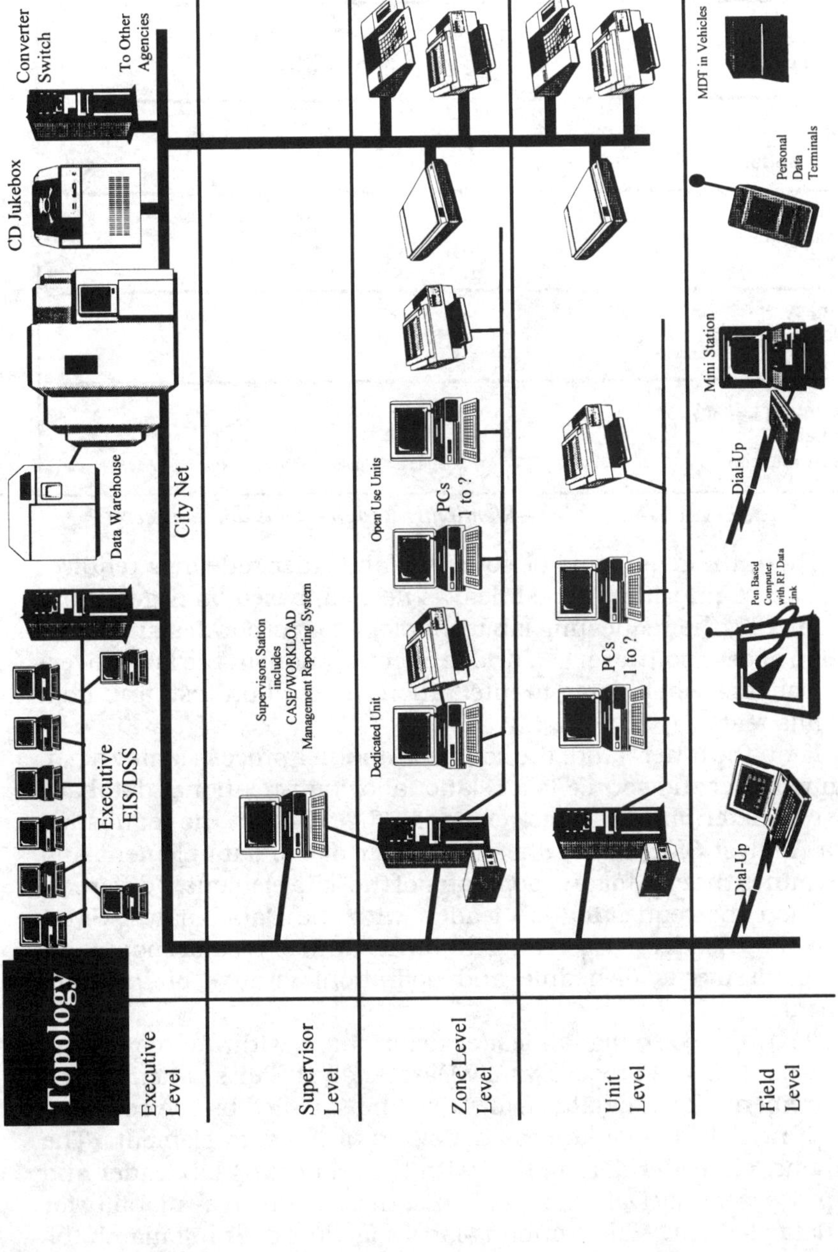

Figure 5-22 Deliverables

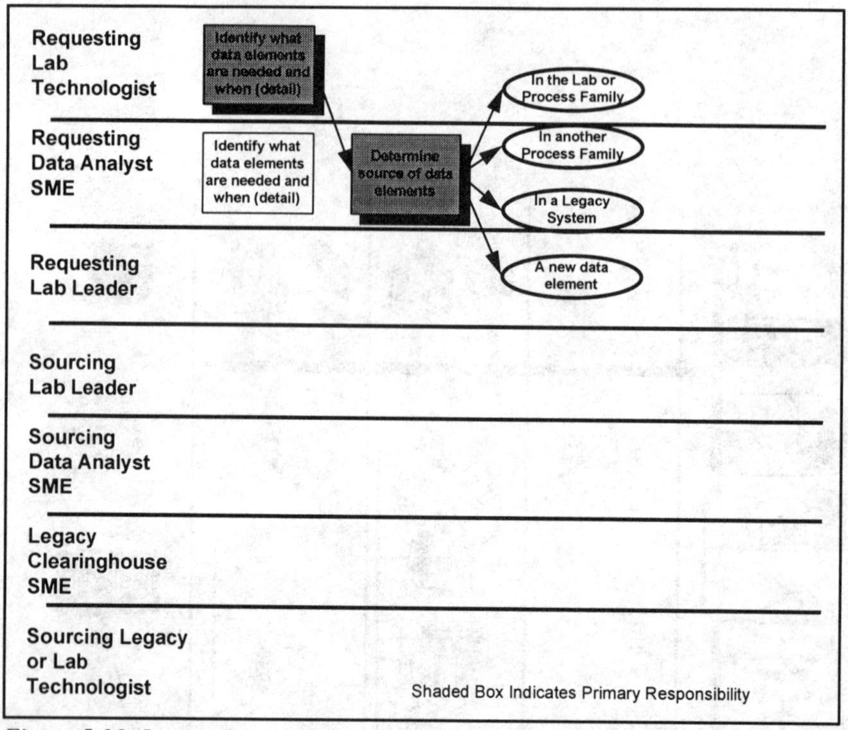

Figure 5-23: Legacy Integration—Identifying Requirements and Sources

Then, the requesting or sourcing lab leader redefines requirements or re-prioritizes schedules, as needed, based on negotiation.

Finally, the requesting lab technologist incorporates any information access software, i.e., bridge or conversion, in the lab deliverable package when going to integration, integration test, and final systems test.

If, on the other hand, the source is another process family's lab, then whether the source is a relational or non-relational database must be determined. If it is relational, Figure 5-25, the requesting Data Analyst SME determines the owner of the data element and determines the creator and populator of the data element, if different.

Then the requesting lab leader, with the Data Analyst SME, gives the lab leader representing the owner and/or creator/populator the requirements (schedule and definition) for use of the data element.

Next, the sourcing lab leader determines, with the requesting lab leader and the process family Data Analyst SMEs, whether the requirements for the data element will be satisfied by the sourcing lab. If not, they negotiate the definition of the data element. The sourcing lab leader determines, with the requesting lab leader and the process family Data Analyst SMEs, the scheduled availability for the data element. If the sourcing lab's schedule does not match the requesting lab's schedule, they negotiate the schedule.

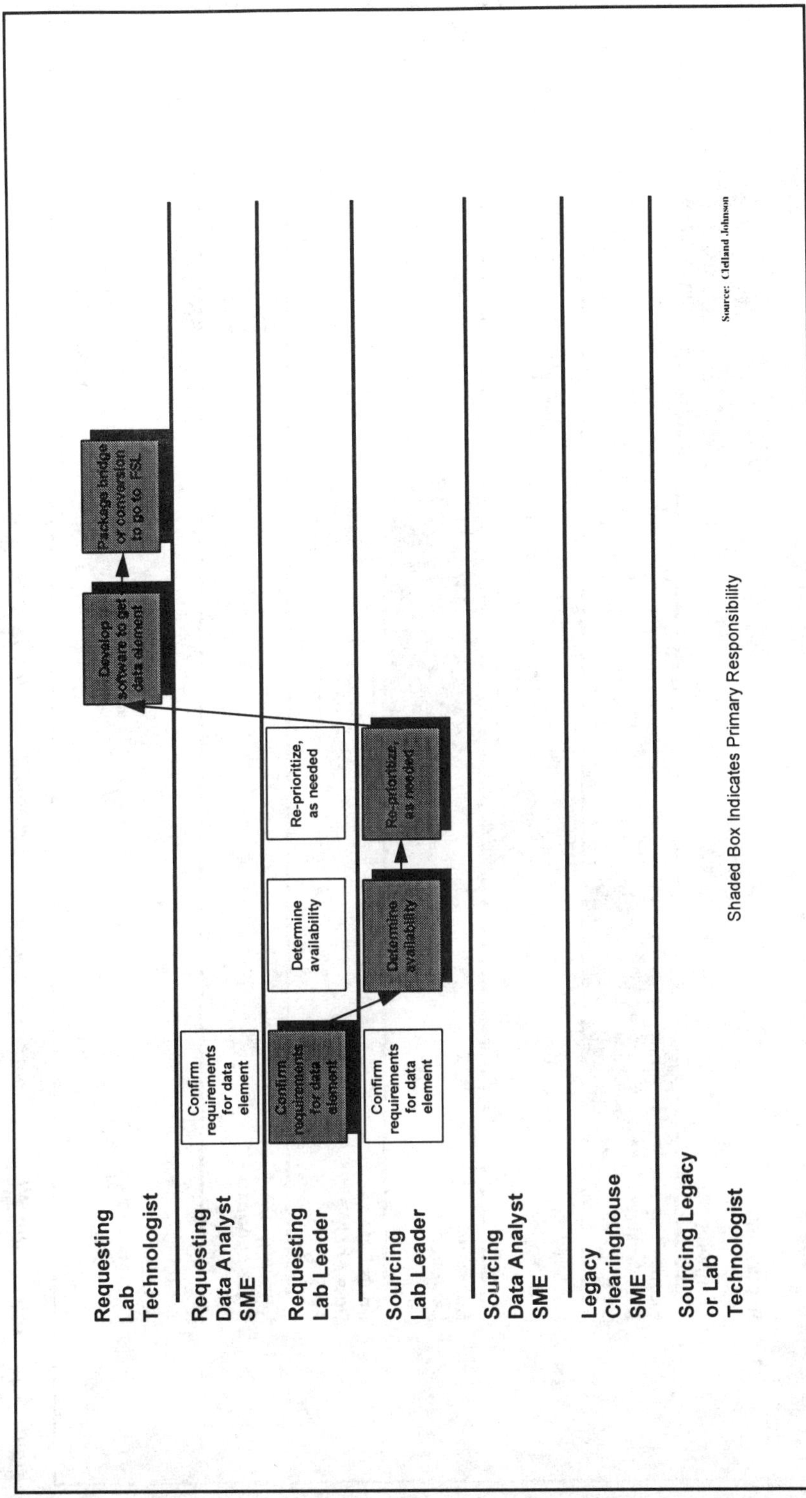

Figure 5-24: Integration When the Source is the Requesting Lab or Process Family

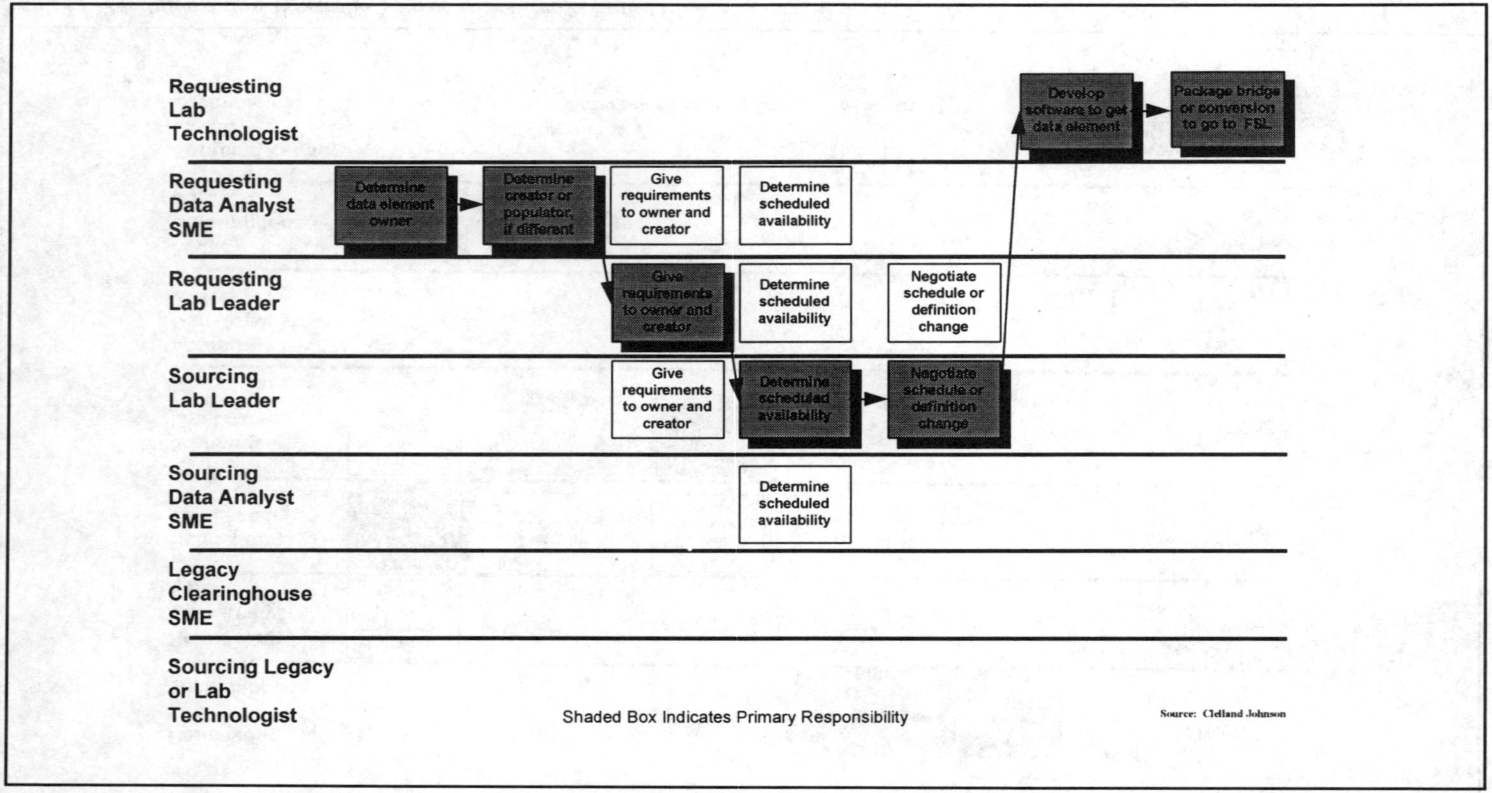

Figure 5-25: Integration When the Source is Another Process Family's Relational Database

Next, the requesting lab technologist develops the software mechanism, e.g., SQL call, to get access to the data element and bring it into the lab's application. Next, the technologist incorporates any information access software, i.e., bridge or conversion, in the lab deliverable package when going to integration and systems test. (Note: Because there is a dependency of one process family on another process family, any changes in the sourcing lab's definition of the data element in question or the scheduled availability of the data element to the requesting lab must be communicated to all concerned (requesting and sourcing I/T integration managers, requesting lab leader, requesting Data Analyst SME, and the Information Data Architect). It is the responsibility of the sourcing lab leader and the sourcing Data Analyst SME to ensure this communication occurs.

Otherwise, if the source is another process family's lab's non-relational database, the sourcing lab must indicate whether the source is temporary or a permanent non-relational data source, Figure 5-26. The requesting Data Analyst SME determines the owner of the data element and determines the creator and populator of the data element, if different.

Next, the requesting lab leader, with the Data Analyst SME, gives the lab leader representing the owner and/or creator/populator the requirements (schedule and definition) for use of the data element.

The sourcing lab leader, in turn, determines if the source system for the data element is a permanent system or a temporary system. A temporary system would be one that is expected to be replaced in a timeframe that would make developing a full-fledged bridge or conversion unacceptable from a cost-to-benefit point of view.

If the source is another process family's lab's non-relational database that is permanent, Figures 5-27a and 5-27b, the sourcing lab leader, if the sourcing system is determined to be a permanent system, determines if the request will best be served through an on-going data bridge or a one-time data conversion. If it is an on-going data bridge, the lab leader determines the on-going cross reference requirements. Once the sourcing system is identified and the determination about the type of bridge or conversion is made, the lab leader determines if any other requests, or expected requests, are of a similar enough nature that this bridge or conversion can become a common object. Next, the lab leader determines, with the requesting lab leader and the process family Data Analyst SME, whether the requirements for the data element will be satisfied by the sourcing lab and what the scheduled availability for the data element is. If the requesting and sourcing reengineering labs do not agree, the lab leaders negotiate the definition and schedule for the data element.

Then, the requesting or sourcing lab leader redefines the requirements or re-prioritizes the schedules, as needed, based on

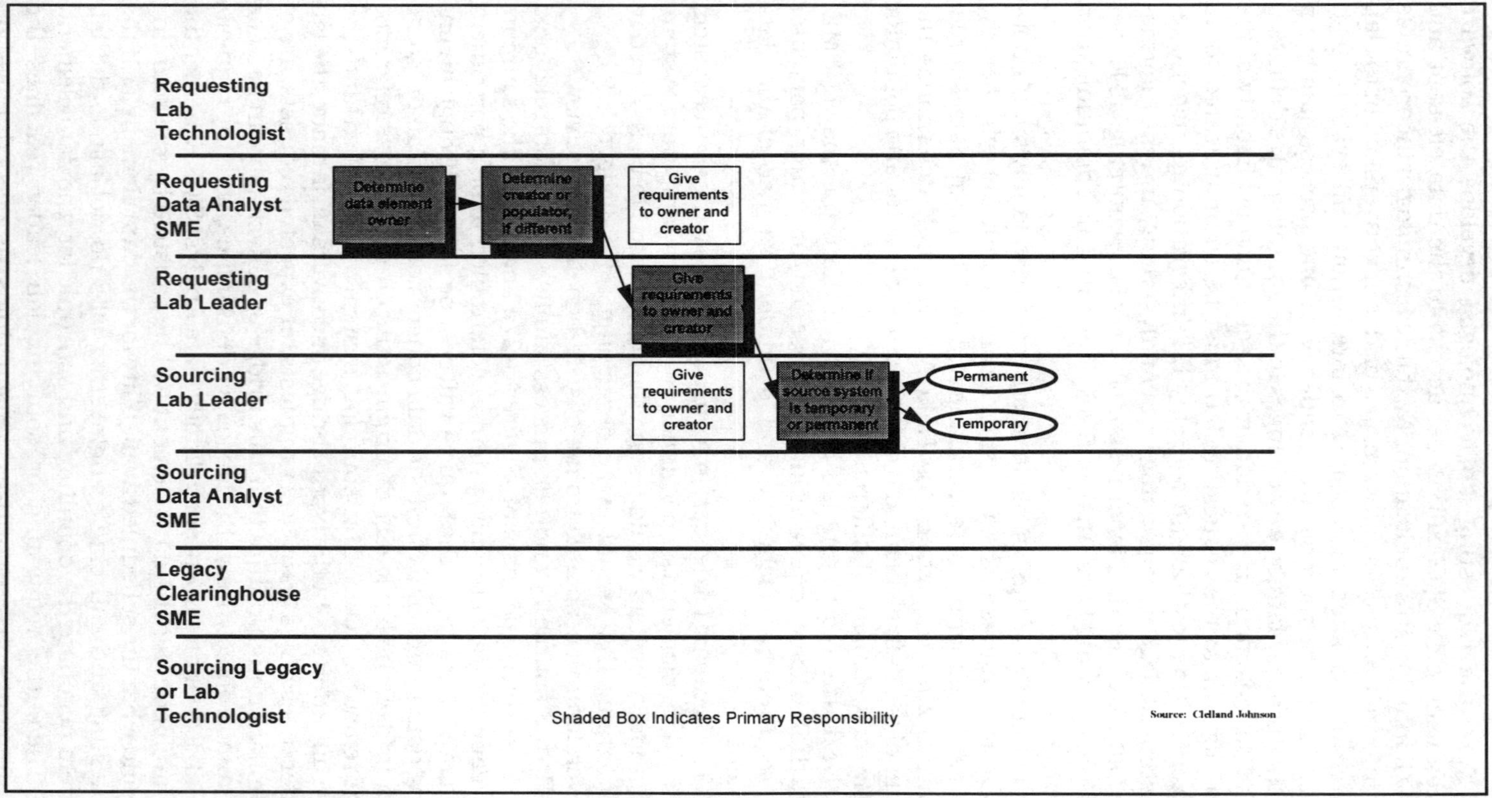

Figure 5-26: Integration When the Source is Another Process Family's Non-Relational Database Source is Permanent or Temporary

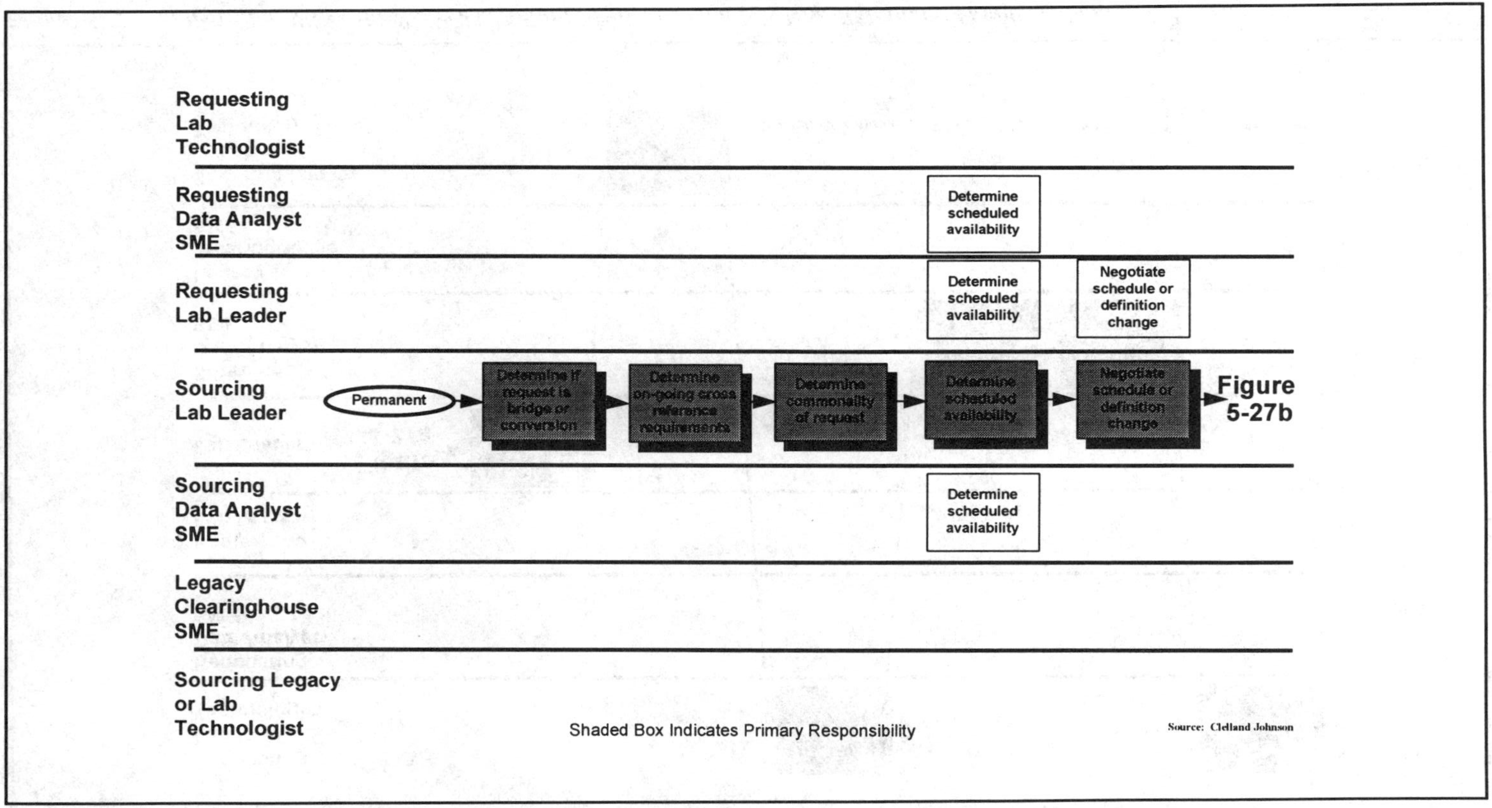

Figure 5-27a: Integration When the Source is Another Process Family's Non-Relational Database -Source is Permanent

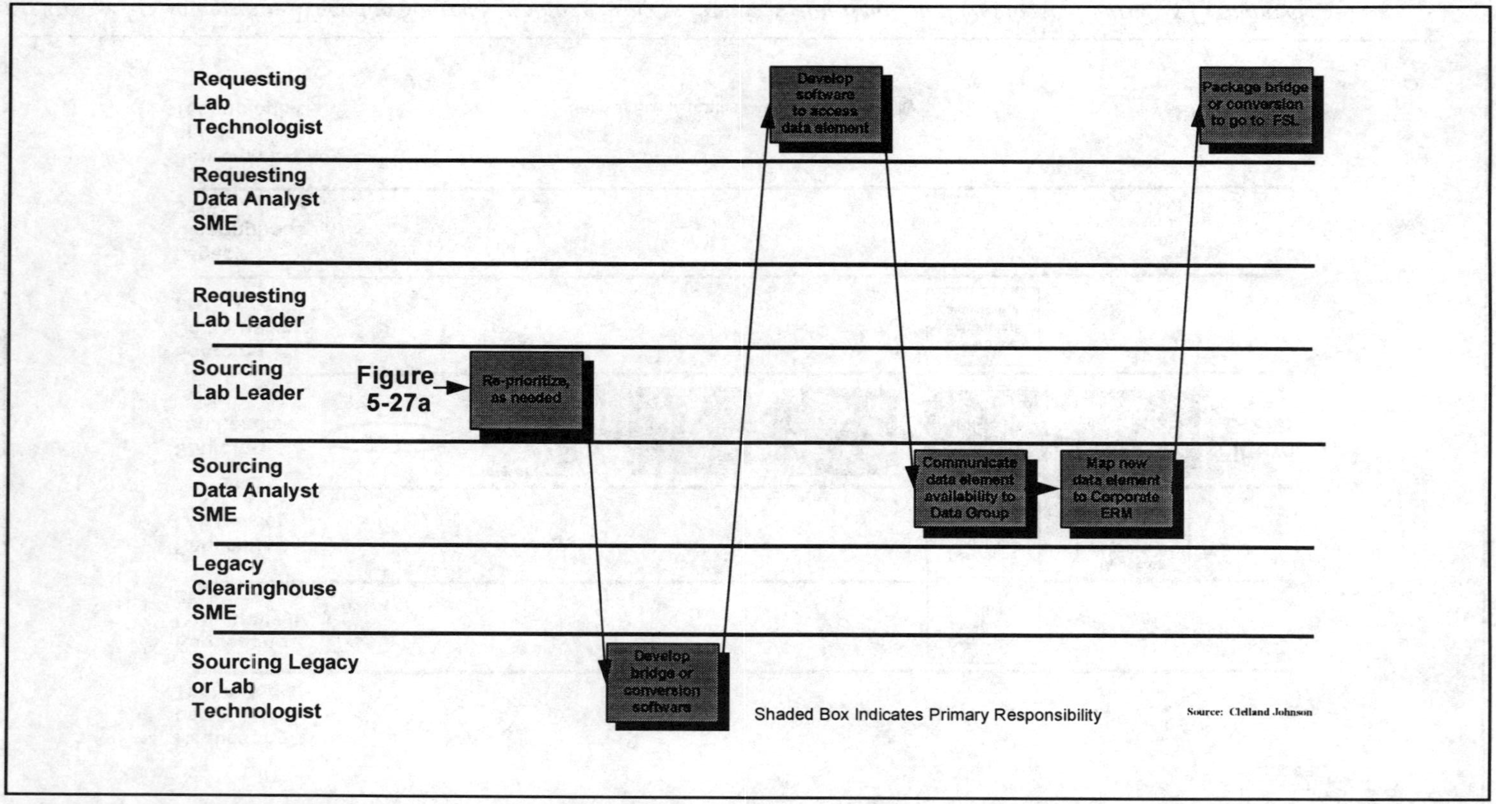

Figure 5-27b: Integration When the Source is Another Process Family's Non-Relational Database-Source is Permanent

negotiation.

Next, the sourcing lab technologist develops the software to accomplish the sourcing portion of bridge or conversion. This could include extracting data from source data store, applying any required cross references or maps to source data, and populating a data store with the data element in "requester-friendly" format. Once tested, the technologist supplies the requesting lab technologist with the software for inclusion with the requesting lab's deliverables.

The requesting lab technologist develops the software mechanism to get access to the data element and bring it into the reengineering lab's application, e.g., SQL or other call.

Next, the sourcing Data Analyst SME communicates data element availability to Information Architect and data group and maps new data element into the Entity Relationship Model (ERM).

The requesting lab technologist then incorporates any information access software, i.e., bridge or conversion, in the lab deliverable package when going to integration and systems test.

If the source is another process family lab's non-relational database that is temporary, Figures 5-28a and 5-28b, the sourcing lab leader, if the sourcing system is determined to be a temporary system, determines if the request will best be served through an on-going data bridge, a one-time data conversion, or some other means, e.g., paper bridge. If it is an on-going data bridge, the lab leader determines the on-going cross reference requirements. Once the sourcing system is identified and the determination about the type of bridge or conversion is made, the lab leader determines if any other requests, or expected requests, are of a similar enough nature that this bridge or conversion can become a common object. Then the lab leader determines, with the requesting lab leader and the Process family Data Analyst SME, whether the requirements for the data element will be satisfied by the sourcing lab and what the scheduled availability for the data element is. If the requesting and sourcing reengineering labs do not agree, the lab leaders negotiate the definition and schedule for the data element.

Then, the requesting or sourcing lab leader redefines requirements or re-prioritizes schedules, as needed, based on negotiation.

Next, the sourcing lab technologist, if an automated bridge or conversion is required, develops software to accomplish sourcing portion of bridge or conversion. This could include extracting data from source data store, applying any required cross references or maps to source data, and populating a data store with the data element in "requester-friendly" format. Once tested, the technologist supplies the requesting lab technologist with the software for inclusion with lab deliverables going to integration and systems test. If a paper bridge or conversion, the technologist defines the process maps, information flows, and templates to accomplish the paper

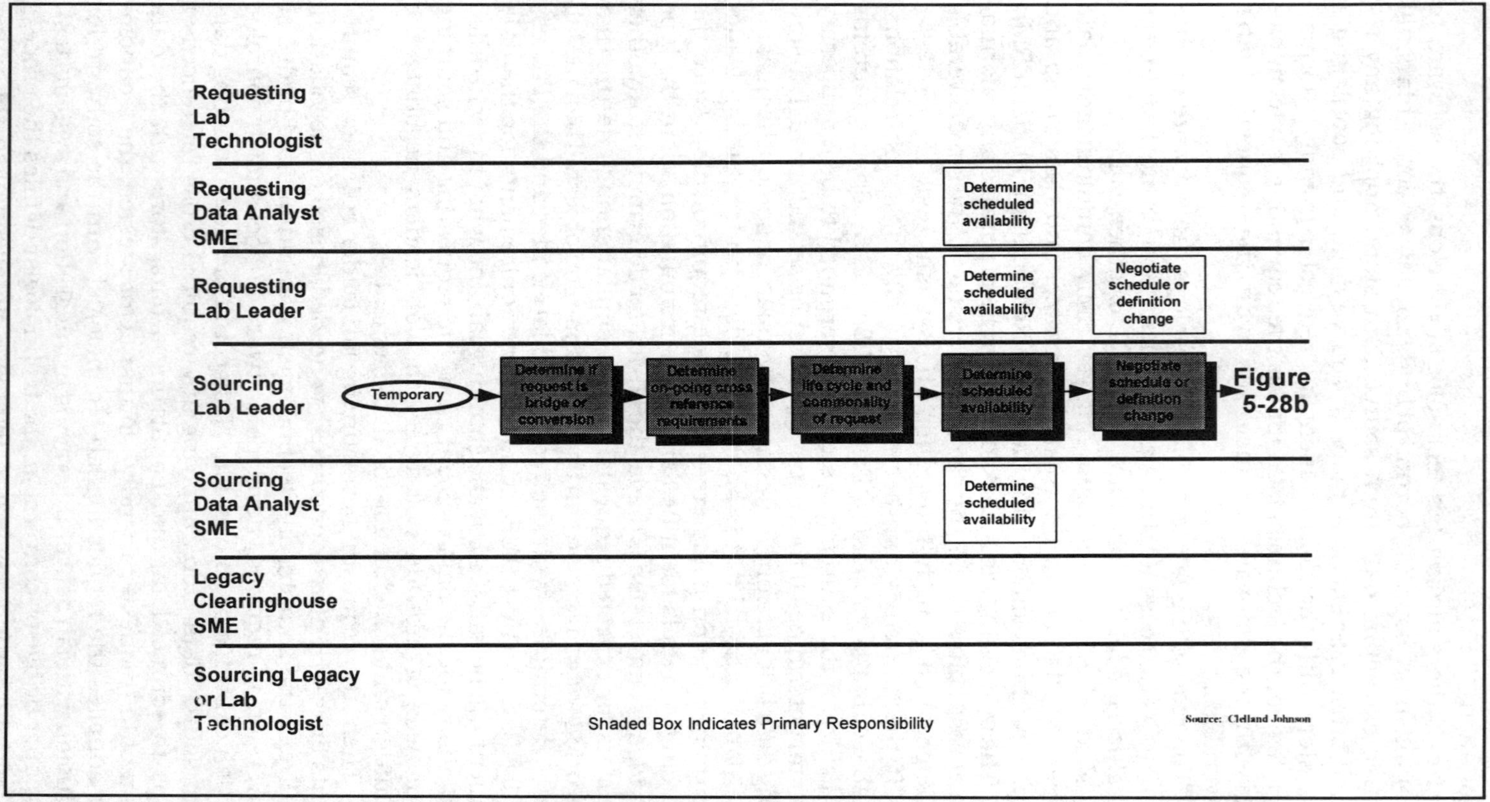

Figure 5-28a: Integration When the Source is Another Process Family's Non-Relational Database-Source is Temporary

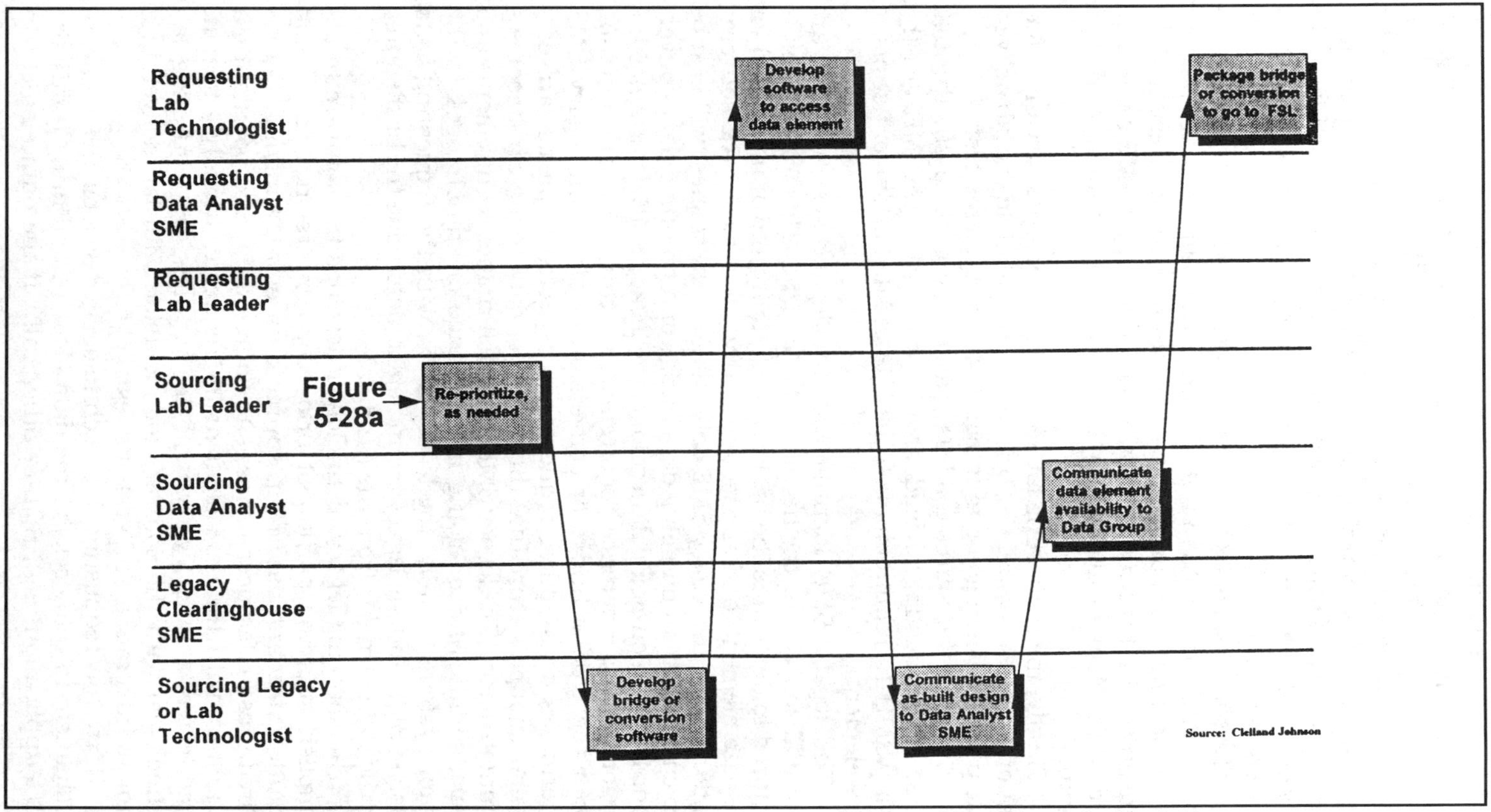

Figure 5-28b: Integration When the Source is Another Process Family's Non-Relational Database - Source is Temporary

bridge or conversion.

The requesting lab technologist, if an automated bridge or conversion, develops the software mechanism, e.g., SQL or other call, to get access to the data element and bring it into the lab's application. If a paper bridge or conversion, the technologist identifies the performers involved and trains them in the use of the process and templates developed to support the paper bridge or conversion.

The sourcing lab technologist, if an automated bridge or conversion, documents the "as-built" design to the Data Analyst SMEs for the requesting and sourcing labs, the Information Architect, and the data group. In this case, the sourcing Data Analyst SME communicates data element availability to Information Architect and data group.

Finally, the requesting lab technologist incorporates any information access software, i.e., bridge or conversion, in the lab deliverable package when going to integration and systems test.

Finally, if the source is a legacy system, Figures 5-29a through 5-29c, the requesting lab leader, with the Data Analyst SME, give the legacy SME the requirements (schedule and definition) for use of the data element.

The legacy SME identifies all the legacy systems that are potential sources for the needed data element. This information is required to determine the best source (quality and applicability) for the data element, and subsequently, the life cycle for the sourcing system. Next, the legacy SME determines if the request will best be served through an on-going data bridge or a one-time data conversion. If it is an on-going data bridge, the legacy SME determines the on-going cross reference requirements. Once the determination about the type of bridge or conversion is made, the legacy SME determines if any other requests, or expected requests, are of a similar enough nature that this bridge or conversion can become a common object. The legacy SME, then determines requirements and responsibilities for on-going maintenance of any changes to the legacy system. Finally, the legacy SME, with the requesting Data Analyst SME and the legacy technologist, determine the best source for the data element from the candidates.

The sourcing legacy technologist develops the software to accomplish sourcing portion of bridge or conversion. This could include extracting data from source data store, applying any required cross references or maps to source data, and populating a data store with the data element in "requester-friendly" format. Once tested, the legacy technologist supplies the requesting lab technologist with the software for inclusion with lab deliverables going to integration and systems test.

Next, the requesting lab technologist develops the software mechanism to get access to the data element and bring it into the Lab's application, e.g., SQL or other call. If the data element in

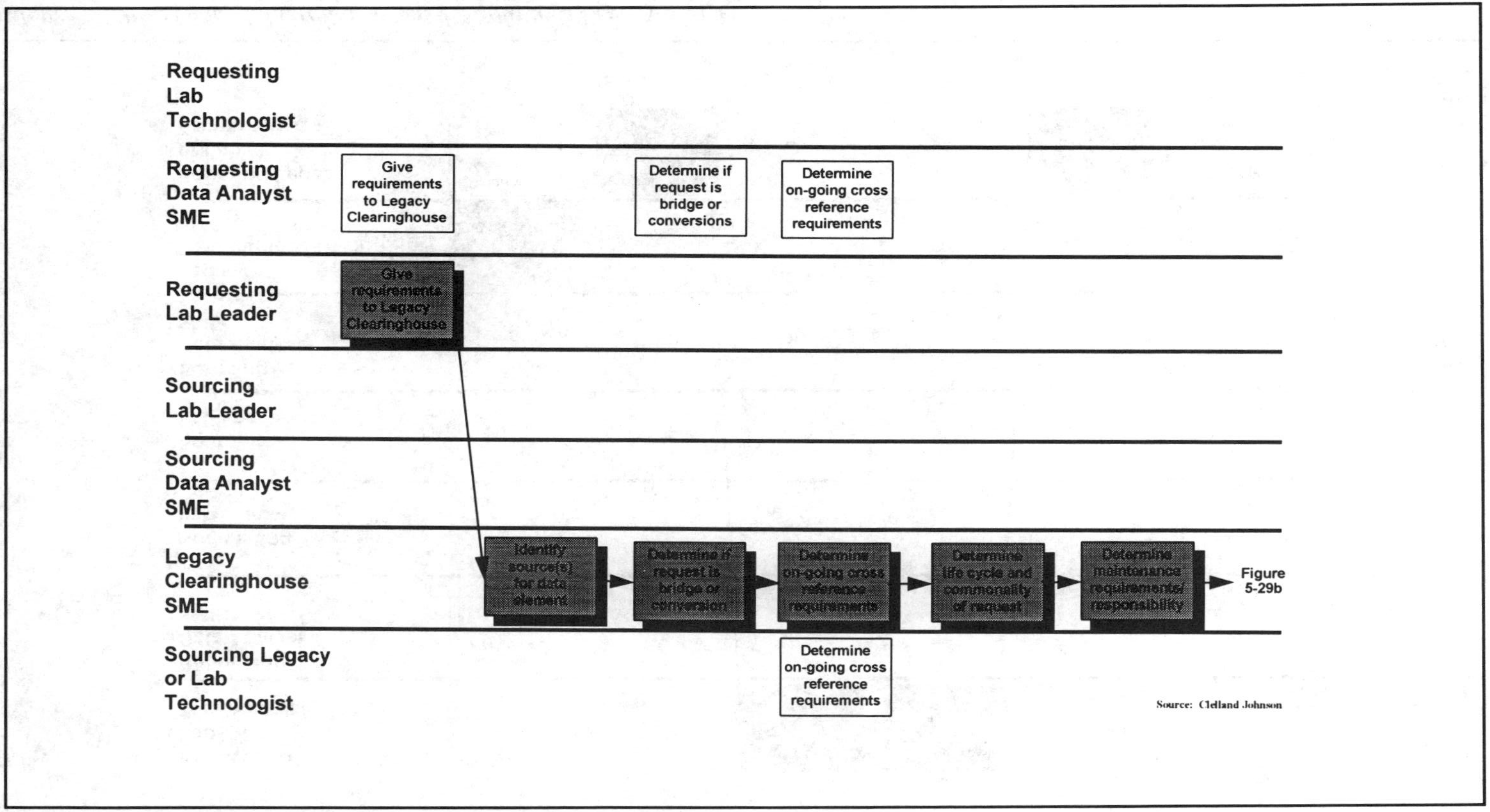

Figure 5-29a: Legacy Integration Shen the Source is Legacy Systems

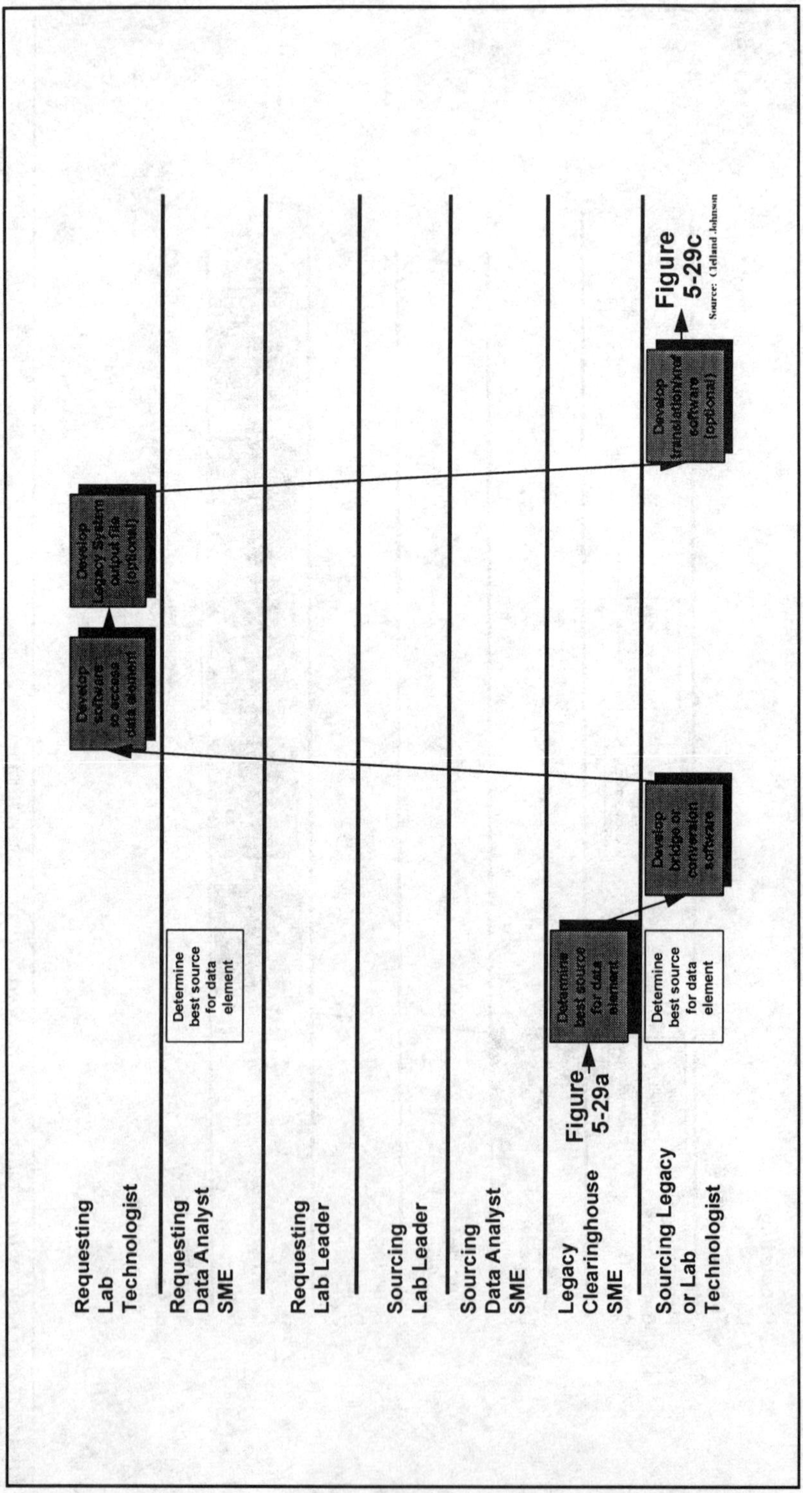

Figure 5-29b: Legacy Integration When the Source is Legacy System (cont.)

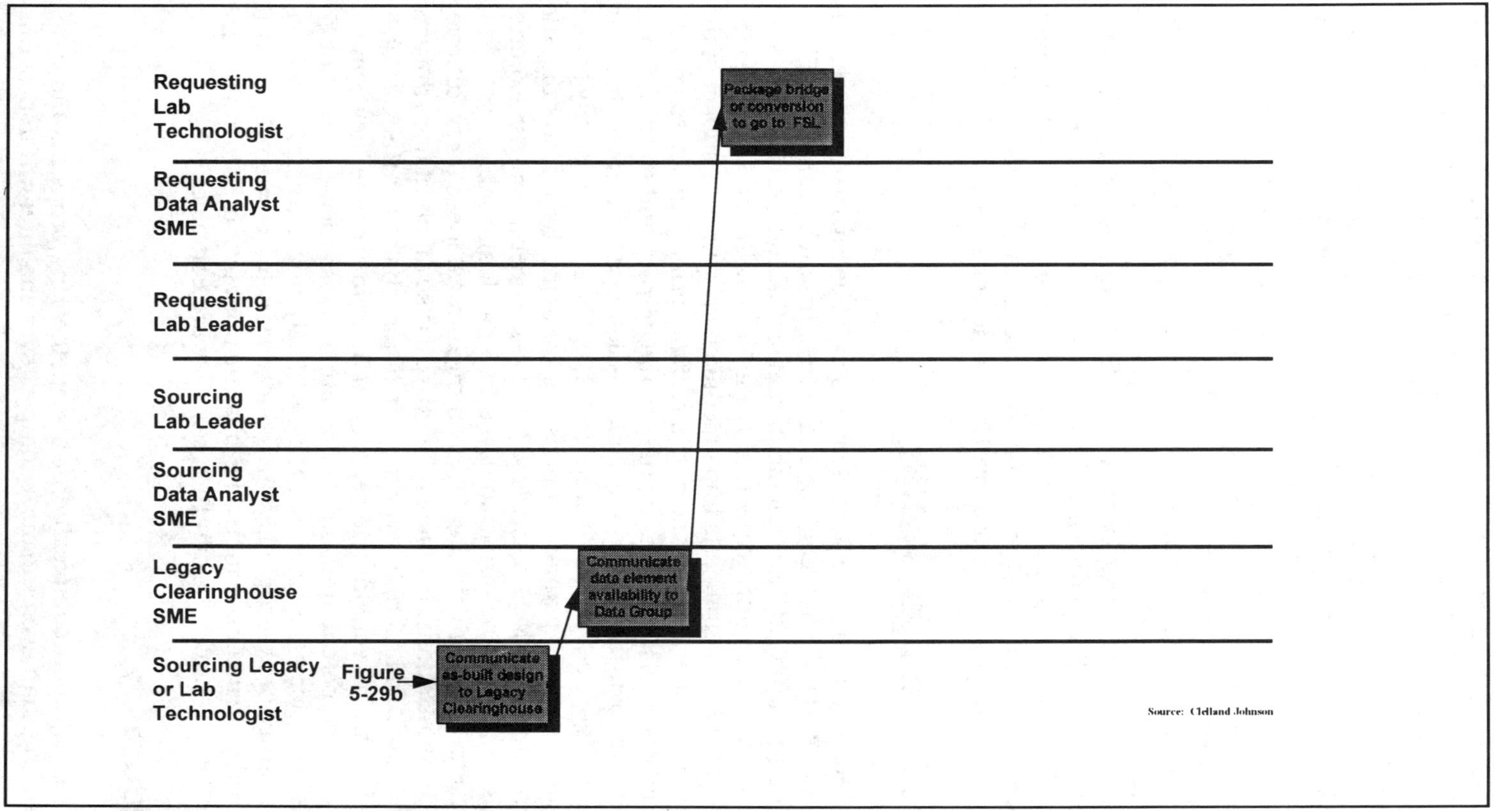

Figure 5-29c: Legacy Integration When the Source is Legacy System (cont.)

question will be used as a source data store for the legacy system that it was retrieved from, the requesting lab must develop the necessary software to produce a "legacy-friendly" formatted file with the updated information.

Next, the sourcing legacy technologist, determines if the legacy system needs to import data from the new system. If so, a "legacy-friendly" formatted file will be produced by the new system. Any software to translate or cross reference the new file into the legacy system will be created by the legacy technologist.

Then, the sourcing lab technologist documents the "as-built" design to the Data Analyst SMEs for the requesting lab, and the legacy SME.

Next the sourcing Data Analyst SME communicates data element availability to Information Architect and data group.

The requesting lab technologist incorporates any information access software, i.e., bridge or conversion, in the lab deliverable package when going to integration and systems test.

Flow-through Staffing

Reengineering lab participants should be involved and participate actively in the reengineering project throughout its life. Flow-through staffing is the implementation of this and the description of the reengineering principle that teams do not "throw stuff over the wall" to other teams. It is implemented by requiring a subset of the staff working in one phase of the reengineering journey to go with their products into the next phase of the journey and so on until the work products themselves are made obsolete by a future reengineering effort, Figure 5-30. Flow-through staffing does not apply only to MIS resources on lab teams; it applies to all staff involved in creating the work products, MIS resources, business leaders, content experts, H/R staff, and any others involved in a particular lab.

Flow-through staffing is one of the hardest ideas for traditional MIS organizations to adhere to because it is so different from the way they have traditionally worked. It is also hard for the business leaders of the reengineering effort to adhere to because they come to rely on competent staff and do not want to loose them. Even though it is hard for all concerned, it is critically important. It provides continuity between phases, it reduces learning curve time, and it provides an incentive for teams creating work products to make sure they are "complete" when they say they are complete.

Summary

Integration complexity for a reengineering project is more demanding than even the most complex systems integration program

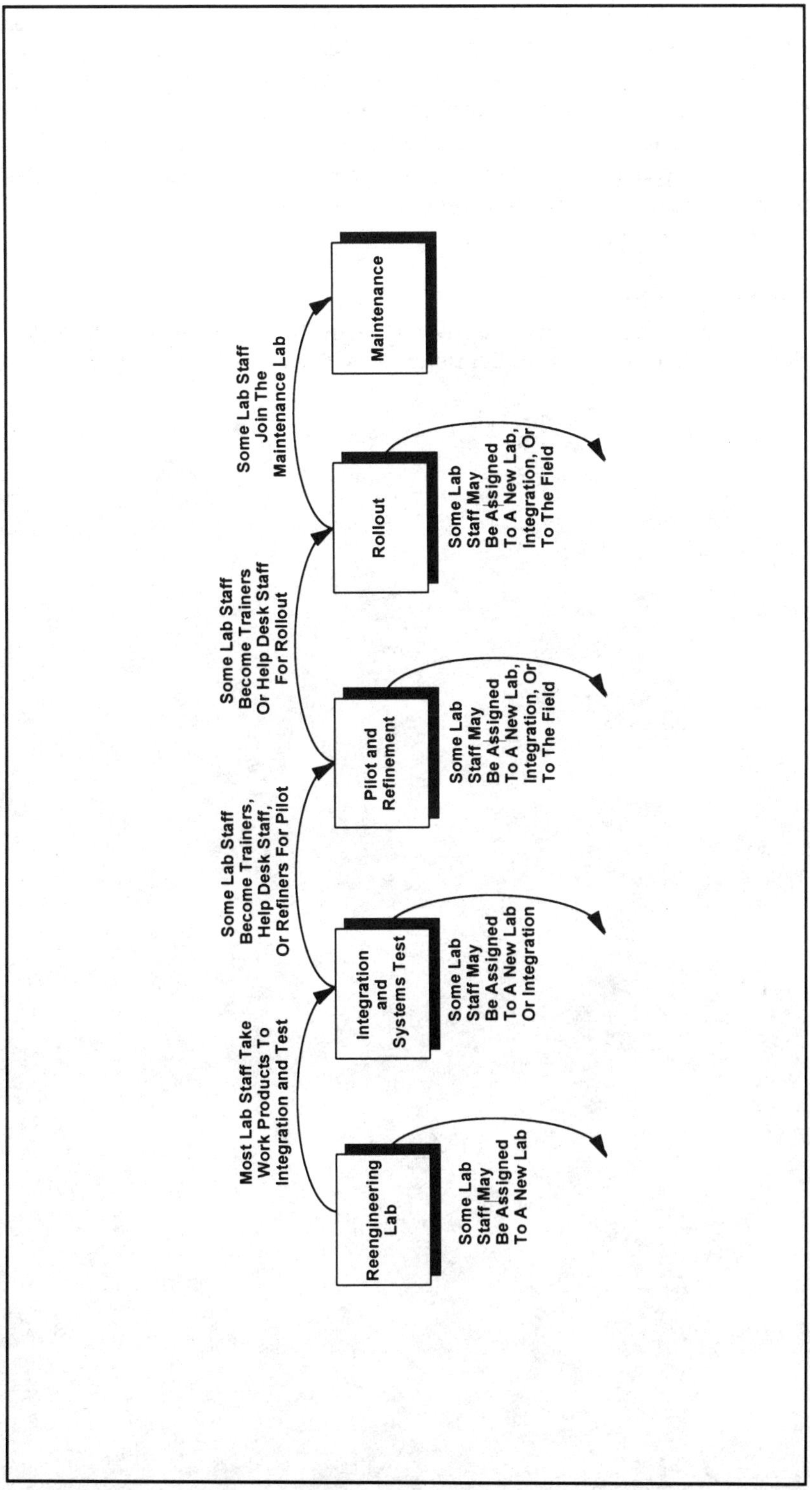

Figure 5-30: Flow-Through Staffing

due to the requirement for a holistic approach to reengineering. Some techniques that reengineering enterprises have used to manage reengineering integration successfully are release planning, identifying business systems implications, conducting sanity checks, identifying critical programs, conducting interventions with Coaches and subject matter experts, using proven integration processes including a legacy systems integration process and using the flow-through staffing model.

Bibliography

Douglas Adams, "Dirk Gently's Holistic Detective Agency," Pocket Books, a division of Simon & Schuster, New York, 1987.

RETOOLING

Reengineering Management Information Systems

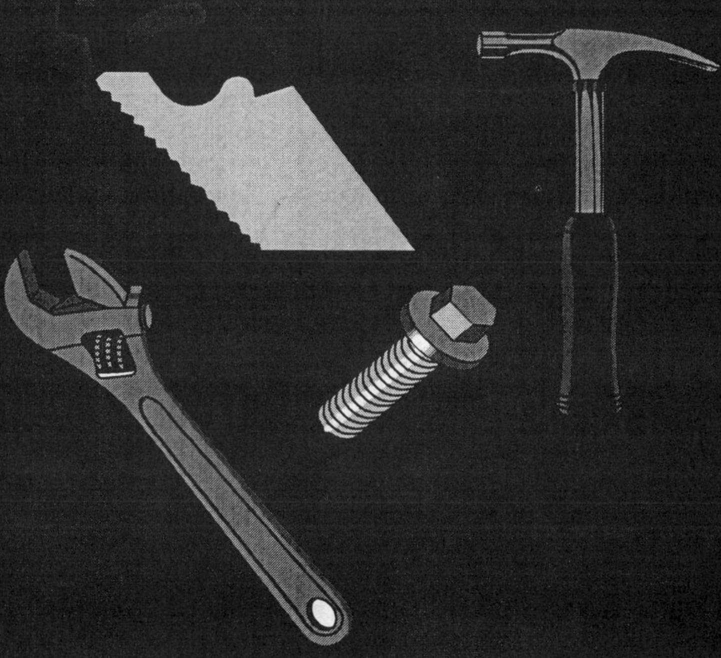

Chapter 6

Infrastructure

MIS Organization

Development Tools and Techniques requires a special architectural composition to help insure success. One cannot merely install the tools and methodologies in the current organization (unless the organization has already undergone significant change to embrace the new client-server world). The following section describes the change needed to the organization in order to set up the proper channels to enable future change to occur.

Once an architecture organization is established it is this new organization that will decide the methodology and new tools to be used for future systems development. This section contains a complete description of an architectural organization structure. There are several new job functions defined that may be performed by one or more persons depending on the size of your organization. This definition is followed by a discussion concerning new tools and techniques and new ways to evaluate, select, install and train for them.

General Architecture

The world of application development is undergoing rapid and deep changes today. Organizations are becoming more user-centered in their approach to developing systems. The user is taking an active role in systems development like never before. MIS organizations are currently ill-equipped to make this change. MIS professionals are used to being in control. They are used to being the "experts." They have spent their entire career being the agents for change.

Today's organization is vastly different. Unless the MIS professional can accept and participate in this change, he will be left behind. Not only are the types of applications being developed changing from traditional mainframe applications to client-server applications, but also the hardware and software environments to create these applications are completely different.

Many of the techniques and standards of just over three years ago are out-of-date with respect to the currently available architectures and tools. Many of the tools that were used three years ago are no longer appropriate to the task at hand. The development world is changing and MIS either has to prepare or be left behind.

The organizational needs of this new development style are different as well. In the past most MIS organizations had a central support function in the name of the Systems Programming team.

Their job was to help the developer assimilate new technology and keep an eye out for new things on the horizon. In the shift to client-server, organizations have usually not setup a similar group to support the new development organization. This group then either grows up on an ad hoc basis due to increasing demand from developers, or the project fails and fingers are unfairly pointed at the project team.

Often the thought is that client-server is an architecture running on an small computer, therefore the support needs are also small. Nothing could be further from the truth. These new environments have the same needs for technical support, controls, backup, recovery, and security as the most robust of the mainframe systems did. Yet, this is often the most overlooked part of a new development organization.

While it may seem possible to convert the current systems programming staff to this new function, to do so would require massive amounts of re-training in different tools, techniques, standards, and styles of support. The sit back and wait style prevalent in a mainframe organization will not be sufficient in a client-server organization. Support in today's MIS team is very pro-active. Support people will visit development teams on a regular basis to assess their needs, suggest the use of new technology, perform high-level integration tasks, and help solve problems before they even occur.

In order to change the mindset we call these people the Architecture Team, not System Programmers. The architecture team has many more talents than the old model of system programming. They have to be attuned to specialized architectures for technology, applications, data and development environments. Without this support the new MIS organization is likely to stumble and fall in its critical initial efforts.

The architecture team centers around the Chief Architect who directs the Application Architect, the Data Architect, the Technical Architect, and the Development Architect. These are new positions, with new responsibilities and roles, that most likely didn't exist in MIS before. Certainly some of their functions existed, a truly large application couldn't have been developed without some of them. But they were never organized in the same way, nor were they held accountable to the user organization for support of the new application in the same way.

General Architecture Structure

The architectural umbrella we see most often is one of evolving client/server computing. For the most part, new applications beginning development are client-server in the sense that the workstation (client) is interfacing to a "black box" (server) that supplies the data required to support the application. Workstations are usually PCs utilizing Windows for both development and production applications. The server can be either a decentralized PC type server with a segmented database or it can be the mainframe computer. In either case the underlying software being used can help to make this dichotomy of location appear transparent to the actual end user.

The data may actually be located at any of several locations in the systems hierarchy. Data can be resident on the workstation itself (either permanently or downloaded just prior to need), it can be on a middle architecture server and available to many clients, or it can remain on the mainframe computer and available to all applications. The actual residence of the data can be specified and changed for each application depending on the specific needs of the application. Considerations that help determine what works best usually depend on:

- type of application,
- volume of data,
- technology available,
- application environment,
- and interfaces required to other applications.

Chief Architect

The Chief Architect is the key individual on the architecture team. It is the Chief Architect's job to make sure that the team's goals and objectives are being met. These will include the goals and objectives of the teams that the Architects are there to support. The Chief Architect is a member of the architecture team and helps to contribute to the team as any other member contributes.

While not a traditional management role, it is, nonetheless, a team leader type of position requiring management level skills. In very large organizations the Chief Architect may indeed be a management or higher-level position. This role needs to be filled with someone who has a strong relationship to the business, understands its needs and goals, and can provide the needed communication link between the business and IT.

Some of the roles and responsibilities of the Chief Architect are:

- **Directs individual architects.** The Chief Architect is the leader of the architecture team. He provides daily general direction concerning architectural issues. The Chief Architect is responsible for

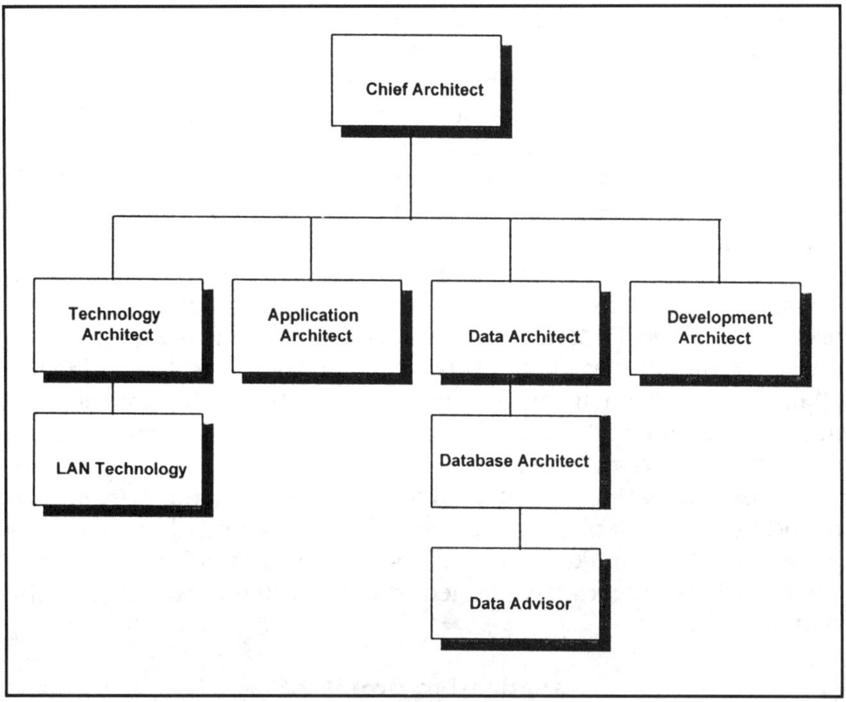

Figure 6.1 Architecture Group Diagram

bringing the business vision to the architecture team.

- **Brings business vision to lower level.** The Chief Architect interfaces with corporate management, such as the CIO to make sure that all architecture decisions fall within the needs of the corporation.
- **Insures smooth integration between architectural components.** The Chief Architect meets regularly with business users and designers from other application groups to ensure that future needs and requirements that are likely to impact the current architecture are taken into account. This provides an early warning to the architecture team about future issues.
- **The Chief Architect also resolves conflicts** among the various architectural disciplines.

Figure 6.1 shows the interrelationships between the Chief Architect and the Application, Data, Technology, and Development Architects. One can also see the need for Data Analysts and Database Analysts in this structure.

Application Architecture

The choices of the application architecture usually dictate the types of tools that can be used in the development process and what type of methodology is used. Mainframe applications will continue to use the traditional methods and tools that have existed and evolved over the past few decades. Client-Server applications will normally require a shift in focus to newer, often less proven tools and techniques. Traditional IS professionals will feel less comfortable with this type of development because of the new techniques and tools required.

Application users, those for whom IT is developing these systems, are usually more adaptable and ready for change than the IS organization itself. Most of these users have been using Windows-based technology in their everyday jobs and have less difficulty changing to this environment. IS traditionalists often have not had much experience with these new architectures and can be much more resistant to change.

The Application Architect plans the navigational issues surrounding education of the users of the system. It is also his responsibility to make sure that the people that will be using the system will be adequately trained in preparation for delivery of the system.

Application Architect

There are several important factors to consider with respect to the Application Architecture.

Consideration must be given to how the application is intended to be used. Different considerations must be given to reporting systems and on-line inquiry systems. The Application Architect must be able to understand the business needs of the organization in order to decide where applications will run and what resources will be required.

The Application Architect needs to understand the overall topography of all applications: both those currently under development and legacy systems that require interfaces. Integration issues are extremely important during the specification of the Application Architecture. In projects past, the major cause of overrun and potential failure was the project team's inability to handle all the integration issues completely and on a timely basis.

Some of the characteristics of the job of Application Architect are:

- **The Application Architect coordinates and manages the various and sundry issues with respect to how the applications will cooperate.** This includes how new applications will work with the legacy applications.
- **Understands business mosaic of applications.** The Application

Architect must be familiar with all applications, both current and planned.

- **Understands business needs and interrelationships.** The Application Architect must be involved in discussions concerning future business needs in order to develop plans with respect to upcoming needs and the interrelationships with legacy systems.
- **Communicates business needs of architecture to development management.** The Application Architect is the main information conduit between business management and development management and designers.
- **Reviews development output for quality and standardization.** The Application Architect is the focal point for control of quality within application development. While the actual QA function may be performed by another group, it is the Application Architect's responsibility to make sure that quality interfaces and standards exist.
- **Communicates with Data Architect on a daily basis to monitor and control utilization of data.** Close integration with the Data Architecture is a key element of the Application Architect's job. Quality systems cannot be created without close integration with the current and evolving data infrastructure.

Challenges to the Application Architect

- **Coordination with subordinate organizations** who are not on a direct reporting relationship can present difficult obstacles the goals and objectives of these groups may not coordinate well with the goals and objectives of the Application Architect. The Chief Architect can be used to resolve any conflicts.
- **Influencing standard and centralized planning** and execution of application development. The Application Architect is one of the few people involved in this style of application development that has a grasp of the complete picture of the elements involved. There are others that understand the complete business picture and some who understand the complete data picture, and still others who understand the technical architecture, but the Application Architect has to have an understanding of how all these pieces fit together. It is with this understanding that the highest degree of integration and cooperation can be accomplished.
- **Understanding diverse needs of a multi-organizational environment**, both business and technical knowledge is essential. The need for this understanding transcends any one of the elements. The Application Architect is the glue that holds many of the pieces together. Certainly this task is very complex and difficult to control. The Application Architect has to be someone on the staff who comes into this effort with a strong understanding of the business and has

a reputation of accomplishment within the organization. This person must also have the respect of those who will be providing information or will be dependent upon the Application Architect for successful delivery of an application.

- **This position needs to be highly empowered** by the Chief Architect in order to be effective. Without strong empowerment this position is doomed to failure. There will be many unpopular decisions that must be made with respect to project scope control and the Application Architect will often feel pulled between many opposing forces. Management will want to move dates and modify deliverables long after lab work has started and the teams are locked into delivery mode. Lab teams will encounter what seems to them to be insurmountable problems in the construction of their business processes and application software. The Application Architect will often have to bring outside forces and influences to bear to make sure not only that the job can be done, but that it be done correctly with as few roadblocks as possible.
- **Must not threaten other internal organizations.** The Application Architect must work extra hard to foster cooperation among various groups to get the job done. There will be many political battles fought and won or lost over who owns the boundaries between the application being constructed and current legacy applications. Some will want to push their scope onto the lab team because "they're in there working on the system anyway." If these scope incursions weren't in the original plan, they cannot be included in the scope on an ad hoc basis or the project will soon be out of control.
- **Interdepartmental communications are key** to successful application implementation. This helps to build in integration during the development process. Constant communication between current lab teams, application maintenance teams and business users will help to make sure that deliverables will meet expectations. One of the main methods of this type of communication is the lab team demo. During this demo, the lab team presents their current approach to solving the business problem to others outside the lab. This is a prime time of communication between the lab team and everyone else. It is during these occasions that others get to offer some of their own ideas and input into the lab process. This input does not necessarily automatically get included in the lab scope, but it is always taken into consideration. If it is not included in the current lab scope, it is usually deferred to be included in the scope of some future lab or initiative.
- **Must foster a team approach.** Because of the nature of the Application Architect's job, this person is one of the key players in the establishment of a team attitude among the Architects.

Data Architecture

The data architecture specifies the definition and philosophy of data retention, data utilization, and general data issues. This architecture specifies most of the statements of direction with respect to data policy and procedures. The Data Architect is the standard bearer for these issues and their resolution.

Data Architect

Some of the characteristics of the job of Data Architect are:

- **Assists project teams during development to help insure that data is being used correctly and efficiently.** The Data Architect may or may not be the Data Administrator or Data Base Administrator depending on the size of the organization and its structure. In large organizations or on large projects the Data Architect will be a position itself, reporting to the Chief Architect with Data Analysts and Database Administrators reporting to it.
- **Reviews development and maintenance of logical and physical data models.** The Data Architect resolves any conflict between the logical model as expressed by the development teams and the physical model needed be the DBAs to create the physical data base. Development teams will usually only develop a logical data model based upon their new business processes. The Data Architect's organization will be called upon to build the physical data model from the logical. This process must be flexible as the logical model is subject to change frequently.
- **Reviews usage of database calls for efficiency and standardization.** This process helps to insure the efficiency and applicability of the database accesses created by the lab teams. Because the lab may not understand the intricacies and limitations of the physical data structures they need a review of their data access in order to prevent runaway data accesses that are injurious to system performance.
- **Enforces data standards across all project teams.** Lab teams will often be unaware of specific data standards as they are pursuing their particular path toward system completion. This is not because they do not have respect for these standards but they are in a constant time crunch and cannot always devote the time necessary to make sure that standards are obeyed.

Challenges to the Data Architect

- **Must understand corporate data model** and work closely with all data groups within the corporation. This is the only way that the corporate data model will continue to represent what is actually happening with respect to the new development in the lab. This often means that data personnel will have to work on the model at unusual times or take unusual steps to insure the integrity of the data model during periods of heavy development.

- **Must coordinate data needs across organizational boundaries** to ensure full integration. Integration across organizational boundaries will be unknown to many of those on lab teams. Their concerns and considerations will often be out of the scope of the lab teams focus. It is incumbent on the Data Architect (and his/her team) to make sure that these needs are understood and met.
- **Needs to build consensus between corporate entities** concerning data ownership and responsibility. Political battles can form around the many facets of data control and ownership during new business design. The Data Architect must help to dissipate the politics surrounding data ownership and build confidence in the new view of the data model. Corporate entities must be made to understand that this type of contention is counter-productive, especially during periods when high productivity is a must to accomplish often ambitious goals.

Technical Architecture

This architecture is where the application actually runs and includes the philosophy of the technical direction of the target architecture. Applications can be resident on PC workstations, middle-level servers or the mainframe computer. Generally today's applications are moving down the hierarchy of hardware to the workstation but there are still many opportunities for continued mainframe development. These decisions are usually made on a case by case basis.

Technical Architect

Some of the characteristics of the job of Technical Architect are:

- **The Technical Architect's job is to make sure that the definition of the technical architecture of the target application environment gets defined** and set up correctly. This includes how the applications will operate and where they will reside.
- **Builds and maintains LAN environment.** This includes communication between the mainframe, middle, and server layers, if present. This position insures that all the necessary components are either planned or installed to fully support the resulting applications being created in the labs.
- **Administers network infrastructure.** While the Technical Architect may not perform all these tasks personally, he/she must make

certain that the infrastructure is administered properly and does not become a burden either on the lab team during development or on the business process performers during testing and installation.

- **Installs infrastructure software and hardware.** Oversees the procurement and installation of various architectural components. This task includes hardware selection, acquisition, installation and maintenance and the maintenance of the appropriate software environment that will reside on the chosen hardware platform.
- **Maintains communications network hardware and software.**

Challenges to the Technical Architect

- **Ensuring that the LAN is available for users and development at all times.** Results are highly dependent on many factors and performance issues. The Technical Architect must be attuned to the daily needs of not only the developers but also the users. There are many demands on the Technical Architect's valuable time. This person must be willing to recognize when these demands are becoming too great and not be worried about asking for additional support. This particular position can often have wide swings of both productivity and scope. There may be weeks when the job is certainly able to be performed by one person and other times when a team of twenty seems too small for the tasks at hand.
- **Keeping the LAN environment as up-to-date as possible.** There will be many technical advances in both hardware and software technology during the life of a multi-lab project. The Technical Architect must be cognizant of the balance that must be struck between maintenance and upgrading and the needs of the lab teams for stability during development and testing.
- **Promotes new usage of LAN environment where it is demonstrably prudent.**
- **Helps determine and plan migrations from one environment to another...** both hardware and software. This task, while necessary, has to be undertaken only when prudent and needed by the business. The days of upgrading technology merely for the sake of having the latest and greatest are gone. Technological advancement must be supported by commensurate demonstrated need by the business.

Development Architecture

The Development Architecture is the complete definition of the environment for developing applications. The environment is determined in large part by the target architecture in which applications will run.

Development Architect

- **The Development Architect will be the main contact and coordinator for Development Tools.** He/she will make sure that all tools are installed and accessible to the various development teams. This Architect will constantly monitor the needs and desires of the lab teams. He/she must also be attuned to the future direction of the organization with respect to technology and research the tools that may be available to simplify the development of applications for new environments.
- **Must understand the business needs for new applications.** Often there will be a long lead time between the development of new applications and their availability as production processes. The toolset must be designed to accommodate the future needs of the application, not just the current architecture.
- **Installs tools/toolsets** necessary to develop applications in the following areas:

    - Methodology
    - CASE philosophy and tool selection, installation and training
    - Application/Program Generators
    - Testing tools
    - Version Control tools
    - Develops training plans for new techniques, software, hardware and tools

    Develops application development standards for :

    - Programming standards
    - GUI design standards
    - Implements and maintains I/S methodology

Challenges to the Development Architect

- **Monitoring and updating development tool environment** as new tools enter the market and are proven viable. Great care must be taken here to avoid unnecessary impact on the lab teams who may already be accustomed to certain tools and techniques. While in the midst of development a change in the toolset could have a strong negative effect. This may not be avoided at all times but strong consideration has to be given to the lab team already working under very strict constraints (Figure 6-2).
- **Insuring that the methodology is being used on all projects.** The methodology must be one that fosters smooth development and does not contain elements or deliverables that are not abso-

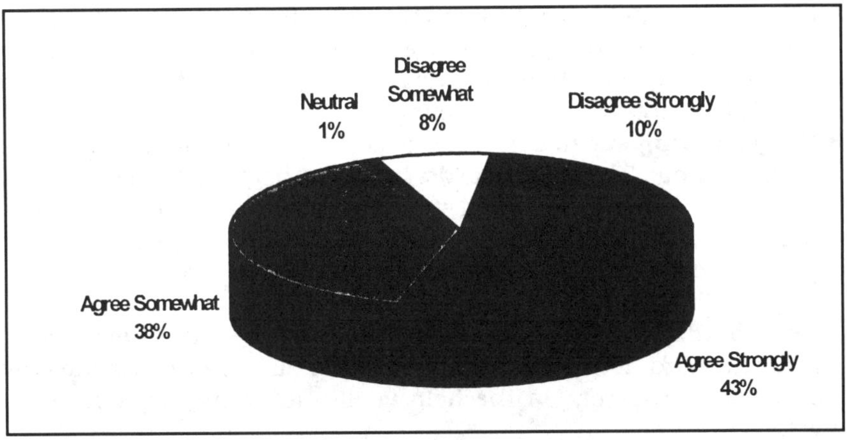

Figure 6.2. Is Technology Transforming Development?

lutely essential. A methodology that is too rigid and requires many deliverables that do not lead directly to the desired result should either be modified for the lab process or discarded in favor of one that does.

- **Must understand whether the current tool set can meet the needs of the developers** to solve business problems. Programming standards cannot be so encompassing or strict that they alone negatively impact project schedules and deliverables.
- **Must coordinate development tool updates between organizations.** The impact caused by these changes affects not only the lab team but also those awaiting deliverable products by the lab team. The business organization must always be consulted during these transitions to assess the impact beyond just what is visible to the development team itself. There may be many factors both in the new business unit and among the labs themselves that can have a negative impact on progress or deliverable quality. We are not saying that the environment must not be changed during this period, just that any changes have to very carefully considered before they are made.
- **Must coordinate development tool training between organizations.** Training can often take personnel away from the environment for long periods of time. For this reason, all training must be planned as much in advance as possible. The impact may not be just to the lab team but may stretch to maintenance organizations and user departments.

There are many other issues that the entire Architecture Team will attack/monitor as a group. As technologies move toward the lab process many of these issues will increase dramatically in importance.

- **Common module development** — This effort needs to get underway at the beginning of the project. Common modules help all teams identify reusability in many forms. This step is necessary as the shift to object-oriented technology occurs.
- **Programming standards** - The need for programming standards is still strong. These standards, however, begin to take on design standards rather than coding standards as the need to specify what the user interface looks like exceeds the need to specify what program code looks like. This is especially true where generators (application or program) are being used.
- **Help facility** - The team needs to specify what kind of help facility is needed and how it will be implemented. In many cases the new application will rely on the help facility to be its major training vehicle.
- **Future direction** - The team needs to understand the future direction that the organization expects to take. This streamlines the process with respect to product and tool choices.
- **Complete Information Systems Plan (ISP)** - An ISP should be developed and maintained. The Architecture Team can be the focal point for this effort under the direction of the CIO.

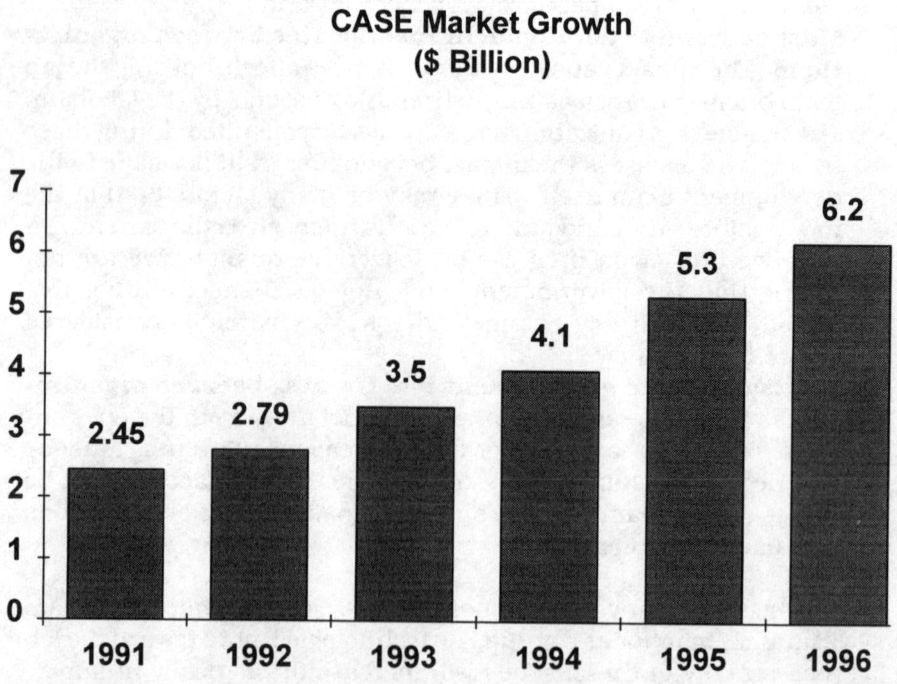

Figure 6.3. CASE Market Growth.

Development Tools and Techniques

Enabling Technologies

In a recent survey (see chart below), when asked whether they thought that technology is transforming the development environment and development culture of MIS, 81 percent of the MIS Managers responding answered that they believed (either "agree strongly" or "agree somewhat") that technology was transforming development. Clearly we are experiencing a revolution of sorts in the development tools area. More tools are available now than at any time in the past twenty years or more. Many of these tools satisfy similar needs as in the case of PowerBuilder and SQLWindows from Gupta. Others have narrowed their scope to very narrow development areas. This makes the process of tool selection and implementation not only confusing but difficult to manage.

The survey also indicates that there is still a tremendous interest in making the use of tools payoff for IS organizations. There is strong support for these tools even though they have not proven to be the standard bearers of increased productivity that they were originally thought. For example, CASE technology has promised (at least in the minds of MIS Managers) to increase the productivity of the MIS staff. These promises were not usually made by the CASE vendors directly, but it is the message heard by the buyers of CASE.

Since the increase in productivity has not been demonstrated, we need to look to other measures in order to gauge the success of tools. Most MIS Managers today are looking to these tools not to increase productivity as much as to build in quality and rigor in the systems development process. Methodologies can begin the process of building in standardization but cannot really enforce those standards. CASE tools, when fully utilized, help to build in the standardization promised by the methodology. As a result the culture responds to this need and begins to adhere to these concepts and procedures more readily.

As organizations standardize their development processes and cultures, the focus can shift from trying to eliminate chaos to that of building in quality. When these tools become fully integrated into the organization some of the effort can begin to shift to a greater concern for satisfaction of user needs than was previously possible. This is aided not only by tool deployment but the way that the tools are used. CASE technology is not enough to help the MIS organization make the kind of improvement in service being demanded by experienced users. These users see the kinds of software that they can buy off-the-shelf and are beginning to apply the same standards to the software being delivered by their own MIS organizations. Whether this is fair or not doesn't matter. The bar has been raised by their experiences and will not be lowered again. These MIS groups are ill-equipped, not only from the perspective of the tools and techniques, but also from their own methodology and experience, to provide software of this quality.

In spite of its failure to deliver on its original promise, the CASE market has grown steadily over the past few years, and is projected to continue growing in the future. The market value of the CASE tool arena is shown in Figure 6-4.

Although an impressive growth curve, the market still remains largely unpenetrated with respect to fully functional, fully integrated CASE tools. While a company may have one, or even two tools to assist in systems development, many of these are stand-alone or are used only on an irregular basis. There are relatively few organizations that have made a full commitment to CASE technology. This is due mainly to the original high level of overstatement of product functionality and payback projected by the CASE vendors combined with the over-optimism of the MIS organization on its ability to adopt and adapt to this technology.

MIS systems of just a few years ago were still largely COBOL mainframe systems. They were the same types of systems that MIS has been building for the past thirty years. They demanded skills from MIS that were readily available. Even with this experience base MIS had difficulty delivering quality systems to its users on time and within budget. Why would we expect, then, that the change to new development tools and client/server systems would be any easier.

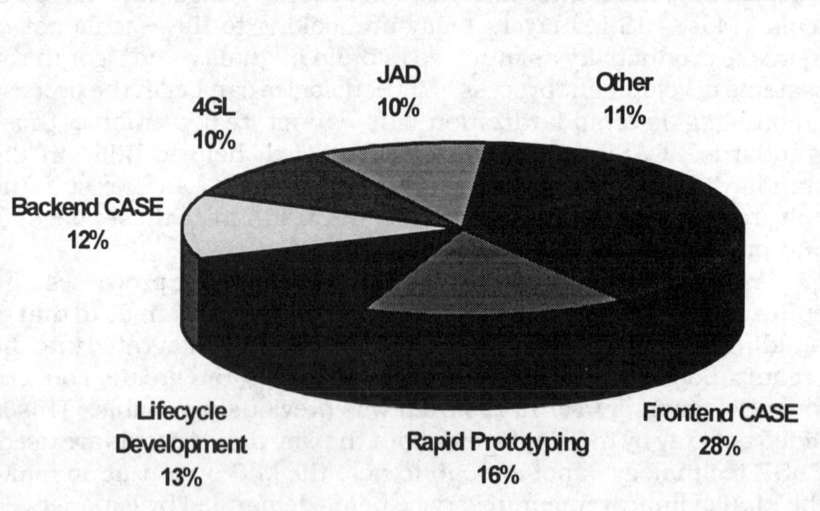

Figure 6.4. What are the Promising Technologies?

We would be producing systems for a largely unknown architecture using techniques and tools that were brand new to us. How could we hope to succeed?

CASE represented a different way of life for the professional developer and unless the organization made a strong commitment to change its entire way of building systems, it was only used on a sporadic basis. Skills built up in support of a specific project were lost during the next project when either a different tool was chosen, or no tool was used at all.

In fact, the user has not seen any real difference in the speed or responsiveness of the MIS organization in order to meet his needs. The same development problems plague the implementation and maintenance process. The same production problems occur on a daily basis. The same people use the same excuses why things do not work. Because of this situation, many companies have begun to relocate the MIS personnel to their user departments. They become responsible for serving a single department, with a focus not experienced before. While this philosophy seems to provide a higher level of service in the user organization, unless it is accompanied with commensurate re-training of the MIS personnel, it is almost certainly doomed to failure.

MIS management has begun to see the light and has begun a search for ways to better serve their corporate users. They still remain focused on the technology, however, to solve their problems. In a poll of promising technology changes, MIS Directors attached importance to their preferences as follows:

It is apparent from the above chart that MIS managers are looking to technology to help solve some of their problems. What is not so apparent is how they intend to link these products to help make a full solution possible. Until these managers take the time to properly choose and integrate tools with a reengineered development process, the full promise of CASE cannot be realized.

There are some tools on the market that attempt to provide such a full function technology solution combined with a change of method. Texas Instruments' The IEF, for example, when implemented properly, can provide assistance from design and planning through code generation. The only difficulty is that such an implementation requires such a major change in the MIS organization that most lose the stomach for it and search elsewhere for a snap-in/snap-out parts integration approach that may be more palatable.

While such a change would seem to be easier to assimilate, it is

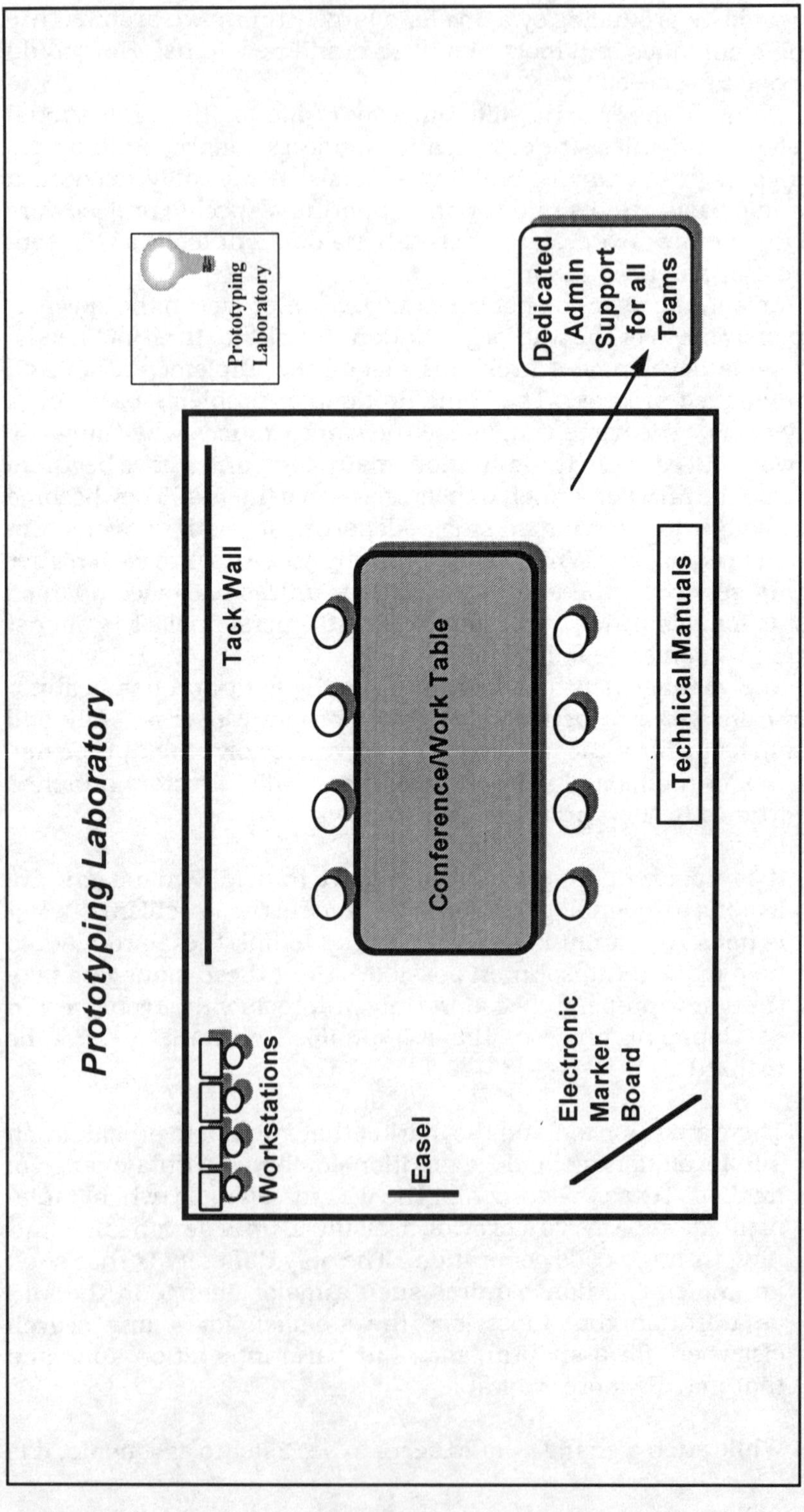

Figure 6.5 General layout diagram.

not driven from within and the entire technology begins to look like a threat to the way MIS perceives its existence. Both approaches are doomed if management cannot step up to the line and provide the leadership and guidance (and money and training) to make it happen.

Our recommendation is to adopt a parts integration approach rather than an integrated single product because it allows some flexibility to respond to the way the organization is today and build a solution that can also be used tomorrow. With parts integration, you can choose a best-in-class tool at each level and integrate it with other tools at other levels. The parts integration approach must be coupled with a complete revamping of the development philosophy and process of the organization. Without this complete change, things will continue along the same path as before, with the same inefficiencies, the same problems, and the same results.

Workshops/Labs

The use of labs for application development requires a strong level of partnership among all parties. All those involved must understand the outcomes of such a new style of development and delivery. Because of the team nature of development and the integration of the products being produced, a high level of facilitation and control must be established. These elements of this style of development are covered in another section of this book.

In this section we will focus on the lab itself. This includes not only the room but also all the infrastructure inside and surrounding the lab.

The physical setup of the laboratory is very important. The environment must be conducive to work. It must be pleasant enough so that the lab team will be able to spend a considerable amount of time inside without feeling totally trapped. The team will spend months working together in this environment. Envision a conference room where you are expected to attend an extended meeting, lasting for weeks, not hours. This process enables one to see many of the considerations that need to be taken into account when constructing the lab space.

Just as you would not like to spend several weeks in a dimly lit, confined space with your fellow workers, members of a lab team need a bright, roomy, fully-equipped space in which to work. Depending upon the size of the actual lab team the room can actually be as small as 20' X 30'. Basic, but required, equipment for the lab includes:

- *Bright wall decor.* The room must be pleasant to work in... the team will be spending their entire working day here for several months.

- *Conference table large enough to provide the entire lab team with a meeting space/work surface as needed.* This will be the major work area for the team. They will use this table for all their materials for discussion, notes during sessions and all the tools to be used in the lab process.
- *Comfortable chairs for all lab team members.* Don't skimp here... uncomfortable chairs can cause productivity to be very low and make the lab team lose focus.
- *Several flip chart easels with paper and markers.* The team will use flip charts to brainstorm new ideas and processes. These will often become permanent pieces of documentation when transferred to other documentation tools.
- *Electronic Marker Board.* Our personal favorite for extreme productivity within the lab team. This board allows the team to express ideas, modify and tweak them until all are satisfied, then push a button to receive a permanent copy of the idea for future use.
- *File/Storage cabinets.* There will be many files established that may not be electronically kept current. This may include documentation available from field organizations, outside vendors, and legacy systems documentation. There will also be many manuals and training materials that will only be available in printed form and will need to be properly filed in order to be easily referenced in the future.
- *Workstations for prototype development and modeling.* The workstations will need to be state-of-the-art computer workstations. The workstations must be easy to use by all members of the lab team. During the course of lab development all team members are usually involved in use of the workstations at one time or another.
- *Laser printer.* The team will have many occasions to print their output for review by others or for review during the lab session itself. A laser printer provides the team the flexibility to iterate through several versions of their deliverables before producing the final version. A printer in the lab facilitates this process.
- *Large television monitor linked to workstations.* There will be occasions when the lab team desires to demonstrate their products to others, sometimes to persons outside of the project. The large screen permits many to see the demonstration at the same time, with one explanation. This monitor can also be used to view training tapes for particular topics in the lab.
- *VCR.* A VCR permits the lab team to view outside tapes during lab sessions. These tapes can include product demonstrations, educational materials or other video subject matter.
- *Overhead projector.* The overhead projector permits the lab team to make presentations to others with respect to lab progress, deliverables, or other simple presentations.

- *Various office supplies and equipment.*

Commitment to lab philosophy

In order for the lab process to succeed there must be a commitment to the overall lab philosophy throughout the organization, or at least among the persons directly involved in the lab effort and their managers. This is a very different process for most MIS professionals to accept. The issues surrounding the lab process as previously discussed are among the most difficult challenges for MIS.

A lab facility can require a significant amount of time in order to be setup correctly and to be ready for use by the lab team. While timeframes may vary widely, they are usually only somewhat dependent upon the ability of the organization to acquire and install the proper tools and equipment. Training in the tools and techniques usually causes more difficulty for the changing organization than the acquisition of the tools themselves. The elements that need consideration for lab setup are:

- Room setup
- Hardware setup
- Software setup
- Outside infrastructure setup

Construction of space can be highly variable depending on space availability, union rules, and suitability of space, once found. Acquisition of equipment to be used in the lab can also present some additional lead time considerations. Depending on corporate purchasing policies the lead time for the following elements can be:

Lab Preparation	**Time frame**
PC Hardware	21-90 days
LAN Hardware/Software	30-90 days
Acquisition/installation of software	30 days
Furniture	1-30 days
A/V Equipment	1-30 days
Communication Materials	30-90 days
Assignment of staff to lab teams	21-90 days

The above time requirements are reasonably predictable. The real problems stem from the organization's commitment and ability to respond to the new training needs of the new team. Extra lead time must take into account the need for advance training before the startup date of the first lab. This may be training in the methodology, the process, the new lab tools, or team building exercises. While some of the training can be accomplished during the lab on a just-in-time basis, much of it needs to be done in advance. In addition, the training process cannot stop here. The teams need constant exposure to new tools and techniques as the environment changes. They need to keep ahead of the curve with respect to tools and methodologies. This is an ongoing training and re-training process that doesn't end.

Notice that one of the longest lead times is related to the assignment of staff to the lab. Companies seem to feel that this can be accomplished quickly but our experience has shown that it is a difficult, arduous task. It takes time to identify those that will leave their old jobs and accept new positions within a lab team. Not only this but it is extremely difficult for the person's organization to let the person go. There are often residual duties that need to be taken care of and turnover to a new person must be arranged. We have seen lab teams fail because the sending organization would not cooperate and let the person spend his/her full time assigned to the lab.

This also becomes very stressful for the lab participant because they have leftover duties that distract from their performance in the lab. Lab teams are true teams and team members feel real guilt when they are constantly pulled from the lab to take care of problems in their old environment.

Hardware - Lab PCs

- Recommended: PC compatible type workstations (3-4 per lab). Choose the fastest equipment your budget will allow. Of course if your environment is different you may substitute comparable equipment. The main consideration is not the specific type but that the hardware chosen is powerful enough to accomplish the tasks undertaken in the lab. This means that the lab team must not feel the need to limit their solution because of limitations that exist in the lab. Basic requirements of a typical system are:

  - 12 MB RAM (more, if possible)
  - 100 MB Disk (most software and data will be stored on the LAN)
  - VGA Graphics (the larger the monitor the better)
  - Related network hardware and software
  - Mouse and mouse pad

- Keyboard
- 3.5" floppy drive
- Switchable connection to large screen monitor in lab (on at least one PC)

- Notebook computer(s) (at least 1 per lab) (similar architecture to workstation).
  - enables entry of notes and information during lab session so that the Lab Scribe is able to participate in lab discussion. It is essential that all lab members participate in all discussions. The notebook computer for use on the lab table enables even the Scribe to take part fully in the definition.
  - enables additional work to be done outside of lab. For extra work the computer can be taken home or used outside the lab room. This allows flexibility to lab team members on doing independent work.
- Printing in the lab room itself is preferred over other network printing unless network printers are very close by the lab(s).

Hardware - Lab Network

- This is highly variable depending on corporate standards in existence, but all labs should be interconnected by LAN/WAN or some type of network interconnection. This may be the main avenue of communication between labs for formal document sharing and integrated discussion databases. In order for each lab team to be able to share data and opinions on a more formal basis than hallway discussion, this facility allows the creation, management and utilization of interlab documents.
- Setup must be transparent to lab users. They should be able to begin work in the lab on the first day with no lab team setup required. Many of the lab participants will be non-IT personnel. Experience has taught us how impatient many of these individuals can be when it comes to sitting and watching while IT types install and test their tools. Indeed, this process can often be harrowing enough that they will not want to use the tools being installed for fear that their work will be at risk. This negative impression should be avoided if possible.
- LAN access facilities should include:

  - Interlab communication of integration issues can be accomplished with a suitable product like Lotus Notes. An E-mail system might prove sufficient but a groupware system like Notes offers many more possibilities for team and inter-team communications. For example, databases can be defined that allow team

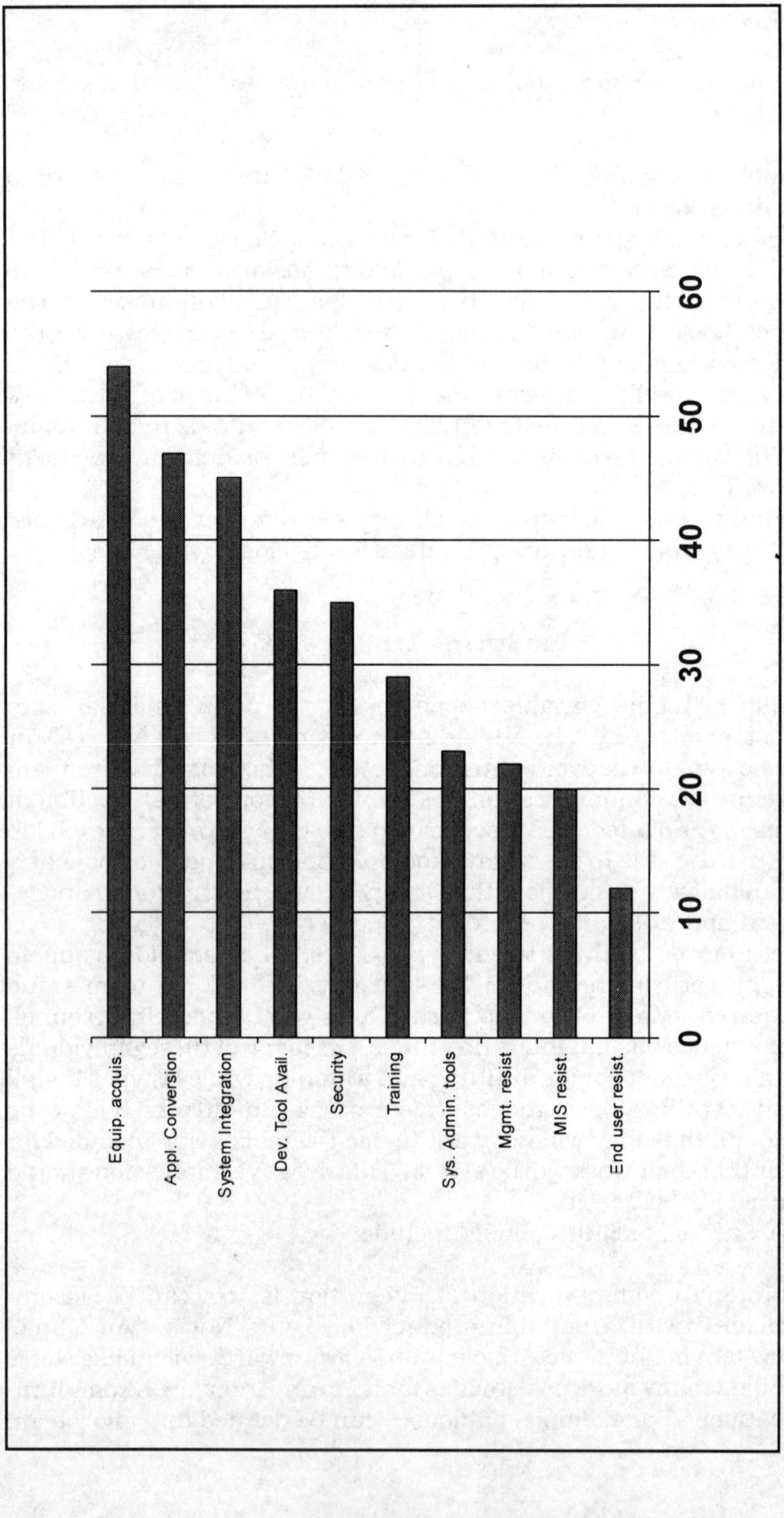

Figure 6.6 Obstacles to Implementing Client/Server Computing.

to share ideas, data, and designs without the need to schedule face-to-face meetings. This is especially useful when taking into account the tight time restrictions among lab teams.

- Interlab use of integrated or cooperative CASE tools to enable significant use of a LAN based repository. The LAN based repository allows lab teams to share their CASE developed models with each other for maximum productivity and accuracy.
- Upward project status reporting can be accomplished via Lotus Notes. This helps satisfy the need to understand status rollups and the impact of the progress of relative lab teams on each other.
- Software version control with a standard product such as PVCS to help maintain versioning and configuration management. This process is not only important within the lab team but also to establish and maintain control over the complex integration and migration issues surrounding complex software development.

Software in the Lab

Tool selection is one of the key elements to help ensure the success of any new development methodology and approach. In the past, IT departments have been able to select tools by using its best and brightest to weed out the few competitors via a features and functions battle. In most of the large shops where single vendor hardware and software was king, there were few other choices to be made architecturally.

In fact, in many cases, your hardware manufacturer's System Engineer spent a significant amount of time helping the systems programming group understand the specifications for some new need or requirement. Oddly (tongue in cheek here), the choice was often a tool from that manufacturer to help meet the need. When it came to competitor's products, their marketing teams were usually selling augmentation products that were designed to assist in the management of the mainframe environment.

Today the situation has changed dramatically. Many of the products like database management systems, operating systems, compilers and editors are treated as commodities. Today's IT organization has to know so much about its own environment that understanding what the options are in any given situation can be next to impossible. Where development was formerly targeted at the mainframe environment with its standard set of tools and techniques, today's targets are not only moving, but are sometimes unknown at the time development is about to begin.

Many companies have undertaken the choice of software for development tools when they were not yet sure what the final target architecture would be. This meant that they sometimes had to choose less than the optimum development tool in order to keep the staff productive and working toward the goal. It is not easy to condone this method of tool selection, but one must recognize it as a sometime necessary evil in our rapidly changing arena of technology. The premature selection process should always be undertaken with care. Choices of the target architecture can take place rather late in the game sometimes and premature choice of development tools can lead to frustration among the technical staff and lost preparation time.

Many IT professionals can remember how we chose software tools in the past. We would follow the best, most rigorous, most convoluted step-by-step process imaginable. First, we would recognize the need for a new tool by reading about something new in a trade journal, or attending one of the endless series of seminars organized to give tool vendors a continuing platform from which to espouse their particular theory of system development. We would follow a procedure something like this:

1. **Identify need (often not user-driven).** If need was a driver at all it was usually some form of desire to increase the acronymic

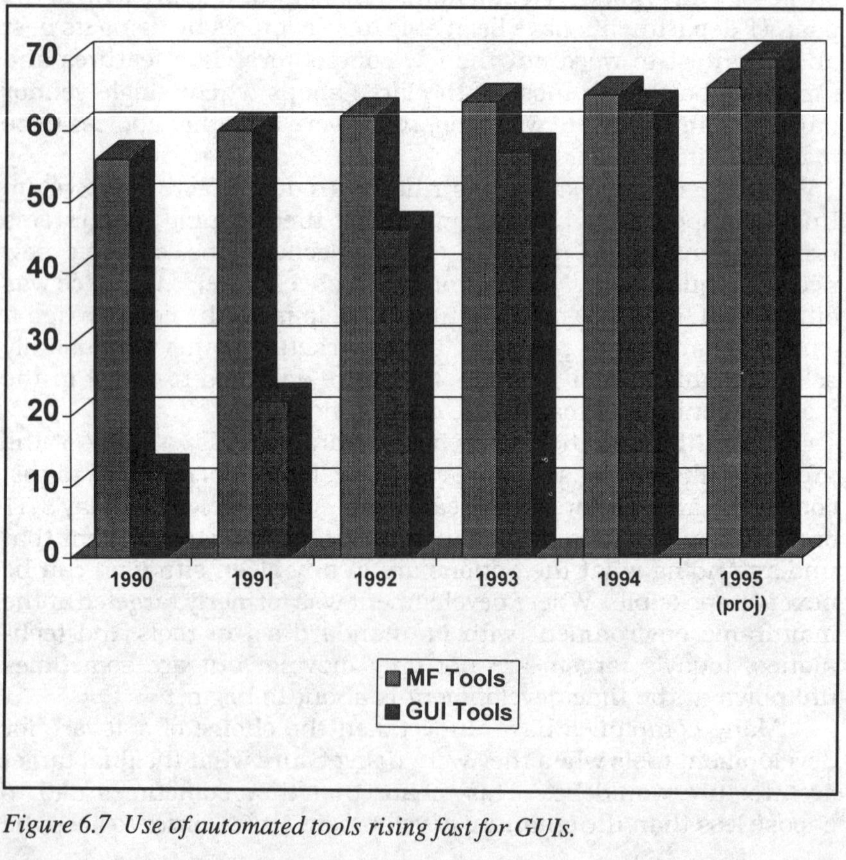

Figure 6.7 Use of automated tools rising fast for GUIs.

graffiti on one's resume. The user's needs or desires for technological change were usually not a part of this equation at all.

2. **Investigate solutions (usually limited in scope).** This investigatory process entailed finding products, some suitable, some not, from sources such as last week's Computerworld or other trade journal.
3. **Organize the tool selection committee (technicians only, please).** Build a committee of technicians whose past major accomplishment with respect to tool selection was that they helped evaluate the upgrade to the previous new release of the mainframe operating system.
4. **Generate large matrix of technical features.** This task probably occupies the selection committee for the longest period of time as the endeavor to include every arcane feature that might exist for the category of products under consideration. These features are included for evaluation whether or not they add any value to the user's solution. This team usually feels that the larger and more complex the matrix, the more complete their investigation will be.
5. **Request product information from vendors with applicable products.** The committee needs all the current marketing literature and technical data to pore through. In most cases they have not planned this process well and will usually demand 1-2 day turnaround from the vendors to supply information. They have little sympathy with vendors who do not immediately grasp the immediacy and urgency of the situation. After all, they need at least a week to fill in the blanks on the matrix (see below).
6. **Begin to fill in the blanks on the matrix.** This arduous process is accomplished based on the information gleaned from the vendor's marketing literature and other materials supplied in step 5 above. Once completed the vendors in question will have little opportunity to review the choices made and encourage any corrections to the hastily made evaluation.
7. **Invite vendors to meet and discuss/demo their product's features to the technical selection team.** The vendor usually has little time to prepare for this process. It can involve a demonstration under the most difficult conditions to a group of people whose main objective is to eliminate products from the long list in order to develop a short list. The main objective of the review team is to find things wrong with a product so that it can be eliminated from further consideration.
8. **Fill in more blanks on the matrix.** This process is largely to determine a technical fit with the company's technical environment and its ability to sustain itself among the other products in the feature war. The shorter the list the simpler the eventual decision will be.
9. **Record some subjective material about competing vendors**

and products. In case of a tie some method needs to exist to select the appropriate vendor.

10. **Add up the "points" scored by each product/vendor.** How else can we determine the product/vendor that can best meet the user's needs. If the preferred vendor looks like it might be eliminated, weighting factors can be applied to sway the voting.
11. **Inform the winning vendor that he is the winner.** It's a fun time when the entire IT organization gets free buttons and T-shirts from the vendor.

We should note that the above process enabled the committee to make a successful choice in the '70s and '80s because there were many similar products on the market that really only differed only in the most basic features. The products had many of the same benefits and the problem being solved was usually technical in nature and the user's needs were only marginally under consideration. For example, when you needed a database the impetus for a new one was usually technically driven, it wasn't the user who asked for it. Whichever DBMS was chosen it was likely to work.

MIS departments today are practicing cocooning. As Faith Popcorn states in The Popcorn Report: Cocooning is to "pull a shell of safety around yourself, so you're not at the mercy of a mean, unpredictable world. Cocooning is about insulation and avoidance, peace and protection, coziness and control — a sort of hyper-nesting." It's a "full-scale retreat into the last controllable (or sort of controllable) environment — your own digs." Today's MIS organization is practicing just such a retreat. They are bombarded from all angles to be the agents of change. The only problem is that they have been traditionally resistant to change.

It's a scary world out there now. Users have gained knowledge of computers and off-the-shelf software that they never had before. Executives are demanding access to more than data, they want information. Consultants visit the user every day with examples of all the exciting things that they can do with technology. There seems to be no practical limit to what MIS is expected to do in the not too distant future. Today's MIS organization is ill-equipped to perform these feats of magic. They are under-trained, overstaffed and don't understand why all these people are asking for all these new things. (The Popcorn Report, Faith Popcorn, HarperCollins Publishers, Inc., NY, NY. Copr. 1992)

After all, today the situation is completely different. The need for a new environment is often driven by direct user demand. Users want systems that are more responsive and pliable and to use technologies that seem familiar to them. This often means a client/server type of architecture with a Windows type of user interface. In order for IT to meet these needs a lot of change needs to occur, and

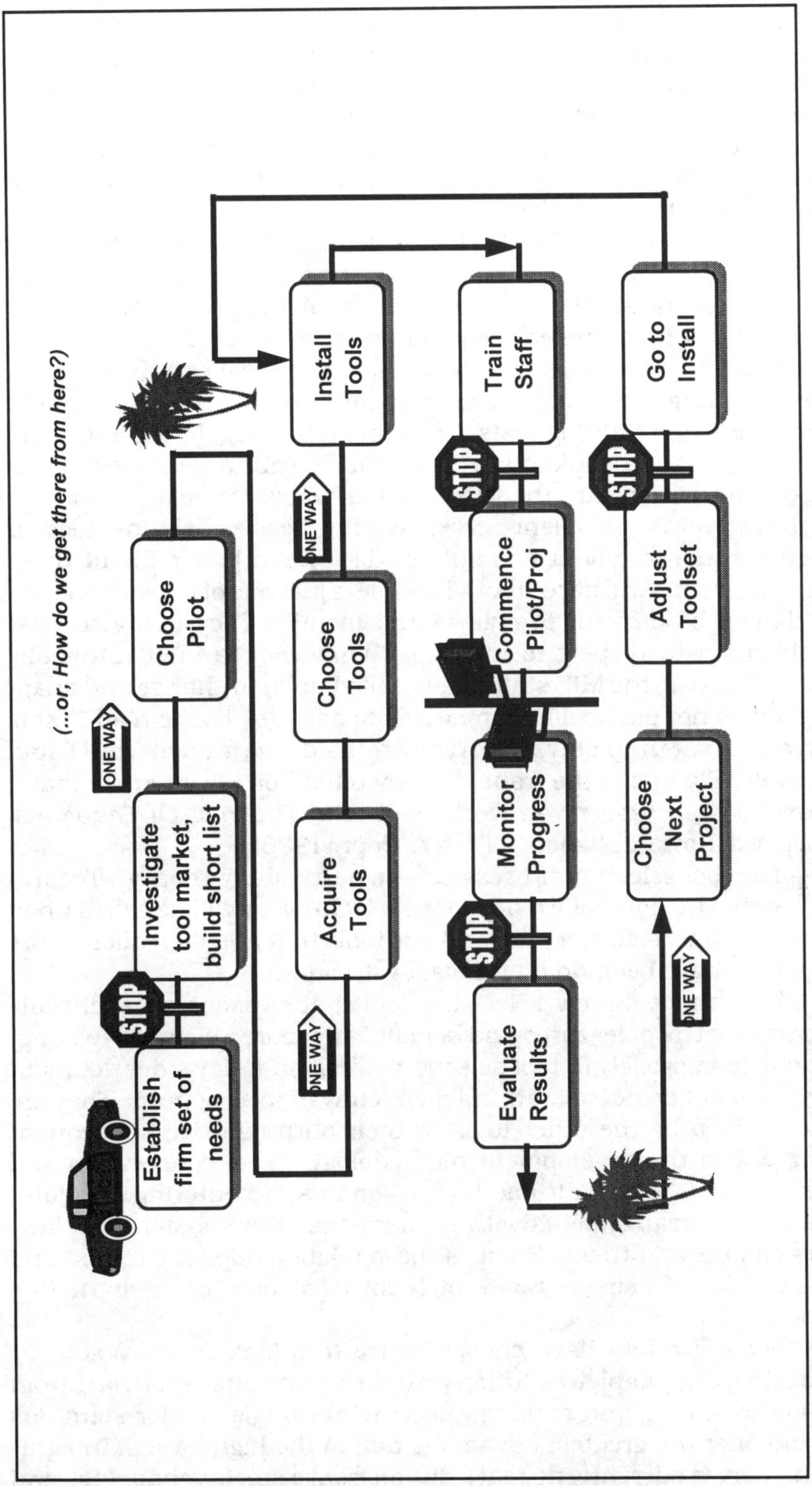

Figure 6.8. Development Toolset Roadmap.

right now, not tomorrow. Some of these factors are covered elsewhere in this book; our focus here is to describe the change needed in the tool selection process which must happen before the MIS staff can be trained in the tools or be prepared to use them.

Indeed, much of MIS management is ignorant of the real problem facing their organization. Figure 6.8 is an example of how out of touch they have become.

The chart shows that MIS management is very concerned with several of the factors involved in implementing client/server systems in their organization. Our experience shows, however, that the problems with equipment acquisition, application conversion and systems integration are all very solvable. The real concerns should center around end-user resistance, MIS resistance, management resistance, and training costs. These areas are largely ongoing, more widespread and people related. Problems with acceptance of any kind of technology are the most difficult to overcome.

However, since client server has not been widely installed or used yet, management has not yet discovered how difficult these latter problems will be to solve. Tool use is just one of these elements. Tools can be difficult to choose and install. They can also pose problems with respect to training. While they are not unusually difficult to use, the MIS staff that is called upon to change and adapt to them is not particularly amenable to change. I once read "...it is difficult to see the picture when you are inside the frame." The IT staff often is fully inside the frame — they often don't even know that a frame exists! (Roger von Oech, *A Kick In The Seat Of The Pants*, Harper & Row Publishers, NY, NY. Copr. 1986)

The tool selection process can be particularly thorny. Technicians who are not really ready for new technology will be called upon to help define, select, install and use tools that are often alien to the way they have been doing things for decades.

We cannot merely select the tool that satisfies an artificially created matrix of features and benefits any more. We need to adopt a holistic approach to tool selection. Tools in today's development environment do not operate independently or in a vacuum. They are often driven by the other tools or their outputs drive subsequent progress in the development methodology. Tool cooperation and integration is at an all-time high. Vendors are entering into joint marketing arrangements with former competitors faster than lawyers can prevent them. Some of these relationships are robust and make a lot of sense. Some of them exist only on a marketing brochure.

Some vendors have chosen to try to attack this problem by providing the complete solution with their own suite of software from vision to testing and maintenance. While single vendor solutions would offer the greatest advantage due to the high level of integration, there is currently no real solution from a single vendor. Several purport such a solution but fall short at one tool level or another. For example, Texas Instruments' The IEF is among the closest toolsets to a completely integrated front-to-back CASE solution. It falls short, however, in several areas.

While strongly rooted in Information Engineering techniques, its program generator cannot satisfy all the user's needs for client/server target architecture. It also has a difficult time gaining widespread acceptance among development professionals because it requires a radical mind shift and a discipline that many do not have. This is not a particular failing of this product, but an inherent problem that is becoming more crucial to solve for today's IT manager.

Development change is placing a tremendous pressure on the IT organization to adapt to new methodologies, techniques, and tools to get their job done. Target architectures are not only different in concept to the developer than anything he has encountered before, but also the tools needed to create software for these target architectures are dramatically different.

Where the systems we have been developing were transaction-based, on-line systems using well-known design and programming techniques, new systems are event-driven, client/server systems using techniques that few of today's MIS organizations understand. Not only is understanding difficult, most of today's IT professionals actually resist this change. In some companies as few as 50 percent of their current IT staff may be able to adapt to a new way of developing systems. The general rule that we have found is that the less-experienced the staff, the more adaptable they will be toward new techniques, methods, and tools. The chart below demonstrates the shift taking place with respect to the demand for tools.

The switch is on. In order to make sure that our future development environment is ready for the new IT professional, a better method for discovering, evaluating and selecting tools must be used. Since we need to center on solving the user's problems and we believe that this solution must not be driven by our current technology. We need to perform a proper investigation each time a major change is projected by the business. Yesterday's investigation techniques will not be sufficient to accomplish this. A better method would be centered on the problem to be solved.

The New Method for Tool Selection

1. **Perform a complete needs analysis from the user's perspective.** The user cannot be ignored any longer in this process. We cannot simply utilize the tools we currently have to implement systems for the user based on our current level of experience. To do so would be to do a disservice to the user and only serves to

continue the declining respect of user's for MIS.

2. **Identify areas where technology is expected to help satisfy these needs.** This is somewhat backwards to the way that we have been doing this. We have all too often built the solution to match the technology on hand, or to what we already knew about the solution. New ideas were looked at askance. Today we need technology evangelists to help point out where technology can be used more effectively.
3. **Canvas vendors of products that seem to fit the general need.** Derive these lists from inquiries into other companies in a similar business. They will be using products closest in nature to those needed. Unless the organization is really on the bleeding edge, the set of tools discovered will be a good starting point for further investigation.
4. **Request contacts from these vendors.** Tell the vendors that you are conducting an investigation of new development tools. Request actual contacts from them of companies of a size and nature similar to your own. The contacts they provide will be your peers and can share a wealth of experience with you about their actual tool use.
5. **Perform a series of short telephone interviews.** Discuss tool usage with these contacts. Be fully prepared, use an interview guide. Explain your process and be willing to share your results with them as a way of thanking them for their assistance.
6. **Record all appropriate data about these companies.** Note which products they use and how happy they are with them. Make special note about their statistics and volumes. These will be invaluable in comparing results later on. Ask them if they know others using the same or similar products. You may be able to expand your interview questions and find out about other products that may be more suitable.
7. **Construct a list of tentatively suitable products and vendors.** Summarize each product's or vendor's important differentiates. Include as much unique information as possible as long as it relates to how the product meets the needs or helps to make an informed decision among similar products.
8. **Form a short list of selected products.** Whittle the selection down to a set of products that are approximately equal and still satisfy the basic needs. The objective is to have a list such that any choice would produce an acceptable solution.
9. **Select a pilot toolset from the short list.** Choose tools that can operate cooperatively with each other. Try to form a logical set that enables an environment similar to the desired final solution.
10. **The pilot toolset can then be installed in a test lab.** A small application can be selected to test the tools. Tool vendors can be invited to assist in demonstrating how their tool not only fits in

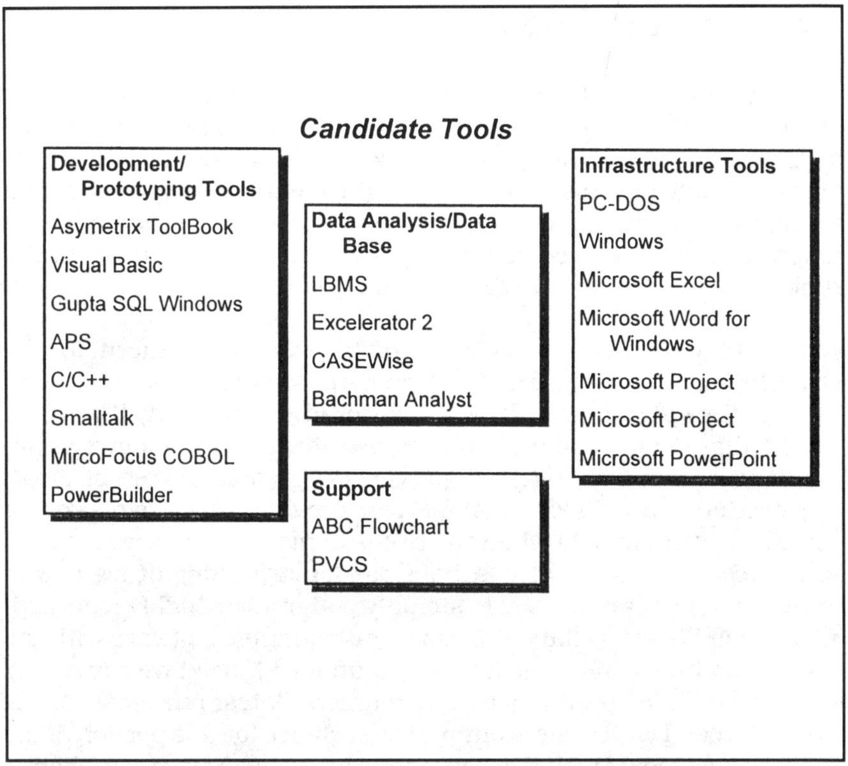

Figure 6.9. Candidate toolset.

the environment, but also adds to the total architecture.

11. **Stay flexible, tools today change rapidly.** Once tools are chosen one must be careful to not think of these choices as final. We are using tools today in our development environments that didn't exist in the market three years ago. New tools enter the marketplace all the time. We cannot allow our solution toolset to stand still until the ultimate tool is either invented or is discovered. New and better choices will be coming along all the time. We need to recognize that development techniques, not tools, must remain stable. While our technicians are trained in the usage of one GUI development tool we can usually switch to a similar competing tool with little or no impact. Often it's the GUI techniques and standards that are important, not the specific syntax of the tool.

Figure 6-9 indicates that tool selection is not a permanent set of choices. Tools change very often in capability and new tools come along every day that may meet the needs of the developer better than those of yesterday.

Evaluate Findings

Once tools are chosen, one must be careful to not think of these choices as final. Toolsets created today can only be expected to last for a somewhat brief time period—in some cases less than two years. One need only look back two years at the tools generally in use then to compare with the tools being used today to understand the magnitude of change going on. Figure 6-9 shows how toolsets will probably evolve in your organization.

- PC-DOS (latest release). OS/2 could be used as a platform for the development toolset. The Development Architect may choose to install the special OS/2 for Windows product offered by IBM. This particular environment allows the user to use all Windows applications without change but provides a greater degree of crash protection than Windows alone can provide. This can prove a useful feature indeed when the needs of many new users is taken into account. Support can be a particularly difficult issue and anything that can be used to simplify it should be highly regarded.
- Microsoft Windows (latest release, or compatible software with the target architecture). The industry standard... need we say more?
- Microsoft Office productivity environment (latest releases). While the Microsoft Office offers our personal choice for this portion of the toolset we recognize that corporations today have often established their own standards for these tools. Other products such as WordPerfect, Lotus 1-2-3, and Persuasion can provide suitable substitutes for these products. The Microsoft suite provides excellent tool integration and data interchange between tools. There will be many occasions when data needs to be transferred between products and the tightest integration provides the highest level of transferability.
- Word for Windows
- Excel
- PowerPoint
- Prototyping environment. Prototyping tools are crucial in the lab environment.
- Asymetrix Toolbook is an excellent choice for this particular level of tool. There is no other product in the marketplace that offers the ability to prototype Windows applications but helps keep the developer away from building too much custom code. It is custom code during prototyping that causes countless problems in the creation and constant improvement of the prototype.
- CASE tools. There are many CASE tools available in today's marketplace. They each have many unique advantages and disadvantages. We recommend Excelerator or LBMS mainly because they are the only LAN smart tools available off the shelf that can

handle the size and complexity of today's system developer.

- Excelerator (Intersolv)
- LBMS (LBMS)
- Development environment (assumes client/server target).

Most of these types of projects are client server in nature. The actual choice of a tool depends upon the type of application being created. If the application is going to operate in a multi-tiered environment accessing data both from a local database and/or a mainframe database (such as DB2) the choice will often be SQLWindows. Gupta's product has many unique features that provide tight integration between the workstation and the database server.

- Gupta SQLWindows (Gupta)
- PowerBuilder has interfaces to other database systems and is often the choice for Sybase or other independent database systems. PowerBuilder has many adherents and is likely often the choice because of the growing number of developers available that already have experience with the product.
- PowerBuilder (Powersoft)
- Either of the two above products could satisfy the needs of today's developer for most of the types of applications being developed. There are an increasing number of other development tools that could be offered as alternatives with similar levels of success. Success can be measured many different ways. If an organization anticipates a shift toward object-oriented methods and techniques, careful consideration to other tools that may be more oriented toward this end. This marketplace is still in a high state of change. Industry leaders have not emerged and the features of these products vary widely and leapfrog each other with each new release. If one is considering this course of action one should carefully consider the following watchouts before proceeding:

- Do not proceed unless you are sure that your staff is amenable to these new techniques and procedures.
- Beware of ambitious productivity or quality claims by those who have little experience with these methods. Properly applied an organization can vastly improve the quality of its products but this requires broad changes among the staff within an organization.
- Be prepared to spend significant amounts of your time and money on product transition and staff training. New methodologies must be acquired, IT staffs will need training both in design and systems development. New tools must be evaluated and acquired and installed.
- There will be little transference of reusability or functionality between old development tools and new development tools.

- Change Management. This is one area that must not be overlooked. Control over new software elements must be established early. This includes not only source modules but also complete production suites of software. This control helps to insure that the proper modules are in production and that when changes are made control over testing and quality assurance is attained.
- PVCS (Intersolv)

Infrastructure

- Audio/Visual
  - Large screen monitor for lab viewing of PC display during development and prototyping
  - VCR for viewing videotapes for educational or miscellaneous purposes
  - Overhead projector
  - Flip charts with easels (at least 2 per lab)
  - Electronic White Marker Board - this is a must for productive time in the lab.
- Large conference/work table (for 12 persons)
- Comfortable seating for 12 at table and seating for PC workstations
- Windows to the outside are highly desired (actual glass, not software)
- Carpeting is highly desired
- Electrical connections must be everywhere including under the conference/work table
- Wall clock
- Tack wall in labs makes posting of work products on the walls for review easy
- The Lab itself should be a room big enough for lab staff comfort. This will be their living quarters for the work day for several months at a time.
- Technical support for lab product instruction, assistance and resolution of hardware/software problems (the lost time element cannot be minimized). This usually consists of a well-defined *Help Desk* function with a roving support function. The amount of roving support needed will vary with the actual number of labs in session at any point in time. The technical support team can either be a group currently performing this task within the organization or a new group set up especially for this task. In either case this team should have the use of certain control and monitoring software to help in problem diagnosis and solution. There are several products on the market today that can help control this activity but among the best is available through the Help Desk Institute in Colorado. Make sure that the tool can track current problems through to their solution and categorize them for future reference. These solutions can help speed solutions to similar

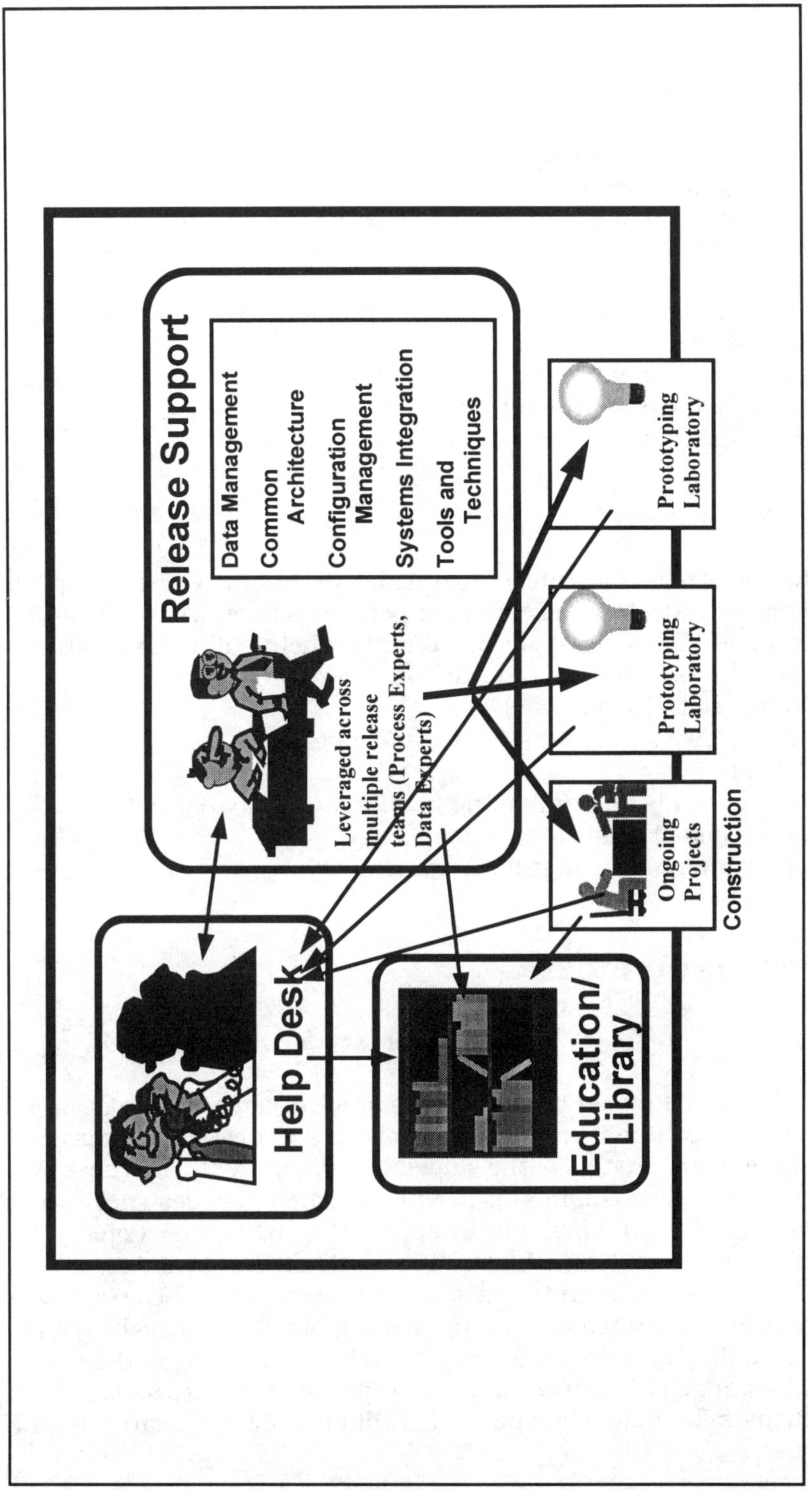

Figure 6.10. Development Environment.

problems as they are reported in the future.

Miscellaneous

- Administrative support
  -1 F/T person per 3 labs
  -Distribute mail, handles phone messages, schedules prototyping demonstrations, arranges travel plans, provides inter-lab communication.
- Individual mail boxes for lab personnel for messages, inter-office and outside mail
- Voice Mail system to minimize lab interruptions
- Coffee/soft drink availability
- Office supplies

Toys

- The use of toys is an integral part of lab productivity. They help lab personnel stay focused for longer periods of time. They add subtle diversions to long discussions and they help build team spirit.
- Examples of suitable lab toys:
  - Koosh balls (#1 favorite)
  - Gak (by Nickelodeon) (#2 favorite)
  - Tile puzzles
  - Magic wands (glitter floating in oil in a transparent stick)
  - Legos (small sets)
  - other interesting, non-noise-making toys

User Involvement

Human Skills Needs

The need for user involvement is much greater in a lab environment. In traditional approaches analysts and designers interacted with the users much like the sloped line in Figure 6-11. There was a lot of involvement in the beginning when the designers were gathering information about the application to be constructed. The user involvement diminished during the detail design and construction phases as the technicians built the system to spec. The user was once again consulted during unit testing (maybe) but really got re-involved during string and application testing. If any of the user's needs changed in the intervening time period they were usually held until installation was complete. This did not always create a happy user.

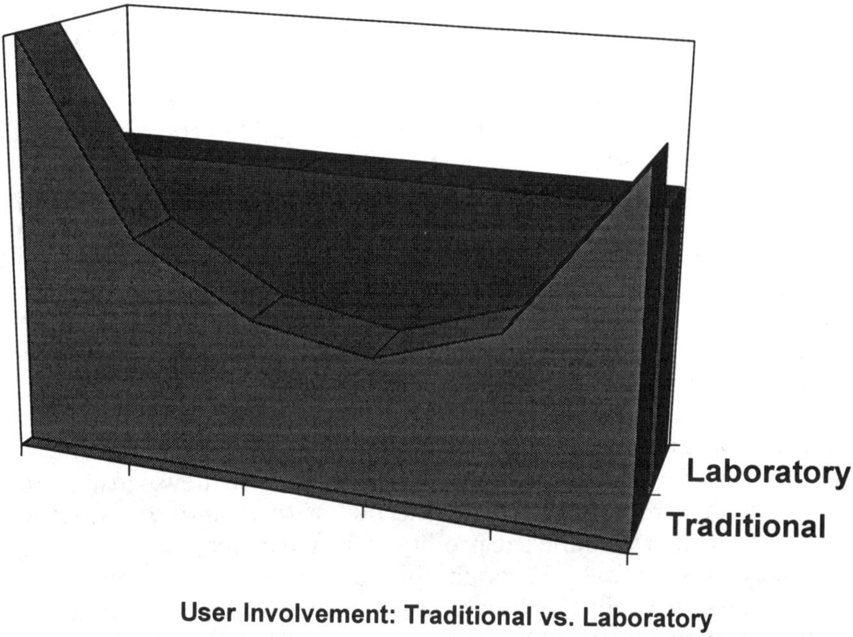

Figure 6.11 User Involvement.

In the second sloped line we can see that the user is involved all the way through the process. There is no gap where someone is off doing something without user involvement. The user is free to (in fact, is encouraged to) suggest changes to the design and implementation of the application. This technique means a greater time commitment from the user but almost guarantees satisfaction when the application is delivered. If we were to weigh this commitment against the amount of re-design and re-tooling needed after the implementation of a less-than-perfect application, we might be surprised at the similar amount of time expended to achieve satisfaction.

User involvement and commitment differences between traditional development and laboratory oriented development

Prototype Analysis

- ***Interactive design.*** The use of interactive design techniques means that facilities must be available to the lab team that enhance their ability to create, review, modify, and demonstrate prototypes of their systems solutions. The lab room itself must be equipped with tools that facilitate the overall control of general lab meetings as well as system development tools that help control the prototyping process.

- ***Modeling.*** Modeling occurs in the lab for nearly all facets of system development. The team creates process models of the redesigned business processes. These models are initially expressed on flip charts but are transferred to the CASE tool as definition becomes more stable and the team becomes more comfortable working with the CASE tool version. Process models, held in the CASE tool are combined with data models to create the underlying system documentation. As the team creates the prototypes the ideas expressed in the prototypes are merged with the definition contained in the process and data models to create a complete picture of the operation and functionality of the new system.
- ***Simulations.*** The team uses these models to create simulations of the new process demonstrating the ability of the new software to support the process. Through the use of these simulations the team continues to refine the prototype from a concept to a working element of software. Through the constant involvement of the users in this process there are no gaps between the functionality of the prototype and the needs of the user. The resultant system meets the user's needs when it is delivered.

CASE Tools

Selection of a Case tool

There are several methods that can be used to select, install and use Case tools. Some of the traditional methods can be vastly improved upon and accelerated. Traditional tool selection usually centered around a team or committee formed to evaluate the various products that may satisfy the needs of the lab. This team usually began by building a matrix with product features listed along the side and vendors supplying products listed at the top. Vendors were then interviewed and products were demonstrated that enabled the team to fill in the blanks on the matrix. In many cases, this analysis did not include any subjective criteria to help evaluate tools and products.

Experience has shown that these product selection teams often did not choose the best tool fit for the organization. They selected the tool that contained the most features, or that satisfied the greatest number of selection criteria. Their efforts often consumed many weeks, even months. Because organizations usually do not plan this task far enough in advance they are usually in a time crunch. This overly cumbersome process usually leads to a delay in selecting the proper tool, resulting in a rush to install the product and train the staff in time for the beginning of the project.

Today's tools are quite sophisticated and often cannot be compared with each other on a feature by feature basis. Many of the more comprehensive tools would have most of the features that the team is searching for. Assuming that this may be the case, the search should actually begin by assessing the actual needs of the lab team, both from an environmental perspective and from the viewpoint of the target architecture. Tools can be quickly eliminated from consideration based upon these criteria and a short list can be developed in days instead of weeks.

The key to this type of selection is tool categorization. Categorization helps to segregate tools based upon their actual usage and fit within the organization. Tools can be categorized as follows:

- Office productivity tools such as word processors, spreadsheets, presentation graphics and diagramming software. Although corporate standards differ greatly for tools in this category, we recommend the Microsoft Office suite of tools due to their widespread base of knowledgeable users, their ability to communicate with each other and trade data and representations of data, and their tight integration with the Windows environment. However, because standards are often already established at many companies, these established tools can be used in place of the Microsoft Office.
- Case tools such as LBMS, Excelerator, and CaseWorks. We recommend these tools mostly due to their ability to use a LAN based repository smartly. These are the major tools that support a full LAN-smart architecture. Users can share the repository across a LAN or WAN with checkin/checkout at a level low enough to not impact all repository users when updating information on the repository. Many CASE tools have other features that are desirable. But, without LAN-based tools the job of the data analyst becomes very difficult.
- Prototyping tools such as Asymetrix' Toolbook for Windows. We recommend Toolbook mainly due to its ability to create robust looking Windows prototypes painlessly and effortlessly. Toolbook is extremely simple to learn. Most lab technicians can become generally proficient in one day.
- Toolbook serves several other useful functions. Since it is not generally able to create complete business applications it prevents the lab team from creating an unnecessarily complex prototype. This feature is extremely important.
- Most technicians create software applications the way they have been trained to create them in the past following the traditional design, specify, code, and test model. Using the lab model of

iterative prototyping the initial prototype must be created quickly without the overhead of significant coding. When we have tried other tools for concept prototyping in the lab the technicians have added significant code to the prototype in order to demonstrate more features of the software.

- Eventually these features must be built in of course, but if they are created too soon they bog down the entire prototype process. The only way to ensure that the prototype is controlled at a high level is to use a tool like Toolbook that cannot build these features in at all. Recommending this process is somewhat controversial because the technicians brought up in the traditional development environment will resist using such "throwaway" prototypes.

The problems with non-throwaway prototypes are as follows:

- prototype is developed incorporating many unique code features of the tool including custom code inserted by the technician
- prototype is reviewed with the user for appropriateness and completeness
- user suggests changes based upon seeing the prototype
- technician resists such change because he has invested a significant amount of time in its creation and debugging
- user is "convinced" to wait and have his suggestions incorporated at a later, more convenient time
- the system is implemented in a Phase 1 - Phase 2 approach that recreates the problems we have always had in software development

The benefits with throwaway prototypes are as follows:

- prototype is developed incorporating no unique code features in a fraction of the time normally used to develop a prototype (hours instead of days)
- user reviews prototype and suggests changes
- changes are quickly reviewed, evaluated and incorporated into the prototype
- the prototype is again executed for suitability

Programming tools, such as Gupta SQLWindows, PowerBuilder and APS, and many others like them, give the developer significant leverage when creating applications. There is a tremendous amount of change in this particular tool group today. Tools such as PowerBuilder and Gupta do many similar things and typically leapfrog each other from release to release with respect to features available. It is difficult to recommend a single tool in this group due to this change and due to specific requirements of the application being constructed in your organization at a particular point in time.

APS is particularly notable due to its ability to create application code for multiple level environments. Some of its utility, however, depends on how flexible your organization is with respect to the target operating environment and where you expect specific application components to execute. If you are targeting a multi-level client/server environment, APS may be just the tool you are looking for. It cannot only build the code needed to support your application, but it can determine where that code executes automatically between the client and the server.

Matching with the Methodology

Once a methodology is chosen it is important to base further tool choices on their respective fit with the methodology. Case tools that can be customized to fit the methodology provide the greatest utility in design and control. To the extent that these tools mirror the methodology the lab team will enjoy greater success in designing, controlling and developing the application. One of the most important features if the applications are being created for a client server environment is a LAN-smart, repository-based Case tool. This tool enables the members of one lab team to communicate with each other and to share the same data model. As definition is filled in, lab teams can use the tools to communicate the design components to each other.

A shared data model is essential to communicate from lab to lab and between labs and data analysts. To the extent that the data model can reflect an inter-lab picture the resultant solution will have a higher level of integration and future enhancements will usually be easier to identify and implement.

Training on the Case Tool

Training on the Case tool can be accomplished in one of several ways. The Case vendor can be contracted to provide training to lab teams either directly or in public classes. Time is of the essence when scheduling the training. If the lab teams are trained too soon they will lose much of their valuable knowledge of the tool before it can be put to use. If training is not scheduled in time coordination between the training vendor may become difficult.

There are many third party training organizations that can provide excellent training as well. They may be priced more reasonably or may have a greater availability of flexibility to meet the team's needs. On-site training is often possible presented by both vendors and third party organizations. Many of these organizations also present train-the-trainer courses so that additional savings can be realized for future classes.

All members of the lab team should be trained in the product as they will all have opportunities to use the tools in the lab. In our experience many of the users on the lab team were as adept at using these tools by IT personnel to help enter data and maintain the model after its creation.

Partnering with the Vendor

If your project is very large or involves many lab teams, an organization may realize additional savings in both time and money by establishing a partnership with a vendor. The vendor may participate in the setup of your lab environment. Vendors can provide installation assistance, customized training, day-to-day consulting to lab teams and insight into product future plans that might otherwise be kept confidential. Understanding these product plans may help decide future architectural direction and enhance the organization's ability respond to the needs of tomorrow.

Support Tools

Drawing/Graphic Packages

The team will need several tools in this category. During the course of a lab team's development they will need a tool to assist in drawing flow charts and process charts on an informal basis, outside of the CASE tool. There will also be many occasions where the lab team needs to prepare presentations to other lab teams, users not working with the lab, and management. These presentations must be well thought out and the use of professional tools will go a long way toward making the best possible impression with these groups. For these choices, it is important that the tools be easy to use and require little formal training. Quick learning and results are needed by the lab team.

Some examples of tools we prefer in this category are:

- ABC Flowchart for ad hoc diagramming. ABC has tremendously increased the features in its product line. The product has been made easier to use and has recently included the diagram sets of various popular methodologies (e.g. CSC Catalyst) into the off-the-shelf product.
- Microsoft PowerPoint for presentation graphics. There are many presentation graphics packages available for purchase. PowerPoint

is among the simpler to use that still contains a host of strong features designed to produce presentation graphics from the simplest to the most complex.

Word processing, spreadsheets, E-Mail

The lab team will need to create a daily log of its design and architectural decisions. They will need to document processes and other items discussed during lab sessions, and they will need to create status reports to management. Spreadsheets will often be used to analyze data, present statistics, and track miscellaneous items. E-Mail systems can be used to facilitate the flow of integration information between lab teams and others in the organization. A more comprehensive system can often be used to organize this integration and discussion points into logical databases.

Some examples of tools in this category are:

- Microsoft Word for Windows (word processing)
- Microsoft Excel (spreadsheet)
- Lotus Notes (E-Mail and information database maintenance)

Other support tools

Version control and configuration management are vital when developing applications in a client/server environment. These functions provide a strong level of control that was often taken for granted in mainframe environments. As software modules are developed by many a team of developers they usually need to be configured into a release for production execution. Manual creation of these configurations is possible, but becomes very difficult to maintain for any but the most trivial systems. In addition, today's modern tools for version control add many levels of security in the control and maintenance of source and object code.

PVCS from Intersolv is such a tool. It has become a de facto industry standard among developers of systems in non-mainframe environments.

From time to time lab teams may need other specialized tools based upon the complexity of the application being created. The use of object-oriented toolsets will become more mainstream in the next few years. This will cause new tools to enter the market for consideration. In addition, many of today's tools will shift toward a more object-oriented approach. Many are already doing so. Of course, this shift also means that current staff must be trained in these new philosophies, techniques and methods as well as the tools built for them. The time and expense associated with this shift cannot be underestimated. It must be offset by demonstrated business need and a strong fit within the architectural direction of the organization.

Project Management

Project management is a key element to the success of the new development environment. Many of the tools and methods used are new to the staff. Traditional elements of project management still apply but need to be modified in order to make certain that the proper products are being produced and that the overall design is complete.

There is a tendency to look at new methods as less controllable than traditional methods. This could not be further from the truth. There is a need to pare down the deliverable products to only those that are essential, but control still needs to be exerted to make sure that standards are adhered to and that quality is under control.

In the past, project management consisted mainly of making sure that all of the products spelled out in the methodology were produced, whether they were necessary or not. Care must be taken to not fall into this trap with new methods and procedures. Project managers need to be much more involved than in the past with the actual solution being produced to make sure that independently produced parts will integrate with other components. In addition, project managers need to make sure that individual teams of developers are following the methodology and are producing according to the schedule.

Time control is very important. Small teams, developing parts of applications independently of each other, have a much greater need for cooperative development and integration. They need to be kept informed not only about their own schedule but also the schedule of those that are developing other components that either they are dependent upon, or that are dependent on them. If any group falls behind and others are not informed, the entire schedule can slip due to delays at integration time. Timebox integration is covered in much greater detail elsewhere in this book.

During the heaviest development period, scope control also becomes critical to overall project control. If any sub-team expands its scope without the knowledge and agreement of the other teams serious schedule delays can result. For example, overlaps or gaps in scope can occur causing major integration problems or wasted time. Scope creep can kill the progress on all but the smallest of projects. It is incumbent on the project manager to make certain that scope is under control at all times and that management is aware of any major changes in scope as soon as they occur.

Project management is at its most critical level during integration of parts and integration testing. It is during this period that the pressure to produce an application can cause the effort to fail. It is too late in the process to change the scope at this time, yet this is just the inclination of the application developer. They may have rushed into integration before they were completely ready and view integration testing as an opportunity to put in these last minute elements.

The project manager must be vigilant and prevent these changes to the extent possible. If necessary, he must send the development team back to the development arena until their product is actually ready for testing. This can be a painful and politically difficult step to take, but it is almost always unavoidable in order to prevent further, deeper problems from occurring.

The next section covers some of the project manager's tools that are available today. These tools do not automate the control over the developers, they merely help the project manager by automating many of the mundane and arithmetic computation portions of the management effort. This frees up time for the manager to maintain and exert control over the development process. The project manager must make sure that he does not fall behind the screen of these tools and become an absentee manager, relying on data and charts, when daily progress assessment and control are what is needed.

If possible, project management should be performed by a team. An administrative project manager can gather data about project progress and enter these data into automated control systems. These reports can be shared with the project manager and upper management and the leaders of individual development efforts so that all parties are informed about progress vs. plan and actual vs. budget expenditures. An overall project manager can then focus his time on product review and progress assessment (not just number rollups) using the administrative project manager as a control and reporting mechanism. A team of experienced integrators can assist the project manager on large projects by helping to insure that integration is happening at all levels.

Tools

Tools available for control of complex projects are quite common and are very easy to use and maintain. Automated tools that reside on a LAN would be most useful but to date these tools do not do an adequate job of rolling up data from many projects on different systems. Two tools in general use that meet the needs of most professionals are Microsoft Project for Windows and ABT's Project Workbench for Windows. Both tools do a good job of assisting the project manager in the process of estimating, planning, reporting and controlling the data associated with a complex project.

While Microsoft Project for Windows is simpler to use for project data entry and planning, ABT's Project Workbench is somewhat simpler to use for weekly time reporting. Microsoft Project is more heavily integrated with other Windows and Microsoft products than ABT's product. For example, data from Microsoft Project can be easily converted into an Excel spreadsheet, manipulated, and converted back into Microsoft Project data. This makes it very easy to perform mass changes on project data and use other facilities that may be more familiar to the project manager.

In the final analysis it doesn't much matter which tool you might have or choose — control must be exerted by the project manager to make things happen. The tool merely exists to report progress or highlight problem areas where attention is needed. Any of the above tools should prove sufficient to monitor and manage the task at hand.

Architecture: Review, Interview, Modification and Documentation Process

Architecture Review Process

The following discussion highlights an alternative approach to defining an architecture without a lengthy market search and recommendation approach.

This process is intended to verify the applicability of the current architecture definition at any corporation. Through a process of investigation and interviews of actual managers/designers at sites with similar architectures we can verify the various architectural elements chosen by an Architecture Committee.

The process should identify candidate architectures that match the architectural needs. If matches cannot be ascertained, the architecture needs may be adjusted to allow a match to be found.

- Identify possible candidate organizations for consideration and investigation (>30 sites).
- Establish technical/business hurdles to eliminate non-applicable candidates.
- Interview candidates to determine technical/business applicability and suitability for further consideration (>5).
- Evaluate all applicable candidate architectures against your organization's needs (at least one).
- If a single applicable candidate architecture cannot be identified, then refine the architecture to permit a candidate architecture to be found.

Architecture Review Process - Overview

- Establish IS Priorities, Architecture Criteria, and Size Criteria. These criteria can be as complex as needed to ensure that the appropriate needs of the organization are met.
- Establish candidate lists from vendors and collective experiences. Candidates to be contacted and interviewed can come from vendors by direct request for similar types of installations. Industry publications can also be investigated to ascertain other organization with similar characteristics and/or architectures.
- Establish and apply hurdles to limit further consideration. These hurdles will help to establish early elimination criteria to quickly narrow the field of vendors to a more manageable number.
- Interview candidates for architectural applicability. Actual telephone interviews will help establish the continued consideration of the candidate organization. Interviews can also reveal other organizations that have similar configurations. Many companies will tell you of others that have similar architectures that they have used to help guide them. Further interviews can then be conducted with these companies to gather more complete information about the desired architecture.
- Document configuration information. Track each interview on a standard sheet to record interview results. (Sample forms follow this section.)
- Determine "Satisfaction" factor for each interview. Rate the interview using a scale to group the most confident results together and to help eliminate those with a low level of confidence.
- Categorize individual products and/or product suites from applicable interviews.
- Evaluate architectural findings with respect to your organization's architecture.
- Create short list of products for further evaluation and consideration (make use of benchmarking, product evaluations, and experience).
- Produce final report of findings.

Architectural Search and Interview Process

Establish IS Priorities, Architecture Criteria, and Size Criteria

Architecture Steering Committee

- Defines the priorities based upon business need, technical direction

- Architecture criteria are determined that meet and/or support the IS priorities
- Size criteria are established that support the business volumes expected for the selected applications
- During the process these criteria may have to be examined and re-evaluated if other sites cannot be found that verify the architectural definition at ABC Corporation

Establish Candidate Lists

- Vendors are interviewed, they may also suggest candidates that could also fit the established criteria

Establish and Apply Hurdles

- A standard must be set outlining criteria that must be met by suggested candidates
- These hurdles must match and support the criteria established by the ABC Corporation Architecture Steering Committee
- As candidates are identified the "hurdle" criteria are applied to accomplish early elimination of non-applicable candidates
- Those that do not meet the criteria are eliminated from further consideration in the process

Interview Candidates for Architectural Applicability

Using an interview guide

- Determine the applicability of each candidate's architecture
- Gather technical and volume data to support further examination
- Establish the degree that the interviewee is satisfied with the architecture implemented.
- Document interview results.

Categorize Products:
Based upon interview and product knowledge:

- Determine which products in the applicable product set are mix and match.
- Determine which products in the applicable product set are product suites and must or should be used in conjunction with each other.

Evaluate Findings:

- If architecture(s) meet the criteria at ABC Corporation and were found to be satisfactory by the interviewed site further evaluation can proceed.
- Determine the exact match of the architecture to the needs of ABC

Corporation.

- Identify gaps between the two architectures.
- Identify products needed to fill gaps.

Create Short List of Products:

- Using selected architecture, list applicable products.
- Identify additional products needed and evaluate suitability using
  - -Benchmarking
  - -Product evaluation
  - -Experience with prior usage
- Review all products for suitability and interoperability

Produce Final Report:

Produce report of conclusions.

- Include:
  - -Process documentation
  - -Interview results
  - -Product reviews
  - -Recommendations

Sample Call Questionnaire

Calling Questionnaire	
Contact Name	
Contact Address	
Contact Phone	
Source	
CallerID	
Date and Time Called	

Questions:

1. What volumes are you processing?	
2. What is your response time?	
3. What tools are you using?	
4. What is the actual tool chain?	
5. Why did you make the change?	
6. What is the benefit?	
7. Would you do it again?	
8. What is your planned next step?	

Sample Telephone Questionnaire for Tool Interview

Information to be gathered during telephone interviews:

Discuss with the interviewee that you are:

- Conducting a market driven review of current state of the art.
- Gathering information to prepare for an RFQ.
- Attempting to talk with some large-scale production sites for assistance in determining architectural, performance and usability choices.
- Wanting to learn what's being used by other large customers.
- Interested in what modeling tools they use for scaling performance and sizing?
- Do you have or are you planning to run a benchmark?
- Do you have partnerships or joint ventures with any hardware/ software vendors?

Customer Site Criteria	**Minimums**
1. Production commercial end user site	Yes or No
2. Transactions per second	Number
3. Multi-tiered architecture	Yes or No
4. No. gigabytes of relational storage accessed by a single system.	Number
5. Number of users.	Number
6. Complex transaction profile (DBMS I/O accesses per txn.)	Describe briefly
7.Response time less than x sec (queue to queue)	Number

Site Information

Site Name	
Contact	
Phone	
Caller	

Data Sheet

	Two Years Ago	Today	Two Years From Now
General DP			
• Organization			
• Primary Objectives			
• Major Projects			
Systems/OS:			
• Mfr./Model			
• Memory			
• CPUs			
Disk:			
• Type (gig)			
• Number			
Terminals/Workstations:			
• Type			
• Configuration			
• Number			
• Dial up or remote			
Network:			
• Type			
• Speed			
• Backbone			
• Tributary			
• Gateways			
DBMS:			
• Types:			
• Largest Size:			
Transaction Manager:			
• Types			
Development Environment:			
• Platform			
• Size/Capacity			
• GUI Tools			
• Code-Generators/CASE			
• Rules Based Systems			
• 4GLs			
• Change Mgmt:			

Utilities			
• Repository/Data Dictionary			
• DB Gateways			
• Object Oriented Methodology			
Office Automation:			
• Recoverability			
• Data Center/OPS Standards			
• Backup & Restore			
• Monitors			
• Network Management			
• Software Distribution			
Performance:			
• End-to-End Time			
• Queue-to-Queue Time			
• Peak TPS:			
• Avg. TPS:			
• Total Daily Transactions:			
• Complexity of Transaction:			
Applications:			
• Number of programs			
• Number of applications			
• Languages used			
• Components of runtime environment			
• Percentage of applications under replacement			
• Number of programmers			
Architecture:			
• What are the system interconnections?			
• How is the data distributed by layer?			
• How is the processing distributed by layer?			
• What is the application life cycle methodology?			
• What is the application view of the data?			
• What are the application-to-application connections?			
• What is the workstation view of the application?			
Results:			
• Reliability			
• Availability			
• Speed of Development			
• Business Effectiveness			

• User Satisfaction			
• Ease of Use			
• Ease of Operation			
• Ease of Installation			
• Ease of Learning			
• Ease of Programming			
• Maintainability			
• Vendor Satisfaction			
• Security			
• Data Integrity			
• Reusability			
• Scalability			
• Openness/ Portability			
• Continuous Operation			
• Adaptability			
• What is largest area of concern?			
• What is the weakest area?			
Cost:			
• Price Performance			
• Largest component			
• Performance/Goals			
• Unexpected costs			

RESKILLING

Reengineering Management Information Systems

Chapter 7

Reskilling the Organization

Facilitating the transformational journey through the use of education provides a foundation for individuals to meet the challenges of change, that is brought about through I/S reengineering. While providing a foundation for the realignment of the I/S organization by modifying the organization structure, only the improvement of the basic skills of these organizations will lead it to the success. During the transition there will be a lack of skills, fear of the new order, and a general lack of experience with working together as a cooperative interactive team with business. The lack of these skills all have the potential for undermining the vision of the future. The skills of the MIS professional today are supportive of the single technology solution. The titles and single tasks focus expertise, and has created an organization of single do's and task activities that cause the organization to be rigid and inward thinking.

The Transformation Journey

The journey is not only for the MIS professional, it needs to include all individuals from the organization that will work hand-in-hand to develop new business solutions. In the alignment of Information Technology and Business Operations the "whole" company must be included in the reskilling process. The transformation must include the rethinking of how company executives, middle and front-line management views and interacts with the new systems professional and combined structures. The Executive team including CEO, CFO, and COO must support the changes that must accrue in how the organization views the implementation of the MIS functions. The transformation will not happen without management of the changes. Executives must integrate the systems organization into the mainstream of the business community and support the new organization. It's important for top management to promote the re-skilling effort by being the first to sign-up. They must be the prime change agent for the transformation. Only through the joint ownership of the solution will the reskilling effort receive the rigor it deserves.

The Challenges of Reskilling Transformation

MIS Managers and Project Leaders

Today's MIS managers and project leaders understand the complex task of running projects, supporting today's systems environment, and controlling staff. In reengineering we require the addition of a whole new dimension to the management role. Managers need to think differently to be tomorrow's leaders. The managers must be reskilled to be responsible for building a positive environment, providing a result-oriented work climate, removing barriers to understanding and cooperation, and providing examples of how to work effectively. MIS managers and project leaders in large and medium-size companies may find it difficult to support changes in the workplace as they move to become more hands on.

Remember it is much easier to modify a process than change a human behavior. Leadership is the key to successful reengineering and it has to start with the managers.

Information Technology Professionals

The current MIS structure that supports development and maintenance work is a world of specialists. In today's new world of business and systems partnerships, the reengineering effort must focus on changing the specialist view of the world. The current business analysts, system analysts, system designers, application programmers need to be transitioned into a caseworker environment, where "business process English" is used as the way to communicate requirements not "technology ease." The challenge is to reskill individuals to communicate technical information from a business point-of-view and keep the information simple. Today technical jargon tends to intimidate business users and slow down the process of development. New paradigms for the definition of "success" for system professionals need to be expressed. The new definition should break the old paradigms of success. Today's measure of success is based on lines-of-code written or being a technology guru. The new definition should combine the old definition with the new definition of success being seen as having the ability to communicate meaningful and creative ideas for specific business goals. The system professionals must share a common set of values with their business partners, where they listen and are viewed as part of the business team. They must be cross-trained in order to provide more flexibility in solving business problems and

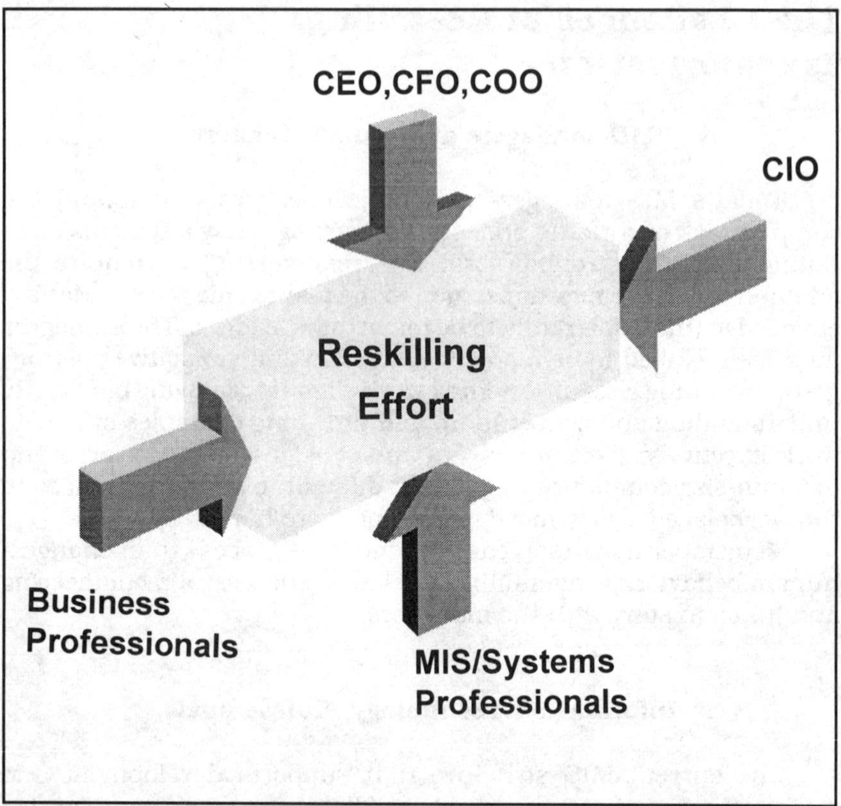

Figure 7.1 The entire organization must be considered when developing a reskilling plan.

getting the job done. They must understand and promote the business goals.

The Business Professional

To provide a complete transition the business community who will work hand-in-hand with the technology professional should have the opportunity to be included in the reskilling of the new organization. This will help to start open communication and promote team dynamics. This is so important in the creation of the new team effort. Business and systems professionals will need to go through the dynamics of team behaviors as they emerge into the high performance team that the reengineering effort is counting on for business results. The business professional should understand some of the technical terminology of the tools that will support the new development process and business solutions. Business professionals include all classifications of business workers affected by the I/S reengineering effort and part of the labs.

Moving Forward

New management styles, new interpersonal considerations, and new communication mechanisms all need to be in order to insure continuous improvements. The tendency when reskilling MIS is to focus on the easy stuff, such as new technology and methodologies. The reskilling process must allow for the development of the softer skills when reengineering of the systems organization. Many organizations have focused only on technology as the solution to drive new capabilities. Therefore, they have spent money and time in technology training only. Very few MIS organizations have included training in the "softer" skills, such as; listening, communication, team dynamics, and conflict management. In the past only managers were offered training that focused on these skills. The reason for this is that in eight out of ten process improvement projects, companies looked to technology that will improve and control the process.

To moving forward, organizations must work together to achieve the best results for the company, using technology to enable change and not to create the change. Some organizations are professing a change in the application development process. However, when looking closely they are only changing the look of the current process, nothing has really changed. In reengineering projects today the most complex issues are the systems groups flexibility of

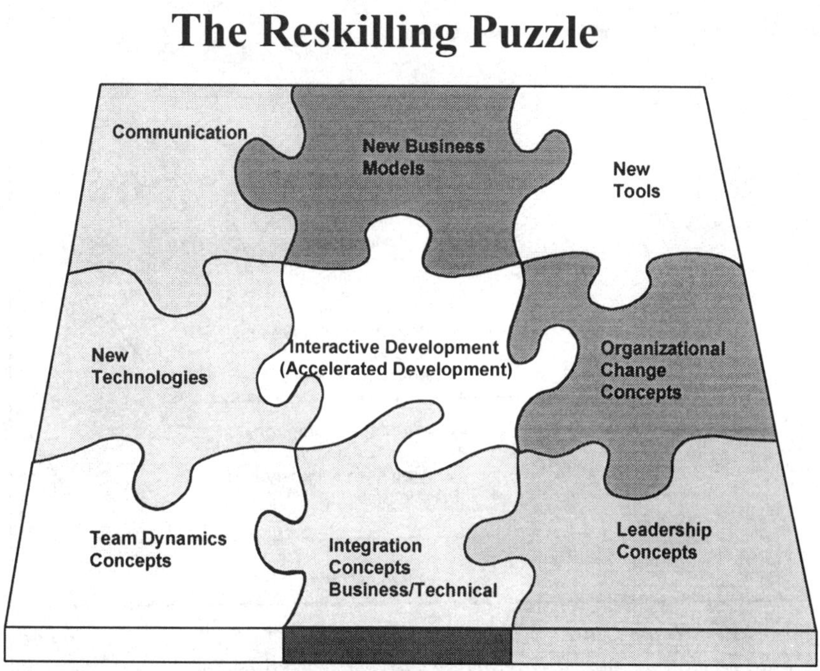

Figure 7.2 The reskilling process combines soft skills and hard skills.

changing their project behaviors to support the rapid development process and team process in the reengineering labs.

What we are seeing is classic computer science skills will not carry systems professionals in today's cooperative interactive development environment. The practices of traditional MIS organizations have continuously slowed development efforts in many organizations making the process of application development too inflexible and unable to meet today's changing business climate. The rapid infusions of new technologies, new worker expectations, and new

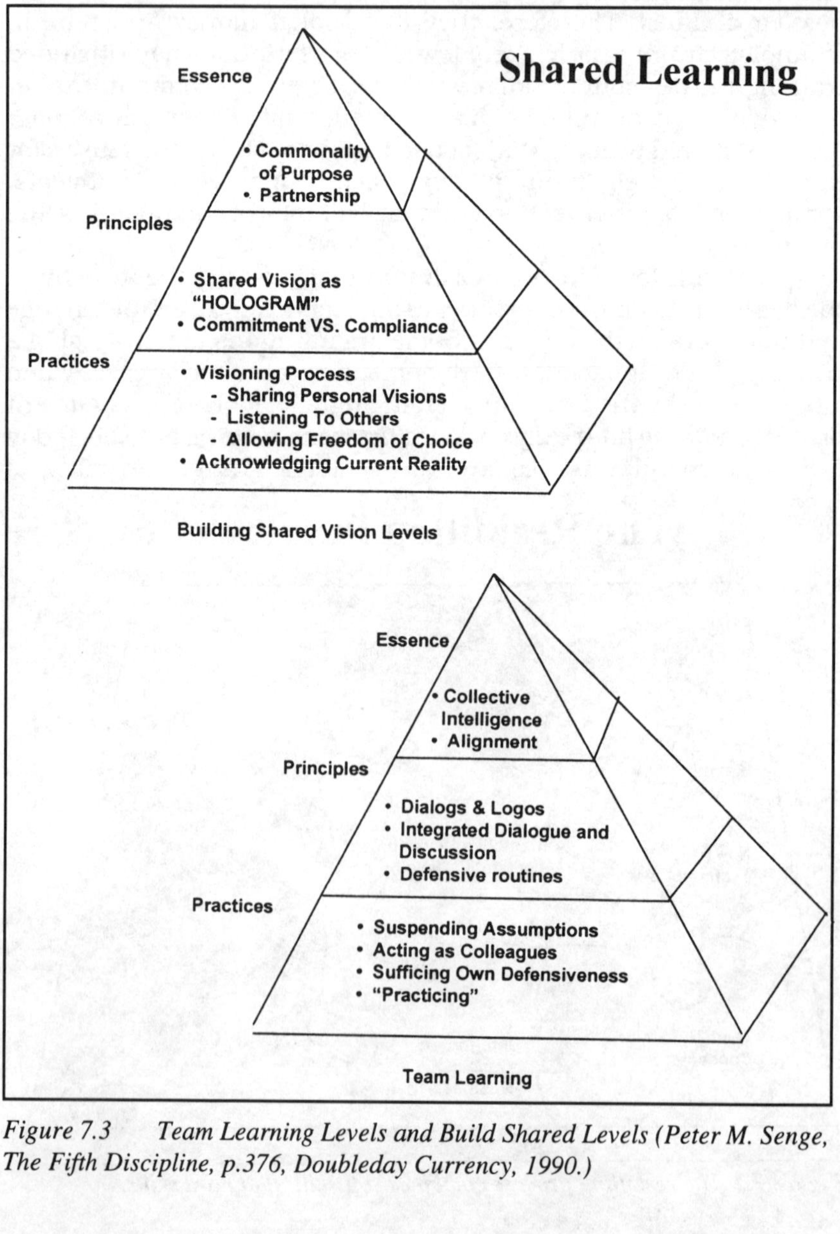

Figure 7.3 Team Learning Levels and Build Shared Levels (Peter M. Senge, The Fifth Discipline, p.376, Doubleday Currency, 1990.)

customer demands of the last few years have not fit well with the restrictive job-works status laden levels of hierarchy, and narrowly focused functions of MIS organizations (Fisher, 1993). The only way to achieve the necessary change in system professionals is to re-skill the organization at all levels. The reskilling process must include new visions, new values and believes, a new structure, and new technical and development skills.

No one should dispute the importance of reskilling the organization in order to successfully achieve optimal performance. The challenges of reskilling agents are to identify programs that will provide individuals with the basic understanding of optimal performance and the skills necessary for high performance communications. These are the building blocks for flexibility, relationships, and appreciation for achieving business results.

Getting Ready for the Transformation

Getting ready for reskilling is not as easy as slecting training courses from a training book. Reskilling is a long process and it takes commitment. An assessment of the organization is a must. Once the assessment is complete, an understanding of the activities ahead will be understood. The process of the assessment includes the evaluation of the current skill levels of individuals, the new skills needed for reengineering efforts and skills required for continued improvement activities. The assessment includes the use of soft-skills, as well as business and technical hard-skills. See figure 7.2.

The First Step

The first step in reskilling the organization is to assess the current skills in order to create a learning plan. Use of the team "learning plan" should best suit the true reskilling needs of an organization in transition. Peter M. Senge describes a learning organization model in his book, *The Fifth Discipline*. See figure 7.3. In short a learning organization is an organization that creates a feedback mechanism for continuous learning and changes based on what is learned over time. The belief that training is a one time event is over. If the organization does not support the concept of a learning organization two years from now the organization will once again be unskilled.

The assessment process of reskilling has eight activities. Keep in mind that the reskilling effort is focused on both the business community and the system community as a "single" community. The assessment of skills should be run as formal workshops. Worksessions are used to do research and gather the needed information for assessing the current knowledge of the organization. See figure 7.4. This will insure that the time is well spent in the initial step of changing the organization and creating the needs introduction to effective teaming and joint development capabilities. The assessment process should not take longer than two months per group. The designed training should be facilitated through team experiences and activities. This will allow the individuals to start building trust and start to experience teaming.

Your schedule of events should include the following steps:

- Assessment initiation
- Identify current skills
- Map the current skills to the new skills
- Assessment of organizational dimensions
- Perform gap analysis and risk assessment
- Identify reskilling alternatives
- Develop a transformation strategy for reskilling

A description of each step should give an idea of the types of activities that need to happen during the assessment. A strong facilitator and scribe should be present at the workshops and worksessions. The assessment will be different for each organization. Some organizations have implemented work team structures and team training already, if you're one of these, you are one step ahead of the game. However, do take the time to assess the results of the structures and team health. In other words, are the teams working together, are they productive, what will be the impact of including development to their list of activities, can they manage change?

Assessment Initiation

The first step of the assessment will be to establish the organizational dimensions surrounded by the activities. The initiation activity will identify who will be involved in the work sessions and their overall roles and responsibilities. This workshop should be conducted with management. This would include CEO, COO, CFO, CIO, Training Director, Human Relations Director, and the team's business manager. This team will provide sponsorship, establish the assessment timetable, and structure the learning feedback process.

Identification of the Current Initiatives and Resources

Through the use of the workshop identify the current initiates and resources that will support the implementation of the reskilling activities. See figure 7.4. The resources include the financial support

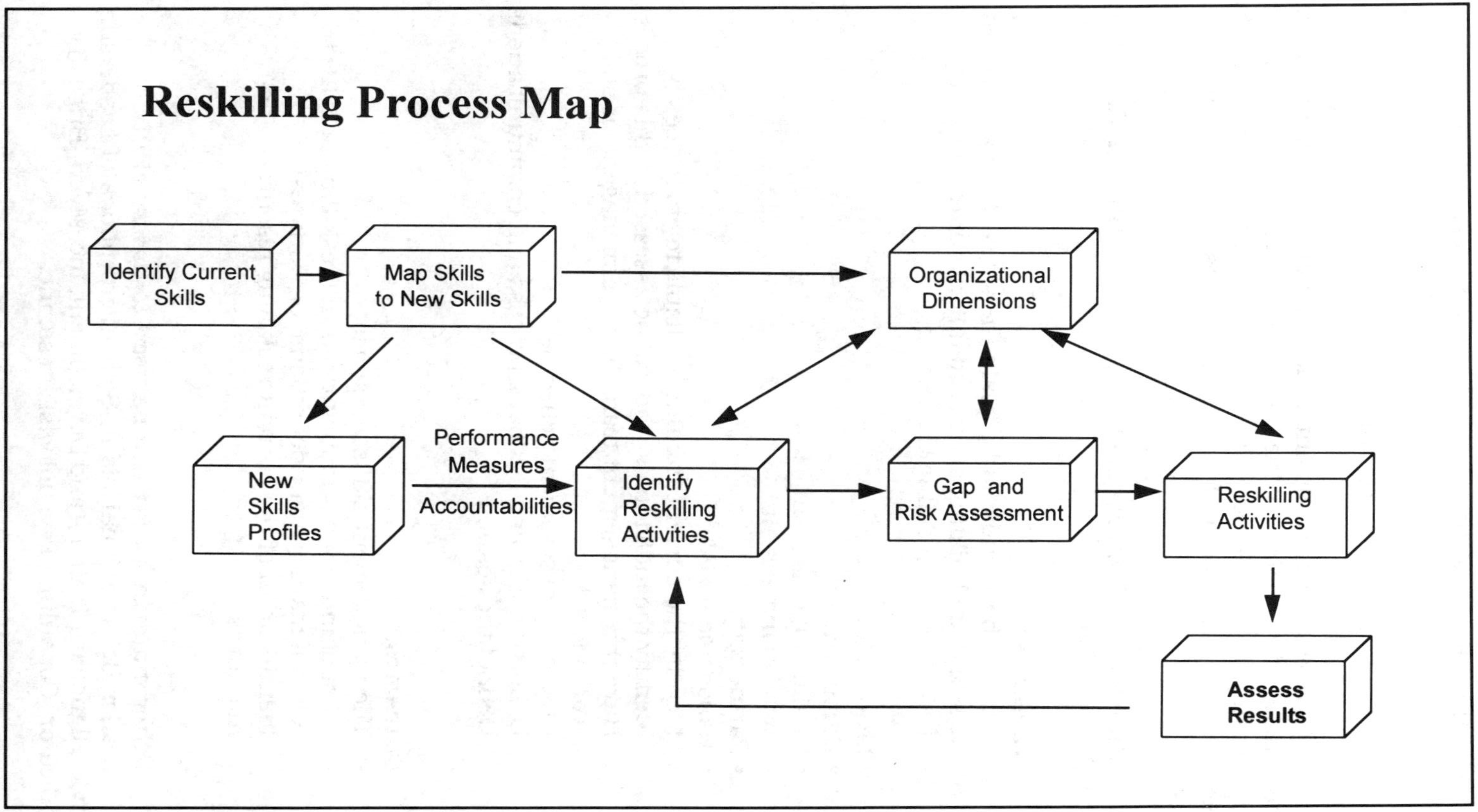

Figure 7.4 The Assessment Process.

to fund this effort and the physical space to conduct the training sessions.

Assessment Initiation Workshop

Objectives: The Assessment Initiation Workshop will introduce the management team to the assessment process and achieve sponsorship for reskilling. The management team will start to identify their strengths and weaknesses to lead the new organization.

Attendees: CEO,COO,CFO,CIO, Director Human Relations, and Director Training.

Procedures:

- Review the agenda and explain the steps of the assessment
- Use a team building activity to talk about team dynamics
- Have the group define the terms:

• Leadership
• Empowerment
• Conflict management
• Stress management
• Partnership
• Management style

- Identify the current training available to employees
- Identify the individuals who will be assessed in this process
- Have the management team fill out a management skill's worksheet
- Create the assessment schedule
- Define the learning feedback process and communications
- Debrief the session

Outcomes:

- The management skills worksheet
- A list of individuals to include in the reskilling activities
- A list of management definitions for work teams
- Identification of the current reskilling resources and initiatives

Other materials that can be used to assess skills:
Leader Behavior Analysis II, Self-A Perceptions of Leadership Style, Blanchard Training and Development, Inc. Myers-Briggs Type Indicator, Consulting Psychologist Press, Inc.

Individual / Title	Sikill Decomposition		Team Management or Employee Management	Trained/ Course	Self-Taugh	Years Used/ When	Job Function Used	Skill Type Business/ Technical	Compensation
	Soft Skills	Hard Skills							

Figure 7.5 Management Skills Worksheet

Individual / Title	Skill Decomposition		Skill Type Business/ Technical	Years Used/ When	Trained/ Course	On-the-Job	Job Function Used	Compensation/ Labor Documented
	Soft Skills	Hard Skills						

Figure 7.6 Team Skills Worksheet.

Individual / New Skill	Skill Decomposition		Course	Self-Taught/ Just-In-Time Classroom	Date Required	Job Function Used	Job Profile Change	Compensation	Labor Issues
	Soft Skills	Hard Skills							

Figure 7.7 Skills Matrix Worksheet.

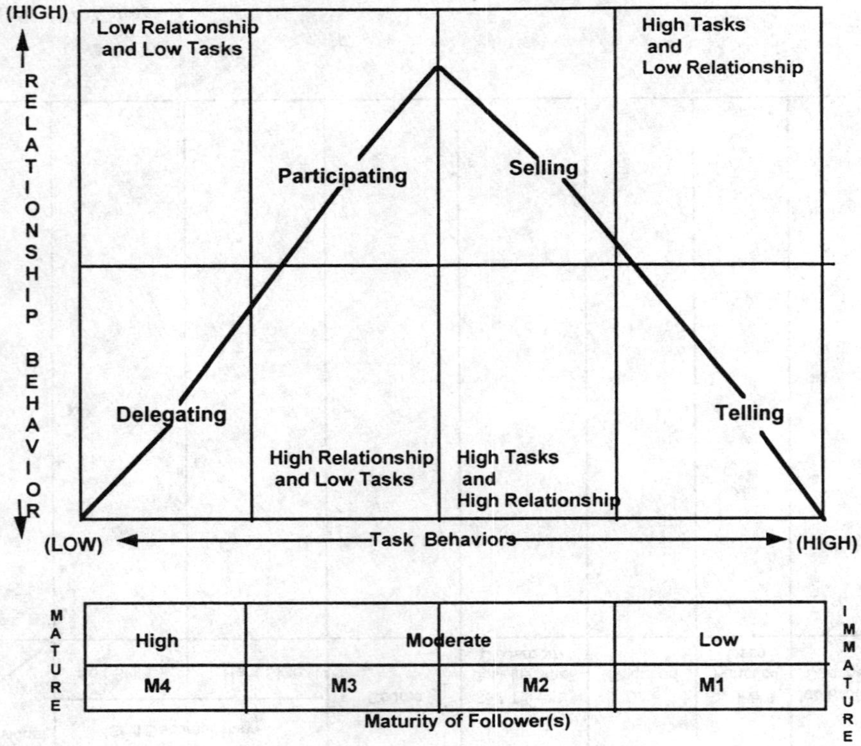

Figure 7.8 Situational Leadership Model (Hersey and K. Blanchard, Management of Organizational Behavior: Utilizing Human Resources, 4th ed., c 1982, p. 152, Prentice-Hall, Inc.

Identify current skills

With the help of the Director of Human Resources or their appointee, start to review the current skills for each of the individuals listed as members of the new process team. Talk to each individual about their current skills, both business and technical. Have each individual fill out the Team Skills Worksheet. See figure 7.7. Collect the worksheets and set the date for the next worksession.

Map the current skills to the new skills

Develop the new skills profiles by mapping the current skills to the new skills needed. See figure 7.8. Once this is completed, work with Human Resources to identify any possible job profiles that need to be changed or compensations that should be documented as part of this process for an individual and the group.

Assessment of Organizational Dimensions

Use a variety of techniques to assess the current values and norms of the organization. The techniques should include a Self-Assessment Survey, a Cultural Survey, and a Change Implication worksession. There are all kinds of survey materials currently on the market. Also there are trained professionals and organizations that specialize in this type of work. It is best to contract with an outside service to either do the assessment surveys or help with the surveys in order to be objective about the information that is gathered.

Perform Gap Analysis and Risk Assessment

Identify the gaps from current skill base to the new process team environment. Create a list of activities or interventions that will need to be completed in order to move from the current environment to the new reengineering environment. Assess the barriers, risks, and assumptions associated with the reskilling of each individual and of the management team which will work within the new environment.

Identify Reskilling Alternatives

Using the information from the Gap Analysis and Risk Assessment define possible reskilling alternatives. This information is used as the foundation for an overall transformation strategy for implementing the new process teams through the reengineering effort.

Develop a Transformation Strategy for Reskilling

Establish a transformation strategy that will maximize opportunities for learning and benefit assessment. The strategy will identify organization transition staffing requirements, reskilling activities, communication and debriefing activities, and a possible pilot project for testing, proving and refining the development process.

The Value of the Assessment

Making the changes that are required to move the business and MIS organizations towards organization commitment and business results takes senior level commitment. The reskilling process addresses all aspects of the development and team environment: physical change, intellectual change, and emotional change. The assessment will identify how prepared the organization is to implement the new organizational design and outline steps needed to make the transition to the changed development environment. This information will drive the reskilling transformation plan, making the transition as easy as possible for the organization and individuals. Without the assessment of the current skill base, the implementation of joint development is based on unrealistic expectations that the systems organization may not be able to live up to. The assessment is only the first step in the reskilling process. Once the assessment is complete the training material must be designed and developed. The training activities need to be outlined and the dates need to be set. The change evaluation mechanism must be put in place.

Putting together the Training Material

There are all kinds of training materials out on the market. Some key course content and concepts that should be taught to management and team members are included in this chapter. Remember, that each group will need to tailor their reskilling program based on the skills assessment. The other key here is that some of the training should be part of a "just-in-time" process. A key consideration on whether to use "just-in-time" training is time to deliver. Business and systems individuals will be learning new ways to develop systems, as well as, dealing with new concepts and team dynamics. Whether formal classroom education or on-the-job just-in-time training, keep in mind adult learning concepts and include the concepts when developing the reskilling activities.

Some Key Concepts to Consider and Teach in the Reskilling Programs

Leadership Concept

Leadership gets results by involving people and management gets results by directing people. To be successful today and in the future, use the traditional management techniques and broaden the leadership dimension of your role. Most of the responsibilities you have now are still important. It's the delivery of these responsibilities that have changed. Management must consider the development of strong self-directed development teams. For a manager this involves growing team members in the "soft-skills" and traditional sales skills such as: negotiations, customer service focused results, communications and business awareness.

Empowerment Concept

Empowerment does not mean doing what every individual wants, too. It means having the ability to make decisions and set limits within the guidelines of the team or organizational procedures. Empowerment should be given as well as received by management and staff. Empowerment should be used to get things done. Empowerment should create energy throughout the organization. If this is not happening, it's probably a result of not understanding what empowerment is or that the individual empowered isn't reskilled in the use of this concept and how it applies to him/her.

Situational Leadership

Situational leadership is a contingency theory that focuses on the workers. The theory states that successful leadership is achieved by selecting the right leadership style based on the worker's maturity level. The maturity level is the ability and willingness of people to take responsibility for directing their own behavior. Situational leadership uses a model of tasks and relationship levels. See figure 7.9. The understanding of this model is very important when reskilling an organization and will help assess the changes in leadership styles as the organization moves through transformation.

Simulation Concept

A simulation is when role playing is used to understand the business changes that are designed and developed. Take the new process and create the day-in-the-life of, this may be a customer, a staff member, or both. Make sure that a walk through of each process is performed and answer the questions: whom am I doing this with, how am I doing this, why am I doing this, when am I doing this, and how long is it taking me? Once these questions are answered make sure that the process supports the business solution and can be implemented quickly. A simulation is similar to the old structured code walk throughs, the difference is that the walk through is based on the new business process. The new team members are jointly responsible for the quality of the designed process and for completeness of the process before it is released. The simulation represents the day-in-the-life of a worker or a process in the new business environment.

Prototype Analysis Concept

Prototype analysis is the process of utilizing a worksession or a lab environment in which the design process is interactive in nature and utilizes activities to set the stage for information gathering. The process identifies activities that drive cooperative design by the team This process utilizes prototyping by either screen or simulation.

The Learning Experience

The learning experience should be based on an adult learning model. The adult learning model that has worked well in the group learning process is Kolb's Model developed in 1975. See figure 7.10. This model has four steps to achieving results in adult learning. These steps are concrete experience, reflections and observations, abstract conceptualizations, and testing and applying concepts in new situations. In order for an adult to effectively learn, the adult must be involved fully in the experience, then reflect on the experience from different perspectives, develop concepts that create the reflections into broad generalizations about the concepts, and apply the generalizations to the future events. If this model is applied to the reskilling training it will provide a mechanism for individuals to reflect on how they feel about an experience and how they will deal with the new experience of team development. This model supports the concepts that underline the accelerated development process discussed in this book.

Things to cover in the Reskilling Training

In this section different training types are listed. It is intended that organizations mix and match the type of training styles needed.

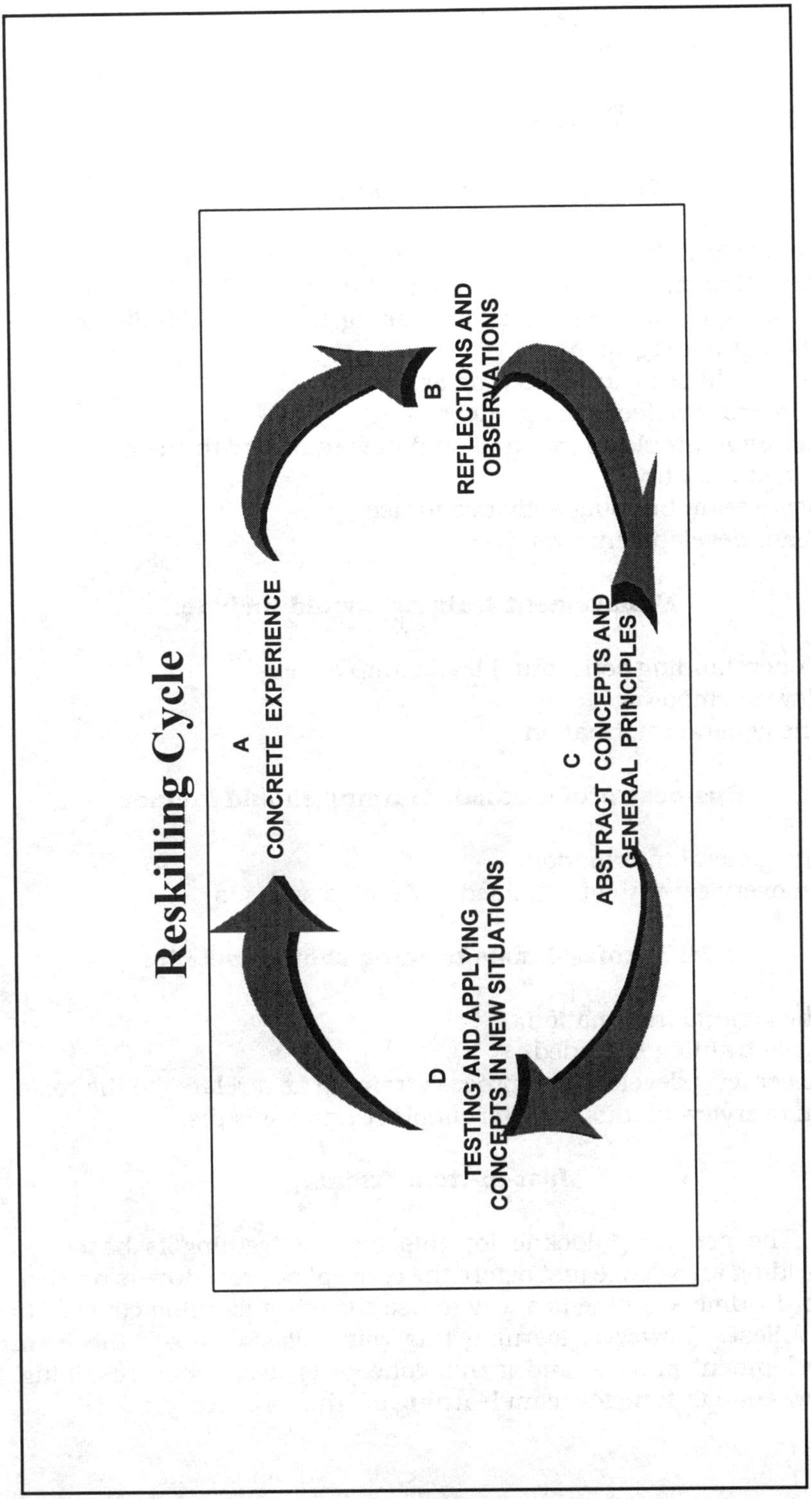

Figure 7.9 The Kolb Model(1975).

This training information is used as a guideline only. Each organization has different training needs.

Classroom Training

The general training should include:

- An accountable model using the empowerment concept
- Team Dynamics which should include the stages of change, diversity, utilizing differences, decision making, consensus building, and conflict management
- Group thinking and listening skills
- Constructive feedback guidelines
- Common problems in teams and how to deal with them
- Facilitation tips
- Some team building activities to use
- Team development overview

Management training should include:

- Understanding conceptual leadership styles
- How to empower
- The general information

Business professionals training should include:

- The general information
- An overview of the tools used to develop systems

MIS professionals training should include:

- The general information.
- Tools training if needed.
- Lower level development process training as it relates to the tools.
- An overview of business terminology and concepts.

Just-in-time Training

The general guideline for this type of training is based on providing knowledge just before the concept or procedure is needed. Just-in-time training is a way to use the adult learning concept to its fullest. However, learning this way will slow down the team development process and if this concept is used when reskilling, allow enough time for team learning on-the-job.

Computer-based, Video and Multi-Media Games

There is a variety of computer-based training programs on the market today. The training programs range from simple concepts about facilitation skills to complex ideas of organizational development and change. The use of computer and video training allows individual's to supplement their team's learning and bring new concepts to the group. This training can be very effective if used in an adult learning activity with the team. Computer-based and video training should be considered in the reskilling plan. The use of multi-media games can be a very effective way of teaching individuals new concepts. It has been proven that this type of learning through fun interaction (games) can teach complex concepts easily by introducing the concept through play. Many companies are using these multi-media games to teach new reengineering concepts to their employees. The only problem with incorporating multi-media games into the reskilling strategy is that multi-media learning mechanisms are difficult to find for highly technical subjects.

A New Meaning of "Success"

"Success" can not be judged in the same way as the old standards by the technology organizations. No longer can we say that development projects are successful because the documentation is signed or that all of the work products are completed or the phases of the development effort are finished. The development of business systems is taking on new dimensions. Today no business stands still. Businesses continually improve and so must the development processes. The focus for development must be based on what can be delivered in small business segments. The developed segments are based on what functions bring the largest value to the business process in the shortest timeframes. The development project may include technology or it may not. Technology should not be the driver for business solutions, it should be the enabler. Success for the system professional has to be redefined. The new definition must be supportive of the new joint development solutions and its impact on the business. Success should be team based and business results focused.

Where Does Reskilling go from Here?

Where do we go from here and how do we get started? First, invest in understanding the process and be committed to providing an environment that is based on leadership principles, joint respect, and business solutions. Start by getting the staff fully trained with cooperative development skills and don't scrimp on the "soft skills." If you're the business executive, remember that MIS organizations are large, old, and heavy with structure and specialization. Remember that the reengineering effort is a process that needs to be given serious support and endorsement or it will fail.

The organization must be assessed as a "learning organization." Continue to reskill and reassess the organization's progress. Make continuous changes, based on learnings and always strive to improve the process.

Keep in Mind

The assessment of the progress of the integrated organization is viewed by management's commitment to the vision and integrated performance targets of a business unit. Successful change starts with executives' commitment and involvement in the reengineering effort.

"Our society has learned a great deal about what works-practically, politically, and morally in the last 100 years. Now learning, not training, needs to become a way of life. Learning happens routinely every day as we go about our business" (Weisbord, 1987). The reskilling activities that need to be implemented at the beginning of this process is only the catalyst for the enhancement of the united work force for development of rapid business results. The production and quality of the results will take commitment to continued learning by those individuals involved. In order not to find the organization in the same shape five years from now, there needs to be a continuous process improvement environment through rewards and recognitions for this on-going requirement.

Notes:

[1] Kimball Fisher, Leading Self-Directed Work Teams, McGraw-Hill, Inc, (1993).

[2] Marvin R. Weisbord, "Productive Workplaces",Jossey-Bass Publishers, (1987).

CHANGE MANAGEMENT

Reengineering Management Information Systems

Chapter 8

Organizational Change

Achieving any of the benefits of reengineering requires organizations to change, essentially to become new reengineered organizations. For years MIS has been forcing change on its business partners. From this perspective, many in MIS believe they are already change agents, but this is a dictatorial view of change; real change is like religion — one must convert before spreading the gospel. By this definition, then, MIS must change to achieve reengineering success. In addition, organizational change is a discipline unlike any other management practice. This chapter describes critical success factors and a process for accomplishing organizational change. Finally, this chapter presents a model of the reengineering-ready MIS organization.

Importance of Change

What is the single greatest impediment to successful MIS support for reengineering? A few hints: It is not lack of standards, proprietary vendor architectures, lack of connectivity options among dissimilar architectures, or cost. It is the fear of, or inability to, change. Organizations typically change as little as possible, rather than as much as necessary. As a result, 70 percent of reengineering projects fail because of people and cultural issues.

One CSC Index study, summarized in Figure 8-1, indicates that change management, communication, and people management are the top three challenges for reengineering projects. Change is hard. It is individual and personal. It requires both intellectual and emotional commitments. Furthermore, it involves both personal and group dynamics.

So, is the ability to change important? While most MIS professionals, indeed most business people believe that "the soft stuff" is unimportant compared to mastering business or technology issues, "the hard stuff," experience indicates that the single most important success-enhancing ability an individual or organization can possess is the ability to change. Indeed, Arie DeGeus says that "the ability to learn may be the only sustainable competitive advantage in highly competitive environments." This is just another way of saying the ability to change is the only sustainable competitive advantage in highly competitive environments.

Change is not something to fear; change is a natural part of life. Growth and aging result in gradual changes. A forest fire or hurricane that causes an ecosystem to renew itself is more dramatic, more radical change. Hurricane Andrew did what appeared to be

Question: What are the three biggest challenges your organization has had to deal with in its reengineering efforts? (Please be specific and rank in order with 1 being the biggest challenge.)

1. Change management	31.5%
2. Communication	21.1%
3. People management	9.0%
4. Defining objectives	8.2%
5. Other	6.5%
6. Existing thinking	6.5%
7. Implementation	4.3%
8. Realizing benefits	2.5%
9. Time management	2.2%
10. Financing	2.2%
11. Prioritization	1.8%
12. Coordinating multiple units	1.4%
13. Technical implementation	1.4%
14. Methodology	1.1%

Source: CSC Index

Figure 8-1 Biggest Challenges of Reengineering.

enormous damage to the Florida Everglades, but in reality the hurricane was good for the Everglades. It took away dead organic material that was "clogging up" the ecosystem; it actually revitalized the Everglades.

MIS is already under pressure to change. MIS is changing from decentralized to centralized control, or vice versa, depending on prevalent management theory. MIS is trying to build what the technology trade press says it should. Business partners are changing from local to global focus and are developing departmental I/T capabilities. But, this degree of change is minor compared to the change that is in store for MIS: business focus and partnership, a new collaborative organizational construct, new technology skills, new management processes, new applications development environment tools, new holistic development techniques, living with ambiguity, and increased complexity.

John Hammitt, Vice President of Information Systems at United Technologies Corporation puts it this way, "For the past twenty years our goal has been simple: 'Keep out of trouble.' We have encouraged people to be afraid to do anything strange. We have to start rewarding people for falling on their faces so that they'll try again."

To make matters worse, the change associated with reengineering is devastatingly hard, especially for MIS. This is not because MIS staff are any less capable, it is just that MIS must achieve the same degree of change as their business partners, but MIS must change first to be able to implement the reengineered business process solutions fast enough to achieve the business case.

For MIS, reengineering requires new ways of thinking and using new techniques, technologies, and tools that most MIS organizations have never used; and that some in MIS do not believe will even work. Indeed, Gartner Group, a firm specializing in information industry analysis, in their September 1992 Strategies for Building Client/Server & Other Next Generation Applications, states that only "five percent of the average IS staff [can] master the intricacies of client/server today (0.8 probability); this will increase to 15 percent by 1997 (0.7 probability)." If MIS is going to have this much trouble with client/server applications development, which is only a small piece of the reengineering puzzle, it will be virtually impossible for MIS to support reengineering projects.

The ability to change is important to MIS for two reasons: initially, to develop a plan to enhance MIS' chances for success in aligning business and MIS visions and supporting reengineering; and, in the longer term, to provide MIS with the skills necessary to include organizational change programs as part of reengineering implementations.

MIS is not the only group that finds change daunting in reengineering. The key lessons learned from recent reengineering projects are all organizational change and change management related:

- "We should have moderated the pace of the effort remembering that the goal is 'ambition and stretch,' not 'do or die.' This is a reflection of the client's culture and is something that could have been changed."
- "Culture is a dominant variable at all times. This is a statement of fact that is not always kept at the forefront of everyone's thinking, but must be."
- "People are the only real critical success factors. Without winning the people over, nothing else really matters."
- "Redesigned business processes must be more robust to include detailed stakeholder profiles, change programs, and transition programs for pilot and rollout implementation."
- "Implementation planning should include the prospective recipients of the changes that will result from the redesigned business processes. Their involvement must start as early in the process as possible and must be substantive, not just for show."

Change management is hard, too. Managing change in itself is a change for most leaders. Managers are unfamiliar with change management as a discipline and it is very different from other management disciplines. To top it off, historically, change management was considered unimportant and of little actual, bottom-line value. Indeed, according to consultant Mimi Lenio (CSC Consulting), "Their background has also taught managers to resist change. Their job has been homeostasis and instilling stability in organizations, not encouraging and managing change."

Consultant Jeanie Dixon Duck likens change management to trying to balance a mobile. Most managers do not have the experience at managing multi-dimensional problems to give them the confidence to manage a change program without significant discomfort. Managers typically use the "mechanistic model, first applied to managing physical work, and [superimpose] it on the new mental model of today's knowledge organization [in an attempt to divide] change into small pieces and then manage the pieces. With change, however, the task is to manage the dynamic, not the pieces...The proper metaphor for managing change is balancing a mobile."

Lenio further defines change management as "taking a systems approach to managing resistance ensuring that compensation and reward systems, other management practices, the organization structure, education and training, and technology all align around the changes to enable personal transition, that is, giving people the capability to change."

Organizational Change Critical Success Factors

Successful organizational change depends on change leaders knowing how the change process works, being able to communicate the right messages at the right times most effectively, and understanding the impediments to change and how to overcome them.

Knowing How Change Works

While not being born with it, everyone develops a predisposition against change. It is not that people resist change, they resist being changed. People fear being forced to change because of the anxiety created by fear of failure and frustration with the inability to master something new. This fear of doing something new is also the fear of change, the fear of getting out of a comfort zone, the fear of being out of control, or even the fear of the perception of being out of control. This anxiety exists, to a greater or lesser extent, in everyone, including every individual in an MIS organization.

Change is personal, voluntary, and must come from within the individual. Because change is voluntary, it is not something that a psychologist can do for an individual or that a manager or consultant can do for an organization.

Change requires making a conscious decision to do, act, feel, or think differently. It also requires both intellectual and emotional commitments. For example, someone may desire to lose weight, quit smoking, become more outgoing, learn a new technology, get a college degree, save more money for retirement, or whatever. Before deciding to achieve a new future state, however, both intellectual and emotional commitments to change must be made. Just deciding intellectually to change, however, is not enough.

It's not until someone feels an emotional need to change that they really start the change process. They may finally decide to lose weight or quit smoking when one of their contemporaries or family members dies from heart disease or lung cancer. They may decide to learn a new technology or get a degree when they are passed over for a promotion. It is this type of jolt to their outlook that is necessary for real change to occur.

After the intellectual and emotional commitments are made, a balancing mechanism between the fear of doing something new and the fear of not changing is required. They must feel that the new course of action will provide them with more safety than the old course and that the future state is attainable. This overriding psychological safety is as part of the vision of the future state. For workers to change, leaders must provide this safety.

Communications and Organizational Change

Today, one can watch CNN and get an update on the entire planet in 30 minutes. As a result, people cannot stand to be without the latest information. If there is an information void, gossip and rumors will fill it. This can be especially devastating to an organizational change program. As a result, communication about the change program must be continuous, complete, and honest. Besides, everyone knows that rumors are much worse and much more negative than anything that is really happening.

Communication must be a priority for everyone involved in the reengineering program. And, it is also important to realize that communication includes not only the scripted messages that are part of the formal communication plan, but also inadvertent messages delivered by change program leaders, senior management, the redesign team, and middle managers. Everything that is said, or not said, speaks volumes in an information void. The most effective communications provide a consistent message that is:

- Simple to understand at all levels of the organization.
- Enthusiastic in explaining how the environment will be better after the change.
- Unrelenting (underscoring senior management's resolve).

• Honest on all matters.

One client adhered to the notion that for someone to comprehend a message, they must hear it seven times in seven ways. As a result, communications programs presented information using different media, or in different venues, or by different senior and middle managers, with the objective of communicating all reengineering-related information "seven-by-seven."

Consultants Steve Stanton, Michael Hammer (Hammer & Co.), and Brad Power (CSC Index) indicate that the communications programs must anticipate what stakeholders will need at each stage of the reengineering program. Messages, media, and timing must all be tailored for each stakeholder group and for each phase of the program. Furthermore, stakeholders undergoing the greatest degree of change must receive the most information, the most inspirational content, and the most personal and organizational support.

For communicating the case for action and the vision, the communications must come from the top and stress why change is necessary, what the change will be (at a high level), how the change will occur (at a high level), and the inevitability of the effect. Also, the communication must include status updates with open discussions of issues, concerns, and problems. During redesign and transition, communications must become more specific for all these topics and, to ease the transition, will include discussions about what will not change.

Understanding Impediments to Change

Organizations are full of "change survivors." Those who have been through downsizings, reorganizations, flattenings, and other change programs and have been able to remain employed without internalizing the changes happening all around them. They typically repeat the mantras: "I'll believe it when I see it," or "It sure sounds great, but what happens when we don't make our numbers?" or "Oh, it's just another management program *du jour*?"

On the other hand, a culture that supports change values creativity, flexibility, immediacy, initiative, controversy, experimentation, and risk-taking. As a result, these organizations look at failure as a part of learning and not as an opportunity to punish. Their decision-making is decentralized and distributed to the staff, not centralized and hierarchical. They approach work by forming nimble, temporary structures and teams to focus on issues and attack problems, not as lumbering dinosaurs unable to get out of their own way.

There are a number of cultural inhibitors to change that an organization may possess. One of the most common is the organization that is too structured. It does not possess the nimbleness to react to a changing environment and, therefore, will be unable to change successfully in the timeframe necessary to make the reengineering effort successful.

On the other hand, is it the organization that is too laid back. This organization responds to whatever comes its way by accepting it, perhaps, maybe, changing their view and processes incrementally, and going on until the next external event forces another change. This is the incarnation of an inertia to stay the course, which may be intentional or may exist because the organization is just too large to change, the proverbial problem of "turning an aircraft carrier."

The opposite end of the spectrum is the organization that is moving and changing too fast, or that is introducing change that is too complex for the individuals in the organization to assimilate. Introducing yet another change program in an organization that has expended all of its assimilation points without allowing the individuals an opportunity to recuperate will lead to unbearable stress and sub-optimal results.

Another type of organization that is likely to exhibit disappointing change results is one that has a series of reward systems that reinforce current behaviors, that explicitly do not reinforce new behaviors, or that punish failure. This is likely when the organization is not fully engaged with the change program or fully in agreement with the need for change as described by the change leaders.

However counter intuitive as it may seem, an organization that has been extremely successful will not necessarily be successful at radical change because "no one in their right mind would change anything around here." The reason is that past success tends to reinforce past behaviors. It promotes thought stagnation, blindness to problems and changes in the external environment, and a commitment to the *status quo*.

Finally, if the environment cannot tolerate mistakes, then the change and learning process must occur in parallel to the production environment. For much the same reason that aircraft pilots' training occurs in flight simulators that never leave the ground, if the production environment cannot tolerate mistakes, the change process must occur in parallel to production.

Successful Organizational Change

Since anxiety is the catalyst for change, what factors can create organizational anxiety? Organizations may fear the threat of loss of industry status, loss of market share, loss of revenues, loss of management or shareholder support, and in extreme cases, an organization may even fear the loss of its life, such as an MIS organization that is being outsourced by its parent company.

What differentiates organizational change from individual change is that every individual must internalize the need, the vision, and the new behaviors. To achieve the individual internalization necessary for change to take place, the case for action, vision, new behaviors, redesigned processes, and transition plans must be communicated to everyone in the organization and translated to a personal level. This will enable every individual to assess the personal cost of change and to make the personal decision to change. One successful approach to organizational change includes:

- Identifying the MIS change leader who will sell changes and ensure executive level commitment to the organizational change program.
- Creating and communicating the case for action and the vision, that is, determining that there is a real need to change, articulating what that need is, envisioning a future in which the problems from the case for action are solved, and communicating these messages. In other words, infecting every individual in the entire organization with the intellectual knowledge that a change will be necessary then giving them a safe means to survive the change.
- Identifying and assembling the redesign leadership team, ensuring the individuals become a high-performance team, and giving them a process to be successful.
- Redesigning the culture, that is, identifying the cultural attributes: values, beliefs, vocabularies, behaviors, thoughts, and feelings, etc., that need to change and how they need to change. Then redesigning the other points of the MIS reengineering diamond including MIS processes, management systems, and I/T deployment. Especially important is working with Human Resources to redesign jobs, skills, organization structures, and reward systems, and to determine training requirements.
- Assessing the readiness of the organization to change, the organization's capability gaps, and estimating the costs of change. Also, identifying MIS stakeholders who will be affected by the changes and assessing the impact of changes on them, as well as understanding the formal and informal organization, authority, power, and communications structures, assessing the power and influence stakeholders have over change, and identifying supporters and obstacles to change.
- Planning the transition by developing a workable implementation plan to move the organization from the current state to the future state, developing contingency plans to overcome expected resistance, identifying any needed support structures to manage change-related stresses, and developing communications programs.
- Validating acceptance and commitment to change.

Leading the Organizational Change Program

No task list, however, will make organizational change successful. A competent leader dedicated to making it successful and executive commitment to the change program are required.

The first and most important decision in an organizational change program is to select and anoint the leader of the change. The leader must be a respected senior manager who will have day-to-day, hands-on responsibility for the program. The leader of a change program cannot be a manager from a staff organization, no matter how senior. Assigning a senior line manager tells the organization that this change is real. In the case of change in an MIS organization, the leader should be the Chief Information Officer.

Being the leader of the organizational change program is not a titular responsibility. This is a real, full-time responsibility. Also, being the leader is hard. Managing change is very different from other management disciplines and requires using skills not always needed day-to-day. Consultants Jim Champy and Don Arnoudse (CSC Index) caution leaders that "reengineering demands more imagination, more patience, more attention, more communications skills, and more persistence than perhaps any other challenge corporate leaders have faced in their careers."

For the staff to believe that the change program is real, the leadership must be active, direct, and visible. Senior- and middle-level management must be directly involved in the change process. In addition, leaders must model the behaviors they expect from the staff. This means the leaders themselves must demonstrate changed behaviors indicating their own internalization of the change process. This will be reflected in changes in decision-making processes that reflect management process changes and demonstrate the attributes of the new organization.

Because change, even organizational change, is so personal (organizational change being the result of individuals in the organization changing collectively to act in some new manner), leaders of change must win their converts one individual at a time. Consultant Vince DiBianca (DiBianca-Berkman) states succinctly that the "leadership challenge is motivating people." And he further provides a list of specific activities to accomplish this:

- Create a rallying cry for your followers.
- Remember that the current and historical management model doesn't work. Management needs to foster flexibility, innovation, teamwork, customer service, employee satisfaction, and overall competitiveness.
- Understand that traditional attempts to restructure organizations

tend to be demoralizing.

- Self-assess and realize that for most leaders, learning how to mobilize people and adapt organizational culture in an integrative way has lagged far behind these realities.
- Remember that the paradigm of authority is bankrupt and to get things done without authority requires leaders to rely on relationships.
- Communicate and model, through words and personal actions, the new set of values needed to support the new business vision.
- Recognize that information is the keystone to successful design and implementation of both business and management processes, and ensure its flow to the right people throughout the change program.

Developing and Communicating a Case for Action and a Vision

The case for action must be widely visible, be believable, generate anxiety, and be personalized. On the other hand, it must not scold. The case for action must be highly visible, understood, and believed by the entire staff. This will require intensive communication so that everyone has the opportunity to see and understand the information. The case for action must be believable. Believing the information means everyone must also understand the information. They may need the economic education to understand the disconfirming information.

Anxiety is essential for change to start, so the case for action must be comprised of anxiety-generating messages. The case for action must be personalized so that every individual in the organization feels anxiety and some responsibility for correcting the situation described in the case for action. It must connect the situation described in the case for action to something each recipient of the message cares about individually and personally. For change to occur, every individual must discover for themselves that if they do not learn something new, they will fail (making them feel guilty) or their job will be in jeopardy (making them feel anxious). The fear of not changing must be greater than the fear of changing.

The case for action must not scold. Consultant Roger Martin cautions framing the case for action in terms that describe the changes that have occurred in the external environment which have, in turn, rendered past practices (which the organization built its success on) ineffectual, and in some cases counter productive. The message must be that the crisis exists, not because people in the organization have damaged something, but because otherwise good practices have just outlived their usefulness. He is emphatic that we must not assign blame for the current crisis, but that we must celebrate the past successes and then put them to rest. This positive reminiscence experience is much like the experience at a New Orleans-style wake.

Once the organization is fearful, unsure, quivering, and afraid to get out of their safety zone, but even more afraid to stand still, they must be directed to a seemingly safe path to achieve the desired changes. The vision will provide this safe harbor. The vision must describe the future and the transition plan that will give the individuals in the organization a psychologically safe route out of the morass described in the case for action. The vision must provide a degree of psychological safety. This is necessary so the anxiety does not cause the organization to become dysfunctional.

The staff must feel that the new behaviors and habits are feasible for them and that changing will not jeopardize their sense of identity and wholeness. They must also feel they have the means to achieve the vision, that is, the capabilities to feel safe to change. This includes any supplemental training or tools needed to achieve the vision.

Assemble Redesign Team

The team who will redesign the MIS culture must be key stakeholders who will become the change leaders of the organization. They must be from the "trenches" of the organization and must be respected by management and staff. Just as the organizational change program leader cannot be from a staff position, this team must be from the line organization to give the change program needed credibility.

Once assembled, they must become a team. The barriers between departments, between organizational levels, and between management and staff must come down. This team will be assigned the responsibility to redesign the organization's future. As a result, it must be given the authority to make decisions that will enable it to carry out that task.

Redesign Culture

Professor Edgar H. Schein of the Massachusetts Institute of Technology defines culture as "a pattern of basic assumptions — invented, discerned, or developed by a given group as it learns to cope with its problem of external adaptation and internal integration — that has worked well enough to be considered valid and, therefore, to be taught to new members as the correct way to perceive, think, and feel in relation to those problems..." Consultant DiBianca describes culture as "the vocabulary we use, the physical and behavioral artifacts we present, even the color shirts we wear." In any event, an organization's culture is its essence and it is that culture which must adapt or adjust for organizational change to take place.

The change leaders will go through an iterative process of developing, testing, recalibrating, and retesting the future culture. They learn what works and what does not by experimentation. The changes they go through will include unlearning, developing new frameworks, creating, sharing, and assimilating information about the organization and the external environment, as well as developing the knowledge to compete successfully in the new external environment, testing, refining, and retesting that knowledge and designing and administering interim or transitional organizational structures.

Change leaders learn to disagree without becoming disagreeable. This is much like the practice of waigaya at Honda - institutionalized conflict in which nothing is out of bounds. It institutionalizes tension so learning can take place. Conflict has human and organizational costs, but it is essential for self-questioning and revitalization.

Consultant DiBianca prescribes engineering breakdowns in the team because "breakdowns lead to break-throughs." Breakdowns occur when it becomes obvious that "business as usual" will no longer work. They provide a new context within which the team can evaluate their strengths and weaknesses and start the redesign process. Breakdowns should happen by design rather than by accident. They should reflect the future vision developed as a result of the case for action.

Assess Readiness

A change readiness assessment gauges organizational commitment, governance structure, adequacy of communications program, capabilities in new needed skills, technological capability, and necessary training and education programs. Assessing the organization's ability to change and readiness for change is instrumental in making change leaders successful in their change efforts.

Consultants and academics have developed change readiness assessment diagnostic tools. Whatever diagnostic tool is used, however, must be modified for each project to emphasize the attributes that the organization wants to promote and the behaviors that the organization wants to discontinue. An example assessment tool for MIS organizations that analyzes values and beliefs, organizational structure, skills and skill levels, staffing processes, processes for aligning with and creating value with the business, internally-focused measurement and management practices, and finally, technical infrastructure and tools is included in Figures 8-2 through 8-7.

It is noteworthy that typical MIS organizations have found their scores lowest in the values and beliefs assessment. The MIS

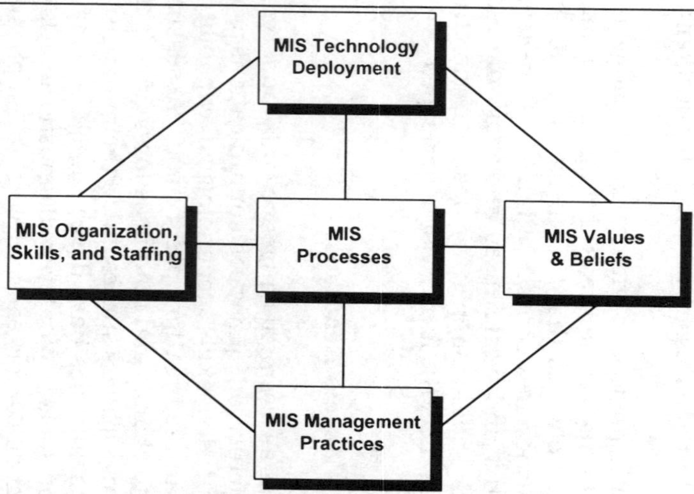

Source: Clelland Johnson

In an effort to assess MIS's readiness to support the rest of the Enterprise during the upcoming reengineering and reinvention activities, we must look at the MIS organization holistically. This holistic view includes process (how we support our business partners and create our work products), in equilibrium with our values and beliefs (how we think, act, and talk about ourselves), our organization, skills, and staffing (how we structure ourselves and make assignments, and the skills we emphasize and value), our management practices (how we look internally, and measure and report our performance), and our technology deployment (the technologies we use and how we apply technologies to solve business problems).

As you complete this survey, keep these definitions in mind. Spend no more than two minutes on each dimension (two minutes per page), answer honestly about the IS organization as you know it, and do not rate any aspect you do not feel qualified to judge.

Figure 8-2 Reengineering-Ready MIS Organization

MIS Processes

We employ traditional analysis, design, and programming techniques	1	2	3	4	5	We use prototyping and simulation
MIS is responsible for deliverables	1	2	3	4	5	We create teams who are responsible for results
Our business partners know what their requirements are at the outset	1	2	3	4	5	We create teams to learn what the requirements are through a process of iterative discovery
The primary MIS contribution to development is technology focus	1	2	3	4	5	We employ a holistic approach to applications development that includes understanding the "big picture" and creating a new business process, new management systems, new jobs, skills, and structures, and new values and beliefs, along with the new information technology
The principle criterion for determining what is and is not in scope for a development effort is the requirements	1	2	3	4	5	The principle criterion for determining scope is time
We use an Information Engineering approach	1	2	3	4	5	We use a business process, business rules and business object approach
Our methodology is a structured "cookbook" methodology that emphasizes deliverables	1	2	3	4	5	Our methodology is not prescriptive, rather it is a flexible framework focusing on results

Source: Clelland Johnson

On the spectrum between these two extreme conditions or states, indicate where the MIS organization currently is in day-to-day practice, i.e., if day-to-day activity is not consistent with stated direction, or published goals, indicate the day-to-day condition, by circling the appropriate number.

Figure 8-3: MIS Processes for Reengineering-Ready MIS

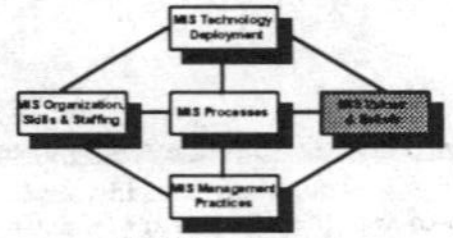

MIS Values & Beliefs

Our business "customers" provide us specifications and we create deliverables to get customer sign-off	1	2	3	4	5	Business "partners" work with MIS in teams to create business value
What we say is not always consistent with what we do; and, we react negatively when confronted with negative news	1	2	3	4	5	MIS enjoys an environment of trust, integrity, "walking the walk," and being honest, not politically correct
MIS is extremely failure-averse, resulting in analysis paralysis and protracted decision-making	1	2	3	4	5	Failure or mistakes are part of learning and change and are not punished. There is a fail fast - win fast approach to validating decisions
MIS management controls MIS	1	2	3	4	5	MIS management leads MIS
MIS is not an enabler, or enables only incremental change	1	2	3	4	5	MIS enables fundamental change, not incremental improvement
MIS owns data and processes	1	2	3	4	5	Business partners own processes, information, etc., and MIS is the steward
MIS drives the change process	1	2	3	4	5	Business processes drive MIS
MIS solutions are perfectly crafted, 100% complete, based on frozen specifications and take a long time	1	2	3	4	5	MIS emphasizes short cycle time; and, decision-making, systems construction, and delivery, are timely rather than 100% accurate
MIS decisions are largely independent of business drivers	1	2	3	4	5	Principles (agreed by business and MIS) drive all decisions and operations

Source: Clelland Johnson

On the spectrum between these two extreme conditions or states, indicate where the MIS organization currently is in day-to-day practice, i.e., if day-to-day activity is not consistent with stated direction, or published goals, indicate the day-to-day condition, by circling the appropriate number.

Figure 8-4 MIS Values and Beliefs for Reengineering-Ready MIS

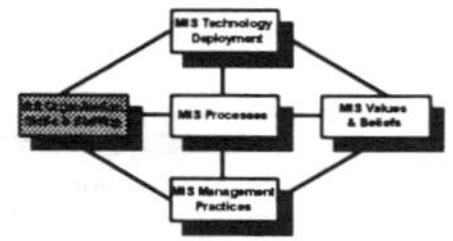

MIS Organization, Skills & Staffing

Our staffs' training is prescribed by management and primarily technology-focused	1	2	3	4	5	We are a learning organization with the staff taking responsibility to identify their own training needs based on the requirements of the MIS organization across all dimensions: process, culture, management, leadership, interpersonal, group dynamics, and technology
Our managers are autocratic, rigid, or inflexible, and emphasize a hierarchical structure of reporting relationships with managers thinking and administering and the staff working on prescribed activities	1	2	3	4	5	MIS leaders are change agents with significant skills in business awareness and coaching
Our staff are technology specialists	1	2	3	4	5	Our staff have a holistic view of their roles within the context of business partnerships and each staff member provides a full range of services to their business partners
Our organization structure is directly linked to the organization of the business causing clear distinctions and barriers between the IS staff supporting different functional areas	1	2	3	4	5	Because MIS has the unique opportunity to look across the entire business, MIS is organized to optimize cross-function, "big picture" thinking and support for our business partners
Our MIS staff is primarily focused internally -- on technology and/or on the IS organization	1	2	3	4	5	Our staff are not just technologists, we have business-aware, "big picture" thinkers in MIS
Our organizational structure is hierarchical with clear distinctions between levels, little direct, two-way communication up and down, and tightly defined job functions, i.e., a typical military-style command and control structure	1	2	3	4	5	We have a matrix organization structure that responds to the needs of our business partners quickly and optimally
MIS staff are rewarded for individual contribution and individual specialization	1	2	3	4	5	Our staff are team oriented and our management rewards the staff for team contributions

Source: Clelland Johnson

On the spectrum between these two extreme conditions or states, indicate where the MIS organization currently is in day-to-day practice, i.e., if day-to-day activity is not consistent with stated direction, or published goals, indicate the day-to-day condition, by circling the appropriate number.

Figure 8-5: MIS Organization, Skills, and Staffing for Reengineering-Ready MIS

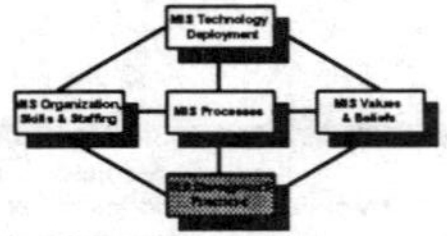

MIS Management Practices

Management emphasizes cost and cost control	1	2	3	4	5	Management emphasizes business value
The measurements MIS uses to evaluate its performance are MIS-based metrics, e.g., system availability, system response time, etc.	1	2	3	4	5	The measurements used to evaluate MIS performance are business-based metrics, e.g., I/T delivery cycle time, successful introduction of new technologies to solve business problems
MIS uses "make it fit" budgeting and estimating	1	2	3	4	5	MIS uses accurate estimating and business case development
MIS management emphasizes managing tasks, deliverables, and checklists	1	2	3	4	5	MIS management focuses on achieving business value
MIS projects are managed independently of one another	1	2	3	4	5	The context for project management is the entire program of interrelated projects, i.e., MIS uses a program management approach
MIS projects often result in project-specific solutions that are not necessarily integrated with a bigger picture	1	2	3	4	5	MIS emphasizes creating integrated business solutions
MIS' primary emphasis in project management is to hand-off deliverables and get the customer's sign-off	1	2	3	4	5	MIS takes responsibility for the results, not just for completing deliverables in a vacuum
MIS projects are "monolithic" resulting in a "big bang" of deliverables that are completed and delivered to the customer at the end of the project	1	2	3	4	5	MIS supports the quick creation of business value by delivering rapid functional releases

Source: Clelland Johnson

On the spectrum between these two extreme conditions or states, indicate where the MIS organization currently is in day-to-day practice, i.e., if day-to-day activity is not consistent with stated direction, or published goals, indicate the day-to-day condition, by circling the appropriate number.

Figure 8-6 MIS Management Practices for Reengineering-Ready MIS

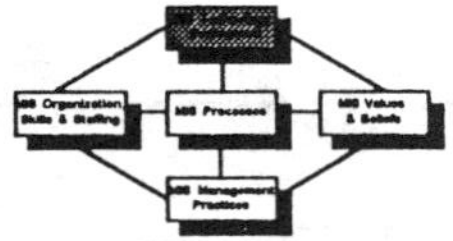

Our technology is proprietary	1	2	3	4	5	Our technology is open
We do not embrace solutions that are "not invented here," and each project may create its own solutions resulting in duplication	1	2	3	4	5	We make a conscious effort to reuse solutions, reapply existing technologies to solve new business problems, and create custom components that integrate across multiple projects
MIS is predominantly too narrowly focused on technology products and tools	1	2	3	4	5	We have an overall architecture addressing information, applications, applications development, and infrastructure which is not product-specific, supports the vast majority (at least 85%) of our requirements, has been communicated widely and understood by the MIS staff, is reviewed and updated periodically, and is adhered to across the board
Every technology product, tool, or architectural decision is "new" and does not take into consideration an overall architecture or previous work	1	2	3	4	5	Our technical and product decisions are taken based on adhering to our architecture and following certain principles about how MIS supports its business partners
Our definitions for enterprise information are data definitions created and organized to match the business' functional stovepipes and not that well integrated	1	2	3	4	5	Our information management systems and definitions view corporate information as an enterprise-wide resource that is defined and managed as such by the business owners of the information

Source: Clelland Johnson

On the spectrum between these two extreme conditions or states, indicate where the MIS organization currently is in day-to-day practice, i.e., if day-to-day activity is not consistent with stated direction, or published goals, indicate the day-to-day condition, by circling the appropriate number.

Figure 8-7 MIS Technology Deployment for Reengineering-Ready MIS

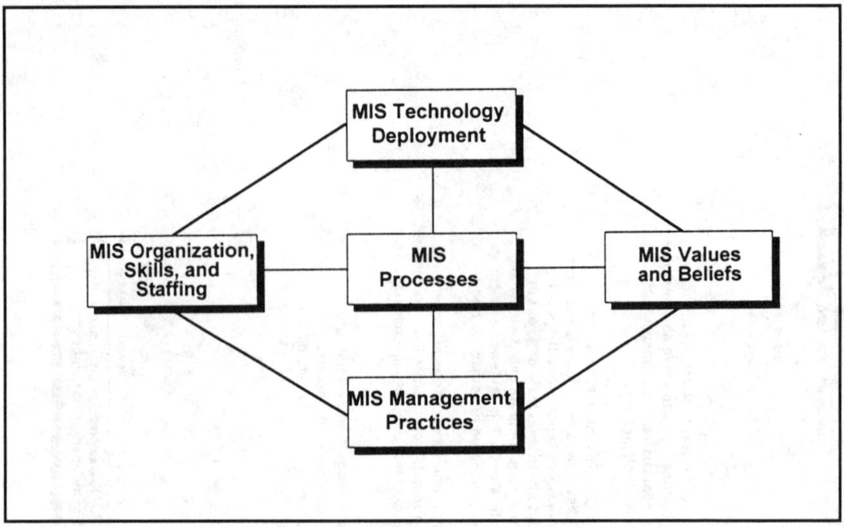

Figure 8-8 MIS Reengineering Diamond.

participants who completed the survey also indicated that values and beliefs are the most important attribute that they should change, but not surprisingly, they expected values and beliefs to be the hardest attribute to change.

The phrase "institutional obstructionism" describes the organized resistance to change that plagues many organizational change programs. Experience indicates that for MIS organizations in particular, the group that is likely to exhibit this behavior is the cadre of middle managers whose world is about to change most drastically. Another group who are likely to cause problems for change leaders are labor unions whose union bosses can manipulate workers to do what's best for the longevity of the union, not what's best for the company, nor indeed the workers themselves and whose primary objective is to keep as many of their members employed as possible, in the highest paying jobs possible, while subdividing the work effort to create the most tightly defined job descriptions possible.

Identify and Manage Stakeholders

Consultants Stanton, Hammer, and Power define change management very narrowly as "anticipating resistance beforehand, and knowing how to diffuse it by gaining the trust and backing of key individuals who will play major roles in the future environment," essentially stakeholder management.

Stakeholders are individuals or homogenous groups who will be affected by the change. Depending on the nature of the current organization and processes and on the future vision for processes and structure, there may be dozens of stakeholder communities.

Stakeholder management is knowing who the stakeholders are, how they are likely to be affected by the change, and what their reactions are likely to be. Armed with this knowledge, the change leaders must then gain intellectual and emotional buy-in from the stakeholders.

Plan Transition

There are investments in training and operational changes that the organization must make to provide an environment of psychological safety. The operational changes include the opportunity to practice new skills, support and encouragement to overcome the fear and shame of making mistakes, coaching and rewards for efforts in the right direction, even if they are not fully successful, and organizational norms that legitimize making mistakes and reward innovative thinking and experimentation.

Pilot testing new processes is the first step in institutionalizing the new processes. Indeed, it is institutionalizing them in a subset of the organization. During pilot testing, we first encounter the difference between the paradigm of individual learning and organization learning. The pilot activity relies on intensive communication and sharing of experiences. It results in the organization's collective assimilation and integration of the new processes with the existing processes.

Validate Results

During institutionalization, artifacts indicating the degree to which the changes are being affected should start to become evident. These could include altered organizational structures, different management systems, new behaviors, new attitudes, different rewards and incentives.

The Reengineering-Ready MIS Organization

Some reengineering practitioners try to distinguish between reengineering MIS and preparing the MIS organization to support reengineering. This is usually an attempt to alleviate the sticker shock project sponsors feel when they realize what reengineering really costs.

Based on the degree of change that MIS organizations involved in reengineering implementation projects have undergone, however, the minimum change required for an MIS organization to support a reengineering project is about 80 percent of the change required to reengineer MIS fully. The difference is so negligible as to be irrelevant. Not going all the way is an example of being penny-wise and pound-foolish.

What is a reengineering-ready MIS organization? How is it different from a traditional MIS organization? Reengineering teams use the concept of the reengineering diamond with business processes supported by jobs, skills, and structures, management practices, values and beliefs, and information technology to represent the need for holistic change. MIS must view itself along analogous dimensions by developing an MIS reengineering diamond like the one in Figure 8-8.

There are a number of behavioral attributes shared among MIS organizations that inhibit the organization's ability to support reengineering. Using the MIS reengineering diamond, these attributes and proposed behaviors to counter them are presented in Figures 8-9 through 8-13. The challenges of changing the MIS organization to prepare to support reengineering or other major business change initiatives are extreme as outlined in Figure 8-14. The two principal aspects of this change are the new technologies and new techniques required, Figures 8-15 and 8-16.

MIS may be accustomed to changing technologies from time to time, but even changing technologies can meet significant resistance. Changing techniques is even more rare and is liable to meet even more resistance. For example, one client MIS organization just finished their new custom-built accounting system. That they custom-built an accounting system is bad enough, but the system is written entirely in IBM 370 assembler language. Why? The company has over 400 assembler programmers in MIS and creating custom applications using assembler language is all they know how to do.

Reengineering Management Support

The primary objective of the reengineering-ready MIS organization is to position the business to succeed in implementing whatever business changes are necessary for survival. MIS management must focus on management issues, not technical issues, foster partnership between MIS and their business partners, measure their performance based on business performance, ensure vision and commitment for success, provide feedback, recognition, and rewards, minimize disruptions and internally-focused management controls, set goals, and then get out of the way. Specifically, MIS will address these tasks in a reengineering project:

- Introduce technological ingredients into business process redesigns and propose I/T alternatives to business partners while not dictating solutions. MIS can participate in the reengineering effort and influence the redesigns through recommendations that will

FROM	TO
• Traditional analysis and design	• Prototyping & simulation
• Technology-focused	• Holistic approach
• Requirement-driven, waterfall approach	• Time-driven approach
• Information Engineering approach	• Business process, Business rules, and Business object approach
• Monolithic Structured Methodology "Cookbook"	• Opportunistic Flexible Methodology Framework
• Stovepipe organization	• Cross-functional organization
• Project-specific deliverables	• Integrated deliverables
• Internally-focused	• Business reengineering-focused
• Development is an MIS activity	• Business reengineering Labs are business tools with IT, H/R, JSS, MS with BP
• MIS responsible for deliverables	• Lab responsible for deliverables
• Users know what the future looks like	• Users learn what the future looks like
• I/T drives process	• Process drives I/T

Source: Clelland Johnson

Figure 8-9 MIS Process Characteristics for Reengineering-Ready MIS.

FROM	TO
• 100% Functionality	• 80%-20% Rule
• Custom (Exclusively)	• Package, integrated, or custom based on requirements
• Perfectly crafted	• Timely
• Big Bang	• Series of small success
• Technology focused	• Business-focused
• Management (Command and control)	• Leadership
• Incremental Improvement	• Fundamental change
• Business customers	• Business partners
• Failure averse	• Fail fast- Win fast
• Disparate and segmented technology	• Standard comprehensive architecture blueprint
• Individual contributors	• Team members
• NIH & project-specific development	• Commonality & reuse
• Hand-offs a sign-offs	• Responsibility for the outcome
• Internally-focused	• Business reengineering focused
• Every decision is "new"	• Principle based decisions
• Frozen specifications	• Evolving specifications
• Analysis paralysis	• Decision-making
• MIS Ownership	• Business partner "power"
• MIS ownership of corporate data	• Business partner ownership; MIS stewardship
• Stovepipe data definitions	• Data definitions supporting cross-functional systems
• Directive	• Participate
• I/T drives process	• Process drives I/T
• Users know what the future looks like	• Users learn what the future looks like

Source: Clelland Johnson

Figure 8-10 MIS Values and Beliefs Characteristics for Reengineering-Ready MIS.

FROM

- Specialists
- Stovepipe Organization
- Training
- Individuals who are internally focused on MIS
- Hierarchy
- Individual Contributors

TO

- Caseworkers
- Cross-functional Organization
- JIT Learning
- MIS staff knowledgeable about the business
- Matrix Organization
- Team Members

Figure 8-11 MIS Organization, Skills, and Staffing Characteristics for Reengineering-Ready MIS.

FROM

- Cost - Based
- Anecdotal
- Big bang
- "Make it fit" budgeting
- Management (command
- and control)
- Tasks and deliverables
- Project management
- Project-specific deliverables
- Hand-offs and sign-offs

TO

- Value - Based
- Metrics - Based
- Series of small successes
- Accurate estimating and business case development
- Leadership
  Achievement of the business case
- Program management
- Integrated deliverables
- Responsibility for the outcome

Figure 8-12 MIS Management Practices Characteristics for Reengineering-Ready MIS.

FROM

- Proprietary
- NIH & Project-Specific Development
- Product- and tool-focused
- Every decision is "new"
- MIS Ownership of Corporate Data
- Stovepipe Data Definitions

TO

- Open
- Commonality and Reuse
- Follow architecture blueprints
- Principles-based decision-making
- Business Partner Ownership
- Data Definitions Supporting Cross-functional Systems

Figure 8-13 MIS Technology Deployment Characteristics for Reengineering-Ready MIS.

MIS Reengineering Challenges

- Information Technology Base Must Change
- MIS Productivity Must Improve
- Information Integration Must Improve and Requires Business Process Ownership
- MIS Must Change Priorities as the Business Requirements Change
- MIS Must Reskill or Retool to Support Reengineering Using the new Technology Base
- MIS and the Enterprise Must Make an Investment in Training
- MIS and the Enterprise May Have to Make an Investment in Consulting
- MIS Must Become More Business Focused and Less Technology Driven
- MIS Has Shorter Timeframes to Deliver Functionality

Source: Clelland Johnso

Figure 8-14 MIS Reengineering Challenges.

New Techniques Required to Support Reengineering

- Accelerated Applications Development
- Business Managed Development vs. MIS Controlled Development
- Continuous Business Partner Involvement and Ownership
- Value- or Business Case-Driven Planning
- Incremental Delivery (Series of Small Successes)
- Client/Server Applications, Distributed Computing Applications, or Distributed Object Computing Applications
- GUI Front-Ends
- Event Driven Applications Processing
- Object Oriented Analysis and Design
- More Parallel or Concurrent Activities Requiring Greater Integration
- Prototyping and Simulation

Source: Clelland Johnson

Figure 8-15 New Techniques Required to Support Reengineering.

New Technologies Required to Support Reengineering

- Interoperability and Open Systems
- Client/Server Design, Implementation, and Management
- RDBMS and Distributed RDBMS Design, Implementation, and Management
- Open Operating Systems Implementation and Operations
- Object Oriented Programming, Management, and Support

Source: Clelland Johnso

Figure 8-16 New Technologies Required to Support Reengineering.

result in the innovative use of technology. This could come in the form of new or unique supporting technologies or in using existing technologies, especially those currently used outside the enterprise's industry, in new ways. This may be the first time MIS has ever been involved in shaping, not just implementing the future.
- Assess and report the business impact of I/T decisions.
- Become a clearinghouse for technical specialists to support business change initiatives. This will include both planned, long-term assignments and ad hoc, short-term technical support and problem fixes.
- Coordinate the relationship between business processes and architectural components.
- Manage I/T integration by identifying, negotiating, and resolving issues, and communicating their resolutions in conjunction with the overall reengineering integration program.
- Design, evolve, and manage the Comprehensive Technical Architecture including process architecture, information architecture, applications architecture, applications development environment architecture, and technology infrastructure architecture. Chapter 4—Comprehensive Technical Architecture describes this process fully.
- Document the current architectures and maintain any pictorial representations of the architectures, enterprise information, and enterprise-wide processes.
- Manage the integration and eventual retirement of legacy systems.
- Coordinate building and deploying architectural components.
- Manage MIS and I/T Critical Programs.
- Maintain MIS synergy by actively involving MIS staff in change, both the change in MIS and in the rest of the enterprise.

Reengineering Lab Support

The other principal and more traditional MIS role in reengineering is preparation for, and support of, reengineering labs. That's where the similarity with past systems projects ends, however. Reengineering labs, unlike typical MIS development efforts or development labs, include all aspects of the reengineering diamond. As a result, MIS participants take a supporting role, not an ownership role in these labs. This means, of course, that the business process owner must take the ownership role. In most cases, the business process owner will want to rely on MIS for project management support which MIS has the most experience with, but it must be the business process owner's decision.

The skills required to support the lab teams are very different from those most MIS staff currently possess. Even the current staff of developers will need different technical skills and, more impor-

MIS Training Curriculum for
Reengineering Lab Support

Lab Facilitation Skills
- ❑ Facilitation
- ❑ Problem Solving
- ❑ Training (How to teach)
- ❑ Team Building
- ❑ Time Management

Project Management
- ❑ MS Project
- ❑ Project Planning
- ❑ Project Scope Management
- ❑ Project Schedule Management
- ❑ Project Estimation

Reengineering Methodology
- ❑ Overall Project Orientation
- ❑ Overview of Reengineering Methodology
- ❑ Design Reviews
- ❑ Deliverables (all points of the diamond)
- ❑ I/T Integration Process
- ❑ Scope Integration
- ❑ Schedule Integration
- ❑ Business Case Integration
- ❑ Process Family Breakout Sessions
- ❑ Current Process Family & Lab Business Scopes/Objectives
- ❑ Lab Readiness & Planning Work in Progress & Completed
- ❑ Lab Environment Overview
- ❑ Communications Mechanisms and Protocols (technical)

I/T Courseware
- ❑ Tool Overviews (MS E-Mail, Windows, Word for Windows, Excel, PowerPoint, Toolbook, LBMS, PowerBuilder, SQL Base, Progress, and Speedware)
- ❑ Tool Detail Training (Toolbook, LBMS, PowerBuilder, SQL Base, Speedware, Sybase (includes transact SQL), and Progress)
- ❑ I/T Program Development
- ❑ Client/Server Computing Overview
- ❑ GUI Screen Development
- ❑ Common Module Development
- ❑ Applications Support and Middleware
- ❑ Data Modeling
- ❑ Logical Data Modeling Overview
- ❑ Logical to Physical Data Modeling Overview
- ❑ Logical Data Modeling Details
- ❑ Logical to Physical Data Modeling Details
- ❑ Testing
- ❑ FSL Overview
- ❑ Program Unit Testing
- ❑ Application String Testing
- ❑ System Testing
- ❑ Package Applications
- ❑ Architecture Overview (Information, Applications, Applications Development Environment, and Technical Infrastructure)
- ❑ UNIX Overview
- ❑ UNIX Fundamentals
- ❑ Operational Procedures Overview

Source: Clelland Johnson

Figure 8-17 MIS Training Curriculum for Reengineering Lab Support.

tantly, their technical skills will not be their most important skills. A typical training curriculum developed for a recent reengineering project is presented in Figure 8-17. Note the emphasis is on facilitation and management skills with secondary emphasis placed on whatever point technologies are required.

Gartner Group estimates "the initial round of formal training for line MIS developers will total roughly a half-year's salary — or $25,000 - $40,000 per developer — factoring in out-of-pocket costs and productivity loss as they hone their new skills. Once the baseline of knowledge has been established, on-going skills updates will be much easier. Figure on $5,000 every 18 months for refreshers and training on new tools."

Organization Structure for Supporting Reengineering

Rigid structures and changing environments are mismatched.

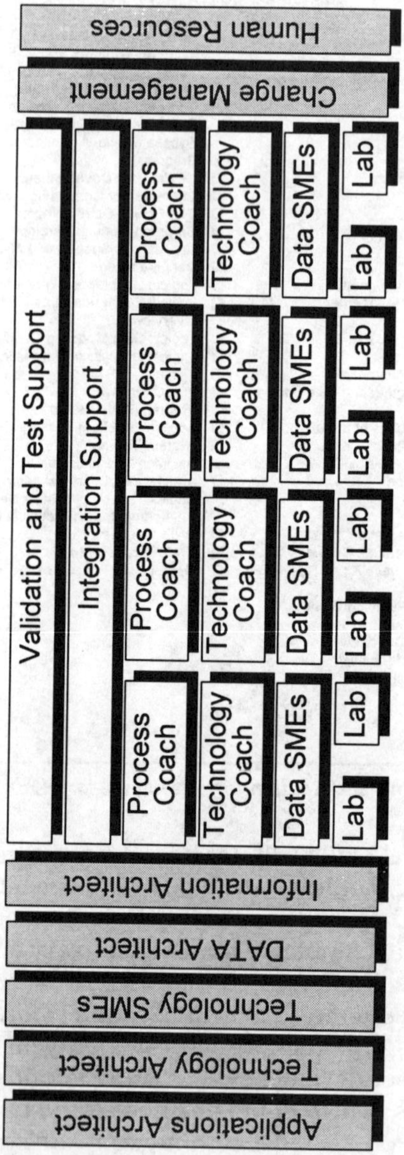

Source: Clelland Johnson

Figure 8-18 Reengineering-Ready Organizational Plaid.

Reengineering-ready MIS organizations are structured more like tents than palaces. Dr. Peter Brews of Babson College elaborates "organizations with rigid structures, narrow skills specialization, formal hierarchy, unambiguous authority structures, and formal integration mechanisms are likely to inhibit" change.

Unlike traditional hierarchical or even traditional matrix organizations which are just hierarchies with matrix managers, the reengineering-ready MIS organization must be organized more like a woven fabric or tartan where the black horizontal stripes and the white vertical stripes intersect to form gray areas. In these gray areas no single individual has total responsibility, but rather everyone involved takes responsibility equally for the success of the effort. As depicted in Figure 8-18, horizontally focused MIS staff directly participating in with business partners in the reengineering labs and vertically focused MIS staff supporting the reengineering lab teams.

The activities that result in a reengineering-ready MIS organization are collectively known as MIS Critical Programs. The notion of critical programs was introduced in Chapter 5 — Reengineering Integration. Briefly, there are a number of activities outside the reengineering labs that are crucial to successful reengineering. These activities typically fall into three categories: Human Resources, Information Technology implementation, and MIS organization. I/T Critical Programs are focused on determining and implementing the technology infrastructure to support the reengineering effort, the MIS technology deployment point of the MIS reengineering diamond. MIS Critical Programs focus the other points of the MIS diamond: MIS processes, MIS values and beliefs, MIS organization, skills, and staffing, and MIS management practices to support reengineering. Examples of MIS Critical Programs are:

- Creating the MIS case for action, the MIS vision, and the MIS organizational change transition plan and preparing and implementing the MIS communications program to publicize the MIS case for action and vision.
- Defining the application building processes to be used by those MIS staff who will be participating directly with the reengineering teams. These processes will be more prototyping- and simulation-based, holistic, time-driven, flexible, cross-functional, integrated, and process-driven than traditional systems development techniques.
- Defining the skills and capabilities required by those MIS staff who will be participating directly with the reengineering teams to be more like caseworkers, not specialists, more able to learn, more knowledgeable about the business, and more team-oriented.

- In the area of MIS management practices, becoming more value-oriented and less cost-oriented, able to deliver a series of small successes rather than a big bang, accurate at developing business cases not just cost estimates, more leaders rather than administrative managers, and more concerned about the outcome and achievement of the business case than sign-offs and checklists.
- Assessing the MIS staff's capabilities and skills and reskilling or retooling the MIS organization to support reengineering—reskilling includes identifying the skills shortfalls and developing an education plan to get the existing staff the required skills; retooling, on the other hand, is the process of identifying the required skills and capacities and looking for an alternate source of those skills in those capacities.
- Determining the level of staffing required by skill. The process for planning staffing for reengineering labs and MIS activities include:
  - Reviewing the Release Plan for a first cut at number of reengineering labs and their timeframes and review with any in-flight reengineering labs for their requirements and projected requirements.
  - Creating a staffing model that depicts the "big picture" requirements.
  - Identifying categories of skills required.
  - Mapping current MIS resources to categories and identify shortfalls of SME and other support resources.
  - Presenting shortfalls to process owners to get their agreement that these are their real requirements, i.e., that these requirements are "show stoppers" and that they would be willing to fund these resources.
  - Identifying alternate sources and acquiring the necessary staff.

This MIS organization and this set of MIS processes and responsibilities will provide the greatest opportunity for success in supporting reengineering.

Summary

Organizational change is important to transition from whatever state currently exists to a future state. Critical success factors for change leaders to master are knowing how change works, being able to communicate about the change effectively, and understanding the impediments to change.

Organizations can only change when every individual in the organization begins to behave, think, feel, and talk differently. Change leaders must translate the fear of not changing into organizational threats or opportunities and then into individual threats or opportunities that will create an emotional inducement to change in such a way that is intellectually sound. Change requires both intellectual and emotional decision-making.

Successful organizational change in a large organization is the result of realizing the need for change, developing a vision of the future state, communicating that vision widely, and enlisting ever-widening circles of change agents who are committed to making the change successful. Each group must experience change firsthand and only then can they become the change agents for enlisting the next group. One client says they have to "walk the walk, not just talk the talk."

The reengineering-ready MIS organization is radically different from the MIS organizations that have evolved over the past 25 years. A reengineering-ready MIS organization is easier to work with, faster and more reliable at delivery, and concerned with the business case, not just funding.

Bibliography

Peter Brews, "Political and Social Processes in Strategy — Promoters and Inhibitors of Organizational Learning," unpublished, February, 1992.

Edgar H. Schein, "How Can Organizations Learn Faster? The Challenge of Entering the Green Room," *Sloan Management Review*, Winter, 1993.

Roger Martin, "Changing the Mind of the Corporation," *Harvard Business Review*, November - December, 1993.

Jeanie Daniel Duck, "Managing Change: The Art of Balancing," *Harvard Business Review*, November - December, 1993.

Steve Stanton, Michael Hammer, & Bradford Power, "From Resistance to Results: Mastering the Organizational Issues of Reengineering," *Insights Quarterly*, Fall, 1992.

James Champy and Donald Arnoudse, "The Leadership Challenge of Reengineering," *Insights Quarterly*, Fall, 1992.

Donald Arnoudse, "Creating Change through Crisis," *Indications*, Vol. 9, No. 1, 1992.

Gartner Group, Inc., *Strategies for Building Client/Server & Other Next Generation Applications*, Stamford, Connecticut, September, 1992.

PROJECT CONTROL

Reengineering Management Information Systems

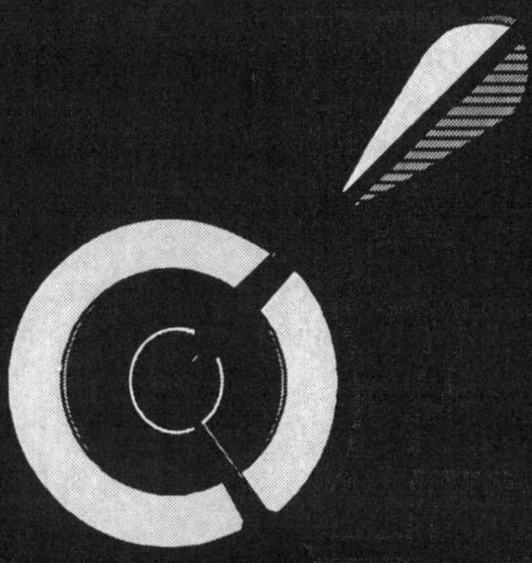

Chapter 9

Project Management

In recent years many MIS organizations have been faced with troubled technology-related projects. Unfortunately, the number of these projects continues to grow. To complicate the issue even more, these projects have been given a fair amount of publicity both internally and externally. Implicit in the new mission of MIS is the mandate of increased service levels and quality of products delivered. In order to achieve our new mission we must enhance the current techniques for managing these initiatives.

This chapter discusses the application of project management concepts, tools, and techniques in the challenging task of reengineering management information systems. (Emphasis is on the unique characteristics of reengineering projects, and the differing approach to organizing and managing them as opposed to the approach used for the more "traditional" project.) Readers will also find this information useful in deciding whether to use internal resources to manage a project or to hire a professional skilled specifically in the area of reengineering management. It should be stated that systems integrators may be able to handle the management of technology or software-related management but may fall short in organizational transformation knowledge critical to managing these efforts.

Project management consists of four components. Planning, organizing, managing tasks and resources are the four key areas of responsibility for managing engagements. These responsibilities are influenced by other factors and control of risks in order to accomplish one or more objectives usually with time and budget con-

Figure 9.1 Four Components of Reengineering Project Management.

straints, and often with constraints dictated by existing ("legacy") systems and the old organization. Although MIS project objectives used to be technical in nature, the objectives of a reengineering project are business related or are closely related to satisfaction of a customers needs, whether internal or external. If they aren't, the project will likely not be perceived as a success by the users.

While it is certainly true that numerous activities make up the day-to-day activities of a project manager the four areas mentioned above certainly are the basics of good project management. However, one must explore the drivers and influences that complicate the management of reengineering projects. Without careful consideration of these factors, the project manager can find himself in jeopardy and risk the project's success.

Project management has been around since the building of the pyramids when it was common practice to kill the project manager at the end of the project to prevent disclosure of the design of the tomb. Unfortunately for us, this practice is still employed — managing a large, complex project is by no means an easy job. When

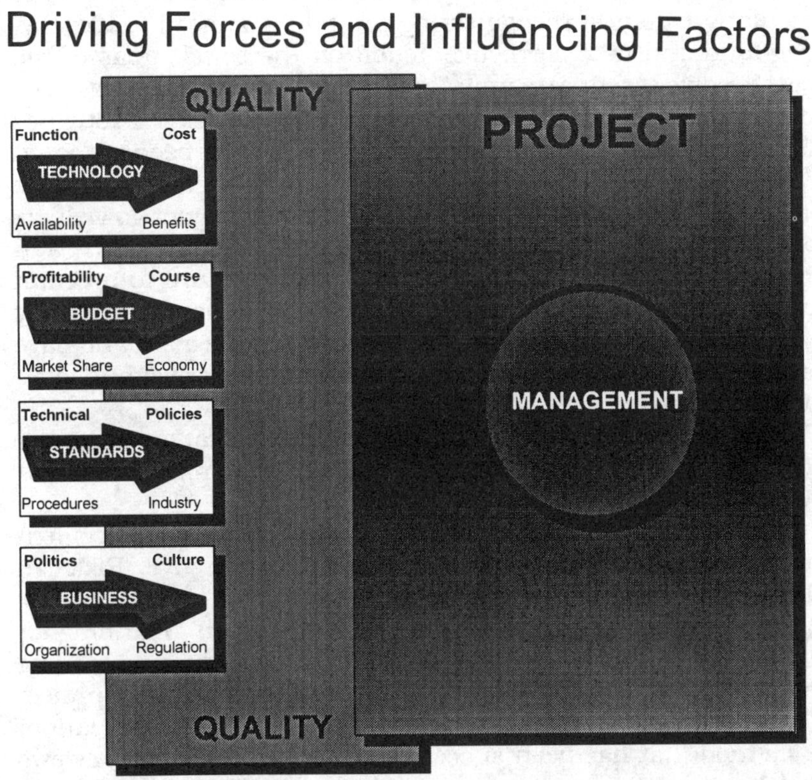

Figure 9.2 This graph depicts the drivers and influences that the project manager must be aware of and consider when managing the project..

something goes awry, the finger pointing starts and the search for someone to hang responsibility on begins. All too often, we search out the guilty and punish the innocent. This is primarily because of perception. Perception in highly changed projects that are associated with reengineering often times overshadows the real issues. We get preoccupied with addressing the symptoms and do not drive to the level of detail required to uncover the underlying illness. All these factors require the project manager's time. This combined with all the other activities with which he is involved, rapidly consume the project manager's time. Time is by far the most valuable commodity for a project manager. Finding tools and techniques that can make more efficient use of this time is essential.

The widespread availability of project management software has helped make the job easier by bringing greater structure and predictability to projects. But tools are not the solution to project management ills or replace the need for a dedicated project manager. Keep in mind, the tools are only as good or useful as the person who uses them. There is still a lot that must be done the old fashioned way by observing, interacting with the project team, asking questions and working with the organizations management. This is particularly true in a reengineering project. The need to identify, understand and take corrective action on the softer areas of the project become essential in projects which entail radical change. The best execution of both the technical and business related activities will fall short of the mark if the organization has not been prepared for the feeling of being overwhelmed that will accompany these projects. If the business and technical activities do not go well, as happens in many cases, we need to identify the difficulty early and take corrective, if not preemptive, measures. Failure to preempt issues in critical areas is by far one of the most common reasons why projects fail. Review of projects that have missed the mark and have been considered a failure — not just because of being over budget — provides valuable insight into why projects fail.

Each and every time MIS fails to meet the expectations, whether it be in terms of functional, budget or delivery, the road to success becomes even rougher to travel.

One tool that is lacking so far is a quantitative measurement system used to look at the project from a risk perspective. Risk can and often does take on many different shapes.

Risks mediation begins with early identification. Planning for activities related to risk mediation is often excluded from resource estimates and schedules. A clear and consistent means of project review is necessary to fulfill the needs of the new MIS organization. One method that has been successfully applied to project reviews and risk mitigation, as we mentioned before, is ***PRISM.***

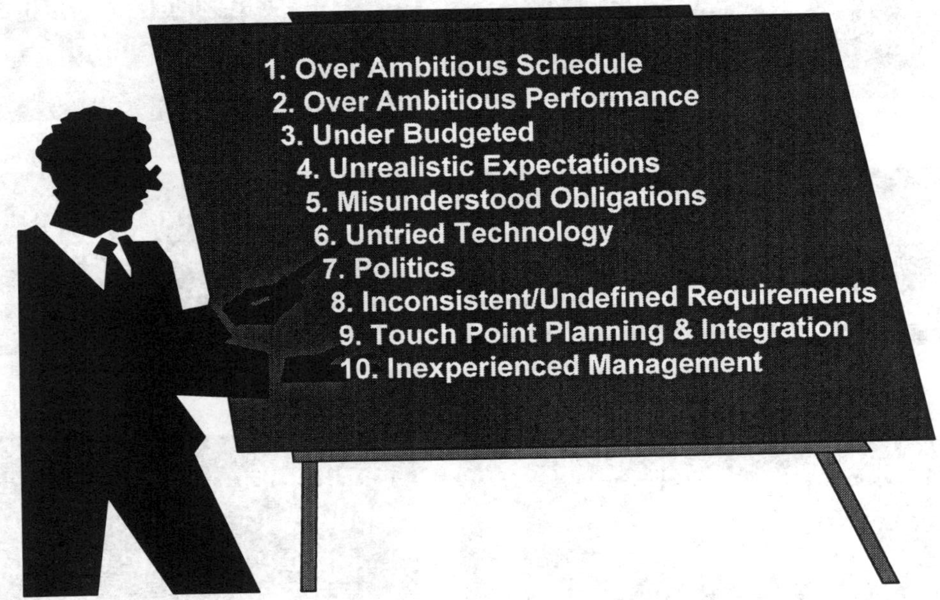

Figure 9.3. The top ten reasons why projects fail

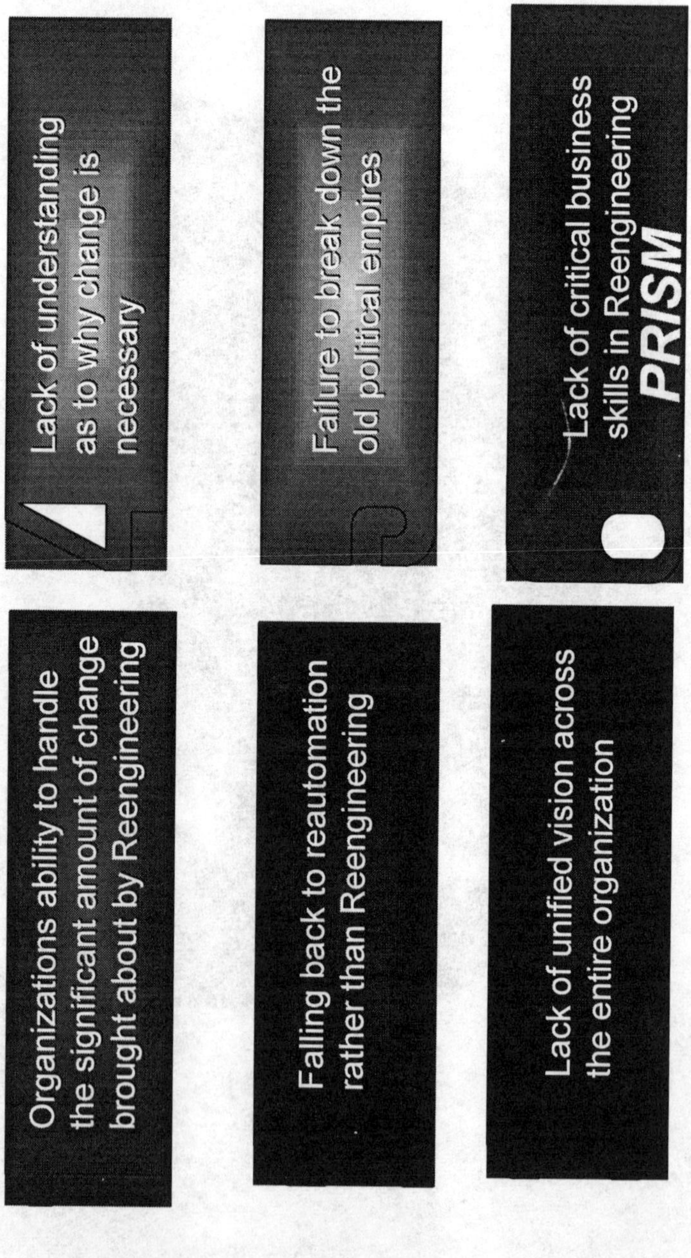

Figure 9.4. This graph represents the major areas of risks in reengineering projects

PRISM/Risk Management

PRISM stands for Project Review: Integrated Systems Management. The primary objective of ***PRISM*** is to manage risk associated with projects that focus on radical redesign of business processes or operations. ***PRISM*** will assist you in determining many different types of risks associated with projects. Early identification of these risks will often determine success in the users eyes or deem the project as just another MIS systems job. Rightly or wrongly, MIS in general has the reputation of projects which are giant black holes where money is thrown. These projects have continued for years and seemingly never end, and we continue to push out delivery in many cases without any notice. The battle cry of the new project manager is "no surprises". *Note: PRISM is the property of Applied Business Intelligence Management Consulting.*

In order to achieve this goal, we must continually assess the progress of the project. In looking at the primary objectives of PRISM, we have identified key focal areas that PRISM addresses.

FOCAL AREAS

PRISM

1. Meeting the needs of the business.

2. Meeting the needs of the users.

3. Meeting management's expectations.

4. Adhering to standards.

5. Meeting budgetary and time requirements.

The focal areas identified above are closely related to the areas identified as those that are critical to managing expectations. Managing expectations is an integral part of overall project management as well as risk mitigation. Failure to properly address these issues will cause a project to encounter difficulty and could lead to disaster. By far the best way to manage risk is to expose risks so that actions can be taken to reduce them or remove the potential hazard altogether.

The ***PRISM*** worksheets (9-1 thru 9-8 in Appendix B) are a mechanism to gather pertinent timely information concerning the status of a project. For example, any method of project review captures a specific snapshot. The dynamics of projects has always

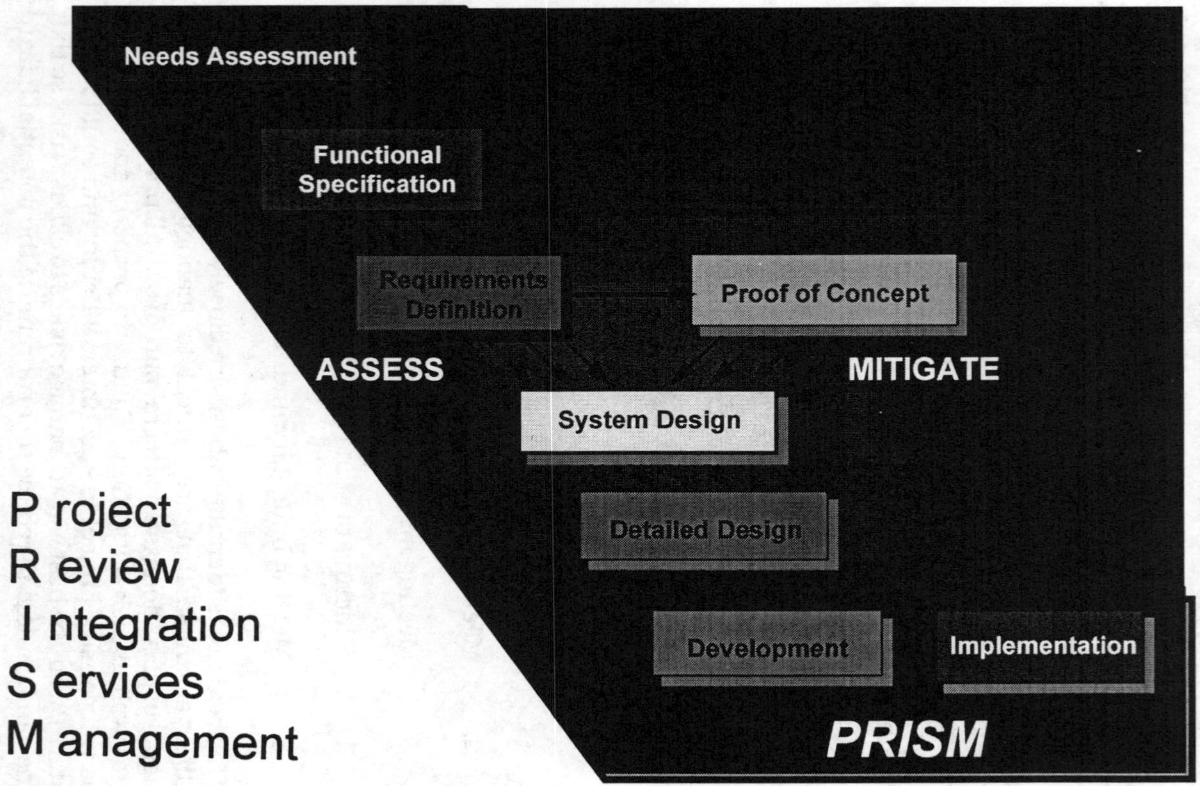

Figure 9.5 The method employed to review and monitor projects must encompass the entire effort cradle-to-grave. PRISM begins at the inception of the project and continues through to implementation.

been a given. However, in the environment of rapid development rapid change is also a given. For the most part management is ill-equipped to deal with the magnitude or speed with which these projects progress. This staggering pace of change is definitely not for the weak at heart and is substantially different from traditional projects. The identification of risks is only part of the activities that must be executed to ensure project success. Once the risks have been identified a treatment must be applied to minimize the exposure. Worksheet 9-9 provides a mechanism of tracking identified risks. Critical to any risk mitigation program, the risk must be assigned to an owner. This individual is responsible for making sure the approved treatment is being administered to the risk and that constant monitoring in accordance with the priority is occurring.

There are only 7 steps involved in a ***PRISM*** review. They are: Planning, Interviews, Development of Preliminary Findings, Conclusions and Recommendations, Communicating via an internal memorandum, Preparation of a treatment plan, and finally, Debriefing with the project staff and the project sponsor. The conclusions and recommendations made at the conclusion of a ***PRISM*** review all focus on enhancing the quality and timeliness of the projects. By making these recommendations at a specific point in time, I do not imply that the project priorities and activities were wrong or mistakes were made. The goal for ***PRISM*** is to highlight the potential future needs and priorities of the project at various points in time. This must take place before these needs become a critical path and stand in the way of project success.

Another key component in risk mitigation deals with identifying the impact of change on the organization and planning and properly positioning the organization to accept change. All too often project teams become so focused on the development and implementation of information systems that they lose sight of the impact changes in one area on another. The disk of change, represented earlier as an octagon, identifies the other areas which may have experienced either direct or ripple effects of the reengineered operations, processes and organization. Careful analysis of potential risks is required to minimize exposure to unanticipated impact which will result in substantial change that the organization may not be able to withstand all at once. Figure 9-6 presents a tool to assist in this effort and identifies the eight areas that may be impacted. The estimated impact in each area is calculated through function point analysis. This is represented by the screen graph in the center of the figure. Significantly out-of-proportion maps should be scrutinized for errors to validate the underlying reasons for the odd distribution. Once established and validated, these figures require review. All eight areas should be revisited and the impact analysis recalculated during every ***PRISM*** review. Updates to the impact analysis calcu-

Reengineering Touch Points Analysis

TOUCH POINT	EXPECTED VALUE	IMPACT VALUE	COMMENTS
1. Business Process	7	7	No Orderly Redesign
2. Measures	6	2	No Investigation
3. Values & Beliefs	5	3	No Investigation
4. Controls	5	3	No Investigation
	5	6	No Investigation
6. Organization	7	4	No Investigation
7. Information Systems	6	9	New Technology Suite
8. Culture	4	2	No Investigation

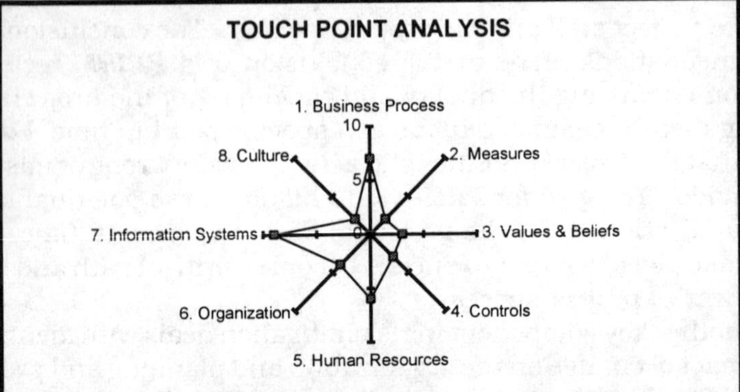

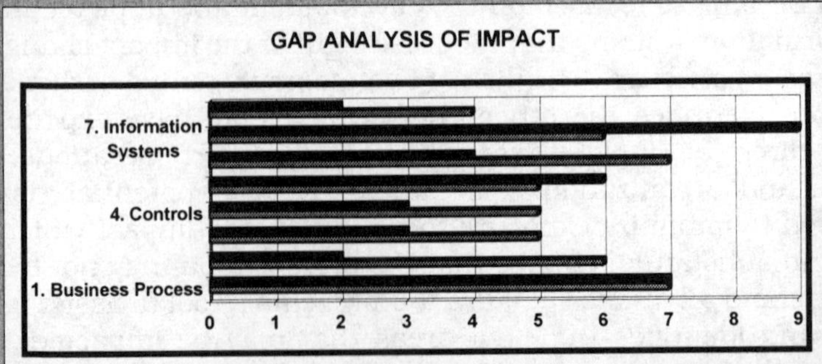

Figure 9.6. In order to manage the risk of radical change, careful, regular monitoring of the impact of the project of associated areas must be conducted. This figure is a graphical representation of one method to quantitatively analyze impact.

lations are input into the table at the top, and the resulting gap analysis is presented in the bar graph at the bottom of the page. This will not only protect management of serious changes that have taken place with regard to impact but will also allow the project staff to take the appropriate corrective measures to once again minimize the exposure to risk. Only through careful monitoring and timely corrective treatment can the risk associated with radical change be managed.

Numerous other activities that serve to mitigate risk go hand-in-hand with good project management. Clearly defined roles and responsibilities are critical to eliminate white areas resulting from misunderstanding as to who has been charged with work in a specific area or where a specific area of responsibility ends.

The Challenges of Reengineering

Reengineering brings new and different challenges to the MIS organization both in terms of the goals and objectives of the typical reengineering project and in the way the project is conducted. This method is different from that of traditional development projects.

Consider what reengineering is expected to accomplish. MIS and its business counterparts expect to work a radical change into one or more business processes. It soon becomes apparent that the users and MIS will have to work together to achieve a set of common objectives. MIS management must now determine how to manage the MIS portion of the reengineering effort. Think about where the business and MIS will be when the project is completed (this is usually called a vision).

VISION

- Order-of-magnitude improvement in the targeted business processes has been achieved resulting in order-of-magnitude improvements to the bottom line.
- Rapid and radical change in the MIS environment has made possible the timely implementation and support of the new processes by the MIS organization.
- The MIS organization has the right mix of skills, knowledge and experience to support future reengineering projects as well as continuous improvement in existing systems.

In order to achieve this vision, MIS initiates a business reengineering project with the following objectives:

1. Rapidly develop computer systems which support the reengineered

business.
2. Work closely with the business community to make certain the new computer systems support the reengineered business with its new business processes.
3. Provide people with the appropriate skills and experience to successfully conclude the MIS project, to operate the new systems environment and to support continuous improvement of the business processes in the future.

The challenge is heightened because reengineering projects are different from other, more "traditional" projects. These differences affect the way the project should be managed, and everyone involved — MIS and business users — need to understand and take into account this new environment in order to succeed. Here are the major differences between reengineering projects and the "traditional" projects.

- The project moves much faster in reengineering. The process is oriented toward delivering new systems within months instead of years. This means that decisions need to be made within hours, not days or weeks. If the project, user or MIS organization is bureaucratic or if senior management does not empower the labs to make decisions, the project will bog down.
- There is much more emphasis on business processes in the reengineering processes than MIS people may be accustomed to. The users are not a distant group; they are involved and working side-by-side with the MIS employees. This will challenge the MIS employees to better understand the business and its issues. They will also be challenged to deal with businessmen who tend to better perform "soft" skills such as motivation and negotiation.
- The reengineering lab environment is a challenge to manage. There must be a great emphasis on knowledge and experience when selecting its members. When a group of these people are together they can be very creative, which means that managing this scope is much more difficult than in a conventional development effort. The challenge is to create an environment which is bound but encourages creativity and rapid progress in order to achieve the desired results in the time allotted.
- Reengineering is intended to bring about radical change in all aspects of the organization, including the cultural aspects. This can be very threatening to employees, particularly if they fear that their jobs are threatened.
- Reengineering projects are often staffed by significant numbers of out-of-town employees, thus creating challenges in the areas of expense control, morale, and team building. While this may or may not apply to MIS people, the effects will be felt by all team members.

- Resolving issues in a client-server environment when used is more difficult than in a "traditional" environment because the components of the MIS infrastructure and the business environment are much more interrelated and interdependent. (There are no discrete values.) If you expect to use client-server, facilitation and leadership skills will become more important since meetings need to be held to identify and resolve issues.

How to meet the challenge

Project management is a boring subject—but only if done well—because there are a lot of simple activities which must be performed well in concert in order for the project to succeed. This is much like Vince Lombardi's view of football that in order to win the players need first to master the fundamentals —blocking and tackling—before they can run complex plays well.

Projects, particularly large mission-critical reengineering projects, must be approached with considerable care. Don't fall into the fairly common trap of assuming that because you have succeeded with smaller or less-complicated projects you will succeed at a reengineering project. Projects of different size need to be managed differently. This is true of conventional projects as well as reengineering projects. A single person can function as both project manager and technical leader in a small (fewer than 10 people) project. For a large project this is fatal. For very large projects of long duration, the functions of that small project manager may be the responsibility of four or more people, depending on the nature of the work to be performed.

Planning, discipline and organization become much more important as the project grows in size and complexity, and time spent in the beginning organizing a reengineering project will pay dividends later on. If that time is not spent in the beginning, you may have to spend orders of magnitude more time later to correct problems.

There are five areas in which careful attention during startup will improve your chances for a successful reengineering project.

1. Selecting an experienced project manger.
2. Using a good, tested project methodology.
3. Comprehensive definition of roles and responsibilities.
4. Organizing (structuring) the project and its relationship to the rest of the organization.
5. Planning and enhancing communications.

Let's look at each one in turn:

1. Selecting an experienced project manager. Studies have shown that projects of any size are much more likely to succeed when there is a formally designated project manager with the responsibility and authority necessary to succeed. Large projects will not succeed without a project manager. Nor is project management a part-time job or an additional assignment, particularly in a reeengineering project.

Even if you hire a systems integrator to manage the project, you will need your own project manager who will be the single point of contact for the systems integrator. It is not a good idea to assume you can simply hire a systems integration firm and then sit back and watch it all happen. You still have to manage the systems integrator to get the results you want.

By the way, notice that I said "project manager with the responsibility and authority to succeed". This is an old story, but I still see project managers being appointed with responsibility for a project but given little or no authority. If this does nothing else, it wastes time by forcing the project manager to seek approval for decisions which he/she should be allowed to make in the course of managing the project. Remember, in a reengineering project, the pace of events is much faster and there is little time for bureaucratic procedures.

General Experience. While the basic skills, such as project planning and controlling, can be learned in the classroom, applying them well comes from experience. In fact, much of what makes a good project manager comes from experience. Often this experience stems from lessons learned in dealing with unforeseen or unplanned events — something no project is without. A good project manager learns from these events, and, without becoming overly cynical, learns how to avoid or deal with similar circumstances in future projects.

Experience in Applying Both Project and Development Methodology. (Not that we are talking about two kinds of methodologies - project and development.) Not only is it necessary to have a development methodology specific to reengineering, but there also needs to be a complimentary project methodology which has been tried and tested by the organization and found to be a sound basis for repeatable successes in reengineering projects. This is discussed further below.

New project managers tend to apply methodologies by reading the documentation. This is dangerous enough in "normal" projects, but it can be catastrophic in reengineering projects. A project manager experienced in methodologies knows from experience what is important and what to emphasize and what to monitor. He/she also knows from experience how to adapt the methodology to a particular set of circumstances since not all parts of the methodology are used every time.

Interpersonal Skills. Reengineering projects usually don't fail because the technology is inappropriate or inadequate; they fail because the people involved in the project do not reach documented agreement on the objectives of the project and how to achieve them. So-called failure of the technology can usually be traced to failure to communicate as well as failure to understand along with personal agendas and hidden agendas. The project manager must be able to deal with these shortcomings and must have good interpersonal or "soft" skills. Particularly valuable are negotiation skills, political savvy and communication skills.

Track Record. Just as you wouldn't want your operation to be the surgeon's first, you don't want your "bet your business" project to be your project manager's first. He/she should have spent at least 10 years in project management and have had some experience with business reengineering. However, nobody is going to have a lot of experience at reengineering — the concept is too new.

Ability to deal with executive management. Successful business reengineering projects require the sponsorship and continuous involvement of executive management. Project managers need to understand what is important to these executives and to be able to deal with them in all sorts of situations, often under pressure.

Responsibilities

- Overall project success
- Risk assessment and mitigation
- Problem resolution process and setting priorities
- Making the tough choices
- Develop an inter-project communications process and keeping management informed
- Makes decisions and drives toward action

The project manager must think and act as the Chief Operations Officer of the project and the area(s) that is/are being addressed by the project. Too often the project manager thinks of himself as a representative of the working team rather than an owner of the resulting product.

Key Success Factors

- Operate on facts
- Everyone is 100 percent engaged on the project
- One Team
- Keep commitments to the team and one another
- Everyone works to understand and support one another

- Discussions are open and honest
- Full alignment on key issues and decisions

2. Project Methodology. Elsewhere in this book there is a discussion of the methodology of business reengineering. As I said previously, there must also be a complementary methodology to manage the project itself. This methodology should have the following attributes:

Flexibility. No two projects are exactly alike, and no one who creates or employs a methodology can anticipate all the possibilities. The methodology should therefore be sufficiently flexible to enable an experienced project manager to deal with any situation.

Supports rapid application development. It should be apparent by now that rapid application development is much different than "normal" application development. And you cannot simply take the traditional development process and speed it up. A good reengineering project methodology complements a good reengineering development methodology, and vice versa.

Scope control. Controlling scope is difficult enough in traditional development projects and, as discussed above, it is much more difficult to control in rapid application development. As with development methodology, the scope control methodology should be specific to rapid application development, which is not the same approach used for traditional development.

Risk assessment and mitigation. Project management is risk management, so the approach to risk assessment and mitigation contained in the methodology is a key to project success. Experience is very important here since the combination of a proven methodology and a project manager's experience will account for lessons learned from hundreds of projects in anticipating the risks in your particular project and taking all possible steps to avoid or mitigate them. ***PRISM*** will be the primary tool used in risk management.

User orientation/involvement. We have already learned that reengineering does not take place without heavy user involvement. This involvement cannot be left to chance; it must be managed. A good reengineering project methodology will account for and manage that involvement from the inception of the project through completion.

Provides for learning and re-skilling. From a people skill point-of-view, this should begin with assessing the skills of the MIS personnel in order to determine what additional skills are needed for project participants. It should also take into account what skills are needed after project completion to operate the new system's environment. Failure to conduct a skills assessment and to provide for re-skilling can cause the project to fail.

3. Roles and Responsibilities. Organization and roles and

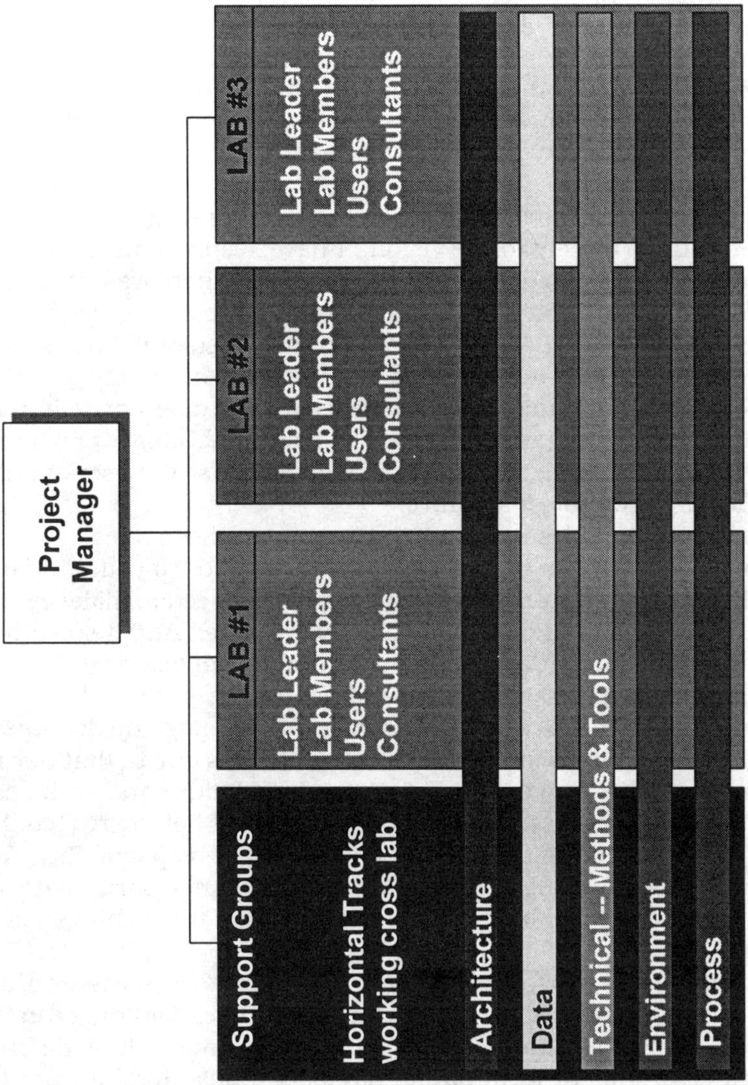

Figure 9.7. Project Management Organizational Structure

responsibilities are related subjects. Since the organization itself will be somewhat determined by the user organization, it makes sense to focus on roles and responsibilities. Remember that there is no one right way to organize, and there is no single organizational structure which is right for all projects. What is more important is that the organization and the roles and responsibilities be agreed upon and documented.

Without clear definition of roles and responsibilities, the project team can waste a lot of time arguing over these during the management of the project. The resulting confusion and lost time will adversely effect the outcome of the project. You need to define these up front, because you will not have time to do so once the project is underway. Some factors to consider are:

- Determine how success will be measured and by whom. This should tie in closely to the vision. I have seen several projects in which there was no definition of success and there was, therefore, no definition of failure. This can cause the project to drag beyond completion because no one can determine when or if it has met its objectives, ("When are we done?"). More serious is the situation where the MIS organization and the users have different definitions of success. At best, this will cause a lot of squabbling over whether the project is completed. At worst, it could cause the user-sponsor to declare the project a failure.
- Determine the roles required and document those roles. Much of this will be driven by the methodologies used, so your guidance will come from that source. Don't ignore the need to make certain everyone understands who is filling what role. And if something changes, document and communicate the change.
- Determine the responsibilities and document them. All corporations have a "political environment". Not defining and documenting responsibilities for a project will subject its fate to that normal human tendency to avoid association with failure and seek association with success. The methodologies will help here, too, but only if you communicate clearly who has what responsibility. You are in a reengineering project, and the participants, particularly the lab members, don't have a lot of time to figure these things out on their own.
- Determine how progress and performance are to be measured, and by whom. A systems integrator can provide useful guidance in this area. Remember that a reengineering project is a different work environment from day-to-day operations, and you need to communicate your project-specific expectations both for the progress of the project and for the performance of individual team members. Remember also that "you get what you inspect, not what you expect".

Progress and performance objectives need to be clear and measurable, and the means for measuring them should be made clear to the project team. Document and publish these measurements.

4. Organization (and staffing). As I said above, staffing will be determined somewhat by the users. The development methodology will doubtfully involve a set of workshops or labs, in which the users and MIS personnel work together to reengineer the business and rapidly develop the MIS infrastructure to support the reengineered business processes.

What's important to MIS? A couple of things you ought to focus on are:

• *The architecture function.* This is a critical success factor. This ongoing function should develop a preliminary architecture, communicate and interpret it to the labs, and make changes based on information from the labs. Failure to manage architecture in this fashion can cause chaos as the labs independently work toward what they think is a common goal. Members of the architecture team and the labs should interact daily.

In the "old days" a single architect might have been enough. Today, a large project will have a systems architect, a data architect, and applications architect, possibly a communications or network architect, and a manager to manage the group.

The business community may or may not understand the need for architecture, so you may have to sell the concept to them. Don't give in on this one - it is too important to the success of the project.

• *Quality people.* Current literature and practice in reengineering emphasize that the businessmen must assign their best people to the project in order to do the best possible job of reengineering the business. MIS personnel must be assigned by applying a similar philosophy. That is why the skills assessment, discussed above, is so critical in determining what skills are needed, evaluating your existing staff against those needs and creating a plan to provide the total mix of skills necessary in the project team even after the project is completed.

5. Planning and Enhancing Communications. I've seen projects fail because of a lack of communication, but I've never seen one fail because of too much communication. Communication, as used here, involves two major activities.

1) Regular formal communications covering all aspects of the project to all interested, involved parties, including stockholders. (Think of this effort as advertising and public relations.) In a large reengineering project, the senior executive sponsor should set the example for good communications by clearly communicating the

objectives of the reengineering effort and by holding periodic informational meetings to report progress against the plan and to give the employees an opportunity to ask questions and express their concerns.

2) Creating and nurturing of a project environment or culture in which free and open communications among the project team is encouraged in every way. "Shoot the messenger" and "Knowledge is power" mind sets can decrease your chances for success. The project manager must take the lead by telling the project team what the rules are and nurture good communications among the team.

Project Manager Profile

The project manager works with the client, MIS and user management to plan, organize and manage tasks and resources to accomplish one or more objectives — usually with time and budget constraints. The objectives will be highly business-oriented.

Reports to: CIO

Responsibilities:

1. Develop a master project plan which includes:

- Project deliverables
- Project dependencies
- Project organization
- Project roles and responsibilities, including any committees formed specifically for the project and other standing committees with project responsibilities
- Identification of risks and a plan to mitigate them
- Project activities including milestones and completion dates
- Project staffing plan containing calendarized requirements for resources/skills
- Project budget listing expenses by category over time
- Change management process which includes management of problems, issues, and changes to scope
- Quality assurance plan
- Communications plan including status reports, their content, frequency and distribution

2. Manage the master project plan, including:

- Progress vs. plan - all areas and subordinate plans
- Expense vs. budget
- Management of risks

3. Develop plans and/or take corrective actions to remedy any problems identified in managing to the master plan (step 2 above).

Tools

You may already be using one of the project management software packages, such as Microsoft Project or Project Workbench. I am familiar with these two and recommend them but, if you are using another one, there is no pressing need for you to change. There are usually greater differences between the non-Windows and Windows versions of the same product than among the products themselves. All produce Gantt charts and CPM networks, and provide for tracking against a plan. Not surprisingly, all are easier to use in the windows version.

Project estimating tools are another matter. Like good project managers, these are developed from experience and are part of the value you get for your money when you hire a systems integrator. Systems integrators typically estimate time and expense for the next project based on previous experience with similar projects.

Estimating tools used in traditional projects are not as useful in business reengineering because of the use of labs and time-boxing. While time-boxing appears to bound by the time and labor estimates, it does not, by itself, manage either one, as many companies have found. That is why systems integrators prefer to conduct business reengineering projects on a time and materials basis rather than fixed-price basis.

Some thoughts on what to measure and what to watch for:

Scope vs. time in a lab. If left to itself, a technician will likely follow a behavior pattern something like this:

First, the staff will decide to add additional functionality or enhance to functionality for which it was originally responsible.

Second, the staff will attempt to deliver a prototype including all the (expanded) functionality in the originally allotted timeframe (the "time box").

Lastly, at some point, the staff will realize that it cannot deliver all the expanded functionality in the originally allotted timeframe and will "de-scope" or "de-commit".

This can result in some original core functionality (upon which other labs or the business itself are dependent) not being provided as part of the prototype given to the integration labs.

In its worst form, this scenario can result in considerable rework in several labs, which means that the rapid application development is now less rapid.

Experienced business reengineering consultants can minimize this problem by actively managing the labs, and not allowing changes in scope to be authorized in or by the lab staff themselves.

Architecture

This has already been discussed above, but it bears reinforcing. The lab staff needs a set of rules governing the relationship of their deliverables to the deliverables of the other lab staff and to legacy systems. If no set of such rules exists, its absence will first be discovered when the lab prototypes are brought together for integration and don't integrate easily or not at all!

There must be a strong architecture function which creates data, application, and technical architectures and interprets them to the lab staff. The architecture should be a living document, not only be interpreted to the staff by the architecture group, but also to be revised to take into account discoveries in the labs which require change to or further definition of the architecture. For this process to work, the architecture group must be in frequent contact with the staff to make certain that the architecture is understood and followed and to make timely revisions as deemed appropriate.

Issue tracing needs. Whether you hire a systems integrator or manage the project yourself, you will need an issue tracking system from the day the project starts. A good systems integrator will always have and use an issue tracking system. I emphasize having the issue tracking system in place the day the project starts because this is another one of those things which will lull you into a sense of complacency; and, by the time you realize the need, you will have a lot of catching up to do. Remember, things move fast in a reengineering project, and you need an issue tracking system which will facilitate the rapid identification, documentation, tracking and closure of issues.

Status Meetings

These meetings present an excellent opportunity to get the decision makers together and to make decisions on key issues that span organizational, political or authoritative boundaries. Unfortunately, these meetings all too often fall into disarray. This is because of loosing sight of what is expected in those meetings and poor planning. To combat this we offer the following guidelines.

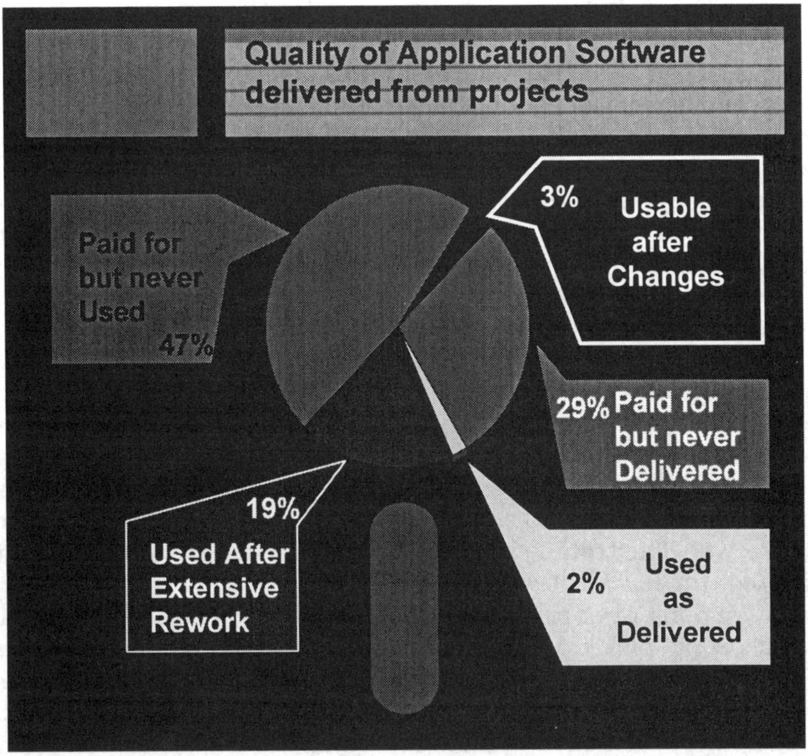

Figure 9.8. Quality of application software delivered from projects.

- Set and adhere to published meeting start and finish times.
- Appoint a timekeeper and scribe responsibilities (scribe notes address decisions only, not a detailed summary of the discussions).
- Follow true time boxing techniques. Set and limit time to present views on a particular problem and, at the end of that time, make a decision.
- Set time aside for risk management discussions and measurement in accordance with the risk management worksheet.
- Do not substitute for persons in the meeting. Key players must make themselves available for this activity.
- Assign a facilitator for every topic. This person is charged with the presentation of all sides of the issue and its resolution.
- Complete prep/post work. Time must be allotted in everyone's schedule to allow them to come to this meeting prepared.
- Set agendas at least one week in advance. Not surprisingly, topics can be interjected into these meetings. Allowing this to happen only prolongs the decisionmaking process which is inefficient.

Politics. Politics is one of the top reasons projects, reengineering or otherwise, fail. Remember, that there is no easy way to transform the culture of an organization, and that many, if not all, the project team will have their own stake in preserving the status quo. And, in case you haven't already noticed, many employees will appear to be strong public supporters of the project objectives but will covertly drag their feet or work actively against those objectives. Establishing free and open communications as discussed above can help to reduce—but not entirely eliminate—this problem. Another method of limiting this exposure is through the use of the Executive Project Sponsor. The clear understanding that this individual will not accept territoralism or politics will serve to calm this type of activity. Keep in mind, this must be reinforced on an ongoing basis.

Just saying you-made-your-dates culture. This has to be the most frequent cause of trouble in projects. I have seen multi-million dollar projects where a full-time administrator who developed a giant project network (usually a Gantt chart) dutifully report completion of each activity without any other valid reason to do so other than the completion date had arrived. The most common reason activities are incorrectly reported as complete is that no one wants to deliver bad news. The trouble with this is that the longer the problem is ignored, the harder it is to fix it.

"We don't need to plan it - we'll just do it". This is another bad habit people pick up from successfully completing small projects. You don't need a plan to mow only your lawn. However, if you are responsible for mowing fifty lawns over a wide geographic area with 10 employees and 10 lawn mowers, some planning is called for. (This may also explain why some landscape businesses grow to a certain size, then either fail to give good service or fail entirely.) The problem is that, in a large project, the effects of poor planning often take weeks or even months to become noticeable. By this time, it may well be too late to recover. In a reengineering project, you can get into more trouble quicker.

Quality Assurance. Quality is now a major force in the conduct of American business and continues to be the subject of articles in American business journals. Many companies have instilled the quality ethic into their culture and have been quite successful as a result. For example, Motorola has actually beaten the Japanese at their own game in part through the use of comprehensive quality management techniques

Quality in MIS projects or systems-related projects have fallen under a great deal of fire in recent years. Numerous software bugs have gained widespread media attention because of their crippling efforts on business and, in some cases, the consumers. Studies on software quality suggest that each and every year tens of millions of dollars are lost because of system failures. Failures related to faulty application software totaled over 24 percent; communications related equipment and software came in at 21 percent; and hardware related failures were responsible for 28 percent of loses. The remainder of the pie is contributed to human errors. When you add the dollars wasted on systems related projects that fail or fail to meet the end users needs, the figure soars into the billions.

Business reengineering projects must be quality driven. Remember, these are "bet-your-business" mission-critical projects, and no one wants their result to be of poor quality. In looking at the results of poor quality in information systems, the breakout of the results looks like this:

Software failures have resulted in: (listed in order of magnitude)

1. Customer Dissatisfaction
2. Lost Productivity
3. User Complaints and Dissatisfaction
4. Lost Revenue
5. Overtime
6. Lost Customers
7. Penalties or Fines

Some important points:

A good systems integrator will have a methodology or approach to quality involving the development and implementation of a quality assurance plan as an integral part of the project plan. A successful reengineering project will have such a plan, and the plan should be implemented not just displayed in someone's bookcase. On a regular basis make absolutely sure the plan has independent project review built in. Furthermore, make sure the reviews are performed.

Managing Expectations

Expectations are an important but often overlooked aspect of any project. Their importance increases significantly in a business reengineering project because of its scope, magnitude and bet-your-business nature.

I have discussed elsewhere the importance of defining success and defining what "done" means. Upon definition, both of these become expectations which must be managed. Suppose, for example, that the MIS organization defines success to mean getting the system installed on time, while the head of a key business unit defines success to mean being able to ship from another warehouse if an item is out of stock in the local warehouse. The project, as started initially, will meet both expectations providing that the desired feature is in the desired timeframe. Now let us suppose that due dates begin to slip and the MIS organization defers this feature into the second wave in order to get the system installed “on time”. The business unit now has an expectation which is not going to be met. It must be managed.

Some Thoughts on the Process

- Set key expectations early in the project.
- Look for expectations which have already been set.

(These first two should be done in a workshop.)

Don’t set expectations that can’t be met. For due dates, consider the old PERT approach providing most optimistic, most pessimistic and most likely due dates. Calculate sick days, vacation days and a certain amount of slack time into the schedule.

Be aware that time and changing circumstances can change expectations. Actively look for these changes and deal with them in an open and honest fashion. Test stakeholders to see if their expectations have changed and identify why the change has occurred.

Communicate!

Lessons Learned

Reengineering Management Information Systems

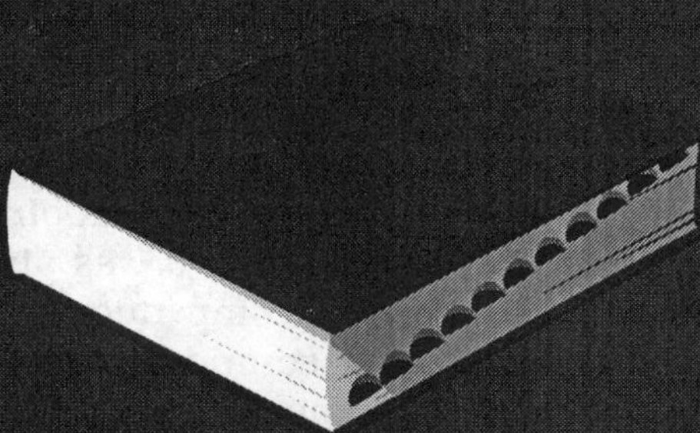

Chapter 10

Reengineering Lessons Learned

As with all breakthroughs in business, reengineering is one of the most publicized topics in the media and business community if not the most publicized. However, reengineering can neither solve all the problems faced by business today, nor be successful in every case. Each time the reengineering approach is applied to a business, it must be tempered in order to fit within the specific parameters of that specific situation. Failure to identify areas that are situationally specific can and will lead to project failure. This article will look at a few areas that are the most common and present actual case histories around the failure. It is important to note that even though these reengineering projects have failed, the approach is still highly valued and should not be overlooked by businesses that require fundamental change in order to grow or, in some cases, survive in today's marketplace.

Scenario #1 Background

The organization involved in this reengineering attempt was a multi-national manufacturer, distributor and sales organization. With over $2 billion in revenue, the organization saw moderate competition rise until three years ago and was able to sustain a moderate level of growth. Recently, competition intensified, profit margins were significantly decreased and market growth slowed. This is typically seen in maturing markets after the initial feeding frenzy that often accompanies hi-tech products. Prior to embarking on the reengineering initiative, the organization went through a series of cost-cutting measures. These measures included a series of staff reductions as well as reductions in non-essential and discretionary spending. Summarizing, all the cream had been skimmed off the top when it came to cost cutting measures. The organization recognized how heavily they relied on information technology in conducting their day-to-day business. The current portfolio of information systems was very fragmented with a significant amount of redundancy that was attributed to customizing software to the various organizational departments. This organizational structure fostered multiple departments all doing portions of a functional business area. This is evidenced by over a dozen sales organizations that were not only divided by product line but by sales type, i.e. location, customer type. After the laboratory team was selected, the initial direction was to identify the basic business processes and select a package software solution that was flexible and could be easily modified to conform to the requirements that would come out of the reengineering activities. The work surrounding identification, evaluation and selection of a software package began. During this timeframe several team members were replaced because of irreconcilable personality characteristics. Once the package selection was made, the focus of this group shifted to concentrating on the reengineering of the business processes. During the preparation that needs to occur prior to initiating the reengineering effort, several significant events occurred that were indeed symptoms to the underlying problem. One of the first symptoms that was noticed was people deviating from the traditional approaches to conducting business. Deeply rooted in the organization these people were ostracized and branded not a team player. In looking at some of the people transitioned off the team in the early stages of software product selection, many of those occurrences were probably contributed to this problem.

The second and even more disturbing event that arose was a declaration by the sales department. They claimed that nothing needed to change with regard to their processes (all 12+ of them). In order to reach the baseline savings and not the stretch goals that were set for the project, the savings would have to come from another department. In other words, there was no fat left to trim in the sales portion of the organization. Next, the MIS organization stepped to the front of the picture. This contingent of the laboratory team stated they already knew 90 percent of the process redesigns that needed to take place and could drive this effort with minimal support and participation from the functional business areas. Already several weeks behind, they did not believe that they would have any trouble meeting the schedule. This schedule, by the way, was extremely tight to start with and would require extraordinary efforts by the entire project team. Additionally, the MIS contingent was looking at the reengineering laboratory methodology and the individuals who were brought in to assist in this specific effort because they had a technique that would feed in the current funtional business process and a miracle would occur producing the reengineered version of the process.

The final event that was clearly the icing on the cake took place at a meeting between the reengineering team and the executive sponsor who discussed the status and direction of the project. The reengineered processes would only create a 10 percent difference in the existing functional processes. Once again, challenges to the way in which fundamental business processes arose. True to form, the individuals making those challenges were transitioned off the reengineering team. Interestingly enough, the individuals transitioned off were the only ones that had expereince in reengineering and the reengineering of functional business processes.

Identified Problems

1. Traditional Thinking. The project team must be comprised of individuals who are open-minded and innovative. These individuals must be motivated to make the necessary changes that are required to meet the goals and objectives set by the executive sponsor. For this to transpire, the individuals that are on the team must be given certain guarantees that a position of at least equal status and compensation will be available to them after they conclude the reengineering project. The second factor that must be considered is their direct supervisors. In order for the reengineering team to function unimpeded by politics and employee/supervisor biases, the reengineering project team should not report to any of the functional business areas undergoing the reengineering.

2. Methodology. The methodology employed to identify a base package based on initial and fundamental functional requirements prior to conducting the reengineering of the business processes it would have to report was risky. However, because of the problems associated with reengineering of the processes a conclusion cannot be drawn whether or not this was a success or failure. At this point, one could not condone or condemn this approach based on this project.

3. Re-automate. Clearly, there is a problem in getting caught up into the re-automate vs. reengineer predicament. The driving force behind any reengineering initiative is to achieve a substantial amount of gains in terms of productivity, efficiency and profitability necessary to meet the goals or stretch goals set for the project and the organization. To achieve this, one has to change. And it has to be a big change! The minor change brought about by re-automating will not provide the magnitude of improvement necessary. Even thought the team is clearly moving in the right direction, the rewards will not match the expectations of the executive sponsor of executive management.

4. Magical Solution. The organization's view of the reengineering laboratory as a Holy Grail and a magical Xanadu that would solve all their problems is not all that uncommon among laypersons. There is no magic involved. Reengineering projects involve hard work, a clear understanding of solid business practices and innovative problem solving and design work that is unbiased by internal politics, turf battles and empires that have been established over the course of business evolution.

Scenario #2 Background

In this instance, the organization deals with a consumer food product. There are actually two distinctive product lines that are hardly related except that they share many of the same distribution channels. They manufacture, sell and distribute their products through a wide variety of channels. The organization is earning just under $1 billion a year in sales and, like everyone else, is suffering from increased competition and demands from a value-conscious consumer for high-quality products. The history of this organziation depicts an extremely lean organization that has a habit of responding to customer needs and market changes very slowly. In order to be successful and competitive, they must change their operations to accommodate the needs of their customers. Another requirement is that the user interface utilize the ease of user supplied by the Graphic User Interface (GUI) technology.

During the first few weeks of the reengineering project it became evident that the project team was made up of staff personnel and outside consultants. The understanding of general business principles, technical principles around the information systems and human resource management techniques did not allow for significant progress in the reengineering and redesign of the business operations and the design of the supporting information systems. The entire reengineering effort could go flawlessly and the project would not be successful without planning a transitional strategy from the old way of doing business and systems to the new processes and information systems. One month out of pilot, the strategy for implementing the redesigns, as well as how the redesigns would be validated prior to placing the products of the reengineering efforts into limited business operations existed. During the design of the remote order-entry process requirements and the supporting information system design, the discussions were led by MIS staff with moderate input from the sales department. This system would be one of only two methods of interface to the customers.

Identified Problems

1. Skill Level. The skill set possessed by the internal staff was lacking in several key areas. Without added support in these areas, the redesigns were only average and would not provide the competitive advantage desired by upper management. Additionally, even though these individuals were uncomfortable with the tasks they had been assigned, they did not speak up because of the repercussions. The culture, so heavily entrenched in the employees, was that of meeting schedules and not needing assistance. Failure in either one of these areas could bring about dismissal.

2. Planning and Validation. The importance of a smooth transition from the old way of conducting business to the new process is critical, even though this would be initially on a limited basis. The business cannot stop to cut over to live operation and the customers cannot be inconvenienced by the organizational changes that would be going on. For this reason, the redesigns needed to be validated prior to being placed into limited operations in pilot. This validation should be in a simulated business environment where the business processes and supporting information systems are exercised. The method of validation should be based on business transactions and not just on testing of the information systems. Failure to uncover flaws in the redesign as a complete package could spell disaster later on in subsequent redesign releases.

3. Customer Involvement. While all of these issues are a concern and could jeopardize the success of the project, one way to ensure failure is not involve your customers in the portions of the redesigns that reach them. The main objective of the reengineering effort is flexibility in meeting the needs of their customers. Customers should have been consulted on how the remote order-entry process would work from a functional standpoint.

Scenario #3 Background

In this project, the organization is a multi-national distributor of consumer products. There are actually two product lines that are very closely related and many share the same distribution channels. The manufacturing facilities are distributed across the world as well as their distribution channels. The organization earns well over $3 billion a year in sales and, like all organizaitions, is suffering from increased competition and a value-conscious-consumer that demands high-quality product even though they are ranked second largest in their market. The history of this organization depicts excessive waste because of redundancies in operations and in the organization's management and operations. The organization has a habit of being extremely sluggish when responding to customer needs and market changes. In order to be successful and competitive, they must change their operations to accommodate the needs of their customers and a changing market. Another requirement is that they need to be able to assess the profitability of individual components of the organization. During the first few weeks of the reengineering project, it became evident that the internal staff that made up the project team did not have the skills and understanding of the overall business strategy or the direction in which the organization was moving. Outside consultants skilled in reengineering were used to supplement the internal staff. However, the lack of understanding of past focus on general business principles, technical principles around the information systems and human resource management techniques hindered the progress in the reengineering and redesign of the business operations and the design of the supporting information systems. The entire reengineering would be at risk if the awareness of the impact on these touch points could not be increased to appropriate levels. In addition, because of poor communication from the top, the first few months of operation required a massive effort to break the traditional thinking of "Why should we do anything different?". Changing the way the organization would conduct business and systems to the new processes and information systems tended to adhere to the old goals and objectives, not necessarily the methods of conducting work. A strategy for implementing the change in management program was defined and invoked. This would begin to communicate in a graphic, easy-to-understand medium the changes that were taking place and, just as important, the drivers that made it necesary to change. The reengineering processes would be defined in an iterative approach and would be reviewed on a regular basis. During the design of the order fulfillment process requirements and the supporting information system design, the discussions were led by business staff from all over the country with moderate input from the international sales department. This system would be the primary method of interface to the customers.

Identified Problems

1. *Cultural Change*. The skill set possessed by the internal staff lacked aptitude in several key areas. Past corporate culture did not promote the software side of business or process management. Without added support programs in these areas, the redesigns would not position the organization to move forward. Additionally, even though highly skilled individuals were added to focus on these areas, the embedded culture was difficult to overcome. The culture was so heavily entrenched in the employees that the executive sponsor would need to lead the charge in this initiative.

2. *Implementation Planning*. The importance of a well-thought-out approach to reengineering of processes and systems must include multiple check points and reviews. It is very easy to get off track, over expand scope and overlook the long-term objectives, instead concentrating on short-term gains. In addition, a smooth orderly transition from the old way of conducting business to the new process is critical and requires a substantial amount of preplanning, even though this would be initially on a limited basis. Like past projects, management was concerned that business operation could not be interrupted during cut over and the customers could be inconvenienced by the organizational changes that would be happening.

3. Executive Sponsor Involvement. No other issue could jeopardize the success of the project more than a lack of visible executive sponsorship. The unquestionable commitment of executive management to these initiatives must be visible at all levels. Any question about the sponsorship needs to be addressed immediately. Extensive use of messages from the executive sponsor detailing the importance and the need for everyone to support these changes will help facilitate the redesign process and transition.

Scenario #4 Background

A major pharmaceutical manufacturer had no MIS function of its own. They relied on outside consultants for the detailed definition of their architecture and the building of their systems. The client is a major competitor in the highly-competitive pharmaceutical industry.

Prior to redefining their environment, most of their development work was centered around mainframe applications. The transition from mainframe to client-server was a major goal of this project. Much of the organization existent at the time was insufficient for the migration.

Identified Problems

Organizational Changes. In order to preserve the current environment and enable full readiness for the upcoming application implementation in client/server, we setup an architecture team consisting of a Chief Architect, an Applications Architect, a Development Environment Architect, a Data Architect, and a Technical Infrastructure Architect. The teamwork provided by these four architects under the direction of the Chief Architect provided a coordination and level of control not previously possible. (A complete description of this architecture team is described elsewhere in this book.)

Each architect provided a focal point for gathering information about his/her particular discipline. In addition, the Data and Application architects provided the ability to make sure that all applications under development would integrate with each other as well as with legacy applications and data.

There were many instances where the Architecture team proved to be the only group within the organization that had the complete "big picture" concerning all the facets of development and how the new application would fit within the business organization. Integration between Data and Application was smooth and nearly flawless. The application worked exactly as expected when delivered because of this tight integration. There were minor problems with some of the screens and associated performance but these were quickly resolved between the Development Environment Architect and the Technical Architect.

Where there might be some disconnects between traditional systems programming support and the application developers we had smooth communications. The architecture team resided and worked with the application development teams on a day-to-day basis. There were no communication lags because the teams worked in close proximity to each other.

The major lesson learned from this engagement is that management of the environment and issues surrounding new development (especially where new architectures are involved) are absolutely essential to the success of the project.

Scenario #5 Background

During an engagement with a major communications corporation we guided the client through the definition of a new laboratory methodology, tools selection process, and reskilling process to make best use of the new environment.

Identified Problems

Methodology. The client had a weak methodology going into the project. They had used a traditional methodology but still did not have complete compliance within the organization. We helped create a methodology for change management that would govern the overall process of system building and maintenance. During this period we also installed a commercially available methodology that would help guide the company through the intricacies of laboratory team development.

We began the process of setting up and coaching the company through the implementation of an accounts payable system with a series of three laboratory teams. These laboratory teams were led by employees of the company and were staffed by employees of the company.

Laboratories commenced on their three-month journey toward installation and customization of an accounts payable package. There were some problems during development but overall the laboratory teams were very successful and completed their major efforts on time. This was nearly a first for this company. A second series of laboratory teams was then started to add further functionality to the application and install more of the package software.

Without a comprehensive methodology to guide them these teams would have floundered and failed to achieve their goals. Their previous methodology would have proven inadequate to the task of helping to manage their laboratory development efforts. Without experienced coaching, failure would have also been likely because no one at the company had ever been through a laboratory development effort before.

Conclusion

Reengineering is by no means a magical solution to the woes of business and MIS. Reengineering in and of itself is a technique that requires skill and tenacity in order to manifest the best chance of success. Organizations must properly prepare themselves as well as the reengineering project team for this undertaking. In preparation for these types of initiatives, executive management must go into this with their eyes wide open and be aware of the political hornet's nest that will be stirred up as a result. Not all organizations can pull this off alone. Politically neutral individuals who are politically savvy are required to keep everyone honest. There is no substitute for the first-hand experience of individuals who have lived through a reengineering initiative.

AUTHORS

Reengineering Management Information Systems

Appendix A

About the Authors

All five authors bring a wealth of experience and varied educational backgrounds to bare on Reengineering of Management Information Systems. Experience such as participation in several reengineering engagements, one being one of the world's largest Reengineering and Systems Development and Implementation projects for a consumer products manufacturer and distributor. It is experience such as this that provides them the firsthand knowledge necessary to guide others through this complex undertaking. Much of their work pioneered the techniques and methods employed to assure the utmost quality of business solutions.

Kevin G. Coleman is an International Management Consultant with over a decade of experience. Kevin has consulted to many of the largest companies in the United States and abroad. He specializes in solving business problems and application of information technology to achieve competitive advantage. During his career he has successfully directed multi-million dollar projects in the public and private sectors. He has consulted to city, state and federal governments and worked in the insurance, manufacturing and consumer products industries. Prior experience in the "Big 6", Kevin was a Manager at Touche Ross and Deloitte & Touche.

Kevin has routinely published in leading trade magazines and has authored multiple chapters in "The Encyclopedia of Computer Science and Technology". In addition, he is often called upon by the media for comments on significant events in the business community. Additionally, he has lectured at such schools as Carnegie Mellon University Graduate School of Industrial Administration, Georgia Institute of Technology, New York University School of Business and the University of Southern California School of Business.

His outstanding reputation in business and industry is evidenced by three U.S. patents, three Excellence in Design awards from Design News, the 1991 Bronze IDEA award from Business Week, and recently he has been named to "Who's Who in the Computer Industry" and is a lifetime member of "Who's Who Worldwide Platinum Edition". In addition, he has been presented a Certificate of Merit from the International Biographical Centre in Cambridge England and their exclusive Meritorious Achievement award.

The combination of his business, technical education, and experience provides the background necessary for innovative solutions to the problems faced in the global business market of the 21st century.

Jim Ettwein is a Management Consultant with a national consulting firm. With over 20 years of management and corporate consulting experience, Jim has served many of the Fortune 1000 companies. His vast experience includes redesign management, Reengineering Lab leadership, design, development and implementation of new processes and information systems. In addition, Jim is an authority in the area of CASE and Productivity tools. During his career Jim has evaluated numerous tools for increasing development productivity.

Jim has lectured and presented to corporate leaders on such topics as: CASE Technology, Reengineering, Methodologies and Strategic Importance of Information Systems. He recently participated in CSC Exchange where reengineering successes and lessons learned were presented.

Jim recently successfully concluded his role in one of the world's largest reengineering engagements for an international beverage company. He is currently involved in two reengineering projects, one for a communications company and the second for a major player in the video music production and broadcasting business.

Clelland Johnson is a Partner with a national management consulting firm providing reengineering implementation and commercial systems integration services. He is an active line consultant and directs the Client/Server computing practice as well as other advanced information technology initiatives. His experience in Business Reengineering, technical architecture, networking strategies and management of computer operations provides the detailed technical and business application knowledge to provide clients a competitive edge in today's marketplace.

Prior experience with Andersen Consulting, Clelland managed system development and implementation projects. He provided technical guidance to many of the Fortune 1000 companies and addressed the middle market and the public sector as well. He assisted clients in the evaluation and selection of hardware and software and the monitoring of emerging technologies that could provide a competitive advantage.

The author of numerous technical papers and articles, Clelland has taught and spoken in Europe, Asia, and North America. He has also spoken at every CSC Exchange to date, the largest conference on Business Reengineering.

Dick Pigman is a Principal in a leading world-wide consulting company and has over thirty years experience in system design and project management. Dick has successfully led major projects involving the reengineering of a major international beverage company, outsourcing of the telecommunications organization from a Fortune 50 manufacturing company, the development and marketing of a picture archiving and communications system (PACS) for a Fortune 50 manufacturing company, and the development and implementation of a public electronic mail system for a major American telecommunications common carrier.

Dick has been engaged by a telephone operating company, a major document management company, and one of the leading computer manufacturers in the US. In addition to project management, his background includes telephone and data systems management, telecommunications network system design and implementation, and computer hardware and software development and support.

Deborah L. Pulak is an Accelerated Development Specialist. She has over fifteen years of experience in development processes, techniques and methods as applied to management information systems. In the last decade she has focused on developing and refining techniques employed in accelerated development of information systems. Deborah authored portions of CSC's Methodology for Business Reengineering, Systems Development and Systems Management, CSC Catalyst X/AD, dealing with the accelerated design and development of business systems.

Deborah held a management position with DuPont's Information Engineering Associates (IEA), a pioneer in the field of rapid application design and development. During this time she contributed to the evolving use of "timeboxing" and "iterative production prototyping", and the fundamental concepts of accelerated development.

During her career, she has consulted to the leaders of the business community, many of them members of the Fortune 1000. She has successfully completed numerous projects in manufacturing, consumer products and insurance. Additionally, she has customized Accelerated Development Methodologies for many clients.

Deborah lectures extensively in the U.S. and abroad. She shares her experience in such areas as Empowerment, Leadership, Team Building as well as on developing Accelerated Development capabilities and implementing these concepts in your organization.

AUTHORS

Reengineering Management Information Systems

Points of Contact

Name		
Kevin G. Coleman	28 Elmcrest Drive P.O. Box 6028 Wheeling, WV 26003	(304) 242-0047
Jim Ettwein	7 Carriage Drive Acton, MA 01720	(508) 263-3511
Clelland Johnson	29 Old Farm Road Hopkinton, MA 01748	(508) 435-3926
Richard Pigman	P.O. Box 690 Victor, New York 14564	(716) 924-8290
Deborah Pulak	13 Wood Drive P.O. Box 548 Atkinson, NH 03811	(603) 362-6343

WORKSHEETS

Reengineering Management Information Systems

Worksheet #1

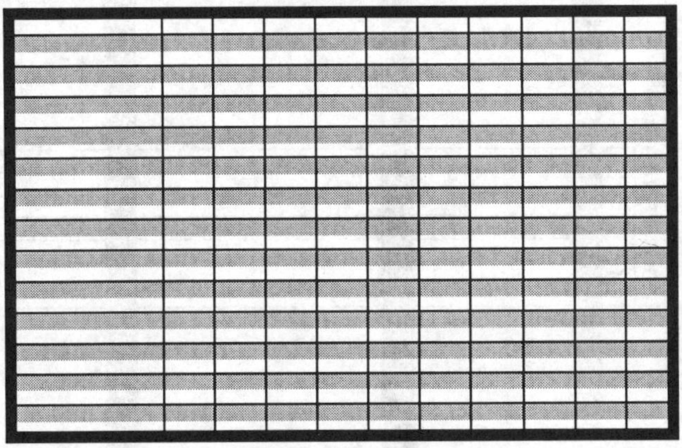

APPENDIX B

MIS Evaluation Worksheet

MIS MANAGEMENT	POOR 0	1	2	3	FAIR 4	5	6	GOOD 7	8	9	COMMENTS
Reporting relationship of MIS within the organization											
Organizational structure											
Areas serviced by MIS											
MIS mission alignment with the organization											
MIS goals as a benefit to the organization											
MIS decentralization											
MIS business focus											
Reporting structure of MIS within the department											
Job descriptions											
Job context											
Job responsibilities											
Job authorities											
Resource balance											
Span of management											
Strategic information's systems plan											
Systems plan											
Executive capability											
Level of administration control											
System development priorities											
System development process											
Change control procedures											
Version control procedures											
Documentation control process											

Worksheet 2-1

Evaluation Worksheet (continued)

MIS MANAGEMENT	POOR 0	1	2	3	FAIR 4	5	6	GOOD 7	8	9	COMMENTS
Approach to management control											
Effectiveness of operating reports											
System and programming reports											
Accounting control											
EDP auditing											
Determination of staffing requirements											
Development plans with staff requirements											
Definition of skill requirements											
Formal interviewing process											
Staff skill base											
Staff backgrounds											
Match with level of MIS sophistication											
Key staff member skill match to MIS											
Personnel policies and procedures											
Recruiting sources											
Selection criteria											
Recruitment results analysis											
Employee training											
Salary scale & benefits											
Performance appraisals (yearly min.)											
Personnel security screening											

Worksheet 2-2

Evaluation Worksheet (continued)

MIS MANAGEMENT	POOR			FAIR			GOOD				COMMENTS
	0	1	2	3	4	5	6	7	8	9	
Career development opportunities											
Criteria for advancement											
Activities rate											
Formal training program											
On-the-job training											
Training plan											

Worksheet 2-3

Evaluation Worksheet (continued)

MIS HARDWARE & SOFTWARE	POOR 0	1	2	3	FAIR 4	5	6	GOOD 7	8	9	COMMENTS
MIS technological base											
MIS sophistication											
Technological age											
Technological match											
Technology monitoring											
MIS operational analysis											
Gathers utilization statistics											
Gathers accounting data											
Gathers CPU utilization											
Gathers disk utilization data											
Monitors idle time											
Tests program execution time											
Monitors rerun time											
Monitors on-line response time											
Monitors multi-program impact											
MIS hardware configuration analysis											
Monitors tape utilization											
Monitors disk utilization Analyzes data access patterns											
Analyzes data access patterns											
Analyzes internal memory management											
Analyzes CPU options											
Analyzes printer utilization											
Analyzes job/production mix											
Analyzes operating procedures											

Worksheet 2-4

Evaluation Worksheet (continued)

MIS HARDWARE & SOFTWARE	POOR			FAIR			GOOD				COMMENTS
	0	1	2	3	4	5	6	7	8	9	
MIS software configuration analysis											
Operating system current release											
Operating system configuration											
Program libraries maintenance											
Multiprogramming level											
Use of utilities											
Efficiency of software											
Programming language match											
Programming techniques											
Software techniques (file organization)											

Worksheet 2-5

Evaluation Worksheet (continued)

	POOR				FAIR			GOOD			
COMPUTER OPERATIONS WORKFLOW	0	1	2	3	4	5	6	7	8	9	**COMMENTS**
Physical arrangements											
Layout of MIS area											
Adequate work space											
Adequate storage space											
Backup facilities											
Scheduling											
Production schedule publication											
Schedule change communication											
Special job request process											
Production reports											
Operations											
Run logs for production jobs											
Job staging											
Job setup process											
Staffing											
Restart procedures											
Emergency communication (pagers)											
Disaster recovery plan											
Distribution											
Written instructions											
Control checks											
Output controls											

Worksheet 2-6

Evaluation Worksheet (continued)

USER SATISFACTION	POOR 0	1	2	3	FAIR 4	5	6	GOOD 7	8	9	COMMENTS
User requirements											
Primary business focus of system											
Frequency of use											
Complete processing functionality											
Processing bottlenecks											
Unnecessary work steps											
Processing schedules											
Mix of on-line/batch											
User documentation											
User interface ease of use											
Output effectiveness											
Level of user confidence											
MIS operation support											
MIS problem resolution											
System reliability											
Accuracy											
Timeliness											
Data security											
System availability											

Worksheet 2-7

Evaluation Worksheet (continued)

USER SATISFACTION	POOR 0	1	2	3	FAIR 4	5	6	GOOD 7	8	9	COMMENTS
Cost-effectiveness											
Operational costs											
Transaction processing costs											
Implementation costs											
Manpower utilization											
Machine utilization											
Maintenance costs											
Technical efficiency											
Efficient system design											
Efficient use of computing equipment											
Number of files & programs											
File-processing techniques											
Flexibility of expansion											
Flexibility for maintenance											
Efficient operating procedures											
Efficient programming practices											
Efficient maintenance practices											

Worksheet 2-8

Staffing, Organization, and Environment

QUESTIONS	YES	NO	COMMENTS
Is there a full-time Project Manager assigned to the project?			
Does the project plan leave the Project Manager free from technical tasks?			
If the project team is large, is it broken up into smaller groups with appropriate team leaders?			
Do the team members have adequate experience for the roles that they are being used to play?			
Have team members been given time and opportunity to receive training in the technologies that they will use?			
At each level, does the team have the right mix of senior and junior people and the right mix of skills?			
Is there sufficient continuity of staff between the early phases and later phases of the life cycle?			

Worksheet 2-9

Staffing, Organization, and Environment (continued)

QUESTIONS	YES	NO	COMMENTS
Does the team trust and respect the project manager, system architect and team leaders?			
Are there mechanisms, such as regular meetings or technical bulletins to encourage the exchange of information among team members?			
Is it clear what the end-product will be?			

Worksheet 2-10

Business System Definition

QUESTIONS	YES	NO	COMMENTS
Does user management want this system?			
Has the executive who is the primary sponsor of the system made his or her ownership of the system clear to the rest of the organization?			
Do the users understand that they must invest a significant amount of time in defining and designing the system?			
Does the project team have ready access to key users?			
Do the users involved in system definition include both decision makers and lower level individuals with a detailed knowledge of the business?			
Is the right level of user providing the right type of input, that is, executives making policy decisions, lower-level users providing information business details?			

Worksheet 2-11

Business System Definition (continued)

QUESTIONS	YES	NO	COMMENTS
Are users deciding the business issues and MIS deciding the technical issues?			
Is the team using workshop techniques such as JAD to involve the users and speed the information gathering process?			
Does everyone clearly understand which issues are business and which technical?			
Have project team members visited the work area of the individuals whom the system will serve and observed how they currently do their jobs?			
Has the project team avoided using a methodology			
Are business policy issues fully understood to be just that, and not disguised as system issues?			

Worksheet 2-12

Business System Definition (continued)

QUESTIONS	YES	NO	COMMENTS
Does the project team include some on which experience in this industry and application?			
Have internal and external auditing requirements been addressed?			
Is adequate consideration given to using existing standard system concepts, packages, or pre-engineered software?			
Has a task to organize and publish the document been scheduled?			
Are key users given ample feedback of requirements prior to final document publication?			
Is there a formal walkthrough scheduled to review the document with the key users?			
Is formal sign-off expected from key users?			

Worksheet 2-13

Manual Procedures and Training

QUESTIONS	YES	NO	COMMENTS
Does the planned user manual provide for several levels of documentation: • Detailed introduction for new clerical users? • Quick reference card or guide for the experienced user? • Management level explanation of how to use the system to achieve business objectives?			
Is there a formal written plan outlining how the manual will be produced?			
Has it been determined what type of people will be needed to produce the manual (technical writers, artists, programmers)?			
Is there a formal written plan describing how training on the new system will be accomplished?			
Has it been determined whether separate training guides will be needed or whether the user manual will be used as the text?			

Worksheet 2-14

General Review Questions

QUESTIONS	COMMENTS
What metrics are used to measure productivity and quality	
How is the project plan developed and maintained • Level of detail • Frequency of update • Reporting	
Need to conduct independent estimates (action item Phil) explosion, Estimates)	
Was software selected before redesign	
Are legacy systems being maintained by different staff	
Is there a legacy system retirement plan	
Is the MRP data realistic	

Worksheet 2-15

General Review Questions

QUESTIONS	COMMENTS
Are projects modularized	
How are user requests prioritized/scrutinized approved (business or technology driven)	
Is ROI conducted	
Benefits managed	
How do you track problems	
Who is responsible for overall project and do they have proper authority	
How much end-user development What tasks	

Worksheet 2-16

General Review Questions

QUESTIONS	COMMENTS
How do these systems fit within the overall vision and direction of the organization and into the SISP	
What level of user participation Project MGMT sign-off Training and documentation	
Change control process (feed back to project sponsor)	
What development standards are you using Do you follow them	
Are user tasks schedule and cost captured.	

Worksheet 2-17

Business Process Change Impact

- A **Business Process (BP)** is defined as a closely related group of business activities which add value to the organization.

– How old are the current business processes?	1 2 3 4 5 New Old
– How well understood are the old processes?	1 2 3 4 5 So So Very Well
– Are Business Processes tied to specific jobs within the organization?	1 2 3 4 5 No Yes
– How different are the new process from the processes currently in use?	1 2 3 4 5 Very Little Totally

Management Level

Worksheet 8-1

Measures Systems Change Impact

- A **Measure (MS)** is defined as a mechanism by which to appraise the processes and results of activities or tasks.

– How old are the current measures?	1 2 3 4 5 New Old
– How well understood are the old measures?	1 2 3 4 5 So So Very Well
– Are new measures tied to specific job performance targets, incentives and bonuses?	1 2 3 4 5 No Yes
– How different are the new measures from the current measures in use?	1 2 3 4 5 Very Little Totally

Management Level

Worksheet 8-2

Values & Beliefs Change Impact

- The **Value & Belief (VB)** is defined as a creed that the organization has placed it's trust and has a conviction for, and that is deemed as having worth.

– How old are the current values & beliefs?	1 2 3 4 5 New Old
– How well understood are the old values & beliefs?	1 2 3 4 5 So So Very Well
– Are values & beliefs tied to specific job targets, incentives and bonuses?	1 2 3 4 5 No Yes
– How different are the new values & beliefs from the current ones in use?	1 2 3 4 5 Very Little Totally

Management Level

Worksheet 8-3

Controls Systems Change Impact

- A **Control (CS)** is defined as a mechanism to check, test or verify the operational characteristics of a business

– How thorough are the current controls?	1 2 3 4 5	Not — Totally
– How well understood are the controls?	1 2 3 4 5	So So — Very Well
– Are the new controls applied to specific areas of risk and not used throughout the organization?	1 2 3 4 5	No — Yes
– How different are the new controls from the current ones in use?	1 2 3 4 5	Very Little — Totally

Management Level

Worksheet 8-4

Human Resources Change Impact

- **Human Resources (HR)** deal with the relationship of people to the organization, their skills, hiring practices and methods of management employed to effectively acquire and retain staff.

– How well are skills matched to jobs?	1 2 3 4 5 Not Totally
– Skill requirements influence hiring?	1 2 3 4 5 So So Yes
– Are the new skills required in specific areas and not used throughout the new processes?	1 2 3 4 5 No Yes
– How different are the new job skills from the current ones?	1 2 3 4 5 Very Little Totally

Worksheet 8-5

Organizational Change Impact

- **Organization (OR)** deals with the structure and reporting lines within the organization. Functional Areas, departments work groups all fall under this heading.

  – How old is the current organizational structure? 1 2 3 4 5 (Old – New)

  – How many reporting layers are there currently? ***(circle 5 for 5 or more layers)*** 1 2 3 4 5

  – How significantly different are the new processes grouped compared to the old processes? 1 2 3 4 5 (So So – Totally)

  – How different will the new reporting relationships, responsibilities and authorities be? 1 2 3 4 5 (Very Little – Totally)

Worksheet 8-6

Information Systems Change Impact

- **Information Systems (IT)** deals with computer hardware, software, tools and techniques that are used in the development, maintenance and operation of systems that support the business.

– How old is the current information infrastructure?	1 2 3 4 5 Old New
– How different is the proposed solution from the current suite of technology?	1 2 3 4 5 Very Little Totally
– How significant will the distribution of technology change with the new approach?	1 2 3 4 5 So So Totally
– How different are the skills necessary to support the new systems?	1 2 3 4 5 Very Little Totally

Worksheet 8-7

Cultural Change Impact

- **Culture (CT)** deals with the intellectual, moral and educational properties of the staff that make up the organization. It represents the integrated pattern of human interaction within the business.

– How well defined is the corporate culture?	1 2 3 4 5	So So … Well
– How well ingrained is the old culture within the staff impacted by this change?	1 2 3 4 5	Very Little … Totally
– How significant will the changes be to the corporate culture with the new approach?	1 2 3 4 5	So So … Totally
– What degree of divination from the old culture will take place under the new systems?	1 2 3 4 5	10^ … 180^

Worksheet 8-8

Information Systems Change Impact

- **Information Systems (IT)** deals with computer hardware, software, tools and techniques that are used in the development, maintenance and operation of systems that support the business.

– How old is the current information infrastructure?	1 2 3 4 5 Old New	
– How different is the proposed solution from the current suite of technology?	1 2 3 4 5 Very Little Totally	
– How significant will the distribution of technology change with the new approach?	1 2 3 4 5 So So Totally	
– How different are the skills necessary to support the new systems?	1 2 3 4 5 Very Little Totally	

Worksheet 8-9

Project Management

QUESTIONS	YES	NO	COMMENTS
Is there a written, detailed, and up-to-date project plan?			
Does the plan show the real understanding of the application and the tasks that need to be done in this phase of the life cycle?			
Are task estimates realistic?			
Does the plan make allowances for sick time, vacation time, and other non-project time? (Loading should not be more than 80 percent except on very short projects).			
Do all tasks have some type of product that they produce?			
Are tasks structured so that it is possible to tell when they are done?			
Is there only one person responsible for a task?			

Worksheet 9-1

Project Management (continued)

QUESTIONS	YES	NO	COMMENTS
Are team members perfectly clear about which tasks they are assigned and when the tasks are due?			
Do team members report progress in writing on a weekly basis?			
Is there a mechanism by which team members and the Project Manager can track hours planned and expended on each task, and thereby variances from plan?			
Are there guidelines to define what "done" means?			
Does Project Manager really understand where the project standards, or is he just managing the numbers?			
Does the Project Manager regularly report project status, including variance in hours and dollars, to management?			
Does the Project Manager have a good relationship with the user?			

Worksheet 9-2

Project Control Worksheet

PROJECT MANAGEMENT	POOR 0	1	2	3	FAIR 4	5	6	GOOD 7	8	9	COMMENTS
Project Plan											
Detailed project plan											
Project Plan updated regularly											
Plan is broken into phases											
Plan shows understanding of lifecycle											
Plan has appropriate millstones											
Actual effort is being tracked against plan											
Project Activities											
Activity descriptions											
Activity dependencies											
Activity responsibilities											
Specific Resources Assigned											
Resource balance is appropriate											
Span of effort is reasonable											
Span of authority matches activities											
Slack time included in activity estimates											
Vacation, sick time and administrative time is estimated and included											
Level of administration control											
Assigned development priorities											
Defined development process											
Change control procedures											
Version control procedures for software & documentation											
Documentation review process											

Worksheet 9-3

Project Control Worksheet continued)

PROJECT MANAGEMENT	POOR			FAIR				GOOD			COMMENTS
	0	1	2	3	4	5	6	7	8	9	
Approach to management control											
Effectiveness of project reports											
Management & tracking reports											
Accounting control & cost tracking											
Project auditing ***(PRISM)***											
Determination of staffing requirements											
Project plans developed with staff requirements considered											
Definition of skill requirements & skills assessed											
Resource availability and commitment defined											
Staff skill base											
Staff backgrounds											
Match with level of role sophistication											
Key staff member skill match to business /technology											
Personnel policies and procedures											
Recruiting sources for temporary or permanent help identified											
Selection criteria defined for business and technical staff											
Recruitment results analysis monitored and feed back											
Employee reskilling defined											
Special salary scale & benefits considered or defined											
Project performance appraisals (at each major milestone)											
Personnel security screening											

Worksheet 9-4

Project Control Worksheet *continued)*

PROJECT MANAGEMENT	POOR 0	1	2	3	FAIR 4	5	6	GOOD 7	8	9	COMMENTS
Task Planning											
Tasks are defined in sufficient detail											
Tasks have defined work product(s)											
Tasks have clearly defined completion criteria											
Only one person is responsible for a task											
Responsibilities											
Resources know what tasks they are responsible for											
Responsible resource reports progress on a weekly basis											
Responsible resource tracks actual effort vs planned effort											
Project Management Role											
Project Manager assigned full time											
Project Manager does not participate in development efforts											
Project Manager understands the project in sufficient detail											
Project Manager Reporting											
Project Manager reports only to the Project Sponsor											
Project Manager holds status meetings at various levels											
Project Manager tracks variances in cost, time, effort and progress											
Project Manager has a good relationship with the team and users											
Project Manager makes sure critical issues get resolved quickly											
Project Manager has sign off responsibility on critical activities											
Project Manager has sign off responsibility on final deliverables											

Worksheet 9-5

Project Control Worksheet *continued)*

PROJECT MANAGEMENT	POOR			FAIR			GOOD				COMMENTS
	0	1	2	3	4	5	6	7	8	9	
User involvement											
Are the users significantly involved in all phases of the project											
Does the Project Manager provide status meeting with the users											
Are the users concerns addressed promptly											
Do the users sign off on key final deliverables											
Project Team											
The project team broken down into smaller groups											
The Project Team is olfadequate size											
The Project Team has proper mix of skills											
The Project Team is kept informed about the entire project											
An appropriate Team Leader is assigned to each group											
The Project Team has been provided necessary training											
Personality conflicts handled within the groups											
Groups are made up of proper mix of senior and junior staff											
Continuity of staff and staff replacements is handled adequately											
Understanding & Relationships											
The Team trust the Project Manager											
The grouped trust their Leader											
The Team shares in the vision & mission of the organization											
The Team is not caught up in internal politics											
The Team openly exchanges ideas and information											
The Team is clear what the end product will be											
The Team clearly understands the business issues being addressed											
The team is not worried about their jobs											

Worksheet 9-6

Project Control Worksheet *continued)*

PROJECT DEFINITION OF BUSINESS ISSUES	POOR 0	1	2	FAIR 3	4	5	6	GOOD 7	8	9	COMMENTS
Management											
There is an Executive Sponsor											
Management recognizes the need the project will fulfill											
The Executive Sponsor has communicated their project ownership											
The Executive Sponsor is highly visible with regard to the project											
Business Knowledge											
The Project Team has access to key users											
The key users understand the investment of their time											
The key users have the detailed business knowledge											
The users have the power to make necessary changes											
The users are involved in technology selection											
The business managers are briefed at key points in the project											
The right level of users have been assigned to provide input											
The users understand the driving factors of their market											
The users take ownership of business issue resolution											
Technical Knowledge											
The Project Manager has a high level understanding of the technology											
The users are technology literate											
The Team has resources who are expert in the technologies											
MIS is involved in technical decision making											
MIS is taking ownership of resolving technical issues promptly											
Technology is being applied to enable business process change											
Benefits of technology are understood, quantified and communicated											
An up-to-date methodology is being employed on the project											

Worksheet 9-7

Project Control Worksheet continued)

OPERATIONS WORKFLOW	POOR			FAIR				GOOD			COMMENTS
	0	1	2	3	4	5	6	7	8	9	
Physical arrangements											
Layout of the LAB area is comfortable											
LAB has adequate work space											
LAB has adequate storage space											
LAB has adequate PCs, software and printing facilities											
Scheduling											
LAB schedules are published and distributed											
LAB Schedule changes are communication											
Special Team building events are scheduled											
LAB training is scheduled in advances											
Operations											
LABs are self governing											
LABs report status on a weekly basis											
LABs work without political bias											
LABs are not troubled by staffing problems											
LABs are following the methodology											
LAB Leader has an Emergency communication (pager)											
LABs have stress reduction events											
Industry Expertise											
Consultants are used to bring outside industry expertise											
Project is looking at best practices or best in class operations											
Out of market examples of world class operations investigated											

Worksheet 9-8

Project Control Worksheet continued)

BUSINESS ANALYSIS	POOR 0	1	2	FAIR 3	4	5	6	GOOD 7	8	9	COMMENTS
User Satisfaction											
Project is primarily business focus of system											
The frequency of use has been defined											
Project represents complete processing functionality											
Processing bottlenecks have been mitigated											
Unnecessary work steps have been eliminated											
Processing schedules and metrics have been evaluated											
Mix of on-line/batch operations have been planned and reviewed											
User documentation is developed at appropriate level											
User interface s have been designed logically and for ease of use											
Reports and other output has been reviewed for effectiveness											
Level of user confidence is high											
MIS is planning operation support											
MIS has a problem tracking and resolution process											
System reliability											
Accuracy requirements for the system are realistic											
Timeliness and delivery for cutover has been evaluated											
Data security and system security has been identified and planned											
System availability has been defined and is realistic											

Worksheet 9-9

Project Control Worksheet *continued)*

MANAGEMENT SATISFACTION	POOR 0	1	2	FAIR 3	4	5	6	GOOD 7	8	9	COMMENTS
Cost-effectiveness											
Operational costs have been properly estimated											
Transaction processing costs have been properly estimated											
Implementation costs have been properly estimated											
Manpower utilization has been reviewed											
Machine utilization has been estimated and is realistic											
Maintenance costs have been planned for over the next 5 years											
Technical efficiency											
Efficiency of the new system design has been reviewed and justified											
Computer equipment has been selected for efficient operation											
Number of files & programs are not excessive											
File-processing techniques are efficient and allow for future growth											
Flexibility of expansion permits the organizational growth for 5 years											
Flexibility for maintenance allows for minimal disruption											
Efficient operating procedures have been defined											
Efficient programming practices have been employed											
Efficient maintenance practices have been employed											

Worksheet 9-10

REFERENCES

Reengineering Management Information Systems

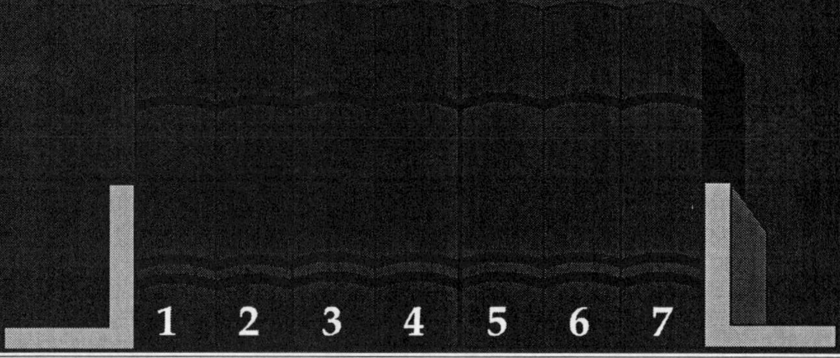

Appendix C

References

"Redesigning Business Operations Management," Advanced Technology Consultants, 1990.

"Measures Definition for Effective Business Management," Advanced Technology Consultants, 1991.

"Strategic Technology Management for Business," Applied Business Intelligence, 1990.

"Advanced Technology Development and Implementation Methodology," Applied Business Intelligence, 1991.

"Business Design and Architecture Development Methodology," Applied Business Intelligence, 1992.

"The Team Handbook," Jarvis Associates, Inc., 1988.

The Popcorn Report, Faith Popcorn, Harper Collins Publishers, N.Y. , N.Y. 1991, 1992

A Kick in the Seat of the Pants, Roger von Oech Harper & Row, N.Y., N.Y. 1986.

A Whack on the Side of the Head, Roger von Oech U.S. Games Systems, Inc., Stamford, CT. 1983, 1990.

Leading Self-Directed Work Teams, Kimball Fisher, McGraw-Hill, Inc., 1993.

Flowcharting with ANSI Standard: A Tutorial, N. Chapin ACM Computing Surveys, Vol. 2, No. 2 (June 1970).

"How Can Organizations Learn Faster? The Challenge of Entering the Green Room" Edgar H. Schun, Sloan Management Review, 1993.

"Getting Them Thru the Wilderness: A Leader's Guide to Transition." William Bridges New Management.

"Dirk Gently's Detective Agency" Douglas Adams Pocket Books, a division of Simon and Shuster, New York, 1987.

Index

SUBMISSION GUIDELINES

If you have a topic or idea that you feel would be a good subject for an **authored** or **edited** book, we invite you to submit a 4-6 page proposal addressing the following areas:

- **Mission:** What is the purpose of the book?
- **Audience:** Whom do you intend this book to address? Included in this section should be a description of the specific group as well as your estimate of the total core audience.
- **Competition:** What other books are on the market that address this same topic, and how will yours differ? What unique characteristics will your proposed book contain to place it above the competition?
- **Timetable for Production:** Give an estimate of when you would have the initial manuscript finished and when the final manuscript would be delivered.
- **Outline:** This section should contain the overall framework or summary of your proposed book as well as a comprehensive list of the table of contents.
- **Sample chapters:** A copy of several chapters of the proposed book (if available) is requested to allow the editorial staff to assess your proposed publication in a more constructive, efficient manner.

Submit your proposal to:

IDEA GROUP PUBLISHING
Olde Liberty Square, Suite 230
4811 Jonestown Road
Harrisburg, PA 17109
Tel: (717) 541-9150 • Fax (717) 541-9159